THE ULTIMATE PUBLIC CAMPGROUND PROJECT

Second Edition

National Park Service Camping

Directory of 1,615 Camping Areas in 37 States

Published by:

Roundabout Publications
PO Box 569
LaCygne, KS 66040

Phone: 800-455-2207
Internet: www.RoundaboutPublications.com

Library of Congress Control Number: 2022936333

ISBN-10: 1-885464-83-5
ISBN-13: 978-1-885464-83-5

Table of Contents

Introduction..................4

Alabama 5

Alaska 7

Arizona 10

Arkansas 16

California 19

Colorado..................27

Florida......................36

Georgia 38

Idaho 40

Indiana.....................42

Kentucky 44

Maine 47

Maryland..................49

Michigan 53

Minnesota 58

Mississippi 60

Missouri....................62

Montana 65

Nevada.....................72

New Jersey................75

New Mexico..............77

New York...................79

North Carolina...........81

North Dakota 87

Oklahoma 89

Oregon.....................91

Pennsylvania.............93

South Carolina 95

South Dakota.................97

Tennessee 99

Texas...........................103

Utah.............................109

Virginia........................118

Washington..................120

West Virginia 138

Wisconsin....................140

Wyoming.....................142

Introduction

Huge portions of public lands, managed by a variety of government agencies, are available to the general public for recreational use. This book will guide you to 1,615 camping areas available from the National Park Service in 37 states.

National Park Service Camping

On August 25, 1916, President Woodrow Wilson approved legislation creating the National Park Service. Today the NPS is made up of more than 400 areas encompassing over 84 million acres. These areas include national parks, seashores, battlefields, and historic sites nationwide. They offer a wide variety of outdoor recreation and educational experiences for the visitor. To learn more about the National Park Service, visit their website: www.nps.gov. Please note that the camping areas accessible only by boat are not included in this guide.

Using This Guide

This guide is especially helpful when used along with Google Maps, Windows Maps, or a GPS device for locating and navigating to each camping area.

State Maps

A state map is provided to aid you in locating the camping areas. A grid overlay on each map is used when cross-referencing with each camping area.

Map Grid Chart & Alphabetical List

Following the state map is a chart showing the camping area ID number(s) located within a map grid. Following this chart is an alphabetical list of each camping area, which is especially helpful when you already know the name of an area. This list provides each location's ID number and map grid location.

Camping Area Details

Camping area details include information about each public camping area within the state. Preceding each location's name is the ID number and map grid location, which is used when referencing the state map.

Details for each camping area generally include the following information:

- Total number of sites or dispersed camping
- Number of RV sites
- Sites with electric hookups
- Full hookup sites, if available
- Water (central location or spigots at site)
- Showers
- RV dump station
- Toilets (flush, pit/vault, or none)
- Laundry facilities
- Camp store
- Maximum RV size limits (if any)
- Reservation information (accepted, not accepted, recommended or required)
- Generator use and hours (if limited)
- Operating season
- Camping fees charged
- Miscellaneous notes
- Length of stay limit
- Elevation in feet and meters
- Telephone number
- Nearby city or town
- GPS coordinates

The Ultimate Public Campground Project

Data for this publication is from The Ultimate Public Campground Project, which was established in 2008 to provide a consolidated and comprehensive source for public campgrounds of all types. Please note that despite our best efforts, there will always be errors to be found in the data. With over 45,000 records in our database, it is impossible to ensure that each one is always up-to-date.

Happy Camping!

Common Abbreviations Used

CG	Campground
CR	County Road
NCA	National Conservation Area
NHP	National Historic Park
NHS	National Historic Site
NM	National Monument
NP	National Park
NPS	National Park Service
NR	National River
NRA	National Recreation Area
NRRA	National River & Recreation Area
NS	National Seashore
NSR	National Scenic River
RA	Recreation Area
TC	Trail Camp
TH	Trail Head
WA	Wildlife Area

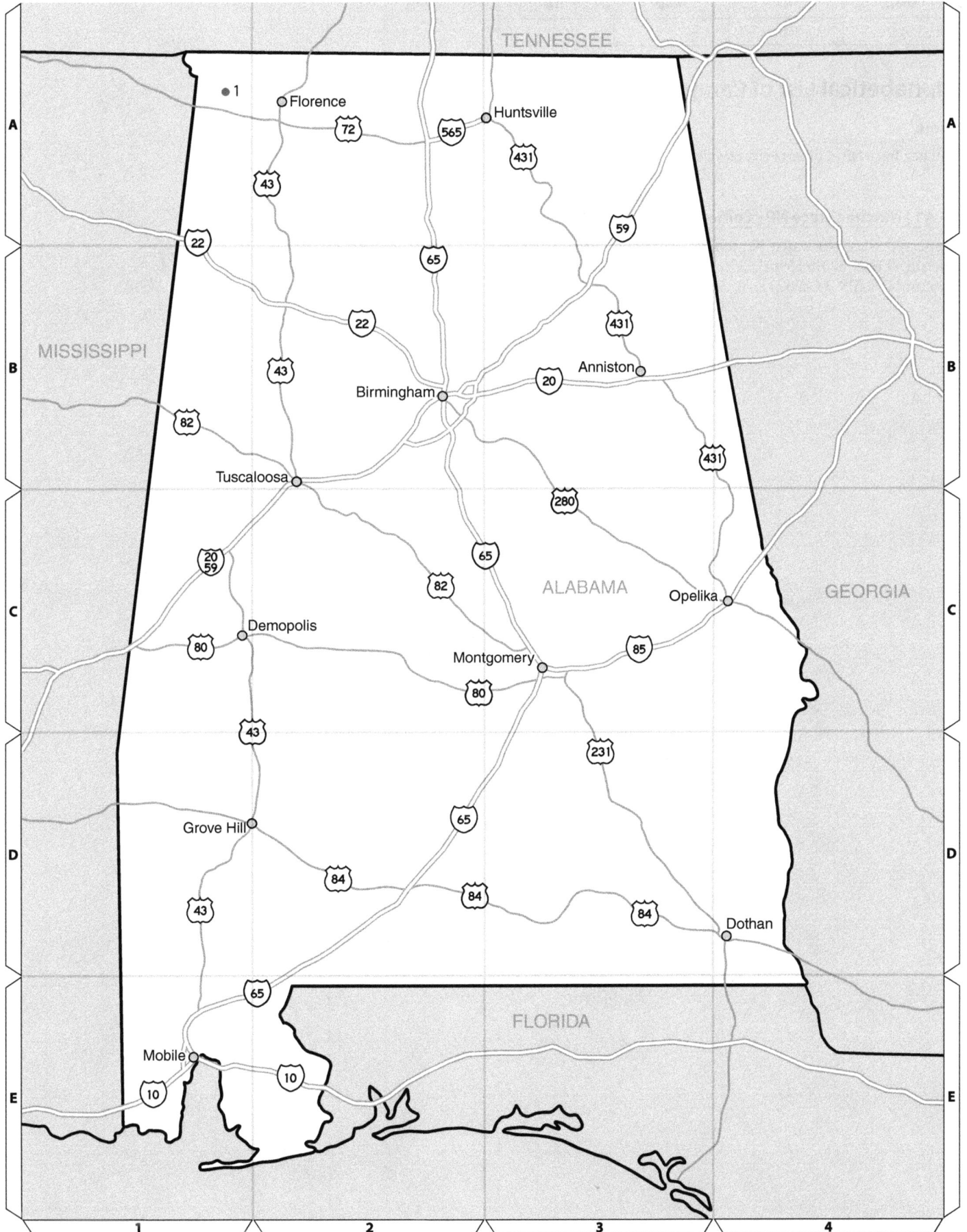

Alabama

TENNESSEE

● 1

○ Florence

72

565

○ Huntsville

431

43

59

22

65

22

431

MISSISSIPPI

43

Anniston

○ Birmingham

20

431

82

○ Tuscaloosa

280

20
59

65

82

ALABAMA

Opelika

○ Demopolis

80

Montgomery

85

GEORGIA

80

43

231

○ Grove Hill

65

84

84

84

○ Dothan

43

65

FLORIDA

○ Mobile

10

10

Map	ID	Map	ID
A1	1		

Alphabetical List of Camping Areas

Name	ID	Map
Natchez Trace NP - Colbert Ferry Bicycle CG	1	A1

1 • A1 | Natchez Trace NP - Colbert Ferry Bicycle CG

Dispersed sites, No water, No toilets, Tents only: Free, Hike-in, Bike-in, Elev: 523ft/159m, Tel: 800-305-7417, Nearest town: Tuscumbia. GPS: 34.836211, -87.951675

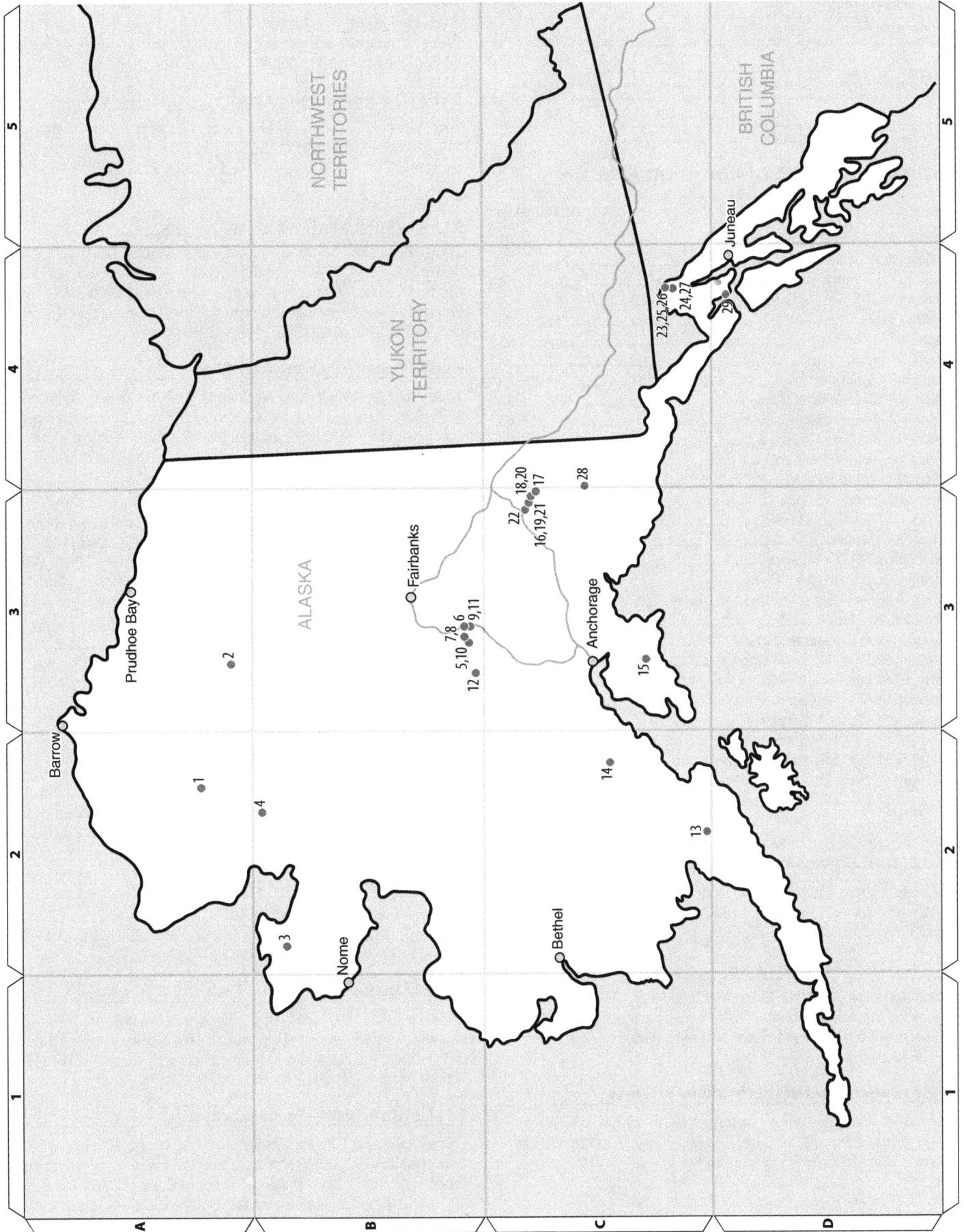

Alaska

ALASKA

NORTHWEST TERRITORIES

YUKON TERRITORY

BRITISH COLUMBIA

Juneau

23,25,26
24,27
29

18,20
22 17
16,19,21
28

Fairbanks

7,8 6
9,11
5,10
12

Anchorage

15

Prudhoe Bay

2

Barrow

1

4

14

13

3

Nome

Bethel

5

4

3

2

1

A

B

C

D

Map	ID	Map	ID
A2	1	C2	13-14
A3	2	C3	15-22
B2	3-4	C4	23-28
B3	5-12	D4	29

Alphabetical List of Camping Areas

Name	ID	Map
Bering Land Bridge National Preserve	3	B2
Chilkoot Trail - Canyon City	23	C4
Chilkoot Trail - Finnegan's Camp	24	C4
Chilkoot Trail - Pleasant Camp	25	C4
Chilkoot Trail - Sheep Camp	26	C4
Denali NP - Igloo Creek	5	B3
Denali NP - Riley Creek	6	B3
Denali NP - Sanctuary River	7	B3
Denali NP - Savage River	8	B3
Denali NP - Second Triple Lake	9	B3
Denali NP - Teklanika River	10	B3
Denali NP - Third Triple Lake	11	B3
Denali NP - Wonder Lake	12	B3
Gates of the Arctic NP	2	A3
Glacier Bay NP - Bartlett Cove	29	D4
Katmai NP - Brooks Camp	13	C2
Kenai Fjords NP - Exit Glacier	15	C3
Klondike Gold Rush NHP - Dyea	27	C4
Kobuk Valley NP - Great Kobuk Sand Dunes	4	B2
Lake Clark NP - Hope Creek	14	C2
Noatak National Preserve - Feniak Lake	1	A2
Wrangell-St. Elias NP - Dead Dog Hill	16	C3
Wrangell-St. Elias NP - Jack Creek Rest Area	17	C3
Wrangell-St. Elias NP - Jumbo Creek	28	C4
Wrangell-St. Elias NP - Kendesnii	18	C3
Wrangell-St. Elias NP - Kettle Lake Wayside	19	C3
Wrangell-St. Elias NP - Nabesna Road Pulloff	20	C3
Wrangell-St. Elias NP - Rock Lake Wayside	21	C3
Wrangell-St. Elias NP - Rufus Creek Wayside	22	C3

1 • A2 | Noatak National Preserve - Feniak Lake

Dispersed sites, No water, No toilets, Tents only: Free, Hike-in, Plane access, Elev: 1445ft/440m, Tel: 907-442-3890. GPS: 68.273955, -158.337245

2 • A3 | Gates of the Arctic NP

Dispersed sites, No water, No toilets, Tents only: Fee unk, Hike-in, Fly-in for 8.4 million acres of wilderness camping, Elev: 2144ft/653m, Tel: 907-692-5494, Nearest town: Anaktuvuk Pass. GPS: 68.136405, -151.737568

3 • B2 | Bering Land Bridge National Preserve

Dispersed sites, No water, No toilets, Tents only: Free, Hike-in, Plane access, Elev: 407ft/124m, Tel: 800-471-2352, Nearest town: Nome. GPS: 65.856225, -164.714858

4 • B2 | Kobuk Valley NP - Great Kobuk Sand Dunes

Dispersed sites, No water, Tents only: Free, Hike-in, Fly-in, Reservations not accepted, Elev: 191ft/58m, Tel: 907-442-3890. GPS: 67.041459, -158.836829

5 • B3 | Denali NP - Igloo Creek

Total sites: 7, RV sites: 0, No water, Vault/pit toilet, Tents only: $17, No fires, Stay limit: 14 days, Open May-Sep, Reservations not accepted, Elev: 2990ft/911m, Tel: 907-683-9532. GPS: 63.609104, -149.585016

6 • B3 | Denali NP - Riley Creek

Total sites: 146, RV sites: 127, Central water, Flush toilet, RV dump, Tents: $17/RV's: $34, Group site: $49, Free Sep-May, Stay limit: 14 days, Generator hours: 0800-1000/1600-2000, Max Length: 40ft, Reservations accepted, Elev: 1624ft/495m, Tel: 907-683-9532. GPS: 63.731286, -148.895365

7 • B3 | Denali NP - Sanctuary River

Total sites: 7, RV sites: 0, No water, Vault/pit toilet, Tents only: $17, Stay limit: 14 days, Open May-Sep, Reservations not accepted, Elev: 2473ft/754m, Tel: 907-683-9532. GPS: 63.722736, -149.473623

8 • B3 | Denali NP - Savage River

Total sites: 33, RV sites: 33, Central water, Flush toilet, No showers, No RV dump, Tents: $27/RV's: $27-34, 3 group sites: $49, Stay limit: 14 days, Generator hours: 0800-1000/1600-2000, Open May-Sep, Reservations accepted, Elev: 2745ft/837m, Tel: 907-683-9532. GPS: 63.716556, -149.259289

9 • B3 | Denali NP - Second Triple Lake

Dispersed sites, No water, No toilets, Tents only: Free, Hike-in, Stay limit: 14 days, Reservations not accepted, Elev: 2086ft/636m, Tel: 907-683-9532. GPS: 63.657296, -148.870608

10 • B3 | Denali NP - Teklanika River

Total sites: 53, RV sites: 53, Central water, Vault/pit toilet, No showers, No RV dump, Tent & RV camping: $29, 3 day mimimum stay, Vehicle cannot leave campsite, Stay limit: 14 days, Open May-Sep, Reservations accepted, Elev: 2546ft/776m, Tel: 907-683-9532. GPS: 63.670682, -149.579466

11 • B3 | Denali NP - Third Triple Lake

Dispersed sites, No water, No toilets, Tents only: Free, Hike-in, Stay limit: 14 days, Reservations not accepted, Elev: 2088ft/636m, Tel: 907-683-9532. GPS: 63.666626, -148.884525

12 • B3 | Denali NP - Wonder Lake

Total sites: 28, RV sites: 0, Central water, Vault/pit toilet, No showers, No RV dump, Tents only: $16, No fires, Stay limit: 14 days, Open Jun-Sep, Reservations accepted, Elev: 2021ft/616m, Tel: 907-683-9532. GPS: 63.453472, -150.863425

13 • C2 | Katmai NP - Brooks Camp

Dispersed sites, Central water, Vault/pit toilet, Tents only: $12, Bear watching, $12/person camping fee, Access by floatplane, Open May-Oct, Reservations accepted, Elev: 53ft/16m, Tel: 907-246-3305, Nearest town: King Salmon. GPS: 58.559868, -155.777565

14 • C2 | Lake Clark NP - Hope Creek

Dispersed sites, No water, No toilets, Tents only: Free, Fly-in access to park, Reservations not accepted, Elev: 2008ft/612m, Tel: 907-235-7903, Nearest town: Port Alsworth. GPS: 60.643856, -153.819771

15 • C3 | Kenai Fjords NP - Exit Glacier

Total sites: 12, RV sites: 0, Central water, Vault/pit toilet, No showers, No RV dump, Tents only: Free, Walk-to sites, Stay limit: 14 days, Reservations not accepted, Elev: 373ft/114m, Tel: 907-422-0535, Nearest town: Seward. GPS: 60.191127, -149.619102

16 • C3 | Wrangell-St. Elias NP - Dead Dog Hill

Dispersed sites, No water, Vault/pit toilet, Tent & RV camping: Free, Reservations not accepted, Elev: 2901ft/884m, Tel: 907-822-7250, Nearest town: Tok. GPS: 62.576805, -143.535583

17 • C3 | Wrangell-St. Elias NP - Jack Creek Rest Area

Dispersed sites, No water, No toilets, Tent & RV camping: Free, Reservations not accepted, Elev: 2907ft/886m, Tel: 907-822-7250, Nearest town: Tok. GPS: 62.464717, -143.103336

18 • C3 | Wrangell-St. Elias NP - Kendesnii

Total sites: 10, RV sites: 10, No water, Vault/pit toilet, Tent & RV camping: Free, Max Length: 30ft, Reservations not accepted, Elev: 3106ft/947m, Tel: 907-822-7250, Nearest town: Tok. GPS: 62.529888, -143.259061

19 • C3 | Wrangell-St. Elias NP - Kettle Lake Wayside

Dispersed sites, No water, No toilets, Tent & RV camping: Free, Reservations not accepted, Elev: 2799ft/853m, Tel: 907-822-7250, Nearest town: Tok. GPS: 62.584625, -143.567487

20 • C3 | Wrangell-St. Elias NP - Nabesna Road Pulloff

Dispersed sites, No water, No toilets, Tent & RV camping: Free, Elev: 3151ft/960m. GPS: 62.522904, -143.222301

21 • C3 | Wrangell-St. Elias NP - Rock Lake Wayside

Dispersed sites, No water, Vault/pit toilet, Tent & RV camping: Free, Reservations not accepted, Elev: 3213ft/979m, Tel: 907-822-7250, Nearest town: Tok. GPS: 62.564166, -143.416688

22 • C3 | Wrangell-St. Elias NP - Rufus Creek Wayside

Dispersed sites, No water, No toilets, Tent & RV camping: Free, Reservations not accepted, Elev: 2278ft/694m, Tel: 907-822-7250, Nearest town: Tok. GPS: 62.655399, -143.836039

23 • C4 | Chilkoot Trail - Canyon City

Total sites: 10, RV sites: 0, No water, Vault/pit toilet, Tents only: $27, Hike-in, 7.5 mi, No tent platforms, Permit required, Reservations required, Elev: 403ft/123m, Tel: 907-983-9200. GPS: 59.620718, -135.328908

24 • C4 | Chilkoot Trail - Finnegan's Camp

Total sites: 6, RV sites: 0, No water, Vault/pit toilet, Tents only: $27, Hike-in, 4.8 mi, 10'x10' tent platforms, Permit required, Reservations required, Elev: 354ft/108m, Tel: 907-983-9200. GPS: 59.574108, -135.331021

25 • C4 | Chilkoot Trail - Pleasant Camp

Total sites: 11, RV sites: 0, No water, Vault/pit toilet, Tents only: $27, Hike-in, 10.5 mi, No tent platforms, Permit required, Reservations required, Elev: 716ft/218m, Tel: 907-983-9200. GPS: 59.634176, -135.302849

26 • C4 | Chilkoot Trail - Sheep Camp

Total sites: 27, RV sites: 0, No water, Vault/pit toilet, Tents only: $27, Hike-in, 13 mi, Most sites have tent platforms, Permit required, Reservations required, Elev: 1141ft/348m, Tel: 907-983-9200. GPS: 59.661303, -135.267996

27 • C4 | Klondike Gold Rush NHP - Dyea

Total sites: 22, RV sites: 15, No water, Vault/pit toilet, Tent & RV camping: $10, Narrow bridge access, Max Length: 26ft, Reservations not accepted, Elev: 49ft/15m, Tel: 907-983-9200, Nearest town: Skagway. GPS: 59.505723, -135.347951

28 • C4 | Wrangell-St. Elias NP - Jumbo Creek

Dispersed sites, No water, No toilets, Tents only: Free, Hike-in, Reservations not accepted, Elev: 2332ft/711m, Tel: 907-822-7250, Nearest town: McCarthy. GPS: 61.503804, -142.895061

29 • D4 | Glacier Bay NP - Bartlett Cove

Dispersed sites, Vault/pit toilet, Tents only: Free, Walk-to sites, 1/4 mile, Permit and orientation required, Stay limit: 14 days, Reservations not accepted, Elev: 76ft/23m, Tel: 907-697-2627, Nearest town: Gustavus. GPS: 58.449679, -135.893704

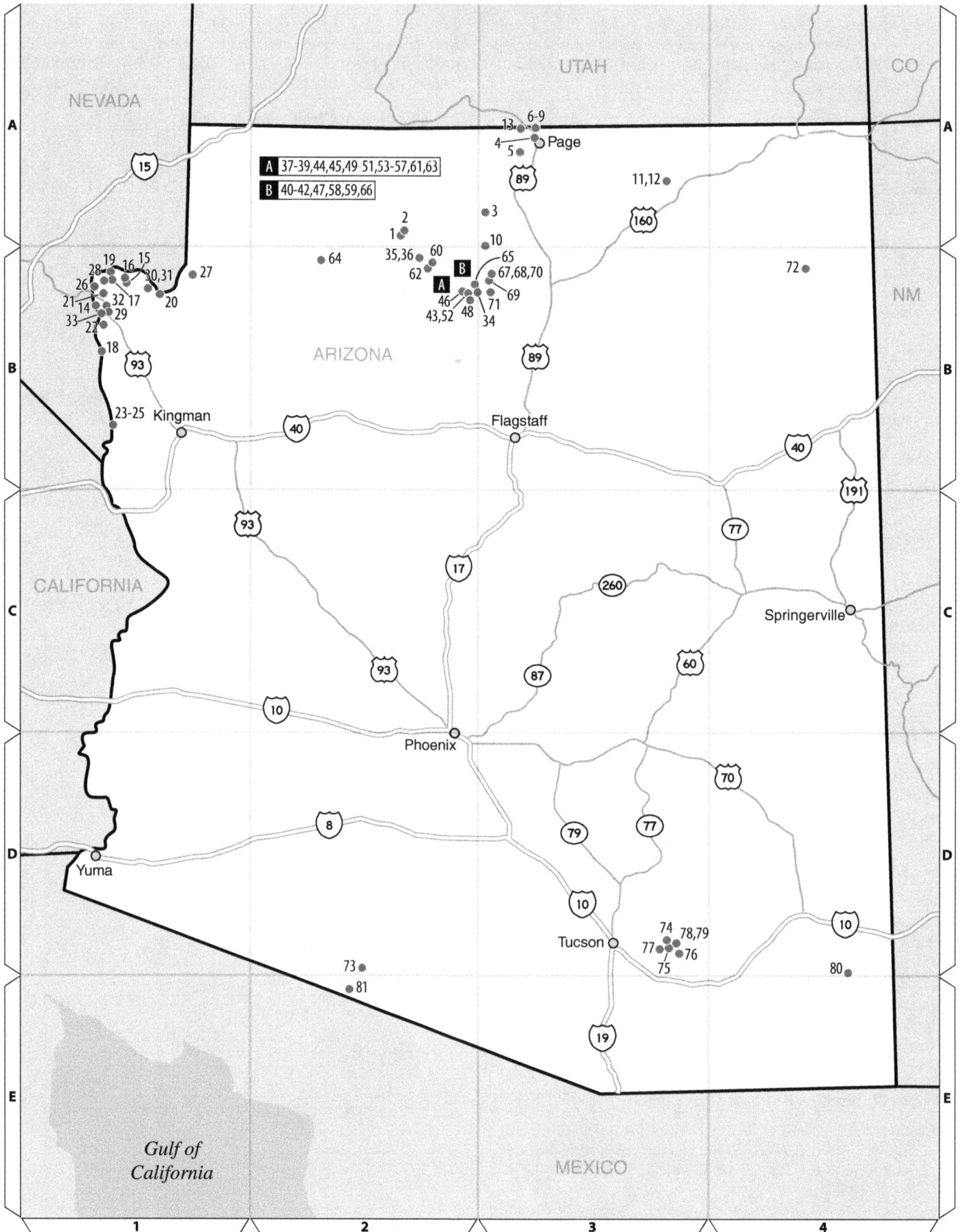

Arizona

UTAH

CO

NEVADA

15

A 37-39,44,45,49 51,53-57,61,63
B 40-42,47,58,59,66

6-9
13
4
5
Page

89

11,12

160

3

2
1

10

35,36 60
62

64

65
B
67,68,70
69

NM

72

19 15
16
28 30,31
26
21 32 17
14 29
33 22
20

27

A
46
43,52 48 71
34

18

93

ARIZONA

89

B

23-25 Kingman

40

Flagstaff

40

191

93

77

17

260

CALIFORNIA

Springerville

C

93

60

87

10

70

Phoenix

8

79 77

D

Yuma

10

19

74 78,79
77 76
75

Tucson

80

73

81

E

Gulf of California

MEXICO

1 2 3 4

Map	ID	Map	ID
A2	1-2	B4	72
A3	3-13	D2	73
B1	14-33	D3	74-79
B2	34-66	D4	80
B3	67-71	E2	81

Alphabetical List of Camping Areas

Name	ID	Map
Canyon De Chelly NM - Cottonwood	72	B4
Chiricahua NM - Bonita Canyon CG	80	D4
Colorado River - Hance	34	B2
Colorado River - Houtata	35	B2
Colorado River - Lower Bass	36	B2
Colorado River - Lower Espejo	67	B3
Colorado River - Palisades Creek	68	B3
Colorado River - South Canyon	3	A3
Colorado River - Tanner	69	B3
Colorado River - Upper Espejo	70	B3
Glen Canyon NRA - Beehive	4	A3
Glen Canyon NRA - Lees Ferry	5	A3
Glen Canyon NRA - Wahweap - Loop 1	6	A3
Glen Canyon NRA - Wahweap - Loops 2-4	7	A3
Glen Canyon NRA - Wahweap - Loops A/B/C/D/F	8	A3
Glen Canyon NRA - Wahweap - Walk-in Tent	9	A3
Grand Canyon NP - Boucher Beach	37	B2
Grand Canyon NP - Bright Angel	38	B2
Grand Canyon NP - Cedar Spring	39	B2
Grand Canyon NP - Cheyava	40	B2
Grand Canyon NP - Clear Creek	41	B2
Grand Canyon NP - Cottonwood Camp	42	B2
Grand Canyon NP - Cottonwood Creek	43	B2
Grand Canyon NP - Desert View	71	B3
Grand Canyon NP - Eremita Mesa	44	B2
Grand Canyon NP - Granite Rapids	45	B2
Grand Canyon NP - Grapevine	46	B2
Grand Canyon NP - Greenland Springs	47	B2
Grand Canyon NP - Hance Creek	48	B2
Grand Canyon NP - Hermit Creek	49	B2
Grand Canyon NP - Hermit Rapids	50	B2
Grand Canyon NP - Horn Creek	51	B2
Grand Canyon NP - Horseshoe Mesa	52	B2
Grand Canyon NP - Indian Gardens	53	B2
Grand Canyon NP - Mather CG	54	B2
Grand Canyon NP - Mather CG - Pine	55	B2
Grand Canyon NP - Mather CG - Sage Group	56	B2
Grand Canyon NP - Monument Creek	57	B2
Grand Canyon NP - Nankoweap	10	A3
Grand Canyon NP - North Rim CG - RV/Tent	58	B2
Grand Canyon NP - North Rim CG - Tent-Only	59	B2
Grand Canyon NP - Point Sublime	60	B2
Grand Canyon NP - Salt Creek	61	B2
Grand Canyon NP - Scorpion Ridge	62	B2
Grand Canyon NP - Tapeats Creek	1	A2
Grand Canyon NP - Thunder River	2	A2
Grand Canyon NP - Trailer Village CG	63	B2
Grand Canyon NP - Tuweep Overlook	64	B2
Grand Canyon NP - Vishnu	65	B2
Grand Canyon NP - Widforss	66	B2
Lake Mead NRA - Black Canyon	14	B1
Lake Mead NRA - Bonelli Bay	15	B1
Lake Mead NRA - Bonelli Landing	16	B1
Lake Mead NRA - Cohenour Mine	17	B1
Lake Mead NRA - Eldorado Powerline	18	B1
Lake Mead NRA - Gilbert Canyon	19	B1
Lake Mead NRA - Greg's Hideout	20	B1
Lake Mead NRA - Horsethief Canyon	21	B1
Lake Mead NRA - Jumbo Wash	22	B1
Lake Mead NRA - Katherine Landing North	23	B1
Lake Mead NRA - Katherine Landing RV Park	24	B1
Lake Mead NRA - Katherine Landing South	25	B1
Lake Mead NRA - Kingman Wash	26	B1
Lake Mead NRA - Pearce Ferry	27	B1
Lake Mead NRA - Pope Mine	28	B1
Lake Mead NRA - Road 63 Site	29	B1
Lake Mead NRA - Temple Bar	30	B1
Lake Mead NRA - Temple Bar RV Park	31	B1
Lake Mead NRA - Two B's Mine	32	B1
Lake Mead NRA - Willow Beach	33	B1
Navajo NM -Canyon View - NPS	11	A3
Navajo NM -Sunset View - NPS	12	A3
Organ Pipe Cactus NM - Alamo Canyon	73	D2
Organ Pipe Cactus NM - Twin Peak	81	E2
Saguaro NP - Douglas Spring	74	D3
Saguaro NP - Grass Shack	75	D3
Saguaro NP - Happy Valley Saddle	76	D3
Saguaro NP - Juniper Basin	77	D3
Saguaro NP - Manning Camp	78	D3
Saguaro NP - Spud Rock Spring	79	D3
Slickrock Corral - NPS	13	A3

1 • A2 | Grand Canyon NP - Tapeats Creek

Dispersed sites, No water, No toilets, Tents only: $10, Hike-in/boat-in, $10+$8/person, Elev: 2680ft/817m, Tel: 928 638-2443, Nearest town: Grand Canyon. GPS: 36.371104, -112.469144

2 • A2 | Grand Canyon NP - Thunder River

Dispersed sites, No water, No toilets, Tents only: $10, Hike-in, $10+$8/person, Elev: 3173ft/967m, Tel: 928 638-2443, Nearest town: Grand Canyon. GPS: 36.392175, -112.451606

3 • A3 | Colorado River - South Canyon

Dispersed sites, No water, No toilets, Tents only: $10, Hike-in/boat-in, $10 permit required, Elev: 2877ft/877m. GPS: 36.502721, -111.857606

4 • A3 | Glen Canyon NRA - Beehive

Total sites: 6, RV sites: 6, No water, No toilets, No showers, No RV dump, Tent & RV camping: $14, Concessionaire, Stay limit: 3 days, Generator hours: 0600-2200, Open all year, Reservations accepted, Elev: 3938ft/1200m, Tel: 928-645-1059, Nearest town: Page. GPS: 36.936028, -111.503523

5 • A3 | Glen Canyon NRA - Lees Ferry

Total sites: 51, RV sites: 51, Central water, Flush toilet, No showers, RV dump, Tent & RV camping: $20, Stay limit: 14 days, Generator hours: 0600-2200, Open all year, Reservations not accepted, Elev:

3202ft/976m, Tel: 928-608-6200, Nearest town: Marble Canyon. GPS: 36.859471, -111.606163

6 • A3 | Glen Canyon NRA - Wahweap - Loop 1

Total sites: 27, RV sites: 0, Water at site, Flush toilet, Pay showers, RV dump, Tents only: $30, Concessionaire, Stay limit: 14 days, Generator hours: 0600-2200, Open all year, Reservations accepted, Elev: 3758ft/1145m, Tel: 928-645-1059, Nearest town: Page. GPS: 36.995488, -111.495393

7 • A3 | Glen Canyon NRA - Wahweap - Loops 2-4

Total sites: 85, RV sites: 85, Water at site, Flush toilet, Pay showers, RV dump, Tents: $30/RV's: $26, Concessionaire, Stay limit: 14 days, Generator hours: 0600-2200, Open all year, Max Length: 40ft, Reservations accepted, Elev: 3777ft/1151m, Tel: 928-645-1059, Nearest town: Page. GPS: 36.995778, -111.497967

8 • A3 | Glen Canyon NRA - Wahweap - Loops A/B/C/D/F

Total sites: 139, RV sites: 139, Elec sites: 139, Water at site, Flush toilet, Pay showers, RV dump, Tents: $46-52/RV's: $68, 139 Full hookups, Concessionaire, Stay limit: 14 days, Generator hours: 0600-2200, Open all year, Max Length: 45ft, Reservations accepted, Elev: 3751ft/1143m, Tel: 928-645-1059, Nearest town: Page. GPS: 36.998919, -111.499857

9 • A3 | Glen Canyon NRA - Wahweap - Walk-in Tent

Total sites: 9, RV sites: 0, Water at site, Flush toilet, Pay showers, RV dump, Tents only: $30, Walk-to sites, Concessionaire, Stay limit: 14 days, Generator hours: 0600-2200, Open all year, Reservations accepted, Elev: 3746ft/1142m, Tel: 928-645-1059, Nearest town: Page. GPS: 36.995779, -111.494605

10 • A3 | Grand Canyon NP - Nankoweap

Dispersed sites, No water, No toilets, Tents only: $10, Hike-in/boat-in, $10+$8/person, Elev: 3793ft/1156m, Tel: 928 638-2443, Nearest town: Grand Canyon. GPS: 36.307674, -111.860256

11 • A3 | Navajo NM -Canyon View - NPS

Total sites: 14, No water, Vault/pit toilet, Tents only: Donation, No open fires, Generator hours: 0600-2200, Open Apr-Sep, Reservations not accepted, Elev: 7287ft/2221m, Tel: 928-672-2700, Nearest town: Kayenta. GPS: 36.685962, -110.541188

12 • A3 | Navajo NM -Sunset View - NPS

Total sites: 31, RV sites: 31, Central water, Flush toilet, No showers, No RV dump, Tent & RV camping: Donation, No open fires, Open all year, Max Length: 28ft, Reservations not accepted, Elev: 7306ft/2227m, Tel: 928-672-2700, Nearest town: Kayenta. GPS: 36.676352, -110.542432

13 • A3 | Slickrock Corral - NPS

Dispersed sites, No water, No toilets, Tent & RV camping: Free, Reservations not accepted, Elev: 4191ft/1277m, Nearest town: Page. GPS: 36.994208, -111.600989

14 • B1 | Lake Mead NRA - Black Canyon

Dispersed sites, No water, No toilets, Tents only: Free, Also hike-in sites, 4x4 required, Elev: 931ft/284m, Tel: 702-293-8990, Nearest town: Las Vegas. GPS: 35.914989, -114.695655

15 • B1 | Lake Mead NRA - Bonelli Bay

Dispersed sites, No water, No toilets, Tent & RV camping: Free, Elev: 1243ft/379m, Tel: 702-293-8990, Nearest town: Kingman. GPS: 36.062182, -114.474159

16 • B1 | Lake Mead NRA - Bonelli Landing

Dispersed sites, No water, No toilets, Tent & RV camping: Free, Elev: 1227ft/374m, Tel: 702-293-8990, Nearest town: Kingman. GPS: 36.083538, -114.485144

17 • B1 | Lake Mead NRA - Cohenour Mine

Dispersed sites, No water, No toilets, Tents only: Free, Also hike-in sites, 4x4 required, Elev: 2775ft/846m, Tel: 702-293-8990, Nearest town: Las Vegas. GPS: 36.076892, -114.579529

18 • B1 | Lake Mead NRA - Eldorado Powerline

Dispersed sites, No water, No toilets, Tents only: Free, Also hike-in sites, 4x4 required, Elev: 1106ft/337m, Tel: 702-293-8990, Nearest town: Las Vegas. GPS: 35.650642, -114.642963

19 • B1 | Lake Mead NRA - Gilbert Canyon

Dispersed sites, No water, No toilets, Tents only: Free, Also hike-in sites, 4x4 required, Elev: 1457ft/444m, Tel: 702-293-8990, Nearest town: Las Vegas. GPS: 36.120983, -114.593768

20 • B1 | Lake Mead NRA - Greg's Hideout

Dispersed sites, No water, No toilets, Tent & RV camping: Free, Elev: 1257ft/383m, Tel: 702-293-8990, Nearest town: Kingman. GPS: 36.001272, -114.230704

21 • B1 | Lake Mead NRA - Horsethief Canyon

Dispersed sites, No water, No toilets, Tents only: Free, Also hike-in sites, 4x4 required, Elev: 2828ft/862m, Tel: 702-293-8990, Nearest town: Las Vegas. GPS: 35.997093, -114.642483

22 • B1 | Lake Mead NRA - Jumbo Wash

Dispersed sites, No water, No toilets, Tents only: Free, Also hike-in sites, 4x4 required, Elev: 1515ft/462m, Tel: 702-293-8990, Nearest town: Las Vegas. GPS: 35.812181, -114.632334

23 • B1 | Lake Mead NRA - Katherine Landing North

Total sites: 47, RV sites: 47, Central water, Flush toilet, Free showers, RV dump, Tent & RV camping: $20, Concessionaire, Open all year, Reservations accepted, Elev: 732ft/223m, Tel: 702-293-8990, Nearest town: Bullhead City. GPS: 35.223992, -114.559135

24 • B1 | Lake Mead NRA - Katherine Landing RV Park

Total sites: 25, RV sites: 25, Elec sites: 25, Water at site, Flush toilet, Free showers, RV dump, No tents/RV's: $35-40, 25 Full hookups, Concessionaire, Open all year, Reservations accepted, Elev: 708ft/216m, Tel: 928-754-3245, Nearest town: Bullhead City. GPS: 35.222963, -114.561891

25 • B1 | Lake Mead NRA - Katherine Landing South

Total sites: 118, RV sites: 118, Central water, Flush toilet, No showers, RV dump, Tent & RV camping: $20, Concessionaire, Open all year, Max Length: 35ft, Reservations accepted, Elev:

748ft/228m, Tel: 702-293-8990, Nearest town: Bullhead City. GPS: 35.223277, -114.556821

26 • B1 | Lake Mead NRA - Kingman Wash

Dispersed sites, No water, No toilets, Tent & RV camping: Free, 4x4 required, Elev: 1250ft/381m, Tel: 702-293-8990, Nearest town: Boulder City. GPS: 36.035985, -114.707712

27 • B1 | Lake Mead NRA - Pearce Ferry

Dispersed sites, No water, No toilets, Tent & RV camping: Free, Elev: 1220ft/372m, Tel: 702-293-8990, Nearest town: Kingman. GPS: 36.116231, -114.001611

28 • B1 | Lake Mead NRA - Pope Mine

Dispersed sites, No water, No toilets, Tents only: Free, Also hike-in sites, 4x4 required, Elev: 3449ft/1051m, Tel: 702-293-8990, Nearest town: Las Vegas. GPS: 36.069036, -114.637126

29 • B1 | Lake Mead NRA - Road 63 Site

Dispersed sites, No water, No toilets, Tents only: Free, Also hike-in sites, 4x4 required, Elev: 2193ft/668m, Tel: 702-293-8990, Nearest town: Las Vegas. GPS: 35.882032, -114.601778

30 • B1 | Lake Mead NRA - Temple Bar

Total sites: 153, RV sites: 153, Central water, No toilets, No showers, RV dump, Tent & RV camping: $20, Open all year, Reservations not accepted, Elev: 1299ft/396m, Tel: 702-293-8990, Nearest town: Temple Bar. GPS: 36.030488, -114.325045

31 • B1 | Lake Mead NRA - Temple Bar RV Park

Total sites: 10, RV sites: 10, Elec sites: 10, Water at site, Flush toilet, Free showers, RV dump, No tents/RV's: $30-35, 10 Full hookups, Concessionaire, Open all year, Elev: 1243ft/379m, Tel: 928-767-3211, Nearest town: Temple Bar. GPS: 36.034276, -114.324018

32 • B1 | Lake Mead NRA - Two B's Mine

Dispersed sites, No water, No toilets, Tents only: Free, Also hike-in sites, 4x4 required, Elev: 2428ft/740m, Tel: 702-293-8990, Nearest town: Las Vegas. GPS: 35.914712, -114.616899

33 • B1 | Lake Mead NRA - Willow Beach

Total sites: 37, RV sites: 28, Elec sites: 28, Water at site, Flush toilet, Free showers, RV dump, Tents: $35/RV's: $60, 28 Full hookups, Concessionaire, No generators, Reservations accepted, Elev: 896ft/273m, Tel: 928-767-4747, Nearest town: Boulder City. GPS: 35.873282, -114.651774

34 • B2 | Colorado River - Hance

Dispersed sites, No water, No toilets, Tents only: $10, Hike-in/boat-in, $10 permit required, Elev: 2582ft/787m. GPS: 36.044228, -111.918906

35 • B2 | Colorado River - Houtata

Dispersed sites, No water, No toilets, Tents only: $10, Hike-in/boat-in, $10 permit required, Elev: 2211ft/674m. GPS: 36.226812, -112.336709

36 • B2 | Colorado River - Lower Bass

Dispersed sites, No water, No toilets, Tents only: $10, Hike-in/boat-in, $10 permit required, Elev: 2200ft/671m. GPS: 36.237868, -112.344943

37 • B2 | Grand Canyon NP - Boucher Beach

Dispersed sites, No water, No toilets, Tents only: $10, Hike-in/boat-in, $10+$8/person, Elev: 2520ft/768m, Tel: 928 638-2443, Nearest town: Grand Canyon. GPS: 36.115468, -112.230538

38 • B2 | Grand Canyon NP - Bright Angel

Total sites: 33, RV sites: 0, Central water, No toilets, Tents only: $10, Hike-in, $10+$8/person, Elev: 6913ft/2107m, Tel: 928-638-7875, Nearest town: Grand Canyon. GPS: 36.100329, -112.095187

39 • B2 | Grand Canyon NP - Cedar Spring

Dispersed sites, No water, No toilets, Tents only: $10, Hike-in, $10+$8/person, Elev: 6119ft/1865m, Tel: 928 638-2443, Nearest town: Grand Canyon. GPS: 36.088926, -112.178166

40 • B2 | Grand Canyon NP - Cheyava

Dispersed sites, No water, No toilets, Tents only: $10, Hike-in, $10+$8/person, Elev: 7395ft/2254m, Tel: 928 638-2443, Nearest town: Grand Canyon. GPS: 36.136745, -112.027084

41 • B2 | Grand Canyon NP - Clear Creek

Dispersed sites, No water, No toilets, Tents only: $10, Hike-in, $10+$8/person, Elev: 7648ft/2331m, Tel: 928 638-2443, Nearest town: Grand Canyon. GPS: 36.114695, -112.011117

42 • B2 | Grand Canyon NP - Cottonwood Camp

Total sites: 25, RV sites: 0, Central water, Vault/pit toilet, Tents only: $10, Hike-in, $10+$8/person, Elev: 6063ft/1848m, Tel: 928 638-7875, Nearest town: Grand Canyon. GPS: 36.170347, -112.040752

43 • B2 | Grand Canyon NP - Cottonwood Creek

Dispersed sites, No water, No toilets, Tents only: $10, Hike-in, $10+$8/person, Elev: 5597ft/1706m, Tel: 928 638-2443, Nearest town: Grand Canyon. GPS: 36.027386, -111.988148

44 • B2 | Grand Canyon NP - Eremita Mesa

Dispersed sites, No water, Tents only: $10, Hike-in, $10+$8/person, Elev: 6368ft/1941m, Tel: 928 638-2443, Nearest town: Grand Canyon. GPS: 36.065203, -112.247585

45 • B2 | Grand Canyon NP - Granite Rapids

Dispersed sites, No water, No toilets, Tents only: $10, Hike-in/boat-in, $10+$8/person, Elev: 5659ft/1725m, Tel: 928 638-2443, Nearest town: Grand Canyon. GPS: 36.097709, -112.184148

46 • B2 | Grand Canyon NP - Grapevine

Dispersed sites, No water, No toilets, Tents only: $10, Hike-in, $10+$8/person, Elev: 6942ft/2116m, Tel: 928 638-2443, Nearest town: Grand Canyon. GPS: 36.036808, -112.022151

47 • B2 | Grand Canyon NP - Greenland Springs

Dispersed sites, No water, No toilets, Tents only: $10, Hike-in, $10+$8/person, Elev: 8504ft/2592m, Tel: 928 638-2443, Nearest town: Grand Canyon. GPS: 36.242283, -111.990585

48 • B2 | Grand Canyon NP - Hance Creek

Dispersed sites, No water, No toilets, Tents only: $10, Hike-in, $10+$8/person, Elev: 6890ft/2100m, Tel: 928 638-2443, Nearest town: Grand Canyon. GPS: 35.998058, -111.970067

49 • B2 | Grand Canyon NP - Hermit Creek

Dispersed sites, No water, Vault/pit toilet, Tents only: $10, Hike-in, $10+$8/person, Elev: 4570ft/1393m, Tel: 928 638-2443, Nearest town: Grand Canyon. GPS: 36.081627, -112.212823

50 • B2 | Grand Canyon NP - Hermit Rapids

Dispersed sites, No water, Vault/pit toilet, Tents only: $10, Hike-in/ boat-in, $10+$8/person, Elev: 4262ft/1299m, Tel: 928 638-2443, Nearest town: Grand Canyon. GPS: 36.099654, -112.209883

51 • B2 | Grand Canyon NP - Horn Creek

Dispersed sites, No water, No toilets, Tents only: $10, Hike-in, $10+$8/person, Elev: 6860ft/2091m, Tel: 928 638-2443, Nearest town: Grand Canyon. GPS: 36.085835, -112.143636

52 • B2 | Grand Canyon NP - Horseshoe Mesa

Dispersed sites, No water, Vault/pit toilet, Tents only: $10, Hike-in, $10+$8/person, Elev: 5502ft/1677m, Tel: 928 638-2443, Nearest town: Grand Canyon. GPS: 36.021844, -111.976102

53 • B2 | Grand Canyon NP - Indian Gardens

Total sites: 35, RV sites: 0, Central water, Vault/pit toilet, Tents only: $10, Hike-in, $10+$8/person, Elev: 6854ft/2089m, Tel: 928-638-7875, Nearest town: Grand Canyon. GPS: 36.085982, -112.124482

54 • B2 | Grand Canyon NP - Mather CG

Total sites: 274, RV sites: 274, Central water, Flush toilet, Pay showers, RV dump, Tent & RV camping: $18, Pine Loop no generators, Generator hours: 070-0900/1800-2000, Open all year, Max Length: 30ft, Reservations accepted, Elev: 7008ft/2136m, Tel: 928-638-7888, Nearest town: Grand Canyon. GPS: 36.050226, -112.120273

55 • B2 | Grand Canyon NP - Mather CG - Pine

Total sites: 55, RV sites: 0, Central water, Flush toilet, Pay showers, RV dump, Tents only: $18, 7 group sites, No generators, Open all year, Reservations accepted, Elev: 7021ft/2140m, Tel: 928-638-7888, Nearest town: Grand Canyon. GPS: 36.049858, -112.117183

56 • B2 | Grand Canyon NP - Mather CG - Sage Group

Total sites: 7, RV sites: 0, Central water, Flush toilet, Pay showers, RV dump, Group site: $50, Generator hours: 0700-0900/1800-2000, Open all year, Reservations accepted, Elev: 6998ft/2133m, Tel: 928-638-7888, Nearest town: Grand Canyon. GPS: 36.049958, -112.119076

57 • B2 | Grand Canyon NP - Monument Creek

Dispersed sites, No water, Vault/pit toilet, Tents only: $10, Hike-in, $10+$8/person, Elev: 6056ft/1846m, Tel: 928 638-2443, Nearest town: Grand Canyon. GPS: 36.082765, -112.186967

58 • B2 | Grand Canyon NP - North Rim CG - RV/Tent

Total sites: 78, RV sites: 78, Central water, Flush toilet, Pay showers, RV dump, Tent & RV camping: $18-25, Generator hours: 0700-0900/1800-2000, Open May-Oct, Max Length: 30ft, Reservations required, Elev: 8312ft/2533m, Tel: 928-638-7888, Nearest town: Grand Canyon. GPS: 36.210499, -112.060405

59 • B2 | Grand Canyon NP - North Rim CG - Tent-Only

Total sites: 12, RV sites: 0, Central water, Flush toilet, Pay showers, RV dump, Tents only: $18, Hike/bike sites: $6, No generators, Open May-Nov, Reservations accepted, Elev: 8310ft/2533m, Tel: 928-638-7888, Nearest town: Grand Canyon. GPS: 36.211092, -112.060972

60 • B2 | Grand Canyon NP - Point Sublime

Dispersed sites, No water, No toilets, Tents only: $8, 4X4 recommended, $10 permit required, Elev: 7487ft/2282m, Tel: 928 638-2443, Nearest town: Grand Canyon. GPS: 36.206868, -112.247861

61 • B2 | Grand Canyon NP - Salt Creek

Dispersed sites, No water, No toilets, Tents only: $10, Hike-in, $10+$8/person, Elev: 6585ft/2007m, Tel: 928 638-2443, Nearest town: Grand Canyon. GPS: 36.085169, -112.163141

62 • B2 | Grand Canyon NP - Scorpion Ridge

Dispersed sites, No water, No toilets, Tents only: $10, Hike-in, $10+$8/person, Elev: 4098ft/1249m, Tel: 928 638-2443, Nearest town: Grand Canyon. GPS: 36.171802, -112.278644

63 • B2 | Grand Canyon NP - Trailer Village CG

Total sites: 84, RV sites: 84, Elec sites: 80, Water at site, Flush toilet, Pay showers, RV dump, No tents/RV's: $65, Dump station near Mather CG, Senior Pass not accepted, Concessionaire, Generator hours: 0800-2200, Open all year, Max Length: 50ft, Reservations accepted, Elev: 7054ft/2150m, Tel: 928-638-2631, Nearest town: Grand Canyon. GPS: 36.05294, -112.1145

64 • B2 | Grand Canyon NP - Tuweep Overlook

Total sites: 9, RV sites: 0, No water, Vault/pit toilet, Tents only: $8, Advance 10 permit required, Must arrive before sunset, No fires, Open May-Oct, Max Length: 22ft, Elev: 4594ft/1400m, Tel: 928 638-7875, Nearest town: Fredonia. GPS: 36.223588, -113.060051

65 • B2 | Grand Canyon NP - Vishnu

Dispersed sites, No water, No toilets, Tents only: Fee unk, Hike-in, $10+$8/person, Elev: 5030ft/1533m, Tel: 928 638-2443, Nearest town: Grand Canyon. GPS: 36.076224, -111.933962

66 • B2 | Grand Canyon NP - Widforss

Dispersed sites, No water, No toilets, Tents only: Fee unk, Hike-in, $10+$8/person, Elev: 7808ft/2380m, Tel: 928 638-2443, Nearest town: Grand Canyon. GPS: 36.183708, -112.085746

67 • B3 | Colorado River - Lower Espejo

Dispersed sites, No water, No toilets, Tents only: $10, Hike-in/ boat-in, $10 permit required, Elev: 2687ft/819m. GPS: 36.120725, -111.824815

68 • B3 | Colorado River - Palisades Creek

Dispersed sites, No water, No toilets, Tents only: $10, Hike-in/boat-in, $10 permit required, Elev: 2692ft/821m. GPS: 36.136372, -111.816428

69 • B3 | Colorado River - Tanner

Dispersed sites, No water, No toilets, Tents only: $10, Hike-in/boat-in, $10 permit required, Elev: 2687ft/819m. GPS: 36.105343, -111.827813

70 • B3 | Colorado River - Upper Espejo

Dispersed sites, No water, No toilets, Tents only: $10, Hike-in/boat-in, $10 permit required, Elev: 2690ft/820m. GPS: 36.126499, -111.820175

71 • B3 | Grand Canyon NP - Desert View

Total sites: 50, RV sites: 50, Central water, Flush toilet, No showers, No RV dump, Tent & RV camping: $18, Stay limit: 7 days, Open Apr-Oct, Max Length: 30ft, Reservations required, Elev: 7464ft/2275m, Tel: 928 638-2443, Nearest town: Grand Canyon. GPS: 36.039649, -111.822164

72 • B4 | Canyon De Chelly NM - Cottonwood

Total sites: 93, RV sites: 93, Central water, Flush toilet, No showers, RV dump, Tent & RV camping: $14, No campfires, Limited facilities in winter, 2 group sites available - $50/night, No senior discount, Generator hours: 0600-2030, Open all year, Max Length: 40ft, Reservations not accepted, Elev: 5541ft/1689m, Tel: 928-674-2106, Nearest town: Chinle. GPS: 36.149843, -109.540222

73 • D2 | Organ Pipe Cactus NM - Alamo Canyon

Total sites: 4, RV sites: 0, No water, Vault/pit toilet, Tents only: $12, Stay limit: 7 days, No generators, Reservations not accepted, Elev: 2484ft/757m, Tel: 520-387-6849, Nearest town: Lukeville. GPS: 32.066522, -112.718001

74 • D3 | Saguaro NP - Douglas Spring

Dispersed sites, No water, Vault/pit toilet, Tents only: $8, Hike-in, 6.3 mi, 3 sites, Reservations required, Elev: 4709ft/1435m, Tel: 520-733-5153, Nearest town: Tucson. GPS: 32.228184, -110.607321

75 • D3 | Saguaro NP - Grass Shack

Dispersed sites, No water, Vault/pit toilet, Tents only: $8, Hike-in, 10 mi, 3 sites, Reservations required, Elev: 5296ft/1614m, Tel: 520-733-5153, Nearest town: Tucson. GPS: 32.183769, -110.592444

76 • D3 | Saguaro NP - Happy Valley Saddle

Dispersed sites, No water, Vault/pit toilet, Tents only: $8, Hike-in, 4.1 mi, 3 sites, Reservations required, Elev: 6127ft/1868m, Tel: 520-733-5153, Nearest town: Tucson. GPS: 32.150541, -110.521598

77 • D3 | Saguaro NP - Juniper Basin

Dispersed sites, No water, Vault/pit toilet, Tents only: $8, Hike-in, 6.9 mi, 3 sites, Reservations required, Elev: 6016ft/1834m, Tel: 520-733-5153, Nearest town: Tucson. GPS: 32.182557, -110.644929

78 • D3 | Saguaro NP - Manning Camp

Dispersed sites, No water, Vault/pit toilet, Tents only: $8, Hike-in, 7.5 mi, 6 sites, Reservations required, Elev: 7952ft/2424m, Tel: 520-733-5153, Nearest town: Tucson. GPS: 32.207353, -110.554981

79 • D3 | Saguaro NP - Spud Rock Spring

Dispersed sites, No water, Vault/pit toilet, Tents only: $8, Hike-in, 5.3 mi, 3 sites, Reservations required, Elev: 7383ft/2250m, Tel: 520-733-5153, Nearest town: Tucson. GPS: 32.204181, -110.532454

80 • D4 | Chiricahua NM - Bonita Canyon CG

Total sites: 22, RV sites: 22, Central water, Flush toilet, No showers, No RV dump, Tent & RV camping: $20, Group site $3/person, Generator hours: 0800-2000, Open all year, Max Length: 29ft, Reservations accepted, Elev: 5374ft/1638m, Tel: 520-824-3560, Nearest town: Willcox. GPS: 32.011467, -109.355144

81 • E2 | Organ Pipe Cactus NM - Twin Peak

Total sites: 208, RV sites: 174, Central water, Flush toilet, Free showers, RV dump, Tent & RV camping: $20, Reservations required Jan-Mar, Stay limit: 21 days, Generator hours: 0800-1000/1600-1800, Open all year, Max Length: 40ft, Reservations required, Elev: 1700ft/518m, Tel: 520-387-6849, Nearest town: Lukeville. GPS: 31.940829, -112.811084

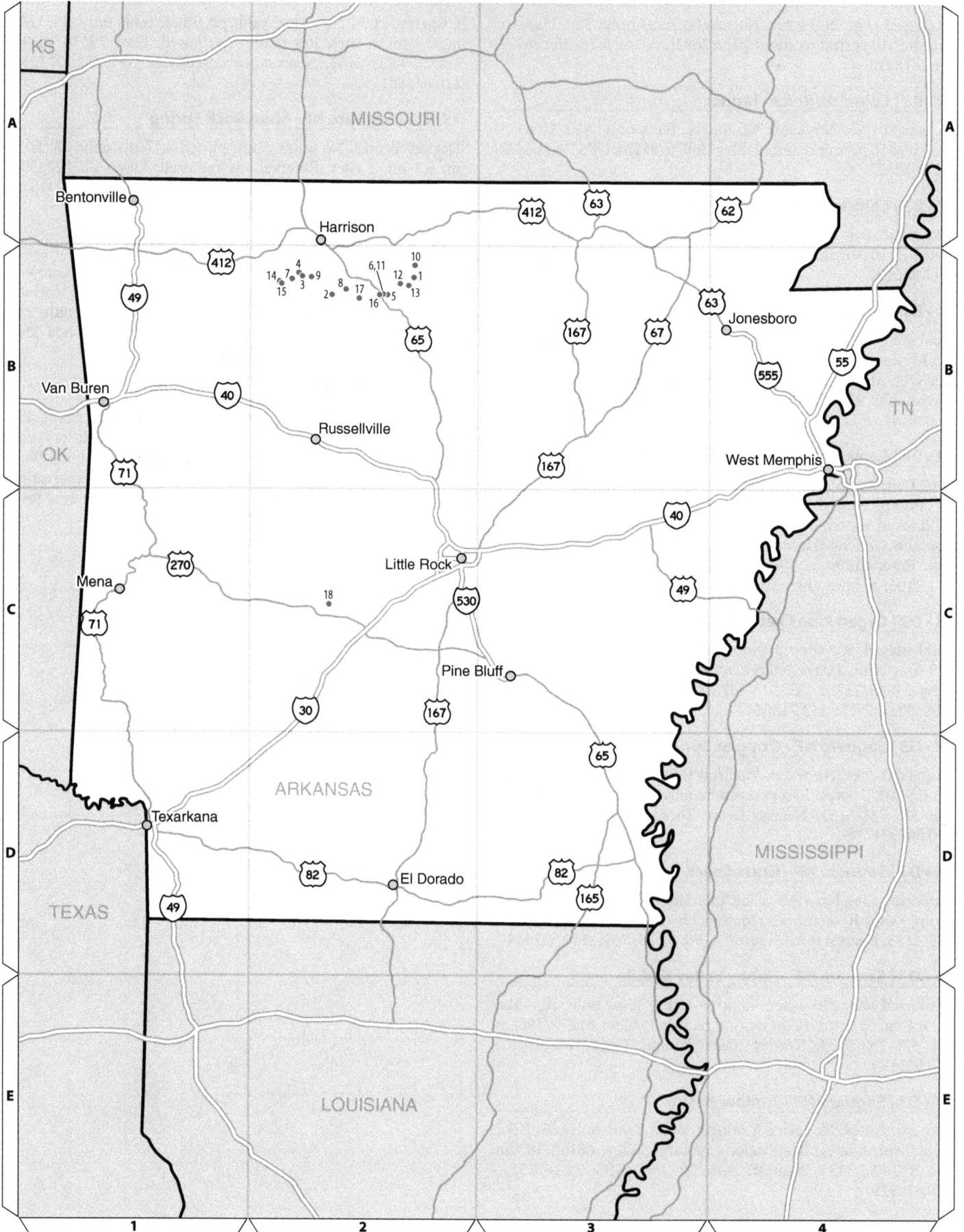

Arkansas

KS

MISSOURI

Bentonville

412

63

62

Harrison

412

49

14 7 4
15 3 9
2 8 17
16

6,11
10
12 1
5 13

65

63

Jonesboro

167

67

55

TN

Van Buren

40

OK

Russellville

167

71

West Memphis

270

40

Mena

Little Rock

49

71

530

18

Pine Bluff

30

167

65

ARKANSAS

Texarkana

MISSISSIPPI

49

82

El Dorado

82

165

TEXAS

LOUISIANA

1 2 3 4

Map	ID	Map	ID
B2	1-17	C2	18

Alphabetical List of Camping Areas

Name	ID	Map
Buffalo NR - Buffalo Point	1	B2
Buffalo NR - Carver	2	B2
Buffalo NR - Erbie	3	B2
Buffalo NR - Erbie Horse Camp	4	B2
Buffalo NR - Gilbert	5	B2
Buffalo NR - Grinders Ferry	6	B2
Buffalo NR - Kyles Landing	7	B2
Buffalo NR - Mt Hersey	8	B2
Buffalo NR - Ozark	9	B2
Buffalo NR - Rush Landing	10	B2
Buffalo NR - Shine Eye	11	B2
Buffalo NR - South Maumee	12	B2
Buffalo NR - Spring Creek	13	B2
Buffalo NR - Steel Creek - Tent	14	B2
Buffalo NR - Steel Creek Horse Camp	15	B2
Buffalo NR - Tyler Bend	16	B2
Buffalo NR - Woolum	17	B2
Hot Springs NP - Gulpha Gorge	18	C2

1 • B2 | Buffalo NR - Buffalo Point

Total sites: 104, RV sites: 83, Elec sites: 83, Water at site, Flush toilet, Free showers, RV dump, Tents: $20/RV's: $30, Group site: $50, Free 15 Nov-14 Mar - Loop B open, Open all year, Reservations accepted, Elev: 508ft/155m, Tel: 870-449-4311, Nearest town: Caney. GPS: 36.070573, -92.555745

2 • B2 | Buffalo NR - Carver

Total sites: 8, RV sites: 8, Central water, Vault/pit toilet, No showers, No RV dump, Tent & RV camping: $16, Free 15 Nov-14 Mar, Open all year, Reservations not accepted, Elev: 778ft/237m, Tel: 870-439-2502, Nearest town: Hasty. GPS: 35.983086, -93.040579

3 • B2 | Buffalo NR - Erbie

Total sites: 16, RV sites: 14, No water, Vault/pit toilet, No showers, No RV dump, Tent & RV camping: Free, 5 group sites: $33, Open Mar-Nov, Reservations not accepted, Elev: 857ft/261m, Tel: 870-439-2502, Nearest town: Jasper. GPS: 36.071318, -93.215626

4 • B2 | Buffalo NR - Erbie Horse Camp

Dispersed sites, No water, Vault/pit toilet, No showers, No RV dump, Tent & RV camping: Free, Open all year, Reservations not accepted, Elev: 990ft/302m, Tel: 870-439-2502, Nearest town: Jasper. GPS: 36.081269, -93.232818

5 • B2 | Buffalo NR - Gilbert

Dispersed sites, No water, Vault/pit toilet, Tents only: Free, Camp on gravel bar, Open all year, Reservations not accepted, Elev: 556ft/169m, Tel: 870-439-2502, Nearest town: St Joe. GPS: 35.986864, -92.715134

6 • B2 | Buffalo NR - Grinders Ferry

Dispersed sites, No water, Vault/pit toilet, Tents only: Free, Camp on gravel bar, Open all year, Reservations not accepted, Elev: 578ft/176m, Tel: 870-439-2502, Nearest town: St Joe. GPS: 35.984893, -92.744116

7 • B2 | Buffalo NR - Kyles Landing

Total sites: 33, RV sites: 0, Central water, Flush toilet, No showers, No RV dump, Tents only: $20, 4x4 high-clearance vehicle recommended, Free 15 Nov-14 Mar - no water, Open all year, Reservations not accepted, Elev: 925ft/282m, Tel: 870-439-2502, Nearest town: Jasper. GPS: 36.055875, -93.280928

8 • B2 | Buffalo NR - Mt Hersey

Dispersed sites, No water, Vault/pit toilet, Tents only: Free, Open all year, Reservations not accepted, Elev: 692ft/211m, Tel: 870-439-2502, Nearest town: St Joe. GPS: 36.009826, -92.952798

9 • B2 | Buffalo NR - Ozark

Total sites: 31, RV sites: 31, Central water, Flush toilet, No showers, No RV dump, Tent & RV camping: $20, Free 15 Nov-14 Mar - no water, Open all year, Reservations not accepted, Elev: 820ft/250m, Tel: 870-439-2502, Nearest town: Jasper. GPS: 36.063982, -93.160128

10 • B2 | Buffalo NR - Rush Landing

Total sites: 12, RV sites: 0, Vault/pit toilet, Tents only: $16, Free 15 Nov-14 Mar - no water, Open all year, Reservations not accepted, Elev: 495ft/151m, Tel: 870-439-2502, Nearest town: Yellville. GPS: 36.125273, -92.549253

11 • B2 | Buffalo NR - Shine Eye

Total sites: 1, No water, Vault/pit toilet, No showers, No RV dump, Tents only: Free, Walk-to/boat-in sites, Camp on gravel bar, Open all year, Reservations not accepted, Elev: 588ft/179m, Tel: 870-439-2502, Nearest town: St Joe. GPS: 35.987884, -92.734501

12 • B2 | Buffalo NR - South Maumee

Total sites: 5, RV sites: 5, No water, Vault/pit toilet, Tent & RV camping: Free, Also boat-in sites, Open all year, Reservations not accepted, Elev: 568ft/173m, Tel: 870-439-2502, Nearest town: Harriet. GPS: 36.039606, -92.635726

13 • B2 | Buffalo NR - Spring Creek

Total sites: 12, RV sites: 0, Vault/pit toilet, Tents only: Free, Open all year, Reservations not accepted, Elev: 551ft/168m, Tel: 870-439-2502, Nearest town: Yellville. GPS: 36.030166, -92.584188

14 • B2 | Buffalo NR - Steel Creek - Tent

Total sites: 26, RV sites: 0, Central water, Flush toilet, No showers, No RV dump, Tents only: $20, Walk-to sites, Free 15 Nov-14 Mar - no water, Open all year, Elev: 1001ft/305m, Tel: 870-439-2502, Nearest town: Ponca. GPS: 36.040994, -93.345552

15 • B2 | Buffalo NR - Steel Creek Horse Camp

Total sites: 14, RV sites: 0, Central water, Flush toilet, No showers, No RV dump, Tents only: $20, Free 15 Nov-14 Mar - no water, Open all year, Elev: 993ft/303m, Tel: 870-439-2505, Nearest town: Ponca. GPS: 36.039641, -93.339131

16 • B2 | Buffalo NR - Tyler Bend

Total sites: 38, RV sites: 28, Central water, Flush toilet, Free showers, RV dump, Tent & RV camping: $20, Also walk-to & group sites, 5 group sites: $50, Open all year, Reservations accepted, Elev: 594ft/181m, Tel: 870-439-2502, Nearest town: St Joe. GPS: 35.987147, -92.759656

17 • B2 | Buffalo NR - Woolum

Dispersed sites, No toilets, Tent & RV camping: Free, Open all year, Reservations not accepted, Elev: 669ft/204m, Tel: 870-439-2502, Nearest town: St Joe. GPS: 35.970919, -92.879962

18 • C2 | Hot Springs NP - Gulpha Gorge

Total sites: 44, RV sites: 44, Elec sites: 44, Water at site, No toilets, No showers, RV dump, Tent & RV camping: $30, 44 Full hookups, Stay limit: 14 days, Generator hours: 0600-2200, Open all year, Reservations not accepted, Elev: 646ft/197m, Tel: 501-620-6715, Nearest town: Hot Springs. GPS: 34.524414, -93.036133

California

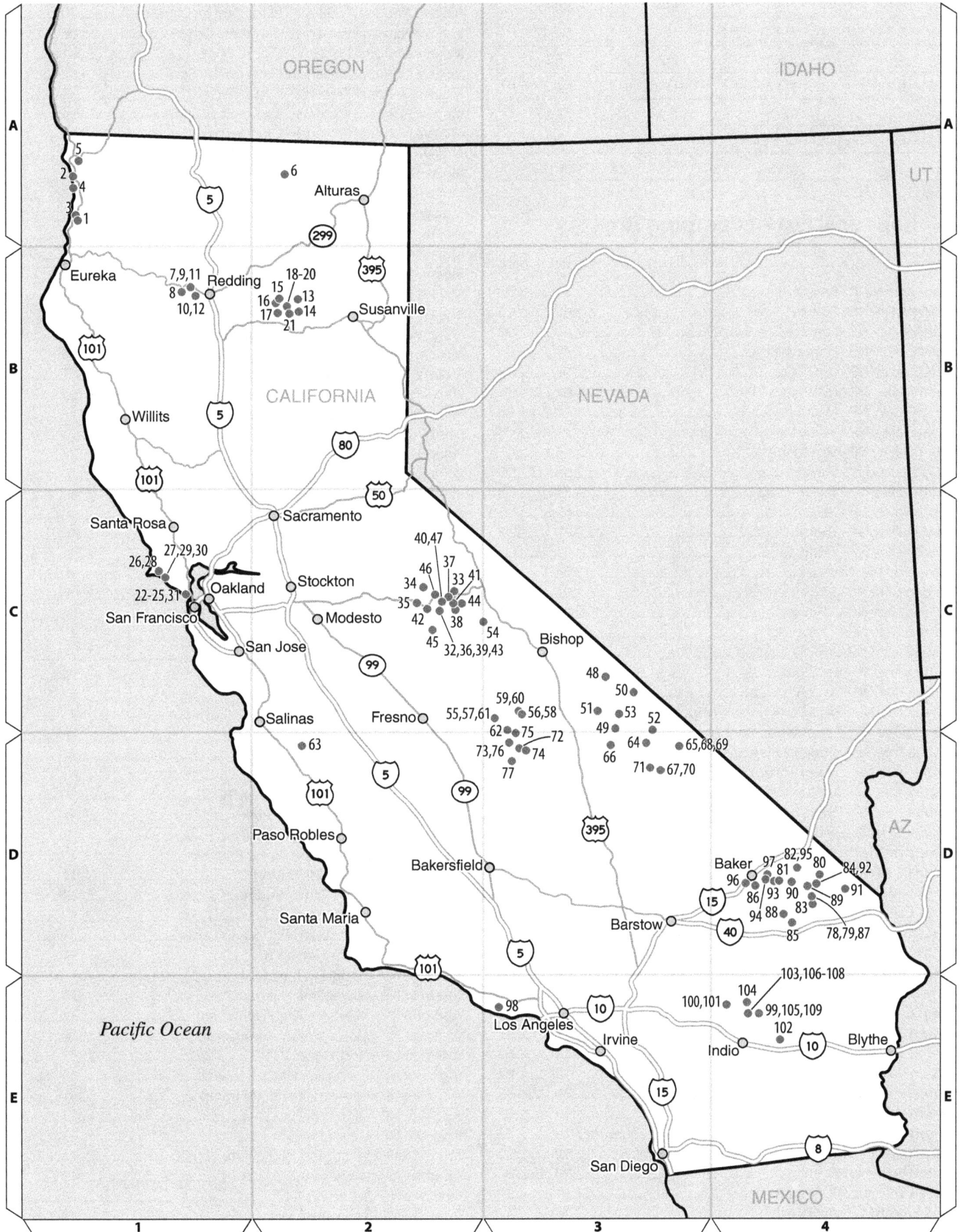

OREGON   IDAHO

UT

5
2
4
3 1

6
Alturas

299

395

Eureka

7,9,11 Redding   18-20
8   15   13
10,12   16   14
      17   Susanville
       21

101

CALIFORNIA   NEVADA

Willits

5

80

50

Santa Rosa   Sacramento

27,29,30
26,28
22-25,31   Oakland   Stockton
San Francisco   Modesto

40,47
37
46   33   41
34   44
35   54
42   38
45   32,36,39,43

San Jose

99

48
50
Salinas   59,60   51   53   52
   63   Fresno   55,57,61   56,58   49   64   65,68,69
                62   75   72   66   71   67,70
                73,76   74
                77

Bishop

5

101

99

395

Paso Robles

Bakersfield

AZ

Baker   97   82,95
    96   81   80   84,92
Santa Maria   86   93   90   89   91
            94   88   83
   Barstow   85   78,79,87

15

40

101

5

10

103,106-108
104
98   100,101   99,105,109
Los Angeles   102
Irvine   Indio   10   Blythe

Pacific Ocean

15

8

San Diego

MEXICO

Map	ID	Map	ID
A1	1-5	C3	48-62
A2	6	D2	63
B1	7-12	D3	64-77
B2	13-21	D4	78-97
C1	22-31	E3	98
C2	32-47	E4	99-109

Alphabetical List of Camping Areas

Name	ID	Map
Death Valley NP - Emigrant	64	D3
Death Valley NP - Eureka Dunes	48	C3
Death Valley NP - Furnace Creek	65	D3
Death Valley NP - Homestake	49	C3
Death Valley NP - Lee Flat	66	D3
Death Valley NP - Mahogany Flat	67	D3
Death Valley NP - Mesquite Spring	50	C3
Death Valley NP - Saline Valley Warm Springs Dispersed	51	C3
Death Valley NP - Stove Pipe Wells	52	C3
Death Valley NP - Sunset	68	D3
Death Valley NP - Teakettle Jct	53	C3
Death Valley NP - Texas Spring	69	D3
Death Valley NP - Thorndike	70	D3
Death Valley NP - Wildrose	71	D3
Devils Postpile NP	54	C3
Golden Gate NRA - Bicentennial	22	C1
Golden Gate NRA - Hawk	23	C1
Golden Gate NRA - Haypress	24	C1
Golden Gate NRA - Kirby Cove	25	C1
Joshua Tree NP - Belle	99	E4
Joshua Tree NP - Black Rock	100	E4
Joshua Tree NP - Black Rock Horse Camp	101	E4
Joshua Tree NP - Cottonwood Springs	102	E4
Joshua Tree NP - Hidden Valley	103	E4
Joshua Tree NP - Indian Cove	104	E4
Joshua Tree NP - Jumbo Rocks	105	E4
Joshua Tree NP - Ryan	106	E4
Joshua Tree NP - Ryan Horse Sites	107	E4
Joshua Tree NP - Sheep Pass Group	108	E4
Joshua Tree NP - White Tank	109	E4
Kings Canyon NP - Azalea	55	C3
Kings Canyon NP - Canyon View Group	56	C3
Kings Canyon NP - Crystal Springs	57	C3
Kings Canyon NP - Moraine	58	C3
Kings Canyon NP - Sentinel	59	C3
Kings Canyon NP - Sheep Creek	60	C3
Kings Canyon NP - Sunset	61	C3
Lassen Volcanic NP - Butte Lake	13	B2
Lassen Volcanic NP - Juniper Lake	14	B2
Lassen Volcanic NP - Lost Creek Group	15	B2
Lassen Volcanic NP - Manzanita Lake	16	B2
Lassen Volcanic NP - Southwest Walk-in	17	B2
Lassen Volcanic NP - Summit Lake Corral Group Equestrian	18	B2
Lassen Volcanic NP - Summit Lake North	19	B2
Lassen Volcanic NP - Summit Lake South	20	B2
Lassen Volcanic NP - Warner Valley	21	B2
Lava Beds NM - Indian Well	6	A2
Mojave National Preserve - Banshee Canyon	78	D4
Mojave National Preserve - Black Canyon Equestrian	79	D4
Mojave National Preserve - Caruthers Canyon	80	D4
Mojave National Preserve - Cinder Cone	81	D4
Mojave National Preserve - Cross on the Rock	82	D4
Mojave National Preserve - D1 Dispersed	83	D4
Mojave National Preserve - East of Rock Springs	84	D4
Mojave National Preserve - Granite Pass	85	D4
Mojave National Preserve - Green Rock Mill	86	D4
Mojave National Preserve - Hole In The Wall	87	D4
Mojave National Preserve - Kelso Dunes	88	D4
Mojave National Preserve - Mid Hills	89	D4
Mojave National Preserve - Mojave Camp	90	D4
Mojave National Preserve - Piute Corral	91	D4
Mojave National Preserve - Pleasant View School	92	D4
Mojave National Preserve - Rainy Day Mine Site	93	D4
Mojave National Preserve - Seventeen Mile Point	94	D4
Mojave National Preserve - Sunrise Rock	95	D4
Mojave National Preserve - Zzyzx Rd Dispersed	96	D4
Mojave National Preserve -Jackrabbits Leg Dispersed	97	D4
Pinnacles NP	63	D2
Point Reyes NS - Coast Camp	26	C1
Point Reyes NS - Glen Camp	27	C1
Point Reyes NS - Sky Camp	28	C1
Point Reyes NS - Stewart Horse Camp	29	C1
Point Reyes NS - Wildcat Camp	30	C1
Redwood NP - 44 Camp	1	A1
Redwood NP - DeMartin	2	A1
Redwood NP - Elam	3	A1
Redwood NP - Flint Ridge	4	A1
Redwood NP - Little Bald Hills Horse Camp	5	A1
Santa Monica Mts NRA - Circle X Ranch Group	98	E3
Sequoia NP - Atwell Mill	72	D3
Sequoia NP - Buckeye Flat	73	D3
Sequoia NP - Cold Springs	74	D3
Sequoia NP - Dorst Creek	62	C3
Sequoia NP - Lodgepole	75	D3
Sequoia NP - Potwisha	76	D3
Sequoia NP - South Fork	77	D3
The Presidio NP - Rob Hill Group	31	C1
Whiskeytown NRA - Brandy Creek RV CG	7	B1
Whiskeytown NRA - Coggins Park	8	B1
Whiskeytown NRA - Dry Creek Group	9	B1
Whiskeytown NRA - Horse Camp Primitive	10	B1
Whiskeytown NRA - Oak Bottom	11	B1
Whiskeytown NRA - Peltier Bridge	12	B1
Yosemite NP - Camp 4	32	C2
Yosemite NP - Glen Aulin High Sierra Camp	33	C2
Yosemite NP - Hetch Hetchy TC	34	C2
Yosemite NP - Hodgdon Meadow	35	C2
Yosemite NP - Lower Pines	36	C2
Yosemite NP - May Lake High Sierra Camp	37	C2
Yosemite NP - Merced High Sierra Camp	38	C2
Yosemite NP - North Pines	39	C2
Yosemite NP - Porcupine Flat	40	C2
Yosemite NP - Sunrise High Sierra Camp	41	C2
Yosemite NP - Tamarack Flat	42	C2
Yosemite NP - Upper Pines	43	C2
Yosemite NP - Vogelsang High Sierra Camp	44	C2
Yosemite NP - Wawona	45	C2
Yosemite NP - White Wolf	46	C2
Yosemite NP - Yosemite Creek	47	C2

1 • A1 | Redwood NP - 44 Camp

Total sites: 4, RV sites: 0, No water, No toilets, Tents only: Free, Hike-in, Free permit required, Elev: 115ft/35m, Tel: 707-465-7335. GPS: 41.232305, -124.01909

2 • A1 | Redwood NP - DeMartin

Total sites: 10, RV sites: 0, Central water, Vault/pit toilet, Tents only: Free, Hike-in, 2-3 miles, Free permit required, Elev: 724ft/221m. GPS: 41.625536, -124.106931

3 • A1 | Redwood NP - Elam

Total sites: 3, RV sites: 0, No water, Vault/pit toilet, Tents only: Free, Hike-in, Free permit required, Elev: 263ft/80m, Tel: 707-465-7335. GPS: 41.264873, -124.02786

4 • A1 | Redwood NP - Flint Ridge

Total sites: 8, RV sites: 0, No water, Vault/pit toilet, Tents only: Free, Hike-in, Free permit required, Elev: 385ft/117m. GPS: 41.525153, -124.078934

5 • A1 | Redwood NP - Little Bald Hills Horse Camp

Total sites: 5, Central water, Vault/pit toilet, Tents only: Free, Hike-in, 4.5 mi, Free permit required, Elev: 1858ft/566m, Tel: 707-465-7335. GPS: 41.768433, -124.038936

6 • A2 | Lava Beds NM - Indian Well

Total sites: 43, RV sites: 43, Central water, Flush toilet, No showers, No RV dump, Tent & RV camping: $10, Stay limit: 14 days, Generator hours: 0800-1000/1500-2000, Open all year, Max Length: 30ft, Reservations not accepted, Elev: 4646ft/1416m, Tel: 530-667-8113, Nearest town: Tulelake. GPS: 41.717507, -121.505069

7 • B1 | Whiskeytown NRA - Brandy Creek RV CG

Total sites: 32, RV sites: 32, Central water, No toilets, No showers, RV dump, No tents/RV's: $15, Units must be self-contained, $7 in winter, Generator hours: 0600-2200, Open Apr-Oct, Max Length: 35ft, Reservations not accepted, Elev: 1306ft/398m, Tel: 530-246-1225, Nearest town: Redding. GPS: 40.616654, -122.574678

8 • B1 | Whiskeytown NRA - Coggins Park

Total sites: 1, RV sites: 0, No water, No toilets, Tent & RV camping: $10, 4x4 recommended, Open all year, Max Length: 25ft, Reservations not accepted, Elev: 4131ft/1259m, Tel: 530-246-1225, Nearest town: Redding. GPS: 40.596142, -122.701725

9 • B1 | Whiskeytown NRA - Dry Creek Group

Total sites: 2, RV sites: 0, Central water, Vault/pit toilet, No showers, No RV dump, Group site: $80, Reservations required, Elev: 1257ft/383m, Tel: 530-242-3412, Nearest town: Redding. GPS: 40.624393, -122.581066

10 • B1 | Whiskeytown NRA - Horse Camp Primitive

Total sites: 2, RV sites: 2, Central water, Vault/pit toilet, No showers, No RV dump, Tent & RV camping: $20, No water in winter, Open all year, Max Length: 25ft, Reservations required, Elev: 1116ft/340m, Tel: 530-246-1225, Nearest town: Redding. GPS: 40.576343, -122.527142

11 • B1 | Whiskeytown NRA - Oak Bottom

Total sites: 120, RV sites: 22, Central water, Flush toilet, Free showers, RV dump, Tents: $25-30/RV's: $25, Walk-to sites, 98 tent sites, Oct 16 to Apr 14: $18 all sites, Generator hours: 0600-2200, Open all year, Reservations accepted, Elev: 1270ft/387m, Tel: 530-359-2269, Nearest town: Redding. GPS: 40.648716, -122.592547

12 • B1 | Whiskeytown NRA - Peltier Bridge

Total sites: 7, RV sites: 0, No water, Vault/pit toilet, Tents only: $20, Open all year, Max Length: 15ft, Reservations required, Elev: 988ft/301m, Tel: 530-246-1225, Nearest town: Redding. GPS: 40.585733, -122.551934

13 • B2 | Lassen Volcanic NP - Butte Lake

Total sites: 101, RV sites: 101, Central water, Flush toilet, No showers, No RV dump, Tents: $15/RV's: $22, $15 when no water, 6 group sites: $62, Generator hours: 0800-1000, 1200-1400, 1700-1900, Open Jun-Oct, Max Length: 35ft, Reservations accepted, Elev: 6152ft/1875m, Tel: 530-595-4480, Nearest town: Old Station. GPS: 40.564248, -121.304292

14 • B2 | Lassen Volcanic NP - Juniper Lake

Total sites: 18, RV sites: 0, No water, Vault/pit toilet, Tents only: $12, Group site: $32, Rough dirt road not suitable for buses/motorhomes/trailers, Generator hours: 0800-1000, 1200-1400, 1700-1900, Open Jul-Oct, Reservations not accepted, Elev: 6867ft/2093m, Tel: 530-595-4480, Nearest town: Chester. GPS: 40.450909, -121.295437

15 • B2 | Lassen Volcanic NP - Lost Creek Group

Total sites: 8, RV sites: 8, Central water, Vault/pit toilet, No showers, No RV dump, Group site: $62, Generator hours: 0800-1000, 1200-1400, 1700-1900, Open Jun-Sep, Max Length: 40ft, Reservations required, Elev: 5679ft/1731m, Tel: 530-595-4480, Nearest town: Redding. GPS: 40.561446, -121.517895

16 • B2 | Lassen Volcanic NP - Manzanita Lake

Total sites: 179, RV sites: 179, Central water, Flush toilet, Pay showers, RV dump, Tent & RV camping: $26, $15 when no water, 5 group sites: &72, Generator hours: 0800-1000, 1200-1400, 1700-1900, Open May-Nov, Max Length: 35ft, Reservations accepted, Elev: 5922ft/1805m, Tel: 530-595-4480, Nearest town: Viola. GPS: 40.531126, -121.562869

17 • B2 | Lassen Volcanic NP - Southwest Walk-in

Total sites: 21, RV sites: 0, Central water, Flush toilet, No showers, No RV dump, Tents only: $16, Walk-to sites, $10 when no water, Generator hours: 0800-1000, 1200-1400, 1700-1900, Open all year, Reservations not accepted, Elev: 6726ft/2050m, Tel: 530-595-4480. GPS: 40.436823, -121.532876

18 • B2 | Lassen Volcanic NP - Summit Lake Corral Group Equestrian

Total sites: 2, RV sites: 2, No water, Vault/pit toilet, Group equestrian site: $37, Open Jun-Sep, Elev: 6735ft/2053m, Tel: 530-595-6121, Nearest town: Redding. GPS: 40.494765, -121.42833

19 • B2 | Lassen Volcanic NP - Summit Lake North

Total sites: 46, RV sites: 46, Central water, Flush toilet, No showers, No RV dump, Tent & RV camping: $24, $15 when no water, Generator hours: 0800-1000, 1200-1400, 1700-1900, Open Jun-Sep, Max Length: 35ft, Reservations accepted, Elev: 6729ft/2051m, Tel: 530-595-4480, Nearest town: Viola. GPS: 40.494354, -121.424238

20 • B2 | Lassen Volcanic NP - Summit Lake South

Total sites: 48, RV sites: 48, Central water, Vault/pit toilet, No showers, No RV dump, Tent & RV camping: $22, Tents or tent-trailers - no RV's, $15 when no water, Generator hours: 0800-1000, 1200-1400, 1700-1900, Open Jun-Sep, Reservations accepted, Elev: 6729ft/2051m, Tel: 530-595-4480, Nearest town: Viola. GPS: 40.48931, -121.42403

21 • B2 | Lassen Volcanic NP - Warner Valley

Total sites: 17, RV sites: 0, Central water, Vault/pit toilet, No showers, No RV dump, Tents only: $17, RV's/trailers not recommended, $12 when no water, Generator hours: 0800-1000, 1200-1400, 1700-1900, Open Jun-Oct, Reservations not accepted, Elev: 5722ft/1744m, Tel: 530-595-4480. GPS: 40.441884, -121.393483

22 • C1 | Golden Gate NRA - Bicentennial

Total sites: 3, RV sites: 0, No water, Tents only: $30, Walk-to sites, 100 yds, No fires, No pets, Stay limit: 3 days, Open all year, Reservations required, Elev: 210ft/64m, Tel: 415-331-1540, Nearest town: Sausalito. GPS: 37.824938, -122.526653

23 • C1 | Golden Gate NRA - Hawk

Total sites: 3, RV sites: 0, No water, Vault/pit toilet, Tents only: Free, Hike-in, 3 to 4 miles , No open fires, No pets, Stay limit: 3 days, Open all year, Reservations required, Elev: 820ft/250m, Tel: 415-331-1540, Nearest town: Sausalito. GPS: 37.853979, -122.520336

24 • C1 | Golden Gate NRA - Haypress

Total sites: 3, RV sites: 0, No water, Tents only: Free, Hike-in, 3/4 mile , No open fires, No pets, Stay limit: 3 days, Reservations required, Elev: 272ft/83m, Tel: 415-331-1540, Nearest town: Sausalito. GPS: 37.860902, -122.545655

25 • C1 | Golden Gate NRA - Kirby Cove

Total sites: 4, RV sites: 0, No water, Vault/pit toilet, Tents only: $30, No pets, Open Mar-Oct, Reservations required, Elev: 115ft/35m, Tel: 415-331-1540, Nearest town: Sausalito. GPS: 37.827462, -122.490916

26 • C1 | Point Reyes NS - Coast Camp

Total sites: 14, RV sites: 0, Central water, Vault/pit toilet, Tents only: $20, Hike-in, Water not dependable, Reservations accepted, Elev: 23ft/7m, Tel: 415-663-8054, Nearest town: San Francisco. GPS: 38.018465, -122.854705

27 • C1 | Point Reyes NS - Glen Camp

Total sites: 12, RV sites: 0, Central water, Vault/pit toilet, Tents only: $20, Hike-in, Water not dependable, Reservations accepted, Elev: 574ft/175m, Tel: 415-663-8054, Nearest town: San Francisco. GPS: 37.989657, -122.78893

28 • C1 | Point Reyes NS - Sky Camp

Total sites: 11, RV sites: 0, Central water, Vault/pit toilet, Tents

only: $20, Hike-in, Water not dependable, Reservations accepted, Elev: 1025ft/312m, Tel: 415-663-8054, Nearest town: San Francisco. GPS: 38.040462, -122.829781

29 • C1 | Point Reyes NS - Stewart Horse Camp

Dispersed sites, Central water, Flush toilet, Free showers, No RV dump, Tent & RV camping: $20, Concession-operated, Reservations accepted, Elev: 180ft/55m, Tel: 415-663-1362, Nearest town: San Francisco. GPS: 38.001835, -122.76124

30 • C1 | Point Reyes NS - Wildcat Camp

Total sites: 5, RV sites: 0, Central water, Vault/pit toilet, Tents only: $20, Hike-in, Water not dependable, Reservations accepted, Elev: 57ft/17m, Tel: 415-663-8054, Nearest town: San Francisco. GPS: 37.970486, -122.790361

31 • C1 | The Presidio NP - Rob Hill Group

Total sites: 4, RV sites: 0, Central water, No toilets, No showers, No RV dump, Group site: $100, Open Apr-Oct, Elev: 407ft/124m, Tel: 415-561-5444, Nearest town: San Francisco. GPS: 37.796617, -122.475432

32 • C2 | Yosemite NP - Camp 4

Total sites: 35, RV sites: 0, Central water, Flush toilet, No showers, No RV dump, Tents only: $6, Walk-to sites, Reservations not accepted, Elev: 4029ft/1228m. GPS: 37.741169, -119.60402

33 • C2 | Yosemite NP - Glen Aulin High Sierra Camp

Dispersed sites, Central water, Vault/pit toilet, No tents/RV's/Cabin(s) only: $152, 8 mi from lodge, Open Jul-Sep, Elev: 7875ft/2400m, Nearest town: Yosemite Valley. GPS: 37.909465, -119.419578

34 • C2 | Yosemite NP - Hetch Hetchy TC

Dispersed sites, Central water, Flush toilet, Tents only: $5, Walk-to sites, Reservations not accepted, Elev: 3976ft/1212m, Tel: 209-372-0200, Nearest town: Mather. GPS: 37.942766, -119.786622

35 • C2 | Yosemite NP - Hodgdon Meadow

Total sites: 105, RV sites: 105, Central water, Flush toilet, No showers, No RV dump, Tent & RV camping: $26, Reservation required Apr-Oct, Generator hours: 0700-0900/1200-1400/1700-1900, Open all year, Max Length: RV-35'/Trlr-27ft, Reservations required, Elev: 4820ft/1469m, Tel: 209-372-0200, Nearest town: Groveland. GPS: 37.79834, -119.86683

36 • C2 | Yosemite NP - Lower Pines

Total sites: 60, RV sites: 60, Central water, Flush toilet, No showers, No RV dump, Tent & RV camping: $26, Generator hours: 0700-0900/1200-1400/1700-1900, Open Mar-Oct, Max Length: RV-40'/Trlr-35ft, Reservations required, Elev: 4045ft/1233m, Tel: 209-372-8502, Nearest town: Yosemite Valley. GPS: 37.740676, -119.567451

37 • C2 | Yosemite NP - May Lake High Sierra Camp

Total sites: 8, RV sites: 0, Central water, Flush toilet, Free showers, No RV dump, No tents/RV's/Cabin(s) only: $159, 16.5 mi from lodge, Open Jul-Sep, Elev: 8342ft/2543m, Nearest town: Yosemite Valley. GPS: 37.844976, -119.490996

38 • C2 | Yosemite NP - Merced High Sierra Camp

Dispersed sites, Central water, Flush toilet, Free showers, No RV dump, No tents/RV's/Cabin(s) only: $159, 14.6 mi from lodge, Open Jul-Sep, Elev: 7241ft/2207m, Nearest town: Yosemite Valley. GPS: 37.739072, -119.406964

39 • C2 | Yosemite NP - North Pines

Total sites: 81, RV sites: 81, Central water, Flush toilet, No showers, No RV dump, Tent & RV camping: $20, Dump station at Upper Pines, Generator hours: 0700-0900/1200-1400/1700-1900, Open Apr-Sep, Max Length: RV-40'/Trlr-35ft, Reservations required, Elev: 4081ft/1244m, Tel: 209-372-8502, Nearest town: Yosemite Valley. GPS: 37.741972, -119.566294

40 • C2 | Yosemite NP - Porcupine Flat

Total sites: 52, RV sites: 52, No water, Vault/pit toilet, Tent & RV camping: $12, Generator hours: 0700-0900/1200-1400/1700-1900, Open Jul-Oct, Max Length: RV-24'/Trlr-20ft, Reservations not accepted, Elev: 8150ft/2484m, Nearest town: Yosemite Valley. GPS: 37.8077, -119.56506

41 • C2 | Yosemite NP - Sunrise High Sierra Camp

Total sites: 9, RV sites: 0, Central water, Flush toilet, Free showers, No RV dump, No tents/RV's/Cabin(s) only: $159, 24.75 mi from lodge, Open Jul-Sep, Elev: 9338ft/2846m, Nearest town: Yosemite Valley. GPS: 37.795146, -119.432542

42 • C2 | Yosemite NP - Tamarack Flat

Total sites: 52, RV sites: 0, No water, Vault/pit toilet, Tents only: $12, Generator hours: 0700-0900/1200-1400/1700-1900, Open Jun-Sep, Reservations not accepted, Elev: 6398ft/1950m, Nearest town: Yosemite Valley. GPS: 37.752151, -119.736508

43 • C2 | Yosemite NP - Upper Pines

Total sites: 238, RV sites: 238, Central water, Flush toilet, No showers, RV dump, Tent & RV camping: $26, Reservation required Mar-Nov, Generator hours: 0700-0900/1200-1400/1700-1900, Open all year, Max Length: RV-35'/Trlr-24ft, Reservations required, Elev: 4078ft/1243m, Tel: 209-372-8502, Nearest town: Yosemite Village. GPS: 37.736308, -119.565609

44 • C2 | Yosemite NP - Vogelsang High Sierra Camp

Total sites: 12, RV sites: 0, Central water, Vault/pit toilet, No showers, No RV dump, No tents/RV's/Cabin(s) only: $152, 6.8 mi hike, Open Jul-Sep, Elev: 10155ft/3095m. GPS: 37.795199, -119.345296

45 • C2 | Yosemite NP - Wawona

Total sites: 93, RV sites: 93, Central water, Flush toilet, No showers, No RV dump, Tent & RV camping: $26, Dump station nearby, Generator hours: 0700-0900/1200-1400/1700-1900, Open all year, Max Length: 35ft, Reservations required, Elev: 3996ft/1218m, Tel: 209-375-9535, Nearest town: Wawona. GPS: 37.547363, -119.678955

46 • C2 | Yosemite NP - White Wolf

Total sites: 74, RV sites: 74, Central water, Flush toilet, No showers, No RV dump, Tent & RV camping: $18, Generator hours: 0700-0900/1200-1400/1700-1900, Open Jul-Sep, Max Length: RV-27'/Trlr-24ft, Reservations not accepted, Elev: 7910ft/2411m, Nearest town: Lee Vining. GPS: 37.869873, -119.649414

47 • C2 | Yosemite NP - Yosemite Creek

Total sites: 75, RV sites: 0, No water, Vault/pit toilet, Tents only: $12, Open Jul-Sep, Reservations not accepted, Elev: 7251ft/2210m. GPS: 37.826666, -119.595669

48 • C3 | Death Valley NP - Eureka Dunes

Dispersed sites, No water, Vault/pit toilet, Tents only: Free, Very rough road, Stay limit: 30 days, Generator hours: 0700-1900, Open all year, Reservations not accepted, Elev: 2878ft/877m, Tel: 760-786-3200. GPS: 37.111733, -117.680938

49 • C3 | Death Valley NP - Homestake

Dispersed sites, No water, Vault/pit toilet, Tent & RV camping: Free, Stay limit: 30 days, Generator hours: 0700-1900, Reservations not accepted, Elev: 3799ft/1158m, Tel: 760-786-3200. GPS: 36.641077, -117.576324

50 • C3 | Death Valley NP - Mesquite Spring

Total sites: 30, RV sites: 30, Water available, Flush toilet, No showers, RV dump, Tent & RV camping: $14, Stay limit: 30 days, Generator hours: 0700-1900, Open all year, Reservations not accepted, Elev: 1791ft/546m, Tel: 760-786-3200, Nearest town: Furnace Creek. GPS: 36.962291, -117.368602

51 • C3 | Death Valley NP - Saline Valley Warm Springs Dispersed

Dispersed sites, No water, No toilets, Tent & RV camping: Free, 4x4 required, For nudists, Stay limit: 30 days, Generator hours: 0700-1900, Reservations not accepted, Elev: 1362ft/415m, Tel: 760-786-3200. GPS: 36.804948, -117.774458

52 • C3 | Death Valley NP - Stove Pipe Wells

Total sites: 190, RV sites: 190, Water available, Flush toilet, No showers, RV dump, Tent & RV camping: $14, Stay limit: 30 days, Generator hours: 0700-1900, Open Oct-Apr, Reservations not accepted, Elev: -20ft/-6m, Tel: 760-786-3200. GPS: 36.607251, -117.146937

53 • C3 | Death Valley NP - Teakettle Jct

Dispersed sites, No water, No toilets, Tent & RV camping: Free, High clearance is required. You'll need a stout vehicle to make this trip. Heavy duty short trailers might be ok, but RVs would not, Stay limit: 30 days, Generator hours: 0700-1900, Reservations not accepted, Elev: 4152ft/1266m, Tel: 760-786-3200. GPS: 36.760214, -117.541894

54 • C3 | Devils Postpile NP

Total sites: 20, RV sites: 20, Central water, Flush toilet, No showers, No RV dump, Tent & RV camping: $20, Stay limit: 14 days, Generator hours: 0600-2200, Open Jun-Sep, Max Length: 25ft, Reservations not accepted, Elev: 7710ft/2350m, Tel: 760-934-2289, Nearest town: Mammoth Lakes. GPS: 37.63145, -119.08524

55 • C3 | Kings Canyon NP - Azalea

Total sites: 110, RV sites: 110, Central water, Flush toilet, No showers, No RV dump, Tent & RV camping: $18, Generator hours: 0900-2100, Open all year, Reservations not accepted, Elev: 6614ft/2016m, Tel: 559-565-3341, Nearest town: Grant Grove. GPS: 36.741699, -118.966064

56 • C3 | Kings Canyon NP - Canyon View Group

Total sites: 16, Central water, Flush toilet, No showers, No RV dump, Group site: $40-$60, No trailers, Generator hours: 0900-2100, Open May-Sep, Reservations accepted, Elev: 4678ft/1426m, Tel: 559-565-3341, Nearest town: Cedar Grove. GPS: 36.78817, -118.66573

57 • C3 | Kings Canyon NP - Crystal Springs

Total sites: 36, RV sites: 36, Central water, Flush toilet, No showers, No RV dump, Tent & RV camping: $18, Reservable group site: $40, Generator hours: 0900-2100, Open May-Sep, Reservations not accepted, Elev: 6745ft/2056m, Tel: 559-565-3341, Nearest town: Grant Grove. GPS: 36.744629, -118.961914

58 • C3 | Kings Canyon NP - Moraine

Total sites: 120, RV sites: 120, Central water, Flush toilet, No showers, No RV dump, Tent & RV camping: $18, Open Memorial and Labor Day weekends, Generator hours: 0900-2100, Open Jul-Aug, Reservations not accepted, Elev: 4754ft/1449m, Tel: 559-565-3341, Nearest town: Cedar Grove. GPS: 36.78572, -118.6607

59 • C3 | Kings Canyon NP - Sentinel

Total sites: 82, RV sites: 82, Central water, Flush toilet, No showers, No RV dump, Tent & RV camping: $22, Generator hours: 0900-2100, Open May-Nov, Reservations accepted, Elev: 4672ft/1424m, Tel: 559-565-3341, Nearest town: Cedar Grove. GPS: 36.79046, -118.67368

60 • C3 | Kings Canyon NP - Sheep Creek

Total sites: 111, RV sites: 111, Central water, Flush toilet, No showers, No RV dump, Tent & RV camping: $18, Generator hours: 0900-2100, Open May-Oct, Reservations not accepted, Elev: 4636ft/1413m, Tel: 559-565-3341, Nearest town: Cedar Grove. GPS: 36.7925, -118.67992

61 • C3 | Kings Canyon NP - Sunset

Total sites: 157, RV sites: 157, Central water, Flush toilet, No showers, No RV dump, Tent & RV camping: $22, 2 group sites ($40) can be reserved, Generator hours: 0900-2100, Open May-Sep, Reservations accepted, Elev: 6621ft/2018m, Tel: 559-565-3341. GPS: 36.737793, -118.96596

62 • C3 | Sequoia NP - Dorst Creek

Total sites: 218, RV sites: 218, Central water, Flush toilet, No showers, RV dump, Tent & RV camping: $22, Group sites: $50-$70, Generator hours: 0800-1100/1700-2000, Open Jun-Sep, Max Length: 50ft, Reservations not accepted, Elev: 6831ft/2082m, Tel: 559-841-3533, Nearest town: Giant Forest. GPS: 36.635323, -118.813269

63 • D2 | Pinnacles NP

Total sites: 134, RV sites: 134, Elec sites: 37, Central water, Flush toilet, Pay showers, RV dump, Tents: $30/RV's: $30-40, No generators, Open all year, Reservations accepted, Elev: 1034ft/315m, Tel: 831-200-1722, Nearest town: Pinnacles. GPS: 36.487724, -121.151845

64 • D3 | Death Valley NP - Emigrant

Total sites: 10, RV sites: 0, Central water, Flush toilet, No showers, No RV dump, Tents only: Free, Stay limit: 30 days, Generator hours: 0700-1900, Open all year, Reservations not accepted, Elev: 2159ft/658m, Tel: 760-786-3200. GPS: 36.496554, -117.227522

65 • D3 | Death Valley NP - Furnace Creek

Total sites: 125, RV sites: 79, Elec sites: 18, Water at site, Flush toilet, Free showers, RV dump, Tents: $22/RV's: $36, Stay limit: 14 days, Generator hours: 0700-1900, Open all year, Reservations accepted, Elev: -197ft/-60m, Tel: 760-786-3200, Nearest town: Furnace Creek. GPS: 36.462856, -116.868853

66 • D3 | Death Valley NP - Lee Flat

Dispersed sites, No water, Vault/pit toilet, Tent & RV camping: Free, Stay limit: 30 days, Generator hours: 0700-1900, Open all year, Reservations not accepted, Elev: 5372ft/1637m, Tel: 760-786-3200. GPS: 36.487404, -117.641801

67 • D3 | Death Valley NP - Mahogany Flat

Total sites: 10, RV sites: 10, No water, Vault/pit toilet, Tent & RV camping: Free, Accessible to high clearance vehicles only - 4x4 may be necessary, Stay limit: 30 days, Generator hours: 0700-1900, Open Mar-Nov, Reservations not accepted, Elev: 8068ft/2459m, Tel: 760-786-3200, Nearest town: Stovepipe Wells. GPS: 36.229904, -117.068609

68 • D3 | Death Valley NP - Sunset

Total sites: 270, RV sites: 270, Central water, Flush toilet, No showers, RV dump, Tent & RV camping: $14, Stay limit: 30 days, Generator hours: 0700-1900, Open Oct-Apr, Reservations not accepted, Elev: -171ft/-52m, Tel: 760-786-3200, Nearest town: Furnace Creek. GPS: 36.459238, -116.864772

69 • D3 | Death Valley NP - Texas Spring

Total sites: 92, RV sites: 45, Central water, Flush toilet, No showers, RV dump, Tent & RV camping: $16, Stay limit: 30 days, No generators, Open Oct-Apr, Reservations not accepted, Elev: 7ft/2m, Tel: 760-786-3200, Nearest town: Furnace Creek. GPS: 36.459124, -116.854567

70 • D3 | Death Valley NP - Thorndike

Total sites: 6, No water, Vault/pit toilet, Tents only: Free, Accessible to high clearance vehicles only - 4x4 may be necessary, Stay limit: 30 days, Generator hours: 0700-1900, Open Mar-Nov, Reservations not accepted, Elev: 7457ft/2273m, Tel: 760-786-3200. GPS: 36.236907, -117.072257

71 • D3 | Death Valley NP - Wildrose

Total sites: 23, RV sites: 11, Central water, Vault/pit toilet, No showers, No RV dump, Tent & RV camping: Free, Stay limit: 30 days, Generator hours: 0700-1900, Open all year, Reservations not accepted, Elev: 4239ft/1292m, Tel: 760-786-3200, Nearest town: Stovepipe Wells. GPS: 36.265895, -117.188276

72 • D3 | Sequoia NP - Atwell Mill

Total sites: 21, RV sites: 0, Central water, Vault/pit toilet, No showers, No RV dump, Tents only: $12, Open May-Oct, Reservations not accepted, Elev: 6657ft/2029m, Tel: 559-841-3533, Nearest town: Silver City. GPS: 36.464225, -118.667869

73 • D3 | Sequoia NP - Buckeye Flat

Total sites: 28, RV sites: 0, Central water, Flush toilet, No showers, RV dump, Tents only: $22, Open Mar-Sep, Reservations accepted, Elev: 2887ft/880m, Tel: 559-841-3533, Nearest town: Three Rivers. GPS: 36.521903, -118.763754

74 • D3 | Sequoia NP - Cold Springs

Total sites: 40, RV sites: 0, Central water, Vault/pit toilet, No showers, No RV dump, Tents only: $12, Also walk-to sites, 9 walk-to sites, Open May-Oct, Reservations not accepted, Elev: 7556ft/2303m, Tel: 559-841-3533, Nearest town: Silver City. GPS: 36.451971, -118.612239

75 • D3 | Sequoia NP - Lodgepole

Total sites: 214, RV sites: 190, Central water, Flush toilet, Pay showers, RV dump, Tent & RV camping: $22, Generator hours: 0800-1100/1700-2000, Open Apr-Nov, Max Length: 42ft, Reservations accepted, Elev: 6765ft/2062m, Tel: 559-841-3533, Nearest town: Giant Forest. GPS: 36.604736, -118.727539

76 • D3 | Sequoia NP - Potwisha

Total sites: 42, RV sites: 42, Central water, Flush toilet, No showers, RV dump, Tent & RV camping: $22, Generator hours: 0900-2100, Open all year, Reservations accepted, Elev: 2211ft/674m, Tel: 559-841-3533, Nearest town: Three Rivers. GPS: 36.517133, -118.800441

77 • D3 | Sequoia NP - South Fork

Total sites: 10, RV sites: 0, No water, Vault/pit toilet, No showers, No RV dump, Tents only: $6, Very rough road, No water in winter - free, Open all year, Reservations not accepted, Elev: 3694ft/1126m, Tel: 559-841-3533, Nearest town: Three Rivers. GPS: 36.35, -118.765

78 • D4 | Mojave National Preserve - Banshee Canyon

Dispersed sites, No water, No toilets, Tent & RV camping: Free, Elev: 4200ft/1280m, Tel: 760 928-2572, Nearest town: Kelso. GPS: 35.038782, -115.398532

79 • D4 | Mojave Nat'l Preserve - Black Canyon Equestrian

Dispersed sites, No water, No toilets, Tent & RV camping: $25, Open all year, Elev: 4317ft/1316m, Tel: 760 928-2572, Nearest town: Kelso. GPS: 35.048676, -115.382948

80 • D4 | Mojave National Preserve - Caruthers Canyon

Dispersed sites, No water, No toilets, Tents only: Free, High-clearance 4x4 recommended, Open all year, Elev: 5574ft/1699m, Tel: 760 928-2572. GPS: 35.231801, -115.301379

81 • D4 | Mojave National Preserve - Cinder Cone

Dispersed sites, No water, No toilets, Tent & RV camping: Free, Open all year, Reservations not accepted, Elev: 3372ft/1028m, Tel: 760 928-2572, Nearest town: Niupton. GPS: 35.192218, -115.767932

82 • D4 | Mojave National Preserve - Cross on the Rock

Total sites: 2, No water, No toilets, Tent & RV camping: Free, Elev: 5035ft/1535m, Nearest town: Barstow. GPS: 35.315198, -115.550823

83 • D4 | Mojave National Preserve - D1 Dispersed

Dispersed sites, No water, No toilets, Tent & RV camping: Free, Open all year, Elev: 3549ft/1082m, Tel: 760 928-2572, Nearest town: Kelso. GPS: 34.982429, -115.388954

84 • D4 | Mojave National Preserve - East of Rock Springs

Dispersed sites, No water, No toilets, Tents only: Free, Open all year, Elev: 4765ft/1452m, Tel: 760 928-2572, Nearest town: Needles. GPS: 35.152892, -115.327264

85 • D4 | Mojave National Preserve - Granite Pass

Dispersed sites, No water, No toilets, Tents only: Free, High-clearance vehicle recommended, Open all year, Elev: 3991ft/1216m, Tel: 760 928-2572. GPS: 34.810571, -115.631682

86 • D4 | Mojave National Preserve - Green Rock Mill

Dispersed sites, No water, No toilets, Tents only: Free, Open all year, Elev: 943ft/287m, Tel: 760 928-2572, Nearest town: Baker. GPS: 35.162835, -116.029715

87 • D4 | Mojave National Preserve - Hole In The Wall

Total sites: 38, RV sites: 38, Central water, Vault/pit toilet, No showers, RV dump, Tent & RV camping: $12, Reservations not accepted, Elev: 4315ft/1315m, Tel: 760 928-2572. GPS: 35.047772, -115.393981

88 • D4 | Mojave National Preserve - Kelso Dunes

Dispersed sites, No water, No toilets, Tent & RV camping: Free, Open all year, Elev: 2526ft/770m, Tel: 760 928-2572, Nearest town: Kelso. GPS: 34.888212, -115.716767

89 • D4 | Mojave National Preserve - Mid Hills

Total sites: 26, RV sites: 26, No water, Vault/pit toilet, No showers, No RV dump, Tent & RV camping: $12, Access road not recommended for RV's, Water available at Hole in the Wall CG, Reservations not accepted, Elev: 5608ft/1709m, Tel: 760 928-2572. GPS: 35.130825, -115.435673

90 • D4 | Mojave National Preserve - Mojave Camp

Dispersed sites, No water, No toilets, Tents only: Free, Open all year, Elev: 3809ft/1161m, Tel: 760 928-2572, Nearest town: Baker. GPS: 35.182205, -115.613697

91 • D4 | Mojave National Preserve - Piute Corral

Dispersed sites, No water, No toilets, Tents only: Free, Open all year, Elev: 3420ft/1042m, Tel: 760 928-2572, Nearest town: Needles. GPS: 35.103765, -115.012521

92 • D4 | Mojave National Preserve - Pleasant View School

Dispersed sites, No water, No toilets, Tents only: Free, Open all year, Elev: 4907ft/1496m, Tel: 760 928-2572, Nearest town: Needles. GPS: 35.155097, -115.334915

93 • D4 | Mojave National Preserve - Rainy Day Mine Site

Dispersed sites, No water, No toilets, Tents only: Free, 4x4 recommended, Open all year, Elev: 2833ft/863m, Tel: 760 928-2572, Nearest town: Baker. GPS: 35.196254, -115.820649

94 • D4 | Mojave National Preserve - Seventeen Mile Point

Dispersed sites, No water, No toilets, Tents only: Free, Open all year, Elev: 1917ft/584m, Tel: 760 928-2572, Nearest town: Baker. GPS: 35.220295, -115.897136

95 • D4 | Mojave National Preserve - Sunrise Rock

Dispersed sites, No water, No toilets, Tents only: Free, Open all year, Elev: 4896ft/1492m, Tel: 760 928-2572. GPS: 35.296804, -115.535676

96 • D4 | Mojave National Preserve - Zzyzx Rd Dispersed

Dispersed sites, No water, No toilets, Tent & RV camping: Free, Open all year, Reservations not accepted, Elev: 1161ft/354m, Tel: 760 928-2572, Nearest town: Baker. GPS: 35.193373, -116.138845

97 • D4 | Mojave Nat' Preserve -Jackrabbits Leg Dispersed

Dispersed sites, No water, No toilets, Tent & RV camping: Free, Open all year, Reservations not accepted, Elev: 2006ft/611m, Tel: 760 928-2572, Nearest town: Baker. GPS: 35.247894, -115.890476

98 • E3 | Santa Monica Mts NRA - Circle X Ranch Group

Total sites: 1, RV sites: 0, Central water, Vault/pit toilet, No showers, No RV dump, Group site: $35-$125, Elev: 1647ft/502m, Tel: 805-370-2301, Nearest town: Malibu. GPS: 34.108473, -118.936778

99 • E4 | Joshua Tree NP - Belle

Total sites: 18, RV sites: 18, No water, Vault/pit toilet, Tent & RV camping: $15, Generator hours: 0700-0900 ,1200-1400, 1700-1900, Open Oct-May, Reservations not accepted, Elev: 3839ft/1170m, Tel: 760-367-3001, Nearest town: Twentynine Palms. GPS: 34.001858, -116.018032

100 • E4 | Joshua Tree NP - Black Rock

Total sites: 99, RV sites: 38, Central water, Flush toilet, No showers, RV dump, Tent & RV camping: $25, Generator hours: 0700-0900 ,1200-1400, 1700-1900, Open all year, Reservations required, Elev: 3999ft/1219m, Tel: 760-367-3001, Nearest town: Yucca Valley. GPS: 34.073588, -116.389986

101 • E4 | Joshua Tree NP - Black Rock Horse Camp

Total sites: 20, RV sites: 20, Central water, Flush toilet, No showers, RV dump, No tents/RV's: $20, Generator hours: 0700-0900 ,1200-1400, 1700-1900, Open all year, Reservations required, Elev: 3984ft/1214m, Tel: 760-367-3001, Nearest town: Yucca Valley. GPS: 34.075637, -116.390172

102 • E4 | Joshua Tree NP - Cottonwood Springs

Total sites: 62, RV sites: 62, Central water, Flush toilet, No showers, RV dump, Tent & RV camping: $25, 3 tent-only group sites: $35-$40, Generator hours: 0700-0900 ,1200-1400, 1700-1900, Open all year, Reservations required, Elev: 3117ft/950m, Tel: 760-367-3001, Nearest town: Indio. GPS: 33.744989, -115.813677

103 • E4 | Joshua Tree NP - Hidden Valley

Total sites: 44, RV sites: 30, No water, Vault/pit toilet, Tent & RV camping: $15, Generator hours: 0700-0900 ,1200-1400, 1700-1900, Open all year, Max Length: 25ft, Reservations not accepted, Elev: 4229ft/1289m, Tel: 760-367-3001. GPS: 34.016663, -116.162687

104 • E4 | Joshua Tree NP - Indian Cove

Total sites: 101, RV sites: 101, No water, Vault/pit toilet, Tent & RV camping: $20, 13 group sites: $35-$50, Generator hours: 0700-0900 ,1200-1400, 1700-1900, Open all year, Reservations required, Elev: 3205ft/977m, Tel: 760-362-4367, Nearest town: 29 Palms. GPS: 34.092835, -116.156232

105 • E4 | Joshua Tree NP - Jumbo Rocks

Total sites: 124, RV sites: 124, No water, Vault/pit toilet, Tent & RV camping: $20, Generator hours: 0700-0900 ,1200-1400, 1700-1900, Open all year, Reservations required, Elev: 4354ft/1327m, Tel: 760-367-3001. GPS: 33.992075, -116.063556

106 • E4 | Joshua Tree NP - Ryan

Total sites: 31, RV sites: 31, No water, Vault/pit toilet, Tent & RV camping: $20, 3 bicycle sites: $5, Generator hours: 0700-0900 ,1200-1400, 1700-1900, Open Oct-May, Reservations not accepted, Elev: 4311ft/1314m, Tel: 760-367-3001. GPS: 33.983069, -116.154369

107 • E4 | Joshua Tree NP - Ryan Horse Sites

Total sites: 4, RV sites: 4, No water, Vault/pit toilet, Tent & RV camping: $20, Generator hours: 0700-0900 ,1200-1400, 1700-1900, Open Oct-May, Reservations required, Elev: 4321ft/1317m, Tel: 760-367-3001. GPS: 33.983024, -116.155318

108 • E4 | Joshua Tree NP - Sheep Pass Group

Total sites: 6, RV sites: 6, No water, Vault/pit toilet, Group site: $35-$50, Generator hours: 0700-0900 ,1200-1400, 1700-1900, Open all year, Reservations required, Elev: 4505ft/1373m, Tel: 760-367-3001, Nearest town: 29 Palms. GPS: 33.999701, -116.119764

109 • E4 | Joshua Tree NP - White Tank

Total sites: 15, RV sites: 15, No water, Vault/pit toilet, Tent & RV camping: $15, Generator hours: 0700-0900 ,1200-1400, 1700-1900, Max Length: 25ft, Reservations not accepted, Elev: 3826ft/1166m, Tel: 760-367-3001, Nearest town: Twentynine Palms. GPS: 33.985363, -116.016524

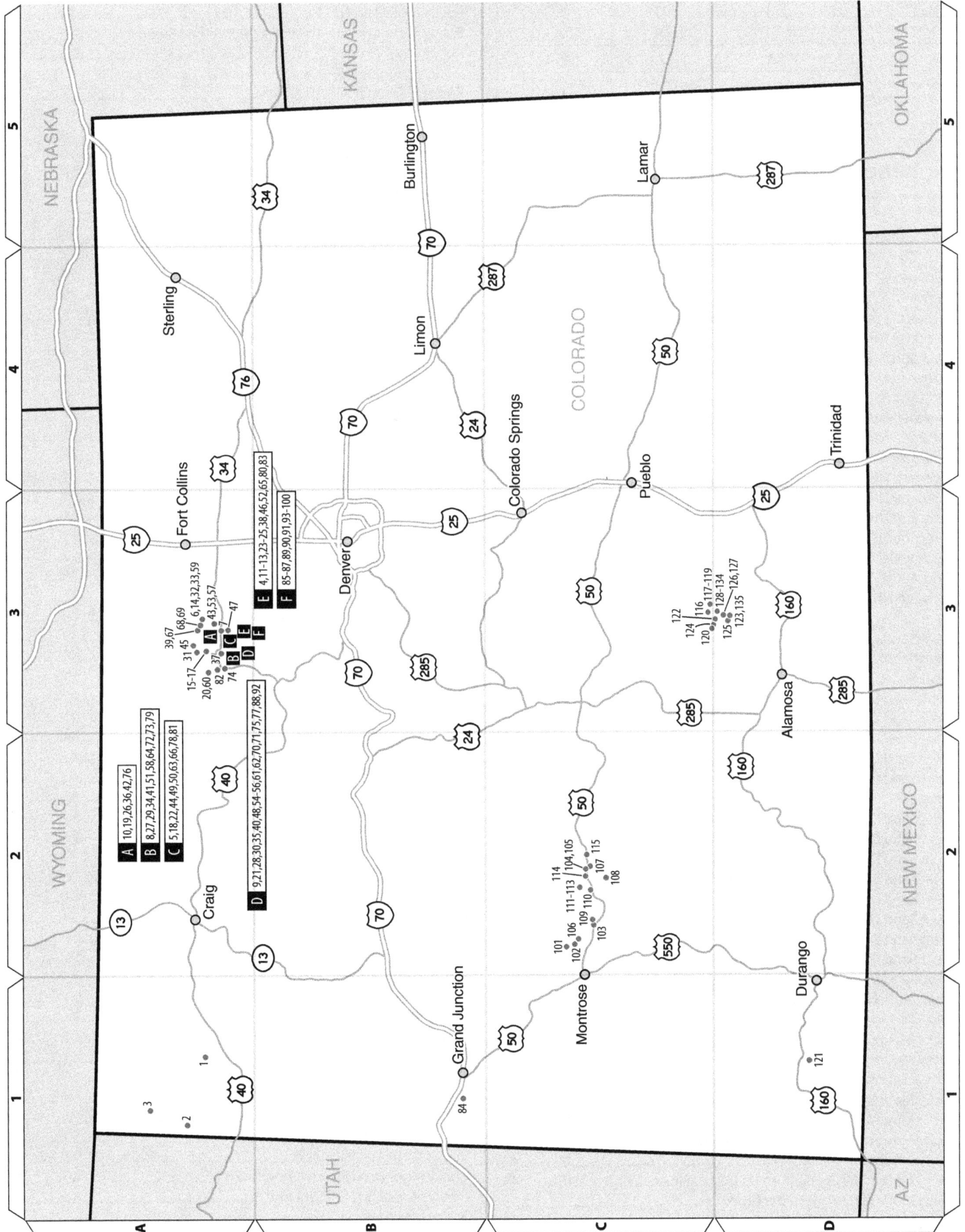

Colorado

NEBRASKA

KANSAS

WYOMING

UTAH

NEW MEXICO

OKLAHOMA

AZ

COLORADO

Sterling

Burlington

Lamar

Fort Collins

Limon

Colorado Springs

Pueblo

Trinidad

Denver

Craig

Grand Junction

Montrose

Alamosa

Durango

A	10,19,26,36,42,76
B	8,27,29,34,41,51,58,64,72,73,79
C	5,18,22,44,49,50,63,66,78,81
D	9,21,28,30,35,40,48,54-56,61,62,70,71,75,77,88,92
E	4,11-13,23-25,38,46,52,65,80,83
F	85-87,89,90,91,93-100

6,14,32,33,59
39,67
68,69
43,53,57
47
31 45
82 37
15-17
20,60
74

A B C D E F

122
124 116 117-119
120 128-134 126,127
125 123,135

114
104,105
111-113
107 115
109 110 108
101 103
102

1
3
2
84
121

287
34
70
287
50
76
34
25
25
25
50
160
160
285
285
24
70
285
70
40
13
50
50
13
550
160

Map	ID	Map	ID
A1	1-3	C2	101-115
A3	4-83	C3	116-120
B1	84	D1	121
B3	85-100	D3	122-135

Alphabetical List of Camping Areas

Name	ID	Map
Black Canyon of the Gunnison NM - North Rim	101	C2
Black Canyon of the Gunnison NM - South Rim	102	C2
Colorado NM - Saddlehorn	84	B1
Curecanti NRA - Cimarron	103	C2
Curecanti NRA - Dry Gulch	104	C2
Curecanti NRA - East Elk Creek Group	105	C2
Curecanti NRA - East Portal	106	C2
Curecanti NRA - Elk Creek	107	C2
Curecanti NRA - Gateview	108	C2
Curecanti NRA - Hermit's Rest	109	C2
Curecanti NRA - Lake Fork	110	C2
Curecanti NRA - Ponderosa Lower	111	C2
Curecanti NRA - Ponderosa Middle	112	C2
Curecanti NRA - Ponderosa Upper	113	C2
Curecanti NRA - Red Creek	114	C2
Curecanti NRA - Stevens Creek	115	C2
Dinosaur NM - Deerlodge Park	1	A1
Dinosaur NM - Echo Park	2	A1
Dinosaur NM - Gates of Lodore	3	A1
Great Sand Dunes NP - Aspen TC	122	D3
Great Sand Dunes NP - Buck Creek TC	123	D3
Great Sand Dunes NP - Cold Creek TC	124	D3
Great Sand Dunes NP - Dunes Camping	125	D3
Great Sand Dunes NP - Escape Dunes TC	126	D3
Great Sand Dunes NP - Indian Grove TC	127	D3
Great Sand Dunes NP - Little Medano TC	128	D3
Great Sand Dunes NP - Medano Lake TC	116	C3
Great Sand Dunes NP - Medano Pass Road Site 11	129	D3
Great Sand Dunes NP - Medano Pass Road Site 12	130	D3
Great Sand Dunes NP - Medano Pass Road Site 13	131	D3
Great Sand Dunes NP - Medano Pass Road Site 14	132	D3
Great Sand Dunes NP - Medano Pass Road Site 15	117	C3
Great Sand Dunes NP - Medano Pass Road Site 16	118	C3
Great Sand Dunes NP - Medano Pass Road Site 17	119	C3
Great Sand Dunes NP - Medano Pass Road Site 9-10	133	D3
Great Sand Dunes NP - Medano Pass Road Sites 1-8	134	D3
Great Sand Dunes NP - Pinon Flats CG	135	D3
Great Sand Dunes NP - Sand Creek TC	120	C3
Mesa Verde NP - Morefield CG	121	D1
Rocky Mountain NP - Andrews Creek	4	A3
Rocky Mountain NP - Arch Rock	5	A3
Rocky Mountain NP - Aspen Knoll Llama	85	B3
Rocky Mountain NP - Aspen Meadow Group	6	A3
Rocky Mountain NP - Aspenglen CG	7	A3
Rocky Mountain NP - Beaver Mill	86	B3
Rocky Mountain NP - Big Meadows Group	8	A3
Rocky Mountain NP - Big Pool	9	A3
Rocky Mountain NP - Bighorn Mt Group/Stock	10	A3
Rocky Mountain NP - Boulder Brook	11	A3
Rocky Mountain NP - Boulder Brook Group	12	A3
Rocky Mountain NP - Boulderfield	13	A3
Rocky Mountain NP - Boundary Creek	14	A3
Rocky Mountain NP - Cache La Poudre Trail Site 2	15	A3
Rocky Mountain NP - Cache La Poudre Trail Site 3	16	A3
Rocky Mountain NP - Campers Creek	87	B3
Rocky Mountain NP - Cats Lair	88	B3
Rocky Mountain NP - Chapin Creek Group	17	A3
Rocky Mountain NP - Cub Creek	18	A3
Rocky Mountain NP - Cutbank	19	A3
Rocky Mountain NP - Ditch Camp	20	A3
Rocky Mountain NP - East Meadow	21	A3
Rocky Mountain NP - Fern Lake	22	A3
Rocky Mountain NP - Finch Lake	89	B3
Rocky Mountain NP - Glacier Basin CG	23	A3
Rocky Mountain NP - Glacier Gorge	24	A3
Rocky Mountain NP - Goblins Forest	25	A3
Rocky Mountain NP - Golden Banner	26	A3
Rocky Mountain NP - Granite Falls	27	A3
Rocky Mountain NP - Gray Jay Group	28	A3
Rocky Mountain NP - Green Mountain	29	A3
Rocky Mountain NP - Grouseberry	30	A3
Rocky Mountain NP - Hague Creek	31	A3
Rocky Mountain NP - Halfway	32	A3
Rocky Mountain NP - Happily Lost	33	A3
Rocky Mountain NP - Haynach Llama	34	A3
Rocky Mountain NP - Hole-in-the-Wall	90	B3
Rocky Mountain NP - Hunters Creek	91	B3
Rocky Mountain NP - July	35	A3
Rocky Mountain NP - Lake Verna	92	B3
Rocky Mountain NP - Lawn Lake	36	A3
Rocky Mountain NP - Little Rock Lake	37	A3
Rocky Mountain NP - Longs Peak	38	A3
Rocky Mountain NP - Lost Lake	39	A3
Rocky Mountain NP - Lower East Inlet	40	A3
Rocky Mountain NP - Lower Granite Falls	41	A3
Rocky Mountain NP - Lower Tileston	42	A3
Rocky Mountain NP - McGregor Mountain	43	A3
Rocky Mountain NP - Mill Creek Basin	44	A3
Rocky Mountain NP - Mirror Lake	45	A3
Rocky Mountain NP - Moore Park	46	A3
Rocky Mountain NP - Moraine Park CG	47	A3
Rocky Mountain NP - North Inlet Group/Stock	48	A3
Rocky Mountain NP - North St. Vrain	93	B3
Rocky Mountain NP - Odessa Lake	49	A3
Rocky Mountain NP - Old Forest Inn	50	A3
Rocky Mountain NP - Onahu Creek	51	A3
Rocky Mountain NP - Ouzel Lake	94	B3
Rocky Mountain NP - Over the Hill	52	A3
Rocky Mountain NP - Pear Lake	95	B3
Rocky Mountain NP - Peregrine	53	A3
Rocky Mountain NP - Pine Marten	54	A3
Rocky Mountain NP - Pine Ridge	96	B3
Rocky Mountain NP - Porcupine	55	A3
Rocky Mountain NP - Ptarmigan	56	A3
Rocky Mountain NP - Rabbit Ears	57	A3
Rocky Mountain NP - Renegade	58	A3
Rocky Mountain NP - Sandbeach Lake	97	B3
Rocky Mountain NP - Silvanmere	59	A3
Rocky Mountain NP - Siskin	98	B3
Rocky Mountain NP - Skeleton Gulch	60	A3
Rocky Mountain NP - Slickrock	61	A3
Rocky Mountain NP - Solitaire	62	A3

Rocky Mountain NP - Sourdough ....63 .... A3
Rocky Mountain NP - South Meadows ....64 .... A3
Rocky Mountain NP - Sprague Lake Grp Accessible Site (WF)..65 .... A3
Rocky Mountain NP - Spruce Lake ....66 .... A3
Rocky Mountain NP - Stormy Peaks ....67 .... A3
Rocky Mountain NP - Stormy Peaks South ....68 .... A3
Rocky Mountain NP - Sugarloaf ....69 .... A3
Rocky Mountain NP - Summerland Park ....70 .... A3
Rocky Mountain NP - Summerland Park Group ....71 .... A3
Rocky Mountain NP - Sunrise ....72 .... A3
Rocky Mountain NP - Sunset ....73 .... A3
Rocky Mountain NP - Tahosa ....99 .... B3
Rocky Mountain NP - Timber Creek CG ....74 .... A3
Rocky Mountain NP - Twinberry ....75 .... A3
Rocky Mountain NP - Upper Chipmunk ....76 .... A3
Rocky Mountain NP - Upper East Inlet ....77 .... A3
Rocky Mountain NP - Upper Mill Creek ....78 .... A3
Rocky Mountain NP - Upper Onahu ....79 .... A3
Rocky Mountain NP - Upper Ouzel Creek ....100 .... B3
Rocky Mountain NP - Upper Wind River ....80 .... A3
Rocky Mountain NP - Ute Meadow Llama ....81 .... A3
Rocky Mountain NP - Valley View ....82 .... A3
Rocky Mountain NP - Wind River Bluff ....83 .... A3

1 • A1 | Dinosaur NM - Deerlodge Park

Total sites: 7, RV sites: 0, Central water, Vault/pit toilet, No showers, No RV dump, Tents only: $10, Walk-to sites, Fee: $6 when no water Oct-Apr, Floods often in spring, Open all year, Max Length: 35ft, Reservations not accepted, Elev: 5614ft/1711m, Tel: 970-374-3000. GPS: 40.446363, -108.512011

2 • A1 | Dinosaur NM - Echo Park

Total sites: 21, RV sites: 17, Central water, Vault/pit toilet, No showers, No RV dump, Tents only: $10, High-clearance vehicles only - access is dependent on weather, Fee: $6 when no water Sep-May, Reservable group site $15, Open all year, Reservations not accepted, Elev: 5108ft/1557m, Tel: 970-374-3000. GPS: 40.526826, -108.982162

3 • A1 | Dinosaur NM - Gates of Lodore

Total sites: 19, RV sites: 19, Central water, Vault/pit toilet, No showers, No RV dump, Tent & RV camping: $10, Fee: $6 when no water Oct-Apr, Road may be impassable in winter, Open all year, Max Length: 35ft, Reservations not accepted, Elev: 5371ft/1637m, Tel: 970-374-3000, Nearest town: Maybell. GPS: 40.727051, -108.887451

4 • A3 | Rocky Mountain NP - Andrews Creek

Total sites: 1, Tents only: $26, Hike-in, 3.6 mi, No open fires, $26 permit required per trip, Reservations accepted, Elev: 10517ft/3206m, Tel: 970-586-1242. GPS: 40.289781, -105.665605

5 • A3 | Rocky Mountain NP - Arch Rock

Total sites: 1, Tents only: $26, Hike-in, 1.6 mi, No open fires, $26 permit required per trip, Reservations accepted, Elev: 8240ft/2512m, Tel: 970-586-1242. GPS: 40.350617, -105.650799

6 • A3 | Rocky Mountain NP - Aspen Meadow Group

Total sites: 1, Tents only: $26, Hike-in, 5.9 mi, Wood fires allowed, $26 permit required per trip, Reservations accepted, Elev: 9453ft/2881m, Tel: 970-586-1242. GPS: 40.497285, -105.539339

7 • A3 | Rocky Mountain NP - Aspenglen CG

Total sites: 51, RV sites: 30, Water available, Flush toilet, No showers, No RV dump, Tent & RV camping: $30, Generators prohibited in loops A and B, Generator hours: 0730-1000/1600-2030, Open May-Sep, Max Length: 30ft, Reservations accepted, Elev: 8212ft/2503m, Tel: 970-586-1206, Nearest town: Estes Park. GPS: 40.399902, -105.593506

8 • A3 | Rocky Mountain NP - Big Meadows Group

Total sites: 1, Tents only: $26, Hike-in, 1.9 mi, No open fires, $26 permit required per trip, Reservations accepted, Elev: 9401ft/2865m, Tel: 970-586-1242. GPS: 40.311035, -105.811623

9 • A3 | Rocky Mountain NP - Big Pool

Total sites: 2, Tents only: $26, Hike-in, 5.0 mi, No open fires, $26 permit required per trip, Location approximate, Reservations accepted, Elev: 8898ft/2712m, Tel: 970-586-1242. GPS: 40.275981, -105.763528

10 • A3 | Rocky Mountain NP - Bighorn Mt Group/Stock

Total sites: 1, Tents only: $26, Hike-in, 6.8 mi, No open fires, $26 permit required per trip, Reservations accepted, Elev: 10378ft/3163m, Tel: 970-586-1242. GPS: 40.443153, -105.604254

11 • A3 | Rocky Mountain NP - Boulder Brook

Total sites: 2, Tents only: $26, Hike-in, 3.9 mi, No open fires, $26 permit required per trip, Reservations accepted, Elev: 10066ft/3068m, Tel: 970-586-1242. GPS: 40.293759, -105.617624

12 • A3 | Rocky Mountain NP - Boulder Brook Group

Total sites: 1, Tents only: $26, Hike-in, 3.9 mi, No open fires, $26 permit required per trip, Reservations accepted, Elev: 10319ft/3145m, Tel: 970-586-1242. GPS: 40.289061, -105.617265

13 • A3 | Rocky Mountain NP - Boulderfield

Total sites: 9, Vault/pit toilet, Tents only: $26, Hike-in, 6.0 mi, No open fires, $26 permit required per trip, Reservations accepted, Elev: 12816ft/3906m, Tel: 970-586-1242. GPS: 40.262184, -105.615446

14 • A3 | Rocky Mountain NP - Boundary Creek

Total sites: 2, Vault/pit toilet, Tents only: $26, Hike-in, 4.6 mi, Wood fires allowed, $26 permit required per trip, Reservations accepted, Elev: 8964ft/2732m, Tel: 970-586-1242. GPS: 40.497736, -105.518619

15 • A3 | Rocky Mountain NP - Cache La Poudre Trail Site 2

Dispersed sites, No water, No toilets, Tents only: $26, Hike-in, Elev: 10154ft/3095m, Tel: 970-586-1242. GPS: 40.471321, -105.734141

16 • A3 | Rocky Mountain NP - Cache La Poudre Trail Site 3

Dispersed sites, No water, No toilets, Tents only: $26, Hike-in, Elev: 10061ft/3067m, Tel: 970-586-1242. GPS: 40.478964, -105.735167

17 • A3 | Rocky Mountain NP - Chapin Creek Group

Total sites: 1, Tents only: $26, Hike-in, 6.1 mi, No open fires, $26 permit required per trip, Reservations accepted, Elev: 10207ft/ 3111m, Tel: 970-586-1242. GPS: 40.463863, -105.731358

18 • A3 | Rocky Mountain NP - Cub Creek

Total sites: 1, Vault/pit toilet, Tents only: $26, Hike-in, 2.2 mi, No open fires, $26 permit required per trip, Reservations accepted, Elev: 8637ft/2633m, Tel: 970-586-1242. GPS: 40.346311, - 105.639795

19 • A3 | Rocky Mountain NP - Cutbank

Total sites: 1, Vault/pit toilet, Tents only: $26, Hike-in, 2.4 mi, No open fires, $26 permit required per trip, Reservations accepted, Elev: 9876ft/3010m, Tel: 970-586-1242. GPS: 40.440305, - 105.627686

20 • A3 | Rocky Mountain NP - Ditch Camp

Total sites: 1, Tents only: $26, Hike-in, 4.6 mi, No open fires, $26 permit required per trip, Also 1 group/stock site, Location approximate, Reservations accepted, Elev: 10243ft/3122m, Tel: 970-586-1242. GPS: 40.458923, -105.867869

21 • A3 | Rocky Mountain NP - East Meadow

Total sites: 1, Tents only: $26, Hike-in, 1.5 mi, No open fires, $26 permit required per trip, Reservations accepted, Elev: 8586ft/ 2617m, Tel: 970-586-1242. GPS: 40.237785, -105.786055

22 • A3 | Rocky Mountain NP - Fern Lake

Total sites: 4, Vault/pit toilet, Tents only: $26, Hike-in, 3.8 mi, No open fires, $26 permit required per trip, Also 1 group site, Reservations accepted, Elev: 9521ft/2902m, Tel: 970-586-1242. GPS: 40.338131, -105.676258

23 • A3 | Rocky Mountain NP - Glacier Basin CG

Total sites: 150, RV sites: 81, Central water, Flush toilet, RV dump, Tent & RV camping: $30, Group sites: $40-$60, Generator hours: 0730-1000/1600-2030, Open May-Sep, Max Length: 35ft, Reservations accepted, Elev: 8629ft/2630m, Tel: 970-586-1206, Nearest town: Estes Park. GPS: 40.328241, -105.594893

24 • A3 | Rocky Mountain NP - Glacier Gorge

Total sites: 1, Tents only: $26, Hike-in, 3.8 mi, No open fires, $26 permit required per trip, Reservations accepted, Elev: 10079ft/ 3072m, Tel: 970-586-1242. GPS: 40.281921, -105.639059

25 • A3 | Rocky Mountain NP - Goblins Forest

Total sites: 6, Tents only: $26, Hike-in, 1.2 mi, No open fires, $26 permit required per trip, Reservations accepted, Elev: 10120ft/ 3085m, Tel: 970-586-1242, Nearest town: Estes Park. GPS: 40.273041, -105.570279

26 • A3 | Rocky Mountain NP - Golden Banner

Total sites: 2, Tents only: $26, Hike-in, 2.5 mi, No open fires, $26 permit required per trip, Reservations accepted, Elev: 9678ft/ 2950m, Tel: 970-586-1242. GPS: 40.451464, -105.627683

27 • A3 | Rocky Mountain NP - Granite Falls

Total sites: 2, Tents only: $26, Hike-in, 5.4 mi, No open fires, $26 permit required per trip, Reservations accepted, Elev: 9885ft/ 3013m, Tel: 970-586-1242. GPS: 40.319688, -105.770782

28 • A3 | Rocky Mountain NP - Gray Jay Group

Total sites: 1, Tents only: $26, Hike-in, 4.9 mi, No open fires, $26 permit required per trip, Reservations accepted, Elev: 9798ft/ 2986m, Tel: 970-586-1242. GPS: 40.230445, -105.735945

29 • A3 | Rocky Mountain NP - Green Mountain

Total sites: 1, Tents only: $26, Hike-in, 1.8 mi, No open fires, $26 permit required per trip, Reservations accepted, Elev: 9459ft/ 2883m, Tel: 970-586-1242. GPS: 40.309433, -105.813008

30 • A3 | Rocky Mountain NP - Grouseberry

Total sites: 1, Tents only: $26, Hike-in, 6.2 mi, No open fires, $26 permit required per trip, Reservations accepted, Elev: 9272ft/ 2826m, Tel: 970-586-1242. GPS: 40.285658, -105.738009

31 • A3 | Rocky Mountain NP - Hague Creek

Total sites: 1, Tents only: $26, Hike-in, 1.6 mi, No open fires, $26 permit required per trip, Also 1 group/stock site, Reservations accepted, Elev: 9748ft/2971m, Tel: 970-586-1242. GPS: 40.517273, -105.742104

32 • A3 | Rocky Mountain NP - Halfway

Total sites: 2, Vault/pit toilet, Tents only: $26, Hike-in, 5.6 mi, No open fires, $26 permit required per trip, Reservations accepted, Elev: 9393ft/2863m, Tel: 970-586-1242. GPS: 40.493674, - 105.530547

33 • A3 | Rocky Mountain NP - Happily Lost

Total sites: 3, Tents only: $26, Hike-in, 6.2 mi, Wood fires allowed, $26 permit required per trip, Reservations accepted, Elev: 9518ft/ 2901m, Tel: 970-586-1242. GPS: 40.498631, -105.550591

34 • A3 | Rocky Mountain NP - Haynach Llama

Total sites: 2, Tents only: $26, Hike-in, 7.2 mi, No open fires, $26 permit required per trip, Reservations accepted, Elev: 10842ft/ 3305m, Tel: 970-586-1242. GPS: 40.336878, -105.753103

35 • A3 | Rocky Mountain NP - July

Total sites: 3, Tents only: $26, Hike-in, 9.7 mi, No open fires, $26 permit required per trip, 1 group site also, Reservations accepted, Elev: 10697ft/3260m, Tel: 970-586-1242. GPS: 40.287118, - 105.702313

36 • A3 | Rocky Mountain NP - Lawn Lake

Total sites: 1, Vault/pit toilet, Tents only: $26, Hike-in, 6.2 mi, No open fires, $26 permit required per trip, Also 5 stock sites, Reservations accepted, Elev: 11005ft/3354m, Tel: 970-586-1242. GPS: 40.468943, -105.631384

37 • A3 | Rocky Mountain NP - Little Rock Lake

Total sites: 1, Tents only: $26, Hike-in, 6.0 mi, No open fires, $26 permit required per trip, Reservations accepted, Elev: 10317ft/ 3145m, Tel: 970-586-1242. GPS: 40.389217, -105.748208

38 • A3 | Rocky Mountain NP - Longs Peak

Total sites: 26, RV sites: 0, Central water, Vault/pit toilet, No showers, No RV dump, Tents only: $30, Reservations not accepted,

Elev: 9298ft/2834m, Tel: 970-586-1206, Nearest town: Estes Park. GPS: 40.274669, -105.557786

39 • A3 | Rocky Mountain NP - Lost Lake

Total sites: 4, Tents only: $26, Hike-in, 9.7 mi, No open fires, $26 permit required per trip, Reservations accepted, Elev: 10747ft/3276m, Tel: 970-586-1242. GPS: 40.506942, -105.600477

40 • A3 | Rocky Mountain NP - Lower East Inlet

Total sites: 1, Tents only: $26, Hike-in, 2.3 mi, No open fires, $26 permit required per trip, Reservations accepted, Elev: 8691ft/2649m, Tel: 970-586-1242. GPS: 40.234865, -105.768669

41 • A3 | Rocky Mountain NP - Lower Granite Falls

Total sites: 2, Tents only: $26, Hike-in, 5.1 mi, No open fires, $26 permit required per trip, Reservations accepted, Elev: 9747ft/2971m, Tel: 970-586-1242. GPS: 40.319311, -105.775402

42 • A3 | Rocky Mountain NP - Lower Tileston

Total sites: 1, Tents only: $26, Hike-in, 6.6 mi, No open fires, $26 permit required per trip, Reservations accepted, Elev: 10755ft/3278m, Tel: 970-586-1242. GPS: 40.451223, -105.611976

43 • A3 | Rocky Mountain NP - McGregor Mountain

Total sites: 2, Tents only: $26, Hike-in, 4.6 mi, No open fires, $26 permit required per trip, Reservations accepted, Elev: 8997ft/2742m, Tel: 970-586-1242. GPS: 40.420753, -105.571594

44 • A3 | Rocky Mountain NP - Mill Creek Basin

Total sites: 1, Tents only: $26, Hike-in, 1.8 mi, No open fires, $26 permit required per trip, Reservations accepted, Elev: 8985ft/2739m, Tel: 970-586-1242. GPS: 40.334888, -105.631416

45 • A3 | Rocky Mountain NP - Mirror Lake

Total sites: 3, Tents only: $26, Hike-in, 6.0 mi, No open fires, $26 permit required per trip, Reservations accepted, Elev: 11044ft/3366m, Tel: 970-586-1242. GPS: 40.536624, -105.696979

46 • A3 | Rocky Mountain NP - Moore Park

Total sites: 2, Tents only: $26, Hike-in, 1.7 mi, No open fires, $26 permit required per trip, Reservations accepted, Elev: 9760ft/2975m, Tel: 970-586-1242. GPS: 40.287185, -105.567006

47 • A3 | Rocky Mountain NP - Moraine Park CG

Total sites: 247, RV sites: 106, Central water, No toilets, No showers, RV dump, Tent & RV camping: $30, 77 sites open in winter: $20, Open all year, Max Length: 40ft, Reservations accepted, Elev: 8143ft/2482m, Tel: 970-586-1206, Nearest town: Estes Park. GPS: 40.359618, -105.600826

48 • A3 | Rocky Mountain NP - North Inlet Group/Stock

Total sites: 1, Tents only: $26, Hike-in, 6.5 mi, Wood fires allowed, $26 permit required per trip, Reservations accepted, Elev: 9287ft/2831m, Tel: 970-586-1242. GPS: 40.286321, -105.735711

49 • A3 | Rocky Mountain NP - Odessa Lake

Total sites: 2, Tents only: $26, Hike-in, 4.1 mi, No open fires, $26 permit required per trip, Reservations accepted, Elev: 10004ft/3049m, Tel: 970-586-1242. GPS: 40.331727, -105.684447

50 • A3 | Rocky Mountain NP - Old Forest Inn

Total sites: 2, Tents only: $26, Hike-in, 1.7 mi, No open fires, $26 permit required per trip, Reservations accepted, Elev: 8363ft/2549m, Tel: 970-586-1242. GPS: 40.349521, -105.660025

51 • A3 | Rocky Mountain NP - Onahu Creek

Total sites: 1, Tents only: $26, Hike-in, 2.4 mi, No open fires, $26 permit required per trip, Location approximate, Reservations accepted, Elev: 9515ft/2900m, Tel: 970-586-1242. GPS: 40.334513, -105.821747

52 • A3 | Rocky Mountain NP - Over the Hill

Total sites: 1, Tents only: $26, Hike-in, 1.3 mi, No open fires, $26 permit required per trip, Location approximate, Reservations accepted, Elev: 8720ft/2658m, Tel: 970-586-1242. GPS: 40.320925, -105.597196

53 • A3 | Rocky Mountain NP - Peregrine

Total sites: 1, Tents only: $26, Hike-in, 2.0 mi, No open fires, $26 permit required per trip, Reservations accepted, Elev: 8261ft/2518m, Tel: 970-586-1242. GPS: 40.427784, -105.536698

54 • A3 | Rocky Mountain NP - Pine Marten

Total sites: 2, Tents only: $26, Hike-in, 7.8 mi, No open fires, $26 permit required per trip, Reservations accepted, Elev: 9577ft/2919m, Tel: 970-586-1242. GPS: 40.278001, -105.719966

55 • A3 | Rocky Mountain NP - Porcupine

Total sites: 2, Tents only: $26, Hike-in, 6.8 mi, Wood fires allowed, $26 permit required per trip, Reservations accepted, Elev: 9376ft/2858m, Tel: 970-586-1242. GPS: 40.284171, -105.729621

56 • A3 | Rocky Mountain NP - Ptarmigan

Total sites: 1, Tents only: $26, Hike-in, 6.7 mi, No open fires, $26 permit required per trip, Reservations accepted, Elev: 9320ft/2841m, Tel: 970-586-1242. GPS: 40.283968, -105.730473

57 • A3 | Rocky Mountain NP - Rabbit Ears

Total sites: 1, Tents only: $26, Hike-in, 1.4 mi, No open fires, $26 permit required per trip, Reservations accepted, Elev: 8109ft/2472m, Tel: 970-586-1242. GPS: 40.426772, -105.526995

58 • A3 | Rocky Mountain NP - Renegade

Total sites: 1, Tents only: $26, Hike-in, 7.3 mi, No open fires, $26 permit required per trip, Reservations accepted, Elev: 10673ft/3253m, Tel: 970-586-1242. GPS: 40.334712, -105.747895

59 • A3 | Rocky Mountain NP - Silvanmere

Total sites: 2, Tents only: $26, Hike-in, 5.6 mi, Wood fires allowed, $26 permit required per trip, Reservations accepted, Elev: 9243ft/2817m, Tel: 970-586-1242. GPS: 40.485004, -105.523408

60 • A3 | Rocky Mountain NP - Skeleton Gulch

Total sites: 1, Tents only: $26, Hike-in, 6.2 mi, No open fires, $26 permit required per trip, Reservations accepted, Elev: 10654ft/3247m, Tel: 970-586-1242. GPS: 40.459859, -105.884263

61 • A3 | Rocky Mountain NP - Slickrock

Total sites: 1, Tents only: $26, Hike-in, 6.0 mi, No open fires, $26 permit required per trip, Reservations accepted, Elev: 10025ft/3056m, Tel: 970-586-1242. GPS: 40.233155, -105.727088

62 • A3 | Rocky Mountain NP - Solitaire

Total sites: 1, Tents only: $26, Hike-in, 6.2 mi, No open fires, $26 permit required per trip, Reservations accepted, Elev: 10119ft/3084m, Tel: 970-586-1242. GPS: 40.231393, -105.725826

63 • A3 | Rocky Mountain NP - Sourdough

Total sites: 1, Tents only: $26, Hike-in, 2.5 mi, No open fires, $26 permit required per trip, Reservations accepted, Elev: 10599ft/3231m, Tel: 970-586-1242. GPS: 40.323248, -105.678678

64 • A3 | Rocky Mountain NP - South Meadows

Total sites: 1, Tents only: $26, Hike-in, 2.0 mi, No open fires, $26 permit required per trip, Location approximate, Reservations accepted, Elev: 9438ft/2877m, Tel: 970-586-1242. GPS: 40.320311, -105.801158

65 • A3 | Rocky Mountain NP - Sprague Lake Group Accessible Site (WF)

Total sites: 1, Tents only: $26, Hike-in, 0.5 mi, No open fires, $26 permit required per trip, Location approximate, Reservations accepted, Elev: 8693ft/2650m, Tel: 970-586-1242. GPS: 40.320515, -105.602758

66 • A3 | Rocky Mountain NP - Spruce Lake

Total sites: 2, Tents only: $26, Hike-in, 4.6 mi, No open fires, $26 permit required per trip, Reservations accepted, Elev: 9663ft/2945m, Tel: 970-586-1242. GPS: 40.342827, -105.687116

67 • A3 | Rocky Mountain NP - Stormy Peaks

Total sites: 1, Tents only: $26, Hike-in, 11.0 mi, No open fires, $26 permit required per trip, Reservations accepted, Elev: 10873ft/3314m, Tel: 970-586-1242. GPS: 40.517924, -105.591249

68 • A3 | Rocky Mountain NP - Stormy Peaks South

Total sites: 1, Tents only: $26, Hike-in, 8.6 mi, No open fires, $26 permit required per trip, Reservations accepted, Elev: 10840ft/3304m, Tel: 970-586-1242. GPS: 40.508726, -105.570536

69 • A3 | Rocky Mountain NP - Sugarloaf

Total sites: 1, Tents only: $26, Hike-in, 8.2 mi, No open fires, $26 permit required per trip, Reservations accepted, Elev: 10118ft/3084m, Tel: 970-586-1242. GPS: 40.505211, -105.568214

70 • A3 | Rocky Mountain NP - Summerland Park

Total sites: 1, Tents only: $26, Hike-in, 1.6 mi, No open fires, $26 permit required per trip, Reservations accepted, Elev: 8581ft/2615m, Tel: 970-586-1242. GPS: 40.263973, -105.789041

71 • A3 | Rocky Mountain NP - Summerland Park Group

Total sites: 1, Group site, Hike-in 1.6 mi, No open fires, $26 permit required per trip, Reservations accepted, Elev: 8516ft/2596m, Tel: 970-586-1242. GPS: 40.260823, -105.795248

72 • A3 | Rocky Mountain NP - Sunrise

Total sites: 1, Tents only: $26, Hike-in, 3.5 mi, No open fires, $26 permit required per trip, Reservations accepted, Elev: 9523ft/2903m, Tel: 970-586-1242. GPS: 40.322573, -105.791608

73 • A3 | Rocky Mountain NP - Sunset

Total sites: 1, Tents only: $26, Hike-in, 3.0 mi, No open fires, $26 permit required per trip, Reservations accepted, Elev: 9502ft/2896m, Tel: 970-586-1242. GPS: 40.321391, -105.794487

74 • A3 | Rocky Mountain NP - Timber Creek CG

Total sites: 98, RV sites: 75, Central water, Flush toilet, No showers, RV dump, Tents: $30-30/RV's: $26, Open May-Oct, Max Length: 30ft, Reservations not accepted, Elev: 9012ft/2747m, Tel: 970-586-1206, Nearest town: Grand Lake. GPS: 40.37904, -105.85204

75 • A3 | Rocky Mountain NP - Twinberry

Total sites: 1, Tents only: $26, Hike-in, 3.0 mi, No open fires, $26 permit required per trip, Location approximate, Reservations accepted, Elev: 8590ft/2618m, Tel: 970-586-1242. GPS: 40.266299, -105.775118

76 • A3 | Rocky Mountain NP - Upper Chipmunk

Total sites: 2, Tents only: $26, Hike-in, 4.2 mi, No open fires, $26 permit required per trip, Reservations accepted, Elev: 10639ft/3243m, Tel: 970-586-1242. GPS: 40.440804, -105.664137

77 • A3 | Rocky Mountain NP - Upper East Inlet

Total sites: 1, Tents only: $26, Hike-in, 6.6 mi, No open fires, $26 permit required per trip, Reservations accepted, Elev: 10202ft/3110m, Tel: 970-586-1242. GPS: 40.228807, -105.716043

78 • A3 | Rocky Mountain NP - Upper Mill Creek

Total sites: 1, Tents only: $26, Hike-in, 1.7 mi, No open fires, $26 permit required per trip, Reservations accepted, Elev: 9061ft/2762m, Tel: 970-586-1242. GPS: 40.333644, -105.631491

79 • A3 | Rocky Mountain NP - Upper Onahu

Total sites: 1, Tents only: $26, Hike-in, 2.8 mi, No open fires, $26 permit required per trip, Location approximate, Reservations accepted, Elev: 9538ft/2907m, Tel: 970-586-1242. GPS: 40.333588, -105.828587

80 • A3 | Rocky Mountain NP - Upper Wind River

Total sites: 1, Tents only: $26, Hike-in, 1.6 mi, No open fires, $26 permit required per trip, Reservations accepted, Elev: 9055ft/2760m, Tel: 970-586-1242. GPS: 40.311047, -105.607349

81 • A3 | Rocky Mountain NP - Ute Meadow Llama

Total sites: 1, Tents only: $26, Hike-in, 2.7 mi, No open fires, $26 permit required per trip, Reservations accepted, Elev: 9432ft/2875m, Tel: 970-586-1242. GPS: 40.363422, -105.649429

82 • A3 | Rocky Mountain NP - Valley View

Total sites: 1, Tents only: $26, Hike-in, 3.2 mi, No open fires, $26 permit required per trip, Reservations accepted, Elev: 10324ft/3147m, Tel: 970-586-1242. GPS: 40.412911, -105.863823

83 • A3 | Rocky Mountain NP - Wind River Bluff

Total sites: 1, Tents only: $26, Hike-in, 1.0 mi, No open fires, $26 permit required per trip, Reservations accepted, Elev: 8742ft/2665m, Tel: 970-586-1242. GPS: 40.317402, -105.586182

84 • B1 | Colorado NM - Saddlehorn

Total sites: 80, RV sites: 80, Central water, Flush toilet, No showers, No RV dump, Tent & RV camping: $22, Loop C: no generators and no trailers, Stay limit: 14 days, Generator hours: 0800-2000, Open all year, Max Length: 40ft, Reservations accepted, Elev: 5755ft/1754m, Tel: 970-858-3617, Nearest town: Fruita. GPS: 39.103027, -108.733154

85 • B3 | Rocky Mountain NP - Aspen Knoll Llama

Total sites: 1, No toilets, Tents only: $26, Hike-in, 2.3 mi, Creek water, No open fires, $26 permit required per trip, Reservations accepted, Elev: 9613ft/2930m, Tel: 970-586-1242. GPS: 40.200372, -105.604926

86 • B3 | Rocky Mountain NP - Beaver Mill

Total sites: 1, No toilets, Tents only: $26, Hike-in, 3.0 mi, Creek water, No open fires, $26 permit required per trip, Reservations accepted, Elev: 9663ft/2945m, Tel: 970-586-1242. GPS: 40.216125, -105.579409

87 • B3 | Rocky Mountain NP - Campers Creek

Total sites: 1, No toilets, Tents only: $26, Hike-in, 2.3 mi, Creek water, No open fires, $26 permit required per trip, Reservations accepted, Elev: 9355ft/2851m, Tel: 970-586-1242. GPS: 40.216291, -105.565223

88 • B3 | Rocky Mountain NP - Cats Lair

Total sites: 1, Tents only: $26, Hike-in, 4.0 mi, No open fires, $26 permit required per trip, Reservations accepted, Elev: 9183ft/2799m, Tel: 970-586-1242. GPS: 40.227157, -105.751267

89 • B3 | Rocky Mountain NP - Finch Lake

Total sites: 2, Vault/pit toilet, Tents only: $26, Hike-in, 4.6 mi, No open fires, $26 permit required per trip, Also 1 group/stock site, Reservations accepted, Elev: 9948ft/3032m, Tel: 970-586-1242. GPS: 40.184328, -105.592393

90 • B3 | Rocky Mountain NP - Hole-in-the-Wall

Total sites: 1, No toilets, Tents only: $26, Hike-in, 1.9 mi, No open fires, $26 permit required per trip, Reservations accepted, Elev: 9175ft/2797m, Tel: 970-586-1242. GPS: 40.216138, -105.561504

91 • B3 | Rocky Mountain NP - Hunters Creek

Total sites: 1, No toilets, Tents only: $26, Hike-in, 3.3 mi, Creek water, No open fires, $26 permit required per trip, Reservations accepted, Elev: 9751ft/2972m, Tel: 970-586-1242. GPS: 40.216951, -105.583743

92 • B3 | Rocky Mountain NP - Lake Verna

Total sites: 1, Tents only: $26, Hike-in, 6.9 mi, No open fires, $26 permit required per trip, Reservations accepted, Elev: 10208ft/3111m, Tel: 970-586-1242. GPS: 40.225896, -105.703004

93 • B3 | Rocky Mountain NP - North St. Vrain

Total sites: 2, Vault/pit toilet, Tents only: $26, Hike-in, 3.5 mi, Creek water, No open fires, $26 permit required per trip, Location approximate, Reservations accepted, Elev: 9789ft/2984m, Tel: 970-586-1242. GPS: 40.212917, -105.624735

94 • B3 | Rocky Mountain NP - Ouzel Lake

Total sites: 1, Vault/pit toilet, Tents only: $26, Hike-in, 4.9 mi, Stream water, No open fires, $26 permit required per trip, Reservations accepted, Elev: 10010ft/3051m, Tel: 970-586-1242. GPS: 40.199665, -105.631342

95 • B3 | Rocky Mountain NP - Pear Lake

Total sites: 1, Tents only: $26, Hike-in, 6.6 mi, No open fires, $26 permit required per trip, Reservations accepted, Elev: 10594ft/3229m, Tel: 970-586-1242. GPS: 40.176813, -105.623303

96 • B3 | Rocky Mountain NP - Pine Ridge

Total sites: 2, Vault/pit toilet, Tents only: $26, Hike-in, 1.4 mi, Creek water, No open fires, $26 permit required per trip, Reservations accepted, Elev: 8916ft/2718m, Tel: 970-586-1242. GPS: 40.200552, -105.588489

97 • B3 | Rocky Mountain NP - Sandbeach Lake

Total sites: 4, Tents only: $26, Hike-in, 4.2 mi, Lake water, No open fires, $26 permit required per trip, Also 1 group site, Reservations accepted, Elev: 10297ft/3139m, Tel: 970-586-1242. GPS: 40.220563, -105.601036

98 • B3 | Rocky Mountain NP - Siskin

Total sites: 1, No toilets, Tents only: $26, Hike-in, 3.7 mi, Creek water, No open fires, $26 permit required per trip, Location approximate, Reservations accepted, Elev: 9864ft/3007m, Tel: 970-586-1242. GPS: 40.210786, -105.619461

99 • B3 | Rocky Mountain NP - Tahosa

Total sites: 1, No toilets, Tents only: $26, Hike-in, 1.7 mi, Creek water, No open fires, $26 permit required per trip, Reservations accepted, Elev: 9113ft/2778m, Tel: 970-586-1242. GPS: 40.198872, -105.593915

100 • B3 | Rocky Mountain NP - Upper Ouzel Creek

Total sites: 1, No toilets, Tents only: $26, Hike-in, 5.6 mi, Creek water, No open fires, $26 permit required per trip, Reservations accepted, Elev: 10561ft/3219m, Tel: 970-586-1242. GPS: 40.197503, -105.642721

101 • C2 | Black Canyon of the Gunnison NM - North Rim

Total sites: 13, RV sites: 13, Central water, Vault/pit toilet, No showers, No RV dump, Tent & RV camping: $16, No water for RV tanks, Stay limit: 14 days, Open Apr-Nov, Max Length: 22ft, Reservations not accepted, Elev: 7753ft/2363m, Tel: 970-641-2337, Nearest town: Montrose. GPS: 38.585222, -107.709383

102 • C2 | Black Canyon of the Gunnison NM - South Rim

Total sites: 88, RV sites: 88, Elec sites: 23, Central water, Vault/pit toilet, No showers, No RV dump, Tents: $16/RV's: $22, No water for RV tanks, Stay limit: 14 days, No generators, Open all year, Max Length: 35ft, Reservations accepted, Elev: 8373ft/2552m, Tel: 970-641-2337, Nearest town: Montrose. GPS: 38.543557, -107.689201

103 • C2 | Curecanti NRA - Cimarron

Total sites: 21, RV sites: 21, Central water, Flush toilet, No showers, RV dump, Tent & RV camping: $16, No water in winter, Open May-Oct, Reservations not accepted, Elev: 6995ft/2132m,

Tel: 970-641-2337, Nearest town: Cimarron. GPS: 38.443791, -107.555258

104 • C2 | Curecanti NRA - Dry Gulch

Total sites: 9, RV sites: 9, Central water, Vault/pit toilet, No showers, No RV dump, Tent & RV camping: $16, Open May-Oct, Reservations not accepted, Elev: 7782ft/2372m, Tel: 970-641-2337, Nearest town: Gunnison. GPS: 38.485728, -107.188735

105 • C2 | Curecanti NRA - East Elk Creek Group

Total sites: 1, RV sites: 1, Central water, Vault/pit toilet, No showers, No RV dump, Group site: $53, Open May-Sep, Reservations required, Elev: 7598ft/2316m, Tel: 970-641-2337, Nearest town: Gunnison. GPS: 38.482749, -107.171704

106 • C2 | Curecanti NRA - East Portal

Total sites: 15, RV sites: 15, Central water, Vault/pit toilet, No showers, No RV dump, Tent & RV camping: $16, Very steep 16% access road, Open May-Oct, Max Length: 22ft, Reservations not accepted, Elev: 6608ft/2014m, Tel: 970-641-2337, Nearest town: Gunnison. GPS: 38.525734, -107.649512

107 • C2 | Curecanti NRA - Elk Creek

Total sites: 160, RV sites: 160, Elec sites: 28, Central water, Flush toilet, Free showers, RV dump, Tents: $16/RV's: $22, No water in winter, Open all year, Reservations accepted, Elev: 7582ft/2311m, Tel: 970-641-2337, Nearest town: Gunnison. GPS: 38.4684, -107.17233

108 • C2 | Curecanti NRA - Gateview

Total sites: 6, RV sites: 0, Central water, Vault/pit toilet, No showers, No RV dump, Tents only: Free, Open May-Oct, Reservations not accepted, Elev: 7959ft/2426m, Tel: 970-641-2337, Nearest town: Gunnison. GPS: 38.384748, -107.243303

109 • C2 | Curecanti NRA - Hermit's Rest

Total sites: 1, RV sites: 0, No water, Vault/pit toilet, Tents only: Free, Hike-in/boat-in, Elev: 10199ft/3109m, Tel: 970-641-2337, Nearest town: Cimarron. GPS: 38.448212, -107.520615

110 • C2 | Curecanti NRA - Lake Fork

Total sites: 90, RV sites: 90, Central water, Flush toilet, Free showers, RV dump, Tent & RV camping: $16, Open Apr-Oct, Reservations accepted, Elev: 7559ft/2304m, Tel: 970-641-2337, Nearest town: Gunnison. GPS: 38.455384, -107.325574

111 • C2 | Curecanti NRA - Ponderosa Lower

Total sites: 5, RV sites: 1, Central water, Vault/pit toilet, No showers, No RV dump, Tent & RV camping: $16, Also walk-to sites, Open May-Oct, Max Length: 24ft, Reservations not accepted, Elev: 7545ft/2300m, Tel: 970-641-2337, Nearest town: Sapinero. GPS: 38.518125, -107.302192

112 • C2 | Curecanti NRA - Ponderosa Middle

Total sites: 16, RV sites: 10, Central water, Vault/pit toilet, No showers, No RV dump, Tent & RV camping: $16, Also walk-to sites, Open May-Oct, Max Length: 35ft, Reservations not accepted, Elev: 7570ft/2307m, Tel: 970-641-2337, Nearest town: Sapinero. GPS: 38.522949, -107.306396

113 • C2 | Curecanti NRA - Ponderosa Upper

Total sites: 7, RV sites: 7, Central water, Vault/pit toilet, No showers, No RV dump, Tent & RV camping: $16, Open May-Oct, Max Length: 25ft, Reservations not accepted, Elev: 7866ft/2398m, Tel: 970-641-2337, Nearest town: Sapinero. GPS: 38.525878, -107.315095

114 • C2 | Curecanti NRA - Red Creek

Total sites: 1, RV sites: 1, No water, No toilets, Tent & RV camping: $16, Also 1 group site - $28, Max Length: 22ft, Reservations not accepted, Elev: 7743ft/2360m, Tel: 970-641-2337, Nearest town: Gunnison. GPS: 38.490419, -107.232242

115 • C2 | Curecanti NRA - Stevens Creek

Total sites: 53, RV sites: 53, Central water, Vault/pit toilet, No showers, No RV dump, Tent & RV camping: $16, Open May-Sep, Reservations accepted, Elev: 7556ft/2303m, Tel: 970-641-2337, Nearest town: Gunnison. GPS: 38.486816, -107.091553

116 • C3 | Great Sand Dunes NP - Medano Lake TC

Dispersed sites, No water, No toilets, Tents only: Free, Hike-in, 3.5 mi, No fires, Free permit required, Reservations not accepted, Elev: 11544ft/3519m, Tel: 719-378-6395, Nearest town: Mosca. GPS: 37.856888, -105.484321

117 • C3 | Great Sand Dunes NP - Medano Pass Road Site 15

Dispersed sites, No water, No toilets, Tent & RV camping: Free, 4x4 required, Open Jun, Reservations not accepted, Elev: 9410ft/2868m, Tel: 719-378-6395, Nearest town: Mosca. GPS: 37.837021, -105.437043

118 • C3 | Great Sand Dunes NP - Medano Pass Road Site 16

Dispersed sites, No water, No toilets, Tent & RV camping: Free, 4x4 required, Open Jun, Max Length: 16ft, Reservations not accepted, Elev: 9461ft/2884m, Tel: 719-378-6395, Nearest town: Mosca. GPS: 37.839158, -105.434743

119 • C3 | Great Sand Dunes NP - Medano Pass Road Site 17

Dispersed sites, No water, No toilets, Tents only: Free, 4x4 required, Reservations not accepted, Elev: 9524ft/2903m, Tel: 719-378-6395, Nearest town: Mosca. GPS: 37.844131, -105.434512

120 • C3 | Great Sand Dunes NP - Sand Creek TC

Dispersed sites, No water, No toilets, Tents only: Free, Hike-in, 7.0 mi, 4x4 required to TH, Free permit required, Reservations not accepted, Elev: 7987ft/2434m, Tel: 719-378-6395, Nearest town: Mosca. GPS: 37.835911, -105.585728

121 • D1 | Mesa Verde NP - Morefield CG

Total sites: 395, RV sites: 267, Elec sites: 15, Central water, Flush toilet, Free showers, RV dump, Tents: $36/RV's: $36-50, 15 Full hookups - reservation required, Open Apr-Oct, Max Length: 46ft, Reservations accepted, Elev: 7861ft/2396m, Tel: 800-449-2288, Nearest town: Cortez. GPS: 37.302218, -108.419253

122 • D3 | Great Sand Dunes NP - Aspen TC

Dispersed sites, No water, No toilets, Tents only: Free, Hike-in, 2.3 mi, 4x4 required to TH, No fires, Free permit required, Reservations not accepted, Elev: 9191ft/2801m, Tel: 719-378-6395, Nearest town: Mosca. GPS: 37.819131, -105.523193

123 • D3 | Great Sand Dunes NP - Buck Creek TC

Dispersed sites, No water, No toilets, Tents only: Free, Hike-in, .5 mi, No fires, Free permit required, Reservations not accepted, Elev: 8416ft/2565m, Tel: 719-378-6395, Nearest town: Mosca. GPS: 37.753492, -105.501862

124 • D3 | Great Sand Dunes NP - Cold Creek TC

Dispersed sites, No water, No toilets, Tents only: Free, Hike-in, 5.5 mi, 4x4 required to TH, No fires, Free permit required, Reservations not accepted, Elev: 8284ft/2525m, Tel: 719-378-6395, Nearest town: Mosca. GPS: 37.827512, -105.569048

125 • D3 | Great Sand Dunes NP - Dunes Camping

Dispersed sites, No water, No toilets, Tents only: Free, Hike-in, 1.5 mi, Pick your spot anywhere outside day-use area, Camp only in good weather - very exposed to elements and blowing sand, No fires, Free permit required, Reservations not accepted, Elev: 8570ft/2612m, Tel: 719-378-6395, Nearest town: Mosca. GPS: 37.753476, -105.534865

126 • D3 | Great Sand Dunes NP - Escape Dunes TC

Dispersed sites, No water, No toilets, Tents only: Free, Hike-in, 1.4 mi, No fires, Free permit required, Reservations not accepted, Elev: 8426ft/2568m, Tel: 719-378-6395, Nearest town: Mosca. GPS: 37.773439, -105.499581

127 • D3 | Great Sand Dunes NP - Indian Grove TC

Dispersed sites, No water, No toilets, Tents only: Free, Hike-in, 2.9 mi, No fires, Free permit required, Reservations not accepted, Elev: 8387ft/2556m, Tel: 719-378-6395, Nearest town: Mosca. GPS: 37.789651, -105.509358

128 • D3 | Great Sand Dunes NP - Little Medano TC

Dispersed sites, No water, No toilets, Tents only: Free, Hike-in, .7 mi, 4x4 required to TH, No fires, Free permit required, Reservations not accepted, Elev: 8754ft/2668m, Tel: 719-378-6395, Nearest town: Mosca. GPS: 37.808246, -105.506783

129 • D3 | Great Sand Dunes NP - Medano Pass Road Site 11

Dispersed sites, No water, No toilets, Tent & RV camping: Free, 4x4 required, Reservations not accepted, Elev: 8855ft/2699m, Tel: 719-378-6395, Nearest town: Mosca. GPS: 37.812269, -105.471848

130 • D3 | Great Sand Dunes NP - Medano Pass Road Site 12

Dispersed sites, No water, No toilets, Tent & RV camping: Free, 4x4 required, Reservations not accepted, Elev: 8908ft/2715m, Tel: 719-378-6395, Nearest town: Mosca. GPS: 37.814407, -105.467773

131 • D3 | Great Sand Dunes NP - Medano Pass Road Site 13

Dispersed sites, No water, No toilets, Tent & RV camping: Free, 4x4 required, Reservations not accepted, Elev: 8926ft/2721m, Tel: 719-378-6395, Nearest town: Mosca. GPS: 37.815721, -105.466444

132 • D3 | Great Sand Dunes NP - Medano Pass Road Site 14

Dispersed sites, No water, No toilets, Tent & RV camping: Free, 4x4 required, Open Jun, Reservations not accepted, Elev: 9188ft/2801m, Tel: 719-378-6395, Nearest town: Mosca. GPS: 37.826293, -105.455707

133 • D3 | Great Sand Dunes NP - Medano Pass Rd Site 9-10

Dispersed sites, No water, No toilets, Tents only: Free, 4x4 required, Reservations not accepted, Elev: 8710ft/2655m, Tel: 719-378-6395, Nearest town: Mosca. GPS: 37.806839, -105.486141

134 • D3 | Great Sand Dunes NP - Medano Pass Rd Sites 1-8

Total sites: 8, RV sites: 8, No water, No toilets, Tent & RV camping: Free, 4x4 required, Reservations not accepted, Elev: 8575ft/2614m, Tel: 719-378-6395, Nearest town: Mosca. GPS: 37.803291, -105.495851

135 • D3 | Great Sand Dunes NP - Pinon Flats CG

Total sites: 88, RV sites: 88, Central water, Flush toilet, No showers, RV dump, Tent & RV camping: $20, 3 group sites: $65-$80, Open Apr-Oct, Max Length: 25ft, Reservations accepted, Elev: 8300ft/2530m, Tel: 719-378-6399, Nearest town: Mosca. GPS: 37.745601, -105.505075

Florida

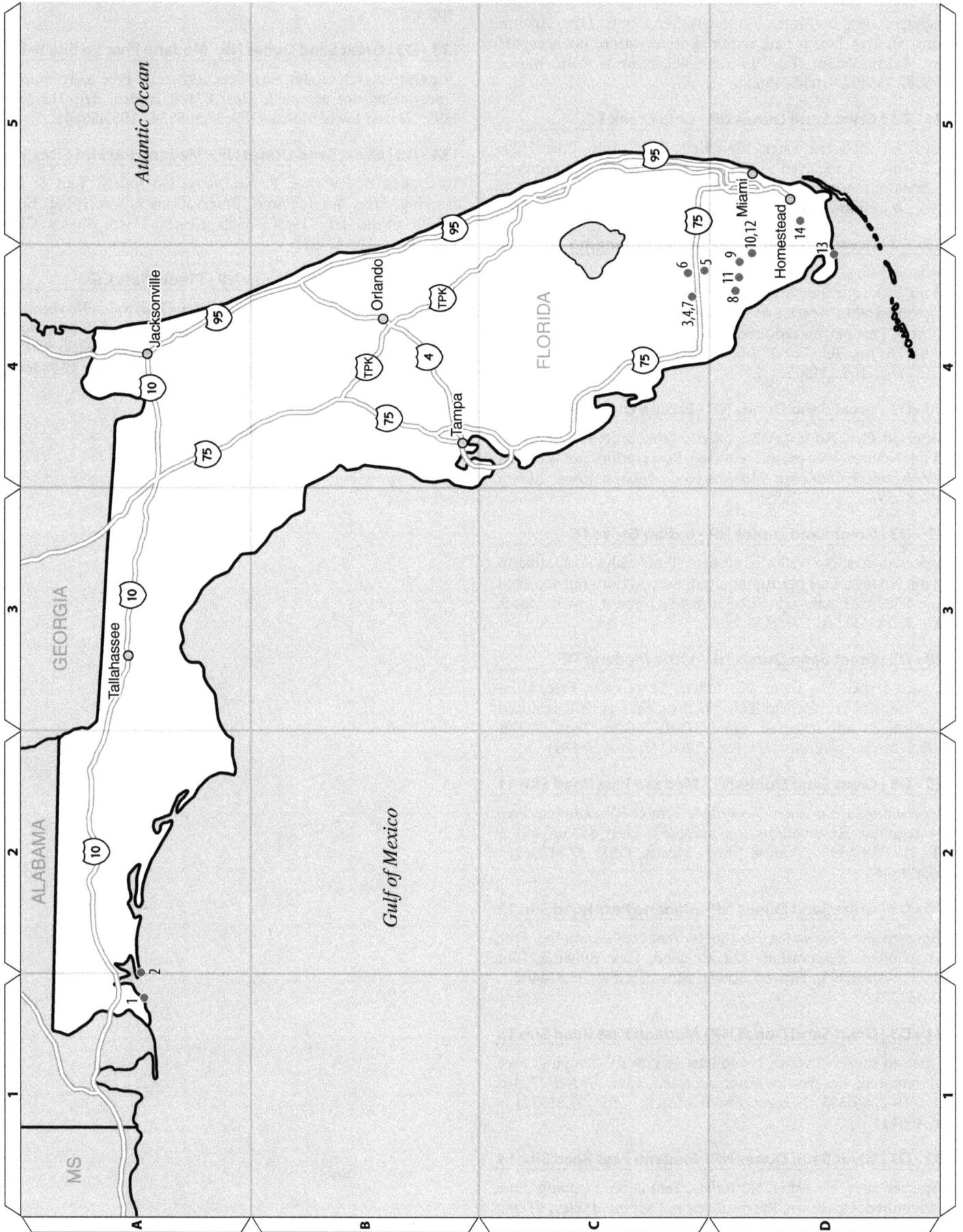

Atlantic Ocean

Gulf of Mexico

GEORGIA

ALABAMA

MS

FLORIDA

Jacksonville

Orlando

Tampa

Tallahassee

Miami

Homestead

3,4,7

6

5

8

11

9

10,12

14

13

1

2

Map	ID	Map	ID
A1	1-2	D4	8-13
C4	3-7	D5	14

Alphabetical List of Camping Areas

Name	ID	Map
Big Cypress NP - Bear Island	3	C4
Big Cypress NP - Burns Lake	8	D4
Big Cypress NP - Gator Head	4	C4
Big Cypress NP - Ivy TC	5	C4
Big Cypress NP - Kissimmee Billy Strand	6	C4
Big Cypress NP - Midway	9	D4
Big Cypress NP - Mitchell's Landing	10	D4
Big Cypress NP - Monument Lake	11	D4
Big Cypress NP - Pinecrest Group	12	D4
Big Cypress NP - Pink Jeep	7	C4
Everglades NP - Flamingo	13	D4
Everglades NP - Long Pine Key	14	D5
Gulf Islands NS - Ft. Pickens	1	A1
Gulf Islands NS - Santa Rosa Island	2	A1

1 • A1 | Gulf Islands NS - Ft. Pickens

Total sites: 200, RV sites: 200, Elec sites: 200, Water at site, Flush toilet, Free showers, RV dump, Tents: $26/RV's: $40, Group tent sites: $20-$30, Stay limit: 14 days, Open all year, Max Length: 50ft, Reservations accepted, Elev: 7ft/2m, Tel: 850-934-2656, Nearest town: Pensacola. GPS: 30.32064, -87.27171

2 • A1 | Gulf Islands NS - Santa Rosa Island

Dispersed sites, No water, No toilets, No tents/RV's: Free, Boondock spot, Elev: 7ft/2m, Nearest town: Pensacola. GPS: 30.347968, -87.054766

3 • C4 | Big Cypress NP - Bear Island

Total sites: 40, RV sites: 0, No water, Vault/pit toilet, Tents only: $10, Access via 20-mile gravel road, Generator hours: 0600-2200, Open all year, Reservations not accepted, Elev: 18ft/5m, Tel: 239-695-1201, Nearest town: Naples. GPS: 26.182974, -81.247652

4 • C4 | Big Cypress NP - Gator Head

Total sites: 9, RV sites: 0, No water, Vault/pit toilet, Tents only: $10, Also hike/bike/ATV accessible, ORV permit required, Generator hours: 0600-2200, Open Aug-Apr, Reservations not accepted, Elev: 18ft/5m, Tel: 239-695-1201, Nearest town: Naples. GPS: 26.223802, -81.267867

5 • C4 | Big Cypress NP - Ivy TC

Dispersed sites, No water, No toilets, Tents only: Free, Hike-in, Free permit required, Open all year, Elev: 12ft/4m, Tel: 239-695-1201, Nearest town: Naples. GPS: 26.126895, -81.059071

6 • C4 | Big Cypress NP - Kissimmee Billy Strand

Dispersed sites, No water, No toilets, Tents only: Free, Hike-in, Several sites in this area, Free permit required, Open all year, Elev: 18ft/5m, Tel: 239-695-1201, Nearest town: Naples. GPS: 26.234084, -81.071583

7 • C4 | Big Cypress NP - Pink Jeep

Total sites: 9, RV sites: 0, No water, Vault/pit toilet, Tents only: $10, Also hike/bike/ATV accessible, ORV permit required, Generator hours: 0600-2200, Open Sep-May, Reservations not accepted, Elev: 38ft/12m, Tel: 239-695-1201, Nearest town: Naples. GPS: 26.216401, -81.295149

8 • D4 | Big Cypress NP - Burns Lake

Total sites: 15, RV sites: 15, No water, Vault/pit toilet, Tent & RV camping: $24, Stay limit: 10-14 days, Generator hours: 0600-2200, Open Aug-Apr, Reservations accepted, Elev: 13ft/4m, Tel: 239-695-1201, Nearest town: Naples. GPS: 25.891752, -81.229856

9 • D4 | Big Cypress NP - Midway

Total sites: 36, RV sites: 26, Elec sites: 26, Central water, Flush toilet, No showers, RV dump, Tents: $24/RV's: $30, Stay limit: 10-14 days, Generator hours: 0600-2200, Open all year, Reservations accepted, Elev: 26ft/8m, Tel: 239-695-1201, Nearest town: Naples. GPS: 25.851435, -80.989364

10 • D4 | Big Cypress NP - Mitchell's Landing

Total sites: 11, RV sites: 11, No water, Vault/pit toilet, Tent & RV camping: $24, Stay limit: 10-14 days, Generator hours: 0600-2200, Open Aug-Apr, Reservations not accepted, Elev: 20ft/6m, Tel: 239-695-1201, Nearest town: Naples. GPS: 25.754785, -80.925916

11 • D4 | Big Cypress NP - Monument Lake

Total sites: 36, RV sites: 26, Central water, No toilets, No showers, No RV dump, Tents: $24/RV's: $28, Stay limit: 10-14 days, Generator hours: 0600-2200, Open Aug-Apr, Reservations accepted, Elev: 10ft/3m, Tel: 239-695-1201, Nearest town: Naples. GPS: 25.867044, -81.113815

12 • D4 | Big Cypress NP - Pinecrest Group

Total sites: 4, RV sites: 0, No water, No toilets, Group site: $30, Stay limit: 10-14 days, Open all year, Reservations accepted, Elev: 23ft/7m, Tel: 239-695-1201, Nearest town: Naples. GPS: 25.762361, -80.919171

13 • D4 | Everglades NP - Flamingo

Total sites: 278, RV sites: 234, Elec sites: 41, Central water, Flush toilet, Free showers, RV dump, Tents: $30-35/RV's: $45-55, Solar-heated showers, Elec sites require reservation Nov-Apr, Group sites: $30, Open all year, Reservations accepted, Elev: 16ft/5m, Tel: Info: 239-695-0124 Res: 855-708-2207, Nearest town: Homestead. GPS: 25.13716, -80.94316

14 • D5 | Everglades NP - Long Pine Key

Total sites: 108, RV sites: 108, Central water, Flush toilet, Free showers, RV dump, Tent & RV camping: $30-35, 1 group site, Open Nov-Apr, Reservations not accepted, Elev: 20ft/6m, Tel: 305-242-7873, Nearest town: Homestead. GPS: 25.400307, -80.655261

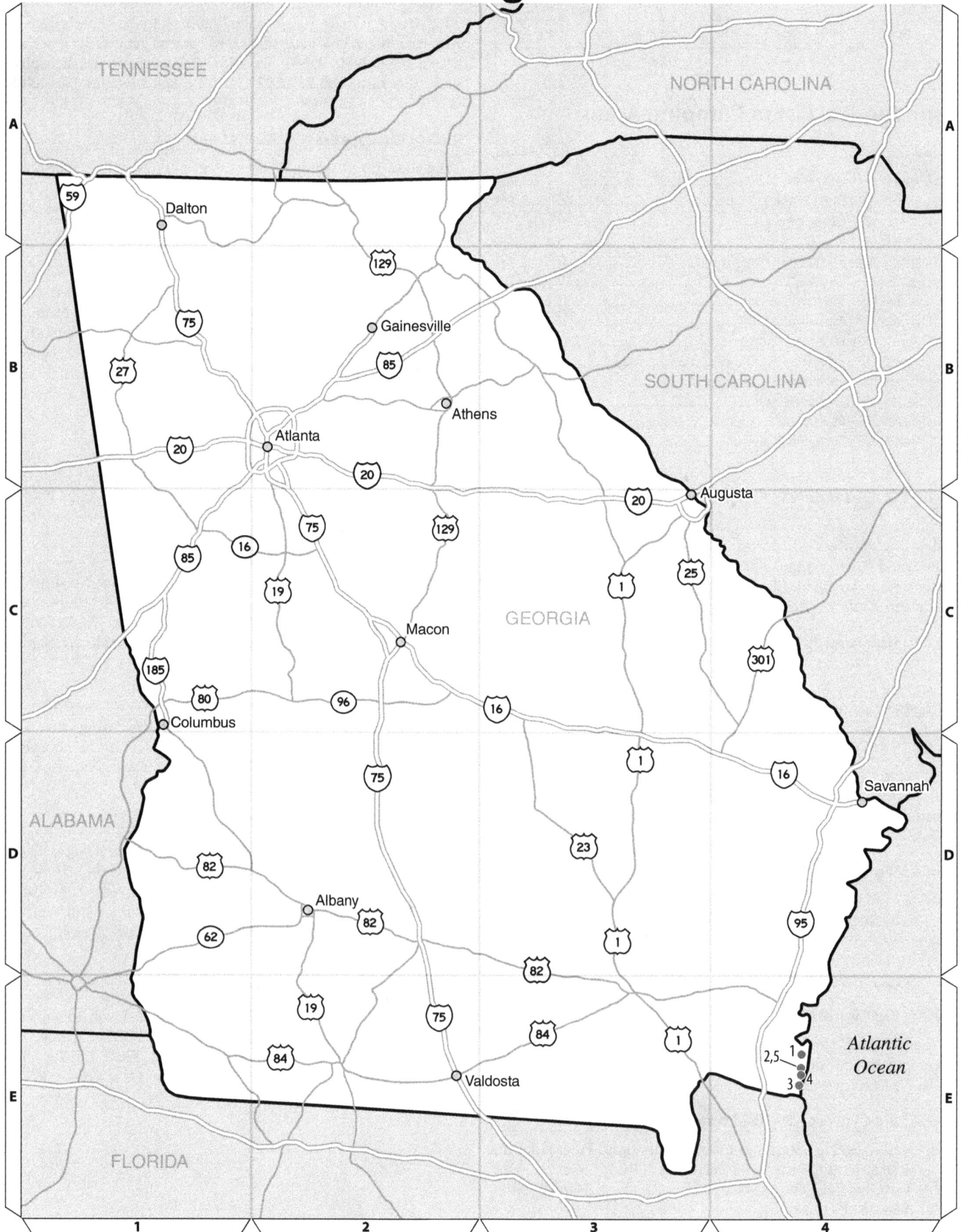

Georgia

TENNESSEE

NORTH CAROLINA

SOUTH CAROLINA

GEORGIA

ALABAMA

FLORIDA

Atlantic Ocean

Dalton

Gainesville

Athens

Atlanta

Augusta

Macon

Columbus

Albany

Valdosta

Savannah

59
129
75
27
85
20
20
75
129
20
1
25
19
185
80
301
96
16
16
75
23
82
82
95
62
19
82
75
84
1
84
1

1
2,5
3
4

Map	ID	Map	ID
E4	1-5		

Alphabetical List of Camping Areas

Name   **ID**   **Map**

Cumberland Island - Brickhill Bluff.. 1 ....E4
Cumberland Island - Hickory Hill .... 2 ....E4
Cumberland Island - Sea Camp .... 3 ....E4
Cumberland Island - Stafford .... 4 ....E4
Cumberland Island - Yankee Paradise... 5 ....E4

1 • E4 | Cumberland Island - Brickhill Bluff

Dispersed sites, No water, No toilets, Tents only: $9, Walk-to sites, Ferry from mainland, 10.5 mile , No fires, No pets, Stay limit: 7 days, Open all year, Reservations required, Elev: 10ft/3m, Tel: 912-882-4336, Nearest town: St. Mary's City. GPS: 30.899938, -81.445538

2 • E4 | Cumberland Island - Hickory Hill

Dispersed sites, No toilets, Tents only: $9, Walk-to sites, Ferry from mainland, 5.5 mile , No fires, No pets, Stay limit: 7 days, Open all year, Reservations required, Elev: 19ft/6m, Tel: 912-882-4336, Nearest town: St. Mary's City. GPS: 30.835937, -81.447892

3 • E4 | Cumberland Island - Sea Camp

Total sites: 16, Central water, Flush toilet, Free showers, No RV dump, Tents only: $22, Walk-to sites, Ferry from mainland, Cold showers, No pets, Stay limit: 7 days, Open all year, Reservations required, Elev: 17ft/5m, Tel: 912-882-4336, Nearest town: St. Mary's City. GPS: 30.764511, -81.462587

4 • E4 | Cumberland Island - Stafford

Dispersed sites, Central water, Flush toilet, Free showers, Tents only: $12, Hike-in, Ferry from mainland, 3.5 mile, No pets, Stay limit: 7 days, Open all year, Reservations required, Elev: 28ft/9m, Tel: 912-882-4336, Nearest town: St. Mary's City. GPS: 30.807996, -81.450833

5 • E4 | Cumberland Island - Yankee Paradise

Dispersed sites, No toilets, Tents only: $9, Walk-to sites, Ferry from mainland, 7.5 mile , No Fires, No pets, Stay limit: 7 days, Open all year, Reservations required, Elev: 20ft/6m, Tel: 912-882-4336, Nearest town: St. Mary's City. GPS: 30.849892, -81.454418

Idaho

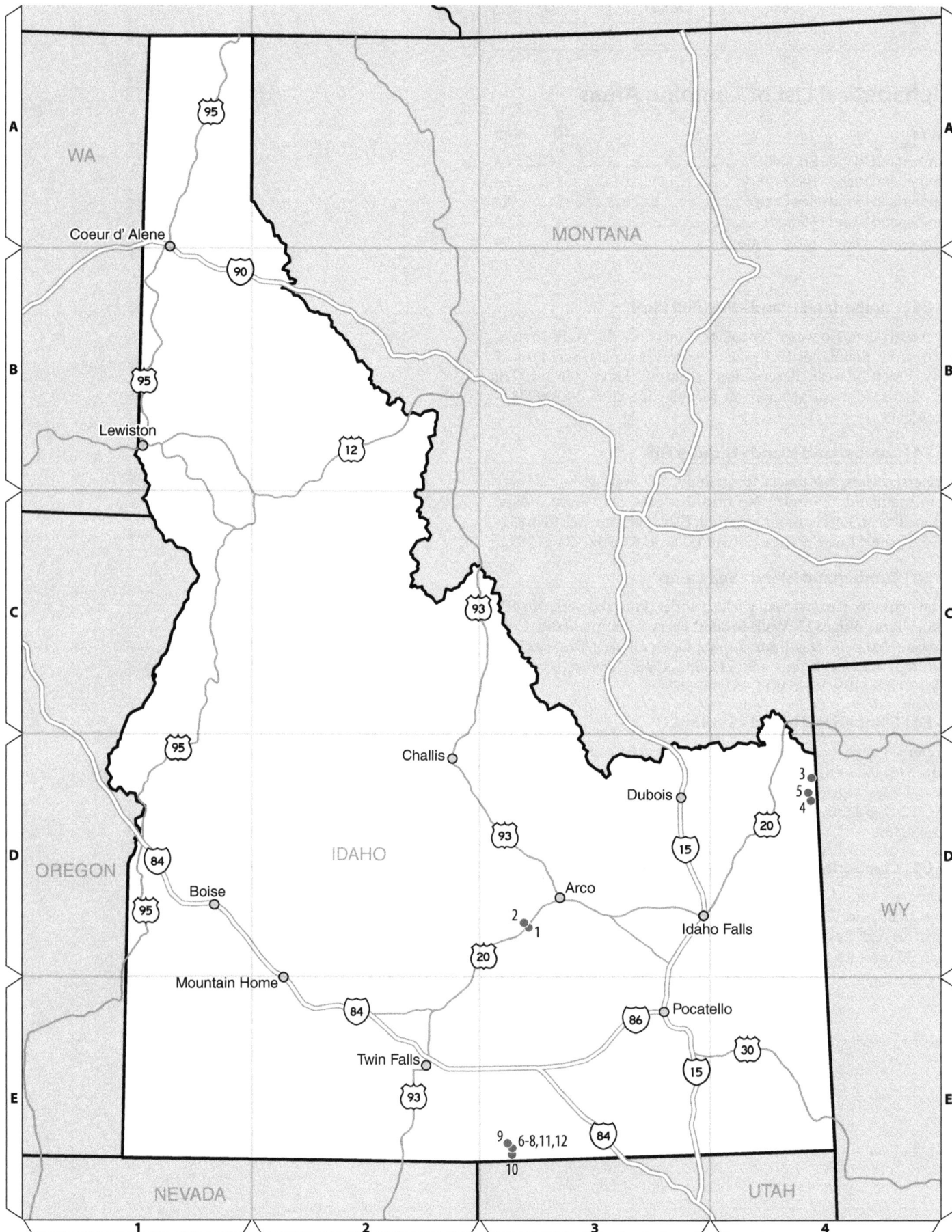

Map	ID	Map	ID
D3	1-2	E3	6-12
D4	3-5		

Alphabetical List of Camping Areas

Name	ID	Map
City of Rocks NR - Bath Rock	6	E3
City of Rocks NR - Bread Loaves	7	E3
City of Rocks NR - Elephant Rocks	8	E3
City of Rocks NR - Finger Rock	9	E3
City of Rocks NR - Twin Sisters	10	E3
City of Rocks NR - Window Arch	11	E3
City of Rocks NR - Window Rock	12	E3
Craters of the Moon NM - Lava Flow CG	1	D3
Craters of the Moon NM - Sunset Cinder Group	2	D3
Yellowstone NP - Buffalo Lake (9A5)	3	D4
Yellowstone NP - Little Robinson Creek (9A7)	4	D4
Yellowstone NP - Robinson Creek (9A6)	5	D4

1 • D3 | Craters of the Moon NM - Lava Flow CG

Total sites: 42, RV sites: 42, Central water, Flush toilet, No showers, No RV dump, Tent & RV camping: $15, $8 off-season, No wood fires, No services in winter, Generator hours: 0600-2200, Open Apr-Nov, Reservations not accepted, Elev: 5882ft/1793m, Tel: 208-527-1335, Nearest town: Arco. GPS: 43.460876, -113.559269

2 • D3 | Craters of the Moon NM - Sunset Cinder Group

Total sites: 1, Central water, Vault/pit toilet, Group site: $30, Open Jun-Sep, Elev: 5847ft/1782m, Tel: 208-527-1335, Nearest town: Arco. GPS: 43.472801, -113.566876

3 • D4 | Yellowstone NP - Buffalo Lake (9A5)

Dispersed sites, Tents only: $3-5, Hike-in, Permit required, 12 person max, Stock allowed, Reservations accepted, Elev: 7720ft/2353m, Tel: 307-344-2160. GPS: 44.327933, -111.074535

4 • D4 | Yellowstone NP - Little Robinson Creek (9A7)

Dispersed sites, Tents only: $3, Hike-in, Permit required, 12 person max, Reservations accepted, Elev: 6360ft/1939m, Tel: 307-344-2160. GPS: 44.190663, -111.081052

5 • D4 | Yellowstone NP - Robinson Creek (9A6)

Dispersed sites, Tents only: $3-5, Hike-in, Permit required, 12 person max, Stock allowed, Reservations accepted, Elev: 6722ft/2049m, Tel: 307-344-2160. GPS: 44.231663, -111.091871

6 • E3 | City of Rocks NR - Bath Rock

Total sites: 13, No water, No toilets, Tents only: $13, Walk-to sites, Stay limit: 14 days, Generator hours: 0700-2200, Reservations accepted, Elev: 6365ft/1940m, Tel: 208-824-5910, Nearest town: Almo. GPS: 42.075908, -113.721152

7 • E3 | City of Rocks NR - Bread Loaves

Total sites: 3, Central water, Vault/pit toilet, No showers, No RV dump, Tents only: $13, Walk-to sites, Stay limit: 14 days, Generator hours: 0700-2200, Reservations accepted, Elev: 6831ft/ 2082m, Tel: 208-824-5910, Nearest town: Almo. GPS: 42.087271, -113.729979

8 • E3 | City of Rocks NR - Elephant Rocks

Total sites: 18, RV sites: 8, No water, Vault/pit toilet, Tent & RV camping: $13, Also walk-to sites, Stay limit: 14 days, Generator hours: 0700-2200, Reservations accepted, Elev: 6273ft/1912m, Tel: 208-824-5910, Nearest town: Almo. GPS: 42.070934, -113.708478

9 • E3 | City of Rocks NR - Finger Rock

Total sites: 4, RV sites: 4, Central water, Vault/pit toilet, No showers, No RV dump, Tent & RV camping: $13, Stay limit: 14 days, Generator hours: 0700-2200, Reservations accepted, Elev: 7244ft/2208m, Tel: 208-824-5910, Nearest town: Almo. GPS: 42.101491, -113.742408

10 • E3 | City of Rocks NR - Twin Sisters

Total sites: 4, No water, Vault/pit toilet, Tents only: $13, Walk-to sites, Stay limit: 14 days, Generator hours: 0700-2200, Reservations accepted, Elev: 6263ft/1909m, Tel: 208-824-5910, Nearest town: Almo. GPS: 42.041563, -113.718513

11 • E3 | City of Rocks NR - Window Arch

Total sites: 16, Central water, Vault/pit toilet, No showers, No RV dump, Tents only: $13, Walk-to sites, Stay limit: 14 days, Generator hours: 0700-2200, Reservations accepted, Elev: 6296ft/1919m, Tel: 208-824-5910, Nearest town: Almo. GPS: 42.072776, -113.713796

12 • E3 | City of Rocks NR - Window Rock

Total sites: 6, Central water, Vault/pit toilet, No showers, No RV dump, Tents only: $13, Walk-to sites, Stay limit: 14 days, Generator hours: 0700-2200, Reservations accepted, Elev: 6686ft/2038m, Tel: 208-824-5910, Nearest town: Almo. GPS: 42.084439, -113.725596

Indiana

MICHIGAN

80 90

1

94

Gary

South Bend

69

30

65

31

30

Fort Wayne

ILLINOIS

24

24

INDIANA

27

OHIO

65

69

31

74

65

70

Richmond

Terre Haute

70

65

37

74

Columbus

50

50

50

65

37

50

231

150

64

64

Evansville

KENTUCKY

Map	ID	Map	ID
A2	1		

Alphabetical List of Camping Areas

Name   **ID**   **Map**

Indiana Dunes NP - Dunewood .... 1 .... A2

1 • A2 | Indiana Dunes NP - Dunewood

Total sites: 66, RV sites: 54, Central water, Flush toilet, Free showers, Tent & RV camping: $25, Also walk-to & group sites, Grup site: $60, Generator hours: 0600-2200, Open Apr-Oct, Reservations accepted, Elev: 653ft/199m, Tel: 219-395-1882, Nearest town: Chesterton. GPS: 41.67054, -86.98344

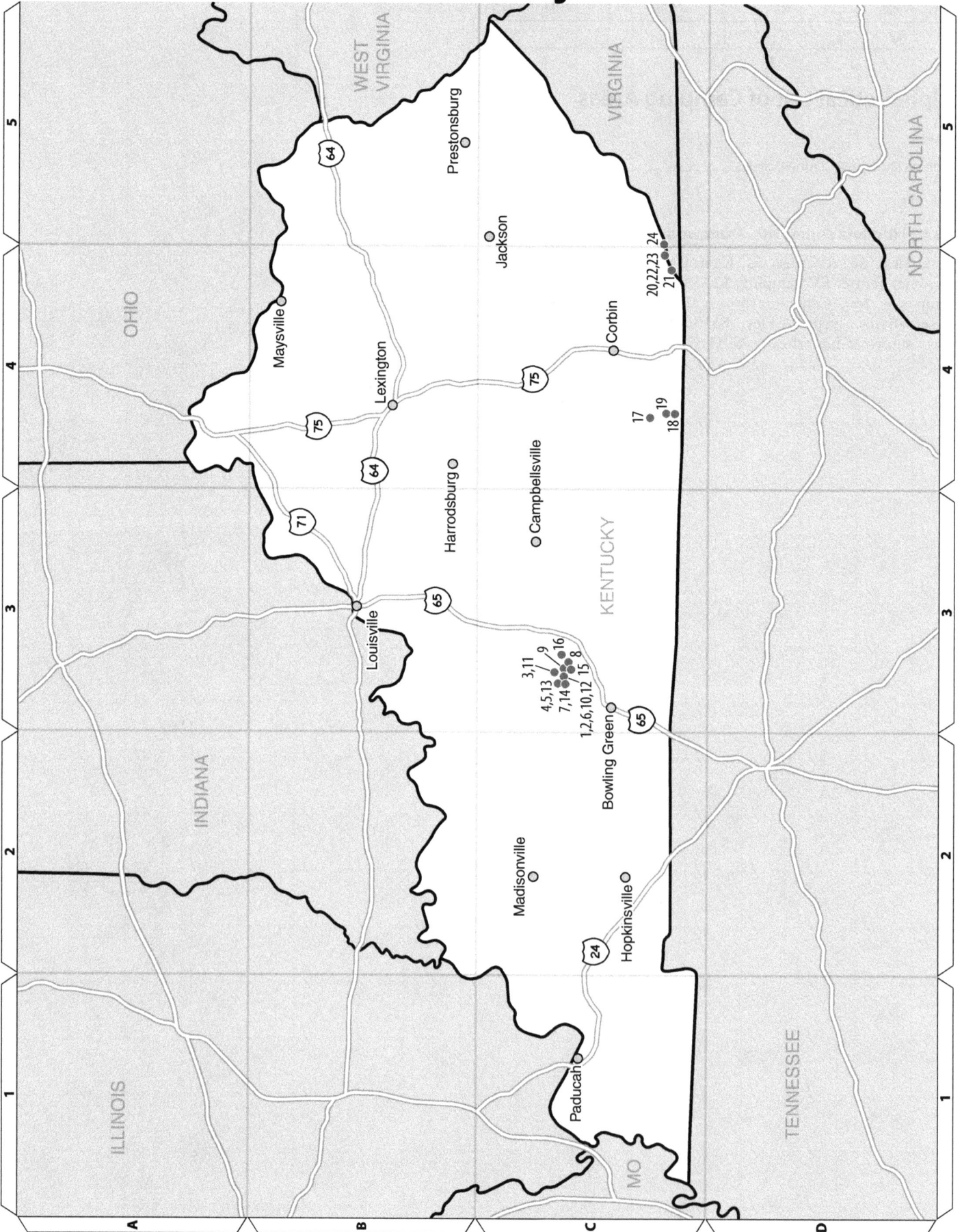

Kentucky

ILLINOIS

OHIO

INDIANA

WEST VIRGINIA

VIRGINIA

NORTH CAROLINA

TENNESSEE

MO

KENTUCKY

Prestonsburg

Jackson

Maysville

Lexington

Corbin

Harrodsburg

Campbellsville

Louisville

Bowling Green

Madisonville

Hopkinsville

Paducah

20,22,23 24
21

17 19
18

3,11 9
16
4,5,13 8
7,14 15
1,2,6,10,12

Map	ID	Map	ID
C3	1-16	C5	24
C4	17-23		

Alphabetical List of Camping Areas

Name	ID	Map
Big South Fork NRRA - Alum Ford	17	C4
Big South Fork NRRA - Bear Creek Horse Camp	18	C4
Big South Fork NRRA - Blue Heron	19	C4
Cumberland Gap NP - Chadwell Gap	20	C4
Cumberland Gap NP - Gibson Gap	21	C4
Cumberland Gap NP - Hensley Camp	22	C4
Cumberland Gap NP - Martins Fork	23	C4
Cumberland Gap NP - White Rocks	24	C5
Mammoth Cave NP - Bluffs TC	1	C3
Mammoth Cave NP - Collie Ridge TC	2	C3
Mammoth Cave NP - Ferguson TC	3	C3
Mammoth Cave NP - First Creek 1 TC	4	C3
Mammoth Cave NP - First Creek 2 TC	5	C3
Mammoth Cave NP - Homestead TC	6	C3
Mammoth Cave NP - Houchins Ferry	7	C3
Mammoth Cave NP - Mammoth Cave	8	C3
Mammoth Cave NP - Maple Springs Group/Equestrian	9	C3
Mammoth Cave NP - McCoy Hollow TC	10	C3
Mammoth Cave NP - Raymer Hollow TC	11	C3
Mammoth Cave NP - Sal Hollow TC	12	C3
Mammoth Cave NP - Second Creek TC	13	C3
Mammoth Cave NP - Three Springs TC	14	C3
Mammoth Cave NP - Turnhole Bend TC	15	C3
Mammoth Cave NP - White Oak TC	16	C3

1 • C3 | Mammoth Cave NP - Bluffs TC

Dispersed sites, Water available, Tents only: Free, Hike-in, Free permit required, 8 person limit, Reservations not accepted, Elev: 596ft/182m, Tel: 270-758-2424, Nearest town: Mammoth Cave. GPS: 37.204847, -86.185936

2 • C3 | Mammoth Cave NP - Collie Ridge TC

Dispersed sites, Water available, Tents only: Free, Hike-in, Free permit required, 8 person limit, Reservations not accepted, Elev: 560ft/171m, Tel: 270-758-2424, Nearest town: Mammoth Cave. GPS: 37.217014, -86.189619

3 • C3 | Mammoth Cave NP - Ferguson TC

Dispersed sites, Water available, Tents only: Free, Hike-in, Free permit required, 8 person limit, Reservations not accepted, Elev: 706ft/215m, Tel: 270-758-2424, Nearest town: Mammoth Cave. GPS: 37.246924, -86.170681

4 • C3 | Mammoth Cave NP - First Creek 1 TC

Dispersed sites, Water available, Tents only: Free, Hike-in, Free permit required, 8 person limit, Reservations not accepted, Elev: 493ft/150m, Tel: 270-758-2424, Nearest town: Mammoth Cave. GPS: 37.224996, -86.228685

5 • C3 | Mammoth Cave NP - First Creek 2 TC

Dispersed sites, Water available, Tents only: Free, Hike-in, Free permit required, 8 person limit, Reservations not accepted, Elev: 489ft/149m, Tel: 270-758-2424, Nearest town: Mammoth Cave. GPS: 37.224924, -86.226394

6 • C3 | Mammoth Cave NP - Homestead TC

Dispersed sites, Water available, Tents only: Free, Hike-in, Free permit required, 8 person limit, Reservations not accepted, Elev: 729ft/222m, Tel: 270-758-2424, Nearest town: Mammoth Cave. GPS: 37.212729, -86.155075

7 • C3 | Mammoth Cave NP - Houchins Ferry

Total sites: 12, RV sites: 0, Central water, Vault/pit toilet, Tents only: $15, Reservations not accepted, Elev: 463ft/141m, Tel: 270-758-2424, Nearest town: Mammoth Cave. GPS: 37.201901, -86.237158

8 • C3 | Mammoth Cave NP - Mammoth Cave

Total sites: 105, RV sites: 41, Elec sites: 6, Central water, Flush toilet, Free showers, RV dump, Tents: $20/RV's: $20-50, 6 Full hookups, 4 group sites: $25, Open all year, Reservations accepted, Elev: 787ft/240m, Tel: 270-758-2424, Nearest town: Mammoth Cave. GPS: 37.182341, -86.096215

9 • C3 | Mammoth Cave NP - Maple Springs Group/ Equestrian

Total sites: 7, RV sites: 4, Elec sites: 2, Central water, Vault/pit toilet, No showers, No RV dump, Tents: $25/RV's: $25-35, 4 equestrian, 3 group sites, Open Mar-Nov, Reservations accepted, Elev: 780ft/238m, Tel: 270-758-2424, Nearest town: Mammoth Cave. GPS: 37.204215, -86.136799

10 • C3 | Mammoth Cave NP - McCoy Hollow TC

Dispersed sites, No water, Tents only: Free, Hike-in, Free permit required, 8 person limit, Reservations not accepted, Elev: 674ft/ 205m, Tel: 270-758-2424, Nearest town: Mammoth Cave. GPS: 37.208069, -86.195753

11 • C3 | Mammoth Cave NP - Raymer Hollow TC

Dispersed sites, Water available, Tents only: Free, Hike-in, Free permit required, 8 person limit, Reservations not accepted, Elev: 720ft/219m, Tel: 270-758-2424, Nearest town: Mammoth Cave. GPS: 37.236023, -86.140545

12 • C3 | Mammoth Cave NP - Sal Hollow TC

Dispersed sites, Water available, Tents only: Free, Hike-in, Free permit required, 8 person limit, Reservations not accepted, Elev: 542ft/165m, Tel: 270-758-2424, Nearest town: Mammoth Cave. GPS: 37.192439, -86.181476

13 • C3 | Mammoth Cave NP - Second Creek TC

Dispersed sites, Water available, Tents only: Free, Hike-in, Free permit required, 8 person limit, Reservations not accepted, Elev: 546ft/166m, Tel: 270-758-2424, Nearest town: Mammoth Cave. GPS: 37.236851, -86.237123

14 • C3 | Mammoth Cave NP - Three Springs TC

Dispersed sites, Water available, Tents only: Free, Hike-in, Free permit required, 8 person limit, Reservations not accepted, Elev:

632ft/193m, Tel: 270-758-2424, Nearest town: Mammoth Cave. GPS: 37.214435, -86.221821

15 • C3 | Mammoth Cave NP - Turnhole Bend TC

Dispersed sites, Water available, Tents only: Free, Hike-in, Free permit required, 8 person limit, Reservations not accepted, Elev: 770ft/235m, Tel: 270-758-2424, Nearest town: Mammoth Cave. GPS: 37.172675, -86.153043

16 • C3 | Mammoth Cave NP - White Oak TC

Dispersed sites, Water available, Tents only: Free, Hike-in, Free permit required, 8 person limit, Reservations not accepted, Elev: 558ft/170m, Tel: 270-758-2424, Nearest town: Mammoth Cave. GPS: 37.215936, -86.051091

17 • C4 | Big South Fork NRRA - Alum Ford

Total sites: 6, RV sites: 6, No water, Vault/pit toilet, Tent & RV camping: $5, Reservations not accepted, Elev: 768ft/234m, Tel: 606-376-5073, Nearest town: Whitley City. GPS: 36.763981, -84.546394

18 • C4 | Big South Fork NRRA - Bear Creek Horse Camp

Total sites: 23, RV sites: 23, Elec sites: 23, Water at site, Flush toilet, Free showers, RV dump, Tent & RV camping: $28, Reservations accepted, Elev: 1301ft/397m, Tel: 606-376-5073, Nearest town: Stearns. GPS: 36.641297, -84.523822

19 • C4 | Big South Fork NRRA - Blue Heron

Total sites: 45, RV sites: 45, Elec sites: 45, Water at site, Flush toilet, Free showers, RV dump, Tent & RV camping: $20, Open Apr-Nov, Reservations accepted, Elev: 1266ft/386m, Tel: 606-376-5073, Nearest town: Stearns. GPS: 36.678333, -84.519118

20 • C4 | Cumberland Gap NP - Chadwell Gap

Dispersed sites, No water, Vault/pit toilet, Tents only: Free, Hike-in, Free permit required, Elev: 3375ft/1029m, Tel: 606-248-2817, Nearest town: Middlesboro. GPS: 36.668704, -83.516691

21 • C4 | Cumberland Gap NP - Gibson Gap

Dispersed sites, No water, Vault/pit toilet, Tents only: Free, Hike-in, Free permit required, Elev: 2839ft/865m, Tel: 606-248-2817, Nearest town: Middlesboro. GPS: 36.637602, -83.604103

22 • C4 | Cumberland Gap NP - Hensley Camp

Dispersed sites, No water, Vault/pit toilet, Tents only: Free, Hike-in, Free permit required, Elev: 3365ft/1026m, Tel: 606-248-2817, Nearest town: Middlesboro. GPS: 36.669479, -83.519556

23 • C4 | Cumberland Gap NP - Martins Fork

Dispersed sites, No water, Vault/pit toilet, Tents only: Free, Hike-in, Free permit required, Elev: 2976ft/907m, Tel: 606-248-2817, Nearest town: Middlesboro. GPS: 36.671429, -83.513481

24 • C5 | Cumberland Gap NP - White Rocks

Dispersed sites, No water, Vault/pit toilet, Tents only: Free, Hike-in, Free permit required, Elev: 3046ft/928m, Tel: 606-248-2817, Nearest town: Middlesboro. GPS: 36.668649, -83.447443

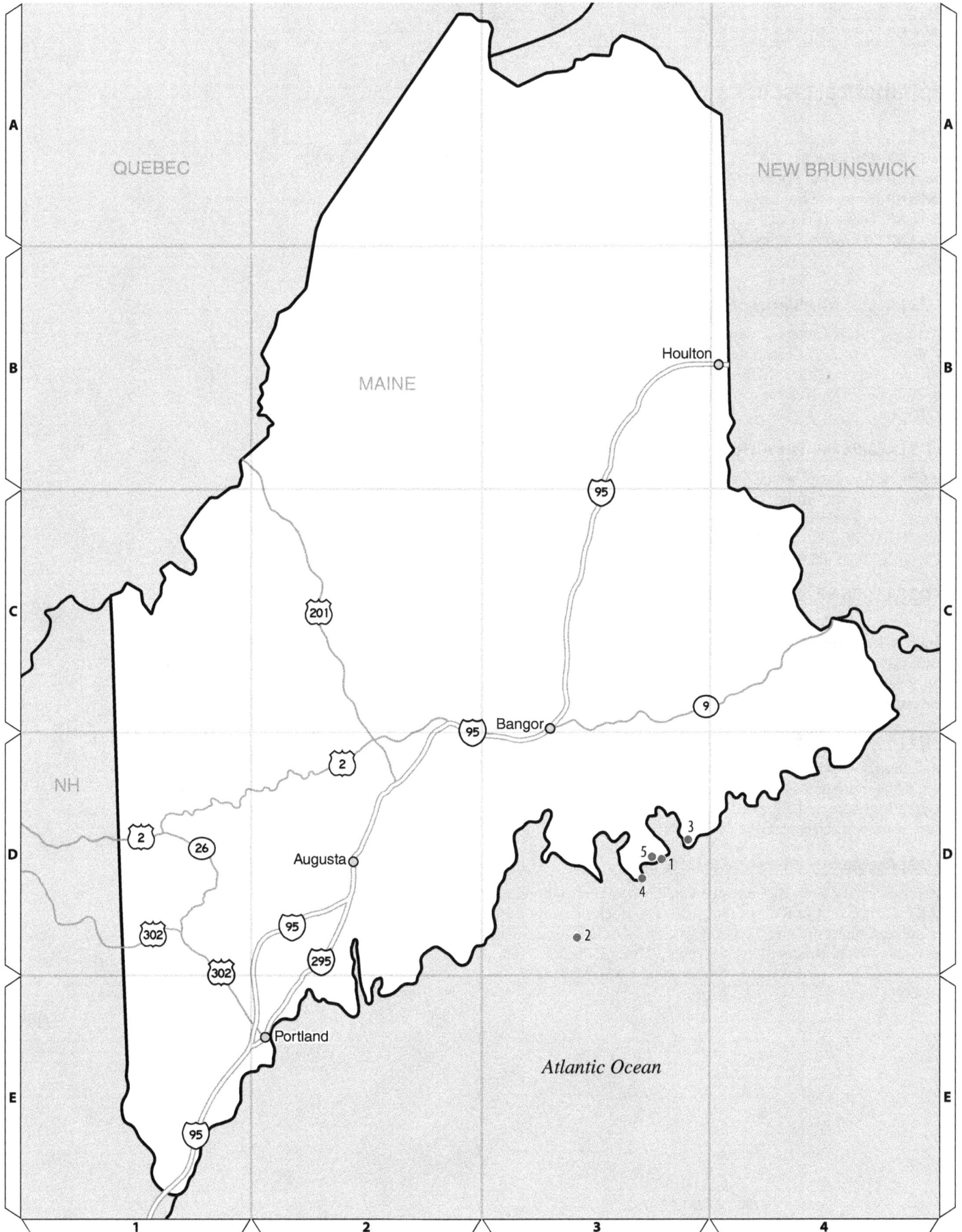

Maine

QUEBEC

NEW BRUNSWICK

A

MAINE

Houlton

B

95

201

C

9

95 Bangor

NH

2

2

26

Augusta

3

5
1

4

302

95

2

295

302

Portland

Atlantic Ocean

95

95

QUEBEC

NEW BRUNSWICK

Map	ID	Map	ID
D3	1-5		

Alphabetical List of Camping Areas

Name	ID	Map
Acadia NP - Blackwoods	1	D3
Acadia NP - Isle Au Haut Duck Harbor	2	D3
Acadia NP - Schoodic Woods	3	D3
Acadia NP - Seawall CG	4	D3
Acadia NP - Wildwood Stables CG	5	D3

1 • D3 | Acadia NP - Blackwoods

Total sites: 281, RV sites: 60, Central water, No toilets, No showers, RV dump, Tent & RV camping: $30, Group sites (4): $60, Open May-Oct, Max Length: 35ft, Reservations accepted, Elev: 20ft/6m, Tel: 207-288-3338, Nearest town: Bar Harbor. GPS: 44.309574, -68.203744

2 • D3 | Acadia NP - Isle Au Haut Duck Harbor

Total sites: 5, Central water, Vault/pit toilet, Shelter: $20, Access by mail boat, 3-day limit, Tents must be inside shelters, Stay limit: 3 days, No generators, Open May-Oct, Reservations required, Elev: 41ft/12m, Tel: 207-288-3338, Nearest town: Stonington. GPS: 44.027876, -68.653304

3 • D3 | Acadia NP - Schoodic Woods

Total sites: 89, RV sites: 78, Elec sites: 78, Water at site, No showers, RV dump, Tents: $22-30/RV's: $30-40, Hike-in and group sites available, 12 hike-in sites, Group site $60, Open May-Oct, Reservations required, Elev: 111ft/34m, Tel: 207-288-3338, Nearest town: Winter Harbor. GPS: 44.381344, -68.068478

4 • D3 | Acadia NP - Seawall CG

Total sites: 214, Central water, No toilets, No showers, Tents: $22/ RV's: $30, Group tent site: $60, Open May-Sep, Max Length: 35ft, Reservations accepted, Elev: 33ft/10m, Tel: 207-288-3338, Nearest town: Southwest Harbor. GPS: 44.240884, -68.304436

5 • D3 | Acadia NP - Wildwood Stables CG

Total sites: 10, RV sites: 10, Central water, Flush toilet, No showers, No RV dump, Tent & RV camping: $15, For stock use only, $25 per horse, Concessionaire, Generators allowed/hours unknown, Open May-Oct, Reservations accepted, Elev: 250ft/76m, Tel: 877-276-3622, Nearest town: Stonington. GPS: 44.314435, -68.249144

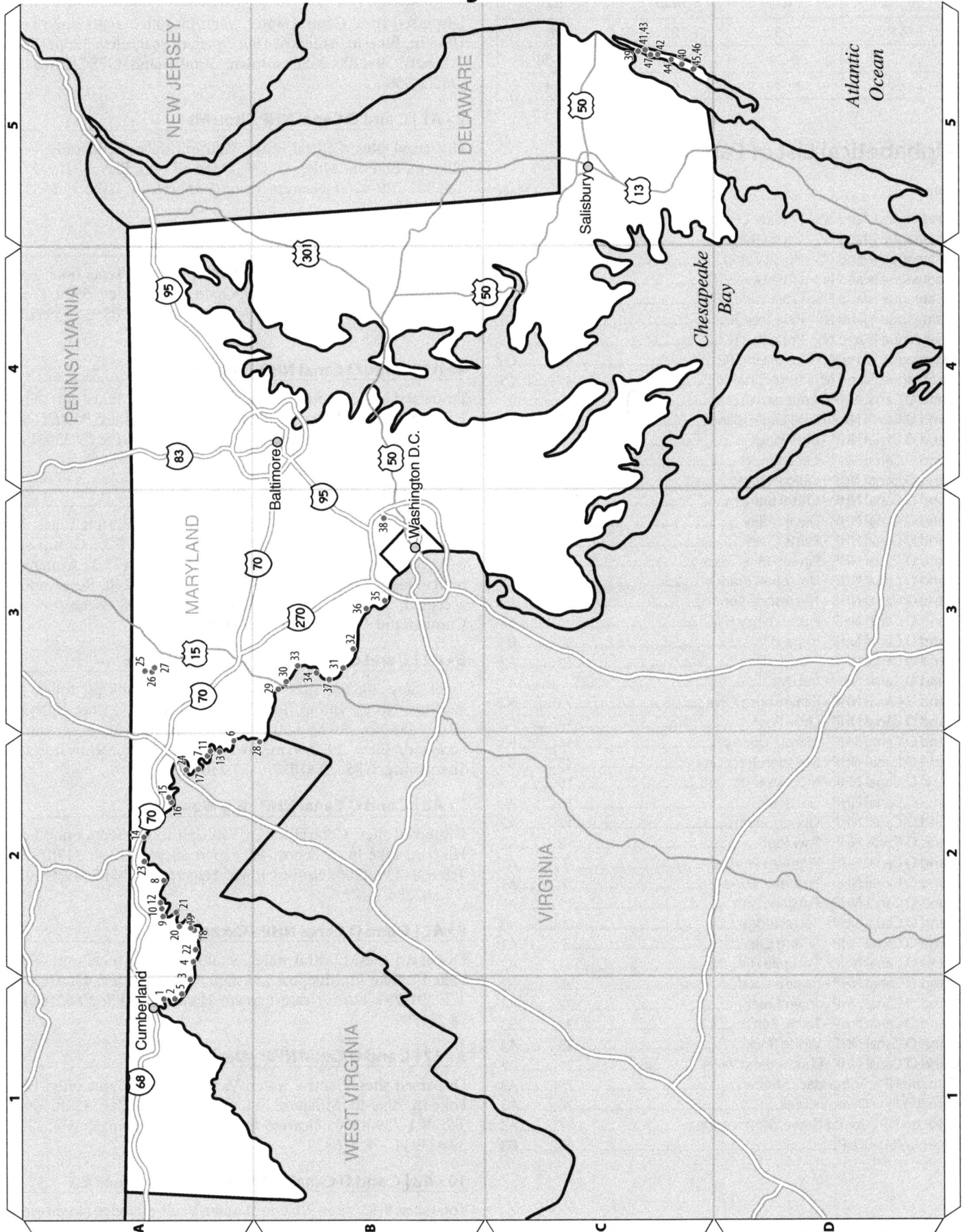

Maryland

Salisbury

Baltimore

Washington D.C.

Cumberland

50

13

301

95

50

83

70

95

50

270

15

70

70

15

68

39
47 41,43
44 42
40
45,46

38

35
36
32
33 31
30
34 37
29

6
7 11
24 13
17
15
16
14

23
8
10 12
9
20 21
3 4 22 19
5 18
1
2
28

Map	ID	Map	ID
A1	1-5	B2	28
A2	6-24	B3	29-38
A3	25-27	C5	39-47

Alphabetical List of Camping Areas

Name	ID	Map
Assateague Island NS - Bayside CG	39	C5
Assateague Island NS - Green Run TC	40	C5
Assateague Island NS - Horse Camp	41	C5
Assateague Island NS - Little Levels TC	42	C5
Assateague Island NS - Oceanside CG	43	C5
Assateague Island NS - Pine Tree TC	44	C5
Assateague Island NS - Pope Bay TC	45	C5
Assateague Island NS - State Line TC	46	C5
Assateague Island NS - Tingles Island TC	47	C5
C and O Canal NHP - Antietam Creek	6	A2
C and O Canal NHP - Bald Eagle Island	29	B3
C and O Canal NHP - Big Woods	7	A2
C and O Canal NHP - Cacapon Jct	8	A2
C and O Canal NHP - Calico Rocks	30	B3
C and O Canal NHP - Chisel Branch	31	B3
C and O Canal NHP - Devils Alley	9	A2
C and O Canal NHP - Evitts Creek	1	A1
C and O Canal NHP - Fifteen Mile Creek CG	10	A2
C and O Canal NHP - Horsepen Branch	32	B3
C and O Canal NHP - Horseshoe Bend	11	A2
C and O Canal NHP - Huckleberry Hill	28	B2
C and O Canal NHP - Indian Flats	33	B3
C and O Canal NHP - Indigo Neck	12	A2
C and O Canal NHP - Iron Mt	2	A1
C and O Canal NHP - Killiansburg Cave	13	A2
C and O Canal NHP - Little Pool	14	A2
C and O Canal NHP - Marble Quarry	34	B3
C and O Canal NHP - Marsden Tract Group	35	B3
C and O Canal NHP - McCoys Ferry	15	A2
C and O Canal NHP - North Mt	16	A2
C and O Canal NHP - Opequon Jct	17	A2
C and O Canal NHP - Paw Paw	18	A2
C and O Canal NHP - Pigmans Ferry	3	A1
C and O Canal NHP - Potomac Forks	4	A1
C and O Canal NHP - Purslane Run	19	A2
C and O Canal NHP - Sorrel Ridge	20	A2
C and O Canal NHP - Spring Gap	5	A1
C and O Canal NHP - Stickpile Hill	21	A2
C and O Canal NHP - Swains Lock	36	B3
C and O Canal NHP - Town Creek	22	A2
C and O Canal NHP - Turtle Run	37	B3
C and O Canal NHP - White Rock	23	A2
C and O Canal NHP -Cumberland Valley	24	A2
Catoctin NP - Adirondack Shelters	25	A3
Catoctin NP - Owen's Creek	26	A3
Catoctin NP - Poplar Grove Youth Group	27	A3
Greenbelt Park NP	38	B3

1 • A1 | C and O Canal NHP - Evitts Creek
Dispersed sites, Central water, Vault/pit toilet, Tents only: Free, Hike-in, Bike-in, Milepost 180, Open all year, Elev: 598ft/182m, Tel: 301-739-4200, Nearest town: Cumberland. GPS: 39.615378, -78.732339

2 • A1 | C and O Canal NHP - Iron Mt
Dispersed sites, Central water, Vault/pit toilet, Tents only: Free, Hike-in, Bike-in, Milepost 175, Open all year, Elev: 581ft/177m, Tel: 301-739-4200, Nearest town: Cumberland. GPS: 39.585328, -78.732281

3 • A1 | C and O Canal NHP - Pigmans Ferry
Dispersed sites, Central water, Vault/pit toilet, Tents only: Free, Hike-in, Bike-in, Milepost 169, Open all year, Elev: 572ft/174m, Tel: 301-739-4200, Nearest town: Old Town. GPS: 39.539923, -78.65734

4 • A1 | C and O Canal NHP - Potomac Forks
Dispersed sites, Central water, Vault/pit toilet, Tents only: Free, Hike-in, Bike-in, Milepost 164.8, Open all year, Elev: 543ft/166m, Tel: 301-739-4200, Nearest town: Old Town. GPS: 39.530619, -78.58855

5 • A1 | C and O Canal NHP - Spring Gap
Total sites: 12, RV sites: 7, Central water, Vault/pit toilet, No showers, No RV dump, Tent & RV camping: $20, Group site: $40, Mid-Nov to Mid-Apr: $10, Milepost 173.3, Generator hours: 0600-2200, Open all year, Max Length: 20ft, Reservations accepted, Elev: 633ft/193m, Tel: 301-739-4200, Nearest town: Cumberland. GPS: 39.563978, -78.715515

6 • A2 | C and O Canal NHP - Antietam Creek
Total sites: 20, RV sites: 0, Central water, Vault/pit toilet, No showers, No RV dump, Tents only: $20, Walk-to sites, Milepost 69.7, Mid-Nov to Mid-Apr: $10, Open all year, Reservations accepted, Elev: 297ft/91m, Tel: 301-739-4200, Nearest town: Sharpsburg. GPS: 39.418776, -77.746332

7 • A2 | C and O Canal NHP - Big Woods
Dispersed sites, Central water, Vault/pit toilet, Tents only: Free, Hike-in, Bike-in, Milepost 82, Open all year, Elev: 317ft/97m, Tel: 301-739-4200, Nearest town: Hagerstown. GPS: 39.491938, -77.802784

8 • A2 | C and O Canal NHP - Cacapon Jct
Dispersed sites, Central water, Vault/pit toilet, Tents only: Free, Hike-in, Bike-in, Milepost 133, Open all year, Elev: 430ft/131m, Tel: 301-739-4200, Nearest town: Hancock. GPS: 39.621844, -78.281399

9 • A2 | C and O Canal NHP - Devils Alley
Dispersed sites, Central water, Vault/pit toilet, Tents only: Free, Hike-in, Bike-in, Milepost 144, Open all year, Elev: 459ft/140m, Tel: 301-739-4200, Nearest town: Berkley Springs, WV. GPS: 39.623944, -78.416329

10 • A2 | C and O Canal NHP - Fifteen Mile Creek CG
Total sites: 9, RV sites: 9, Central water, Vault/pit toilet, No showers, No RV dump, Tent & RV camping: $20, Group site $40, Mid-

Nov to Mid-Apr: $10, Milepost 140.9, Generator hours: 0600-2200, Open all year, Max Length: 20ft, Reservations accepted, Elev: 456ft/139m, Tel: 301-739-4200, Nearest town: Pratt. GPS: 39.624847, -78.385792

11 • A2 | C and O Canal NHP - Horseshoe Bend

Dispersed sites, Central water, Vault/pit toilet, Tents only: Free, Hike-in, Bike-in, Milepost 80, Open all year, Elev: 295ft/90m, Tel: 301-739-4200, Nearest town: Hagerstown. GPS: 39.483206, -77.789962

12 • A2 | C and O Canal NHP - Indigo Neck

Dispersed sites, Central water, Vault/pit toilet, Tents only: Free, Hike-in, Bike-in, Milepost 139, Open all year, Elev: 450ft/137m, Tel: 301-739-4200, Nearest town: Berkley Springs, WV. GPS: 39.629842, -78.366927

13 • A2 | C and O Canal NHP - Killiansburg Cave

Dispersed sites, Central water, Vault/pit toilet, Tents only: Free, Hike-in, Bike-in, Milepost 75.3, Open all year, Elev: 308ft/94m, Tel: 301-739-4200, Nearest town: Sheperdstown, WV. GPS: 39.458909, -77.796749

14 • A2 | C and O Canal NHP - Little Pool

Dispersed sites, Central water, Vault/pit toilet, Tents only: Free, Hike-in, Bike-in, Milepost 120, Open all year, Elev: 395ft/120m, Tel: 301-739-4200, Nearest town: Hancock. GPS: 39.686063, -78.116208

15 • A2 | C and O Canal NHP - McCoys Ferry

Total sites: 12, RV sites: 12, Central water, Vault/pit toilet, No showers, No RV dump, Tent & RV camping: $20, Group site: $40, Mid-Nov to mid-Apr: $10, Tunnel access limits vehicle height to 10' 3", Milepost 110.4, Generator hours: 0600-2200, Open all year, Max Length: 20ft, Reservations accepted, Elev: 433ft/132m, Tel: 301-739-4200, Nearest town: Williamsport. GPS: 39.608195, -77.969038

16 • A2 | C and O Canal NHP - North Mt

Dispersed sites, Central water, Vault/pit toilet, Tents only: Free, Hike-in, Bike-in, Milepost 109, Open all year, Elev: 376ft/115m, Tel: 301-739-4200, Nearest town: Hancock. GPS: 39.601221, -77.978187

17 • A2 | C and O Canal NHP - Opequon Jct

Dispersed sites, Central water, Vault/pit toilet, Tents only: Free, Hike-in, Bike-in, Milepost 90.2, Open all year, Elev: 337ft/103m, Tel: 301-739-4200, Nearest town: Hagerstown. GPS: 39.516841, -77.862319

18 • A2 | C and O Canal NHP - Paw Paw

Total sites: 10, RV sites: 0, Central water, Vault/pit toilet, No showers, No RV dump, Tents only: $20, Walk-to sites, Mid-Nov to mid-Apr: $10, Milepost 156.1, Open all year, Reservations accepted, Elev: 529ft/161m, Tel: 301-739-4200, Nearest town: Paw Paw, WV. GPS: 39.531938, -78.465681

19 • A2 | C and O Canal NHP - Purslane Run

Dispersed sites, Central water, Vault/pit toilet, Tents only: Free, Hike-in, Bike-in, Milepost 156, Open all year, Elev: 526ft/160m, Tel: 301-739-4200, Nearest town: Paw Paw, WV. GPS: 39.536434, -78.463813

20 • A2 | C and O Canal NHP - Sorrel Ridge

Dispersed sites, Central water, Vault/pit toilet, Tents only: Free, Hike-in, Bike-in, Milepost 154, Open all year, Elev: 498ft/152m, Tel: 301-739-4200, Nearest town: Paw Paw, WV. GPS: 39.570918, -78.452678

21 • A2 | C and O Canal NHP - Stickpile Hill

Dispersed sites, Central water, Vault/pit toilet, Tents only: Free, Hike-in, Bike-in, Milepost 148, Open all year, Elev: 463ft/141m, Tel: 301-739-4200, Nearest town: Paw Paw, WV. GPS: 39.582077, -78.399589

22 • A2 | C and O Canal NHP - Town Creek

Dispersed sites, Central water, Vault/pit toilet, Tents only: Free, Hike-in, Bike-in, Milepost 162, Open all year, Elev: 539ft/164m, Tel: 301-739-4200, Nearest town: Old Town. GPS: 39.523333, -78.544563

23 • A2 | C and O Canal NHP - White Rock

Dispersed sites, Central water, Vault/pit toilet, Tents only: Free, Hike-in, Bike-in, Milepost 126, Open all year, Elev: 418ft/127m, Tel: 301-739-4200, Nearest town: Hancock. GPS: 39.678407, -78.209702

24 • A2 | C and O Canal NHP -Cumberland Valley

Dispersed sites, Central water, Vault/pit toilet, Tents only: Free, Hike-in, Bike-in, Milepost 95, Open all year, Elev: 349ft/106m, Tel: 301-739-4200, Nearest town: Williamsport. GPS: 39.564335, -77.865744

25 • A3 | Catoctin NP - Adirondack Shelters

Total sites: 2, No water, Vault/pit toilet, Hike-to shelter: Free, No tents, Hike-in 3 mi, Open all year, Reservations required, Elev: 1511ft/461m, Tel: 301-663-9388, Nearest town: Thurmont. GPS: 39.677188, -77.484402

26 • A3 | Catoctin NP - Owen's Creek

Total sites: 51, RV sites: 51, Central water, Flush toilet, Free showers, No RV dump, Tent & RV camping: $30, Open May-Oct, Max Length: 22ft, Reservations accepted, Elev: 1339ft/408m, Tel: 301-663-9388, Nearest town: Thurmont. GPS: 39.659625, -77.484934

27 • A3 | Catoctin NP - Poplar Grove Youth Group

Total sites: 3, No water, Vault/pit toilet, No showers, No RV dump, Group site: $35, Open Mar-Dec, Reservations required, Elev: 1514ft/461m, Tel: 301-663-9388, Nearest town: Thurmont. GPS: 39.655854, -77.476022

28 • B2 | C and O Canal NHP - Huckleberry Hill

Dispersed sites, Central water, Vault/pit toilet, Tents only: Free, Hike-in, Bike-in, Milepost 62.9, Open all year, Elev: 285ft/87m, Tel: 301-739-4200, Nearest town: Hancock. GPS: 39.342792, -77.756526

29 • B3 | C and O Canal NHP - Bald Eagle Island

Dispersed sites, Central water, Vault/pit toilet, Tents only: Free,

Hike-in, Bike-in, Milepost 50.3, Open all year, Elev: 219ft/67m, Tel: 301-739-4200, Nearest town: Point of Rocks. GPS: 39.286701, -77.552839

30 • B3 | C and O Canal NHP - Calico Rocks

Dispersed sites, Central water, Vault/pit toilet, Tents only: Free, Hike-in, Bike-in, Milepost 48.2, Open all year, Elev: 217ft/66m, Tel: 301-739-4200, Nearest town: Point of Rocks. GPS: 39.263803, -77.522006

31 • B3 | C and O Canal NHP - Chisel Branch

Dispersed sites, Central water, Vault/pit toilet, Tents only: Free, Hike-in, Bike-in, Milepost 30.5, Open all year, Elev: 195ft/59m, Tel: 301-739-4200, Nearest town: Leesburg, VA. GPS: 39.099782, -77.471102

32 • B3 | C and O Canal NHP - Horsepen Branch

Dispersed sites, Central water, Vault/pit toilet, Tents only: Free, Hike-in, Bike-in, Milepost 26, Open all year, Elev: 192ft/59m, Tel: 301-739-4200, Nearest town: Gaithersburg. GPS: 39.069487, -77.397937

33 • B3 | C and O Canal NHP - Indian Flats

Dispersed sites, Central water, Vault/pit toilet, Tents only: Free, Hike-in, Bike-in, Milepost 42.4, Open all year, Elev: 219ft/67m, Tel: 301-739-4200, Nearest town: Point of Rocks. GPS: 39.233626, -77.462701

34 • B3 | C and O Canal NHP - Marble Quarry

Dispersed sites, Central water, Vault/pit toilet, Tents only: Free, Hike-in, Bike-in, Milepost 38.1, Open all year, Elev: 204ft/62m, Tel: 301-739-4200, Nearest town: Poolesville. GPS: 39.180457, -77.489696

35 • B3 | C and O Canal NHP - Marsden Tract Group

Total sites: 1, RV sites: 0, Central water, Vault/pit toilet, No showers, No RV dump, Group site: $40, Milepost 11.5, Open all year, Elev: 89ft/27m, Tel: 301-739-4200, Nearest town: Potomac. GPS: 38.976019, -77.213777

36 • B3 | C and O Canal NHP - Swains Lock

Total sites: 5, Central water, Vault/pit toilet, Tents only: Free, Hike-in, Bike-in, Milepost 16.6, Open all year, Elev: 170ft/52m, Tel: 301-739-4200, Nearest town: Potomac. GPS: 39.031172, -77.243754

37 • B3 | C and O Canal NHP - Turtle Run

Dispersed sites, Central water, Vault/pit toilet, Tents only: Free, Hike-in, Bike-in, Milepost 34.5, Open all year, Elev: 197ft/60m, Tel: 301-739-4200, Nearest town: Poolesville. GPS: 39.140291, -77.515909

38 • B3 | Greenbelt Park NP

Total sites: 174, RV sites: 174, Central water, Flush toilet, Free showers, RV dump, Tent & RV camping: $20, Open all year, Reservations required, Elev: 177ft/54m, Tel: 301-344-3944, Nearest town: Greenbelt. GPS: 38.979485, -76.900257

39 • C5 | Assateague Island NS - Bayside CG

Total sites: 24, RV sites: 24, Central water, Vault/pit toilet, Free showers, No RV dump, Tent & RV camping: $30, Cold showers, Generator hours: 0600-2200, Open all year, Reservations required, Elev: 10ft/3m, Tel: 410-641-3030, Nearest town: Ocean City. GPS: 38.20799, -75.16172

40 • C5 | Assateague Island NS - Green Run TC

Dispersed sites, No water, Vault/pit toilet, Tents only: $10, Hike-in/boat-in, 7-day backcountry permit required/$10 per person, Open all year, Reservations required, Elev: 3ft/1m, Tel: 410-641-3030, Nearest town: Ocean City. GPS: 38.080038, -75.213494

41 • C5 | Assateague Island NS - Horse Camp

Total sites: 2, RV sites: 2, Central water, Vault/pit toilet, Tent & RV camping: $50, Open Oct-Apr, Reservations required, Elev: 3ft/1m, Tel: 410-641-3030, Nearest town: Ocean City. GPS: 38.192863, -75.157482

42 • C5 | Assateague Island NS - Little Levels TC

Dispersed sites, No water, Vault/pit toilet, Tents only: $10, Hike-in, 7-day backcountry permit required/$10 per person, Open all year, Reservations required, Elev: 3ft/1m, Tel: 410-641-3030, Nearest town: Ocean City. GPS: 38.152996, -75.173456

43 • C5 | Assateague Island NS - Oceanside CG

Total sites: 100, RV sites: 41, Central water, Vault/pit toilet, Free showers, RV dump, Tent & RV camping: $30, Cold showers, Generator hours: 0600-2200, Open all year, Reservations required, Elev: 3ft/1m, Tel: 410-641-3030, Nearest town: Ocean City. GPS: 38.19788, -75.15585

44 • C5 | Assateague Island NS - Pine Tree TC

Dispersed sites, No water, Vault/pit toilet, Tents only: $10, Hike-in/boat-in, 7-day backcountry permit required/$10 per person, Open all year, Reservations required, Elev: 3ft/1m, Tel: 410-641-3030, Nearest town: Ocean City. GPS: 38.113203, -75.193807

45 • C5 | Assateague Island NS - Pope Bay TC

Dispersed sites, No water, Vault/pit toilet, Tents only: $10, Hike-in/boat-in, 7-day backcountry permit required/$10 per person, Open all year, Reservations required, Elev: 3ft/1m, Tel: 410-641-3030, Nearest town: Ocean City. GPS: 38.047868, -75.234152

46 • C5 | Assateague Island NS - State Line TC

Dispersed sites, No water, Vault/pit toilet, Tents only: $10, Hike-in/boat-in, 7-day backcountry permit required/$10 per person, Open all year, Reservations required, Elev: 5ft/2m, Tel: 410-641-3030, Nearest town: Ocean City. GPS: 38.044486, -75.231418

47 • C5 | Assateague Island NS - Tingles Island TC

Dispersed sites, No water, Vault/pit toilet, Tents only: $10, Hike-in/boat-in, 7-day backcountry permit required/$10 per person, Open all year, Reservations required, Elev: 3ft/1m, Tel: 410-641-3030, Nearest town: Ocean City. GPS: 38.177789, -75.175889

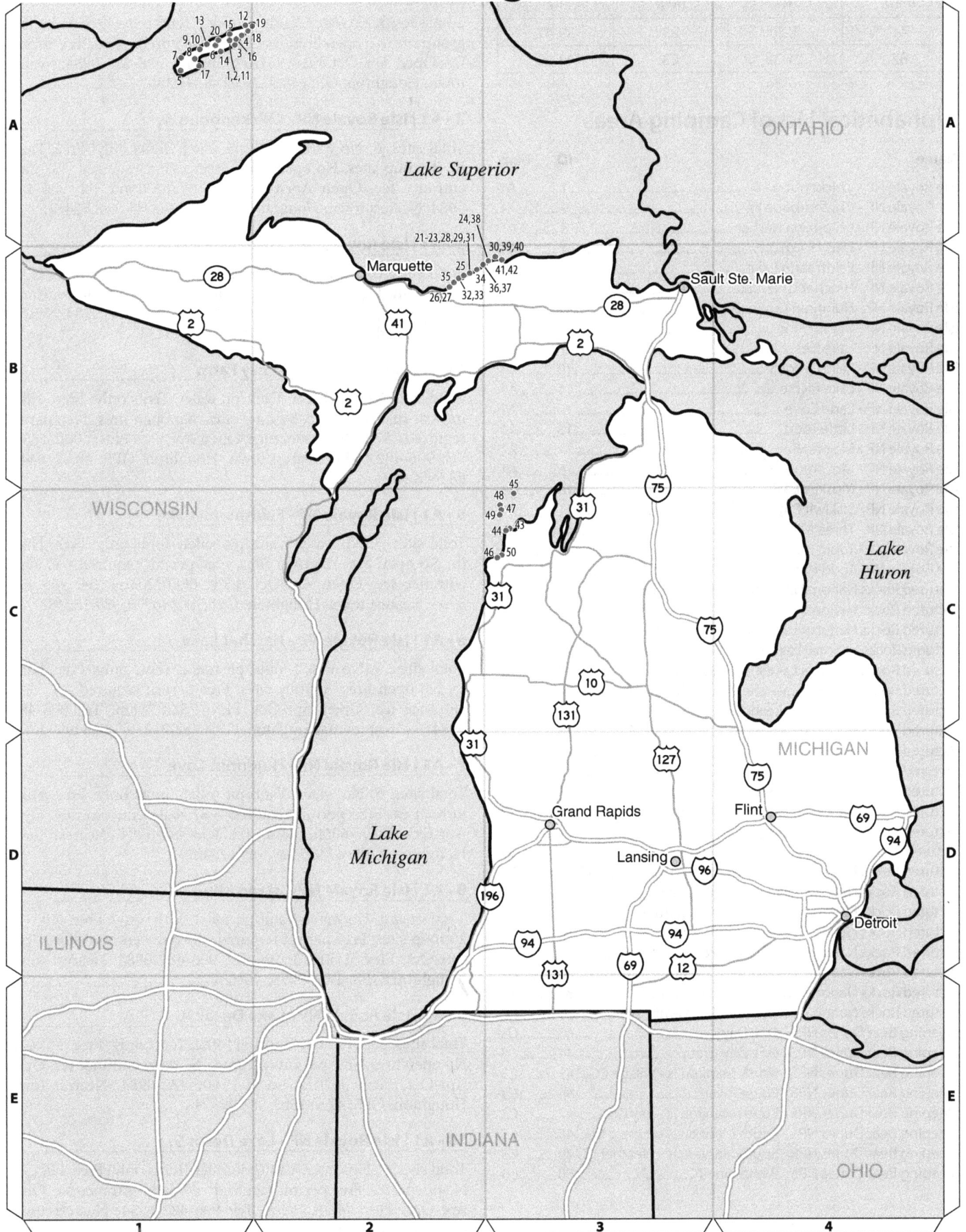

Michigan

13
20 15 12 19
9,10   4 18
7 8   6   3 16
5   17   14   1,2,11

Lake Superior

24,38
21-23,28,29,31
30,39,40
25   41,42
35   34
26,27 32,33 36,37

Marquette

Sault Ste. Marie

ONTARIO

28

2

41

2

2

28

45
48
49 47
44 43
46 50

31

75

Lake
Huron

31

WISCONSIN

75

10

131

75

127

MICHIGAN

31

Grand Rapids

Flint

75

69

94

Lansing

96

D

196

Lake
Michigan

94

Detroit

ILLINOIS

94

131   69   12

INDIANA

OHIO

Map	ID	Map	ID
A1	1-20	B3	39-42
B2	21-38	C3	43-50

Alphabetical List of Camping Areas

Name	ID	Map
Isle Royale NP - Chickenbone E.	1	A1
Isle Royale NP - Chickenbone W.	2	A1
Isle Royale NP - Chippewa Harbor	3	A1
Isle Royale NP - Daisy Farm	4	A1
Isle Royale NP - Feldtmann Lake	5	A1
Isle Royale NP - Hatchet Lake	6	A1
Isle Royale NP - Huginnin Cove	7	A1
Isle Royale NP - Island Mine	8	A1
Isle Royale NP - Lake Desor N.	9	A1
Isle Royale NP - Lake Desor S.	10	A1
Isle Royale NP - Lake Richie	11	A1
Isle Royale NP - Lane Cove	12	A1
Isle Royale NP - Little Todd	13	A1
Isle Royale NP - Malone Bay	14	A1
Isle Royale NP - McCargoe Cove	15	A1
Isle Royale NP - Moskey Basin	16	A1
Isle Royale NP - Siskiwit Bay	17	A1
Isle Royale NP - Three Mile	18	A1
Isle Royale NP - Tobin Harbor Dock	19	A1
Isle Royale NP - Todd Harbor	20	A1
Pictured Rocks National Lakeshore - Au Sable Group TC	39	B3
Pictured Rocks National Lakeshore - Au Sable Point TC	40	B3
Pictured Rocks National Lakeshore - Beaver Creek TC	21	B2
Pictured Rocks National Lakeshore - Beaver Lake Group TC	22	B2
Pictured Rocks National Lakeshore - Beaver Lake TC	23	B2
Pictured Rocks National Lakeshore - Benchmark TC	24	B2
Pictured Rocks National Lakeshore - Chapel Beach TC	25	B2
Pictured Rocks National Lakeshore - Cliffs Group TC	26	B2
Pictured Rocks National Lakeshore - Cliffs TC	27	B2
Pictured Rocks National Lakeshore - Coves Group TC	28	B2
Pictured Rocks National Lakeshore - Coves TC	29	B2
Pictured Rocks National Lakeshore - Hurricane River	30	B2
Pictured Rocks National Lakeshore - Little Beaver Lake	31	B2
Pictured Rocks Nat'l Lakeshore - Masse Homestead Grp TC	41	B3
Pictured Rocks National Lakeshore - Masse Homestead TC	42	B3
Pictured Rocks National Lakeshore - Mosquito Group TC	32	B2
Pictured Rocks National Lakeshore - Mosquito River TC	33	B2
Pictured Rocks National Lakeshore - Pine Bluff TC	34	B2
Pictured Rocks National Lakeshore - Potato Patch TC	35	B2
Pictured Rocks National Lakeshore - Sevenmile Group TC	36	B2
Pictured Rocks National Lakeshore - Sevenmile TC	37	B2
Pictured Rocks National Lakeshore - Twelvemile Beach	38	B2
Sleeping Bear Dunes NPS - D.H. Day	43	C3
Sleeping Bear Dunes NPS - D.H. Day Group	44	C3
Sleeping Bear Dunes NPS - North Manitou Is - Village CG	45	C3
Sleeping Bear Dunes NPS - Platte River	46	C3
Sleeping Bear Dunes NPS - South Manitou Is - Bay CG	47	C3
Sleeping Bear Dunes NPS - South Manitou Is - Poppie CG	48	C3
Sleeping Bear Dunes NPS - South Manitou Is - Weather CG	49	C3
Sleeping Bear Dunes NPS - White Pine TC	50	C3

1 • A1 | Isle Royale NP - Chickenbone E.

Total sites: 3, No water, Vault/pit toilet, Tents only: Free, Hike-in, 1 group site, No open fires, Free permit required - $7 daily entrance fee, Open Apr-Oct, Elev: 761ft/232m, Tel: 906-482-0984, Nearest town: Houghton. GPS: 48.072733, -88.693803

2 • A1 | Isle Royale NP - Chickenbone W.

Total sites: 6, No water, Vault/pit toilet, Tents only: Free, Hike-in, 3 group sites, No open fires, Free permit required - $7 daily entrance fee, Open Apr-Oct, Elev: 675ft/206m, Tel: 906-482-0984, Nearest town: Houghton. GPS: 48.063715, -88.724615

3 • A1 | Isle Royale NP - Chippewa Harbor

Total sites: 6, No water, Vault/pit toilet, Tents only: Free, Hike-in/boat-in, 1 group site, Free permit required - $7 daily entrance fee, Open Apr-Oct, Elev: 621ft/189m, Tel: 906-482-0984, Nearest town: Houghton. GPS: 48.029077, -88.650433

4 • A1 | Isle Royale NP - Daisy Farm

Total sites: 22, No water, Vault/pit toilet, Tents only: Free, Hike-in/boat-in, 16 shelters, 3 group sites, No open fires, Free permit required - $7 daily entrance fee, Open Apr-Oct, Elev: 606ft/185m, Tel: 906-482-0984, Nearest town: Houghton. GPS: 48.091644, -88.595036

5 • A1 | Isle Royale NP - Feldtmann Lake

Total sites: 5, No water, Vault/pit toilet, Tents only: Free, Hike-in, No open fires, 2 group sites, Free permit required - $7 daily entrance fee, Open Apr-Oct, Elev: 668ft/204m, Tel: 906-482-0984, Nearest town: Houghton. GPS: 47.846979, -89.182482

6 • A1 | Isle Royale NP - Hatchet Lake

Total sites: 5, No water, Vault/pit toilet, Tents only: Free, Hike-in, No open fires, 3 group sites, Free permit required - $7 daily entrance fee, Open Apr-Oct, Elev: 781ft/238m, Tel: 906-482-0984, Nearest town: Houghton. GPS: 48.021239, -88.849972

7 • A1 | Isle Royale NP - Huginnin Cove

Total sites: 5, No water, Vault/pit toilet, Tents only: Free, Hike-in/boat-in, Free permit required - $7 daily entrance fee, Open Apr-Oct, Elev: 605ft/184m, Tel: 906-482-0984, Nearest town: Houghton. GPS: 47.935109, -89.176402

8 • A1 | Isle Royale NP - Island Mine

Total sites: 4, No water, Vault/pit toilet, Tents only: Free, Hike-in, 2 group sites, Free permit required - $7 daily entrance fee, Open Apr-Oct, Elev: 1181ft/360m, Tel: 906-482-0984, Nearest town: Houghton. GPS: 47.930258, -89.039722

9 • A1 | Isle Royale NP - Lake Desor N.

Total sites: 3, No water, Vault/pit toilet, Tents only: Free, Hike-in, No open fires, Free permit required - $7 daily entrance fee, Open Apr-Oct, Elev: 867ft/264m, Tel: 906-482-0984, Nearest town: Houghton. GPS: 47.981005, -88.993748

10 • A1 | Isle Royale NP - Lake Desor S.

Total sites: 7, No water, Vault/pit toilet, Tents only: Free, Hike-in, No open fires, Free permit required - $7 daily entrance fee, Open Apr-Oct, Elev: 884ft/269m, Tel: 906-482-0984, Nearest town: Houghton. GPS: 47.969521, -88.975549

11 • A1 | Isle Royale NP - Lake Richie

Total sites: 4, No water, Vault/pit toilet, Tents only: Free, Hike-in, 2 group sites, No open fires, Free permit required - $7 daily entrance fee, Open Apr-Oct, Elev: 641ft/195m, Tel: 906-482-0984, Nearest town: Houghton. GPS: 48.051188, -88.686631

12 • A1 | Isle Royale NP - Lane Cove

Total sites: 5, No water, Vault/pit toilet, Tents only: Free, Hike-in/boat-in, No open fires, Free permit required - $7 daily entrance fee, Open Apr-Oct, Elev: 612ft/187m, Tel: 906-482-0984, Nearest town: Houghton. GPS: 48.144581, -88.557232

13 • A1 | Isle Royale NP - Little Todd

Total sites: 4, No water, Vault/pit toilet, Tents only: Free, Hike-in/boat-in, 3 group sites, Free permit required - $7 daily entrance fee, Open Apr-Oct, Elev: 615ft/187m, Tel: 906-482-0984, Nearest town: Houghton. GPS: 48.020245, -88.926822

14 • A1 | Isle Royale NP - Malone Bay

Dispersed sites, No water, Vault/pit toilet, Tents only: Free, Hike-in/boat-in, Free permit required - $7 daily entrance fee, Open Apr-Oct, Elev: 617ft/188m, Tel: 906-482-0984, Nearest town: Houghton. GPS: 47.984055, -88.800637

15 • A1 | Isle Royale NP - McCargoe Cove

Total sites: 9, No water, Vault/pit toilet, Tents only: Free, Hike-in/boat-in, 3 group sites, Community fire-ring only, Free permit required - $7 daily entrance fee, Open Apr-Oct, Elev: 620ft/189m, Tel: 906-482-0984, Nearest town: Houghton. GPS: 48.087476, -88.708477

16 • A1 | Isle Royale NP - Moskey Basin

Total sites: 8, No water, Vault/pit toilet, Tents only: Free, Hike-in/boat-in, 2 group sites, No open fires, Free permit required - $7 daily entrance fee, Open Apr-Oct, Elev: 614ft/187m, Tel: 906-482-0984, Nearest town: Houghton. GPS: 48.064295, -88.643954

17 • A1 | Isle Royale NP - Siskiwit Bay

Total sites: 6, No water, Vault/pit toilet, Tents only: Free, Hike-in/boat-in, Community fire-ring, 3 group sites, Free permit required - $7 daily entrance fee, Open Apr-Oct, Elev: 613ft/187m, Tel: 906-482-0984, Nearest town: Houghton. GPS: 47.890429, -88.998052

18 • A1 | Isle Royale NP - Three Mile

Total sites: 12, No water, Vault/pit toilet, Tents only: Free, Hike-in/boat-in, 3 group sites, No open fires, Free permit required - $7 daily entrance fee, Open Apr-Oct, Elev: 617ft/188m, Tel: 906-482-0984, Nearest town: Houghton. GPS: 48.123412, -88.530437

19 • A1 | Isle Royale NP - Tobin Harbor Dock

Dispersed sites, No water, Vault/pit toilet, Tents only: Free, Hike-in/boat-in, Free permit required - $7 daily entrance fee, Open Apr-Oct, Elev: 611ft/186m, Tel: 906-482-0984, Nearest town: Houghton. GPS: 48.149104, -88.495978

20 • A1 | Isle Royale NP - Todd Harbor

Total sites: 6, No water, Vault/pit toilet, Tents only: Free, Hike-in/boat-in, 3 group sites, Community fire-ring only, Free permit required - $7 daily entrance fee, Open Apr-Oct, Elev: 610ft/186m, Tel: 906-482-0984, Nearest town: Houghton. GPS: 48.052689, -88.822684

21 • B2 | Pictured Rocks Nat'l Lakeshore - Beaver Creek TC

Dispersed sites, No water, Vault/pit toilet, Tents only: $5, Hike-in/boat-in, 6 sites, Stream/lake water, $5/person, $15 reservation fee, Reservations accepted, Elev: 646ft/197m, Tel: 906-387-2607, Nearest town: Grand Marais. GPS: 46.577077, -86.350273

22 • B2 | Pictured Rocks National Lakeshore - Beaver Lake Group TC

Dispersed sites, No water, No toilets, Group site, Paddle-in/hike-in, Lake water, $5/person, $15 reservation fee, Reservations accepted, Elev: 622ft/190m, Tel: 906-387-2607, Nearest town: Munising. GPS: 46.557241, -86.344618

23 • B2 | Pictured Rocks Nat'l Lakeshore - Beaver Lake TC

Dispersed sites, No water, No toilets, Tents only: $5, Hike-in/boat-in, Lake water, $5/person, $15 reservation fee, Reservations accepted, Elev: 615ft/187m, Tel: 906-387-2607, Nearest town: Munising. GPS: 46.558637, -86.339939

24 • B2 | Pictured Rocks National Lakeshore - Benchmark TC

Dispersed sites, No water, Vault/pit toilet, Tents only: $5, Hike-in/boat-in, 6 sites, $5/person, $15 reservation fee, Reservations accepted, Elev: 647ft/197m, Tel: 906-387-2607, Nearest town: Grand Marais. GPS: 46.647075, -86.200885

25 • B2 | Pictured Rocks Nat'l Lakeshore - Chapel Beach TC

Dispersed sites, No water, Vault/pit toilet, Tents only: $5, Hike-in/boat-in, 6 sites, No fires, Stream/lake water, $5/person, $15 reservation fee, Reservations accepted, Elev: 638ft/194m, Tel: 906-387-2607, Nearest town: Munising. GPS: 46.546799, -86.442667

26 • B2 | Pictured Rocks Nat'l Lakeshore - Cliffs Group TC

Dispersed sites, No water, Vault/pit toilet, Group site, Hike-in, $5/person, $15 reservation fee, Reservations accepted, Elev: 826ft/252m, Tel: 906-387-2607, Nearest town: Munising. GPS: 46.485519, -86.556737

27 • B2 | Pictured Rocks National Lakeshore - Cliffs TC

Dispersed sites, No water, Vault/pit toilet, Tents only: $5, Hike-in, 3 sites, $5/person, $15 reservation fee, Reservations accepted, Elev: 834ft/254m, Tel: 906-387-2607, Nearest town: Munising. GPS: 46.473348, -86.570593

28 • B2 | Pictured Rocks Nat'l Lakeshore - Coves Group TC

Dispersed sites, No water, Vault/pit toilet, Group site, Hike-in, $5/person, $15 reservation fee, Reservations accepted, Elev: 689ft/210m, Tel: 906-387-2607, Nearest town: Munising. GPS: 46.560847, -86.395918

29 • B2 | Pictured Rocks National Lakeshore - Coves TC

Dispersed sites, No water, Vault/pit toilet, Tents only: $5, Hike-in/boat-in, Lake water, $5/person, $15 reservation fee, Reservations accepted, Elev: 645ft/197m, Tel: 906-387-2607, Nearest town: Munising. GPS: 46.568061, -86.372147

30 • B2 | Pictured Rocks Nat'l Lakeshore - Hurricane River

Total sites: 21, RV sites: 21, Central water, Vault/pit toilet, No showers, No RV dump, Tent & RV camping: $25, $15 Nov-Apr - no services, Several generator-sites, Stay limit: 14 days, Generator hours: 0800-2000, Open all year, Max Length: RV-36ft, Tr-42ft, Reservations required, Elev: 630ft/192m, Tel: 906-387-2607, Nearest town: Munising. GPS: 46.66684, -86.16519

31 • B2 | Pictured Rocks Nat'l Lakeshore - Little Beaver Lake

Total sites: 8, RV sites: 8, Central water, Vault/pit toilet, No showers, No RV dump, Tent & RV camping: $25, $15 Nov-Apr, Stay limit: 14 days, Generator hours: 0800-2000, Open all year, Max Length: RV-36ft, Tr-42ft, Reservations required, Elev: 604ft/184m, Tel: 906-387-2607, Nearest town: Munising. GPS: 46.558503, -86.362376

32 • B2 | Pictured Rocks Nat'l Lakeshore - Mosquito Grp TC

Dispersed sites, No water, Vault/pit toilet, Tents only: $5, Hike-in, Paddle-in/hike-in group site, No fires, Stream/lake water, $5/person, $15 reservation fee, Reservations accepted, Elev: 637ft/194m, Tel: 906-387-2607, Nearest town: Munising. GPS: 46.524813, -86.493346

33 • B2 | Pictured Rocks Nat'l Lakeshore - Mosquito River TC

Dispersed sites, No water, Vault/pit toilet, Tents only: $5, Hike-in/boat-in, 5 sites, No fires, Stream/lake water, $5/person, $15 reservation fee, Reservations accepted, Elev: 637ft/194m, Tel: 906-387-2607, Nearest town: Munising. GPS: 46.526933, -86.492175

34 • B2 | Pictured Rocks National Lakeshore - Pine Bluff TC

Dispersed sites, No water, Vault/pit toilet, Tents only: $5, Hike-in/boat-in, 5 sites, Lake water, $5/person, $15 reservation fee, Reservations accepted, Elev: 648ft/198m, Tel: 906-387-2607, Nearest town: Grand Marais. GPS: 46.586291, -86.328652

35 • B2 | Pictured Rocks Nat'l Lakeshore - Potato Patch TC

Dispersed sites, No water, Vault/pit toilet, Tents only: $5, Hike-in, 3 sites, $5/person, $15 reservation fee, Reservations accepted, Elev: 767ft/234m, Tel: 906-387-2607, Nearest town: Munising. GPS: 46.497267, -86.530148

36 • B2 | Pictured Rocks Nat'l Lakeshore - Sevenmile Grp TC

Dispersed sites, No water, No toilets, Group site, Paddle-in/hike-in, Lake/stream water, $5/person, $15 reservation fee, Reservations accepted, Elev: 624ft/190m, Tel: 906-387-2607, Nearest town: Grand Marais. GPS: 46.620479, -86.257277

37 • B2 | Pictured Rocks National Lakeshore - Sevenmile TC

Dispersed sites, No water, No toilets, Tents only: $5, Hike-in/boat-in, 5 sites, Stream/lake water, $5/person, $15 reservation fee, Reservations accepted, Elev: 647ft/197m, Tel: 906-387-2607, Nearest town: Grand Marais. GPS: 46.619212, -86.258967

38 • B2 | Pictured Rocks Nat'l Lakeshore - Twelvemile Beach

Total sites: 36, RV sites: 36, Central water, Vault/pit toilet, No showers, No RV dump, Tent & RV camping: $25, $15 Nov-Apr - no services, Stay limit: 14 days, Generator hours: 0800-2000, Open all year, Max Length: RV-36ft, Tr-42ft, Reservations required, Elev: 604ft/184m, Tel: 906-387-2607, Nearest town: Munising. GPS: 46.6427, -86.21105

39 • B3 | Pictured Rocks Nat'l Lakeshore - Au Sable Grp TC

Dispersed sites, No water, Vault/pit toilet, Group site, Paddle-in/hike-in, Lake water, $5/person, $15 reservation fee, Reservations accepted, Elev: 633ft/193m, Tel: 906-387-2607, Nearest town: Grand Marais. GPS: 46.671121, -86.136591

40 • B3 | Pictured Rocks Nat'l Lakeshore - Au Sable Point TC

Dispersed sites, No water, Vault/pit toilet, Tents only: $5, Hike-in/boat-in, 6 sites, $5/person, Lake water, $15 reservation fee, Reservations accepted, Elev: 632ft/193m, Tel: 906-387-2607, Nearest town: Grand Marais. GPS: 46.669203, -86.135022

41 • B3 | Pictured Rocks National Lakeshore - Masse Homestead Goup TC

Dispersed sites, No water, No toilets, Group site, Hike-in, $5/person, $15 reservation fee, Reservations accepted, Elev: 889ft/271m, Tel: 906-387-2607, Nearest town: Grand Marais. GPS: 46.648116, -86.094244

42 • B3 | Pictured Rocks National Lakeshore - Masse Homestead TC

Dispersed sites, No water, No toilets, Tents only: $5, Hike-in, $5/person, $15 reservation fee, Reservations accepted, Elev: 891ft/272m, Tel: 906-387-2607, Nearest town: Grand Marais. GPS: 46.647677, -86.091696

43 • C3 | Sleeping Bear Dunes NPS - D.H. Day

Total sites: 88, Central water, Vault/pit toilet, No showers, RV dump, Tent & RV camping: $20, Generator hours: 0900-1800, Open Apr-Nov, Reservations required, Elev: 604ft/184m, Tel: 231-334-4634, Nearest town: Maple City. GPS: 44.898955, -86.020793

44 • C3 | Sleeping Bear Dunes NPS - D.H. Day Group

Total sites: 1, RV sites: 0, Central water, Vault/pit toilet, Group site: $40, Open May-Oct, Reservations required, Elev: 600ft/183m, Tel: 231-326-4700, Nearest town: Maple City. GPS: 44.891673, -86.042464

45 • C3 | Sleeping Bear Dunes NPS - North Manitou Is - Village CG

Total sites: 8, No water, Vault/pit toilet, No showers, No RV dump, Tents only: $10, Hike-in, Access by ferry, Camping is allowed almost anywhere on the island except within 300 feet of Lake Michigan high water mark/lakes/streams/ponds/springs/buildings or other camps - permit required, Reservations not accepted, Elev: 627ft/191m, Tel: 231-325-5881, Nearest town: Leland. GPS: 45.129363, -85.980527

46 • C3 | Sleeping Bear Dunes NPS - Platte River

Total sites: 170, RV sites: 146, Elec sites: 68, Central water, Flush toilet, Pay showers, RV dump, Tents: $22/RV's: $26-31, Open all year, Max Length: 40ft, Reservations accepted, Elev: 614ft/187m, Tel: 231-325-5881, Nearest town: Empire. GPS: 44.715468, -86.116249

47 • C3 | Sleeping Bear Dunes NPS - S Manitou Is - Bay CG

Total sites: 25, Vault/pit toilet, Tents only: $10, Walk-to sites, Access by ferry, Reservations not accepted, Elev: 590ft/180m,

Tel: 231-325-5881, Nearest town: Leland. GPS: 45.019597, -86.102343

48 • C3 | Sleeping Bear Dunes NPS - South Manitou Is - Poppie CG

Total sites: 7, Vault/pit toilet, Tents only: $10, Hike-in, Access by ferry, Reservations not accepted, Elev: 592ft/180m, Tel: 231-325-5881, Nearest town: Leland. GPS: 45.046804, -86.114886

49 • C3 | Sleeping Bear Dunes NPS - South Manitou Is - Weather CG

Total sites: 20, Vault/pit toilet, Tents only: $10, Hike-in, Access by ferry, Reservations not accepted, Elev: 600ft/183m, Tel: 231-325-5881, Nearest town: Leland. GPS: 45.000901, -86.113757

50 • C3 | Sleeping Bear Dunes NPS - White Pine TC

Total sites: 6, No water, Vault/pit toilet, Tents only: $10, Hike-in, Reservations not accepted, Elev: 600ft/183m, Tel: 231-325-5881, Nearest town: Frankfort. GPS: 44.727242, -86.096738

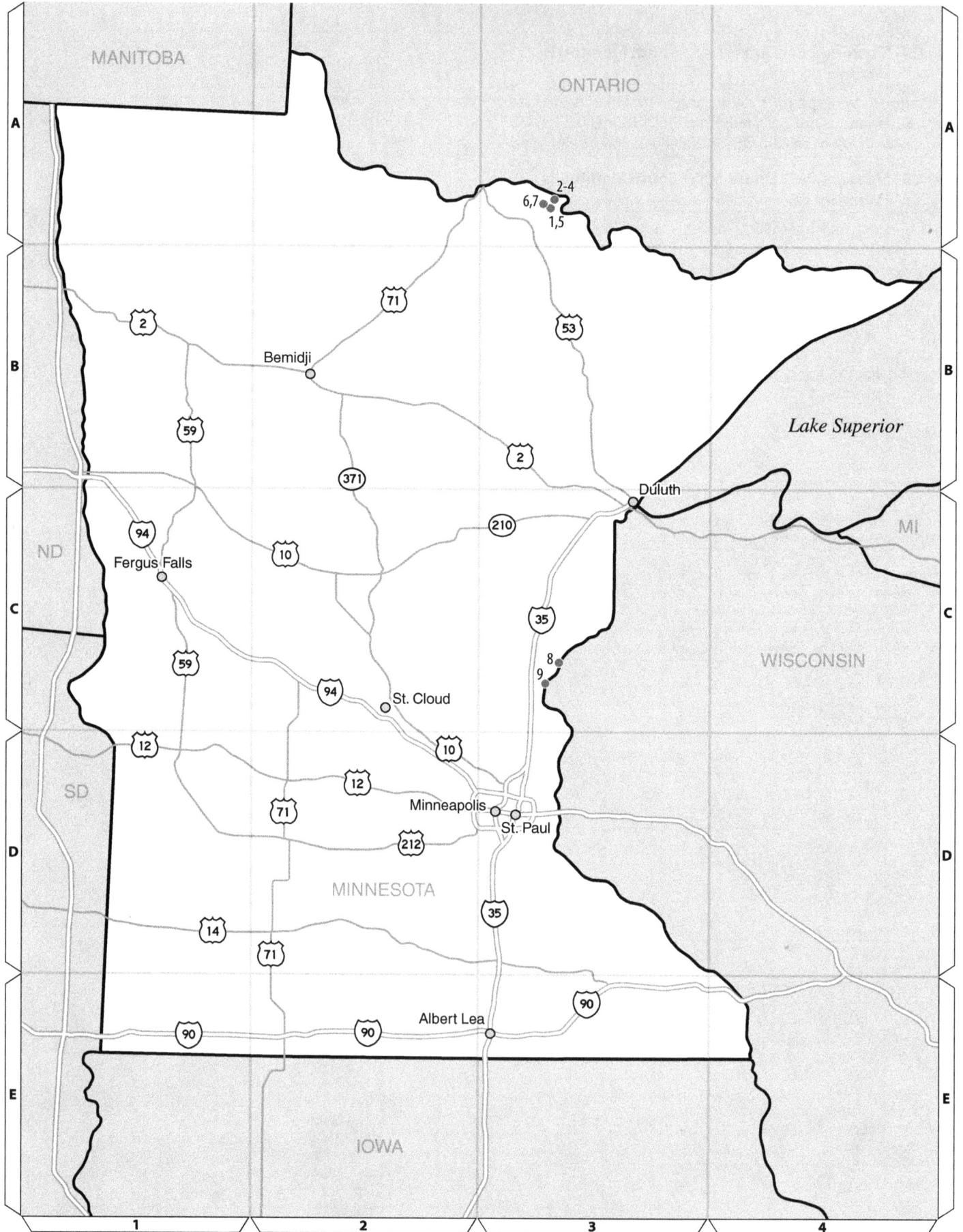

Minnesota

MANITOBA

ONTARIO

2-4

6,7

1,5

71

53

2

Bemidji

Lake Superior

59

371

94

210

Duluth

ND

10

MI

Fergus Falls

35

59

8

94

9

St. Cloud

WISCONSIN

12

10

12

MINNESOTA

71

Minneapolis

212

St. Paul

SD

35

14

71

90

90

Albert Lea

90

90

IOWA

Map	ID	Map	ID
A3	1-7	C3	8-9

Alphabetical List of Camping Areas

Name	ID	Map
St Croix NSR - Snake River Landing	8	C3
St Croix NSR -Old Railroad Bridge Landing	9	C3
Voyageurs NP - B-1 Agnes Lake	1	A3
Voyageurs NP - B-13 Peary Lake	2	A3
Voyageurs NP - B-3 Brown Lake	3	A3
Voyageurs NP - B-5 Cruiser Lake	4	A3
Voyageurs NP - B-6 Ek Lake	5	A3
Voyageurs NP - B-7 Jorgens Lake	6	A3
Voyageurs NP - B-8 Little Shoepack Lake	7	A3

1 • A3 | Voyageurs NP - B-1 Agnes Lake

Dispersed sites, No water, No toilets, Tents only: $16, Hike-in, <10 people, Stay limit: 7 days, Reservations accepted, Elev: 1154ft/352m, Tel: 218-283-6600, Nearest town: International Falls. GPS: 48.468263, -92.814355

2 • A3 | Voyageurs NP - B-13 Peary Lake

Dispersed sites, No water, Vault/pit toilet, Tents only: $16, Hike-in/boat-in, <10 people, Stay limit: 7 days, Reservations accepted, Elev: 1148ft/350m, Tel: 218-283-6600, Nearest town: International Falls. GPS: 48.523626, -92.769549

3 • A3 | Voyageurs NP - B-3 Brown Lake

Dispersed sites, No water, No toilets, Tents only: $16, Hike-in, <10 people, Stay limit: 7 days, Reservations accepted, Elev: 1196ft/365m, Tel: 218-283-6600, Nearest town: International Falls. GPS: 48.513058, -92.788349

4 • A3 | Voyageurs NP - B-5 Cruiser Lake

Dispersed sites, No water, No toilets, Tents only: $16, Hike-in, <10 people, Stay limit: 7 days, Reservations accepted, Elev: 1256ft/383m, Tel: 218-283-6600, Nearest town: International Falls. GPS: 48.499061, -92.800633

5 • A3 | Voyageurs NP - B-6 Ek Lake

Dispersed sites, No water, No toilets, Tents only: $16, Hike-in, <10 people, Stay limit: 7 days, Reservations accepted, Elev: 1153ft/351m, Tel: 218-283-6600, Nearest town: International Falls. GPS: 48.468585, -92.837305

6 • A3 | Voyageurs NP - B-7 Jorgens Lake

Dispersed sites, No water, No toilets, Tents only: $16, Hike-in, <10 people, Stay limit: 7 days, Reservations accepted, Elev: 1208ft/368m, Tel: 218-283-6600, Nearest town: International Falls. GPS: 48.482785, -92.849853

7 • A3 | Voyageurs NP - B-8 Little Shoepack Lake

Dispersed sites, No water, No toilets, Tents only: $16, Hike-in, <10 people, Stay limit: 7 days, Reservations accepted, Elev: 1222ft/372m, Tel: 218-283-6600, Nearest town: International Falls. GPS: 48.489033, -92.875853

8 • C3 | St Croix NSR - Snake River Landing

Dispersed sites, No water, Vault/pit toilet, Tent & RV camping: Free, Free permit required, Nothing larger than van/pu, Reservations not accepted, Elev: 802ft/244m, Nearest town: Grantsburg. GPS: 45.823304, -92.764713

9 • C3 | St Croix NSR -Old Railroad Bridge Landing

Dispersed sites, No water, Vault/pit toilet, No showers, No RV dump, Tents only: Free, Free permit required, Reservations not accepted, Elev: 774ft/236m, Nearest town: Rush City. GPS: 45.702573, -92.872682

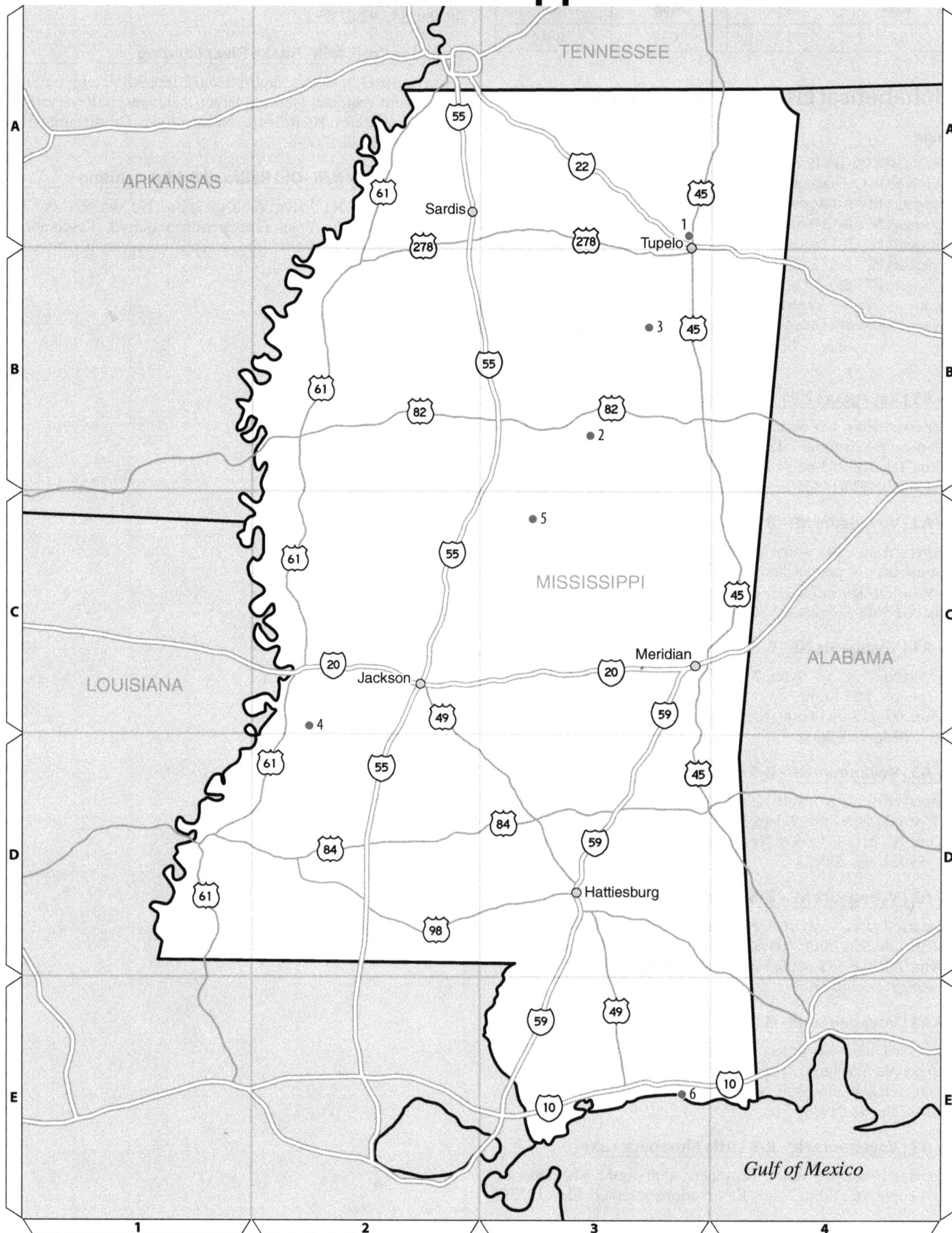

Mississippi

TENNESSEE

ARKANSAS

Sardis

Tupelo

1

3

2

5

MISSISSIPPI

Meridian

ALABAMA

LOUISIANA

Jackson

4

Hattiesburg

Gulf of Mexico

Map	ID	Map	ID
A3	1	C3	5
B3	2-3	E3	6
C2	4		

Alphabetical List of Camping Areas

Name	ID	Map
Gulf Islands NS - Davis Bayou	6	E3
Natchez Trace NP - Jeff Busby	2	B3
Natchez Trace NP - Kosciusko Bicycle CG	5	C3
Natchez Trace NP - Rocky Springs	4	C2
Natchez Trace NP - Tupelo Bicycle CG	1	A3
Natchez Trace NP -Witch Dance Bicycle CG	3	B3

1 • A3 | Natchez Trace NP - Tupelo Bicycle CG

Dispersed sites, Central water, Vault/pit toilet, Tents only: Free, Bike-in, Water at Visitors Center, Open all year, Reservations not accepted, Elev: 318ft/97m, Tel: 800-305-7417, Nearest town: Tupelo. GPS: 34.330993, -88.711382

2 • B3 | Natchez Trace NP - Jeff Busby

Total sites: 24, RV sites: 24, Central water, Flush toilet, No showers, No RV dump, Tent & RV camping: Free, Open all year, Reservations not accepted, Elev: 459ft/140m, Tel: 800-305-7417, Nearest town: Ackerman. GPS: 33.416691, -89.266241

3 • B3 | Natchez Trace NP -Witch Dance Bicycle CG

Dispersed sites, Central water, No toilets, No showers, No RV dump, Tents only: Free, Bike-in, Open all year, Reservations not accepted, Elev: 399ft/122m, Tel: 800-305-7417, Nearest town: Houston. GPS: 33.911131, -88.940144

4 • C2 | Natchez Trace NP - Rocky Springs

Total sites: 20, RV sites: 20, Central water, Flush toilet, No showers, No RV dump, Tent & RV camping: Free, Open all year, Reservations not accepted, Elev: 207ft/63m, Tel: 800-305-7417, Nearest town: Port Gibson. GPS: 32.086627, -90.799167

5 • C3 | Natchez Trace NP - Kosciusko Bicycle CG

Total sites: 3, Central water, Vault/pit toilet, No showers, No RV dump, Tents only: Free, Bike-in only, Open all year, Reservations not accepted, Elev: 418ft/127m, Tel: 800-305-7417, Nearest town: Kosciusko. GPS: 33.037248, -89.580147

6 • E3 | Gulf Islands NS - Davis Bayou

Total sites: 51, RV sites: 51, Elec sites: 51, Water at site, Flush toilet, Free showers, RV dump, Tent & RV camping: $22, Group site: $20-$30, Open all year, Max Length: 60ft, Reservations accepted, Elev: 46ft/14m, Tel: 228-875-3962, Nearest town: Ocean Springs. GPS: 30.397171, -88.795714

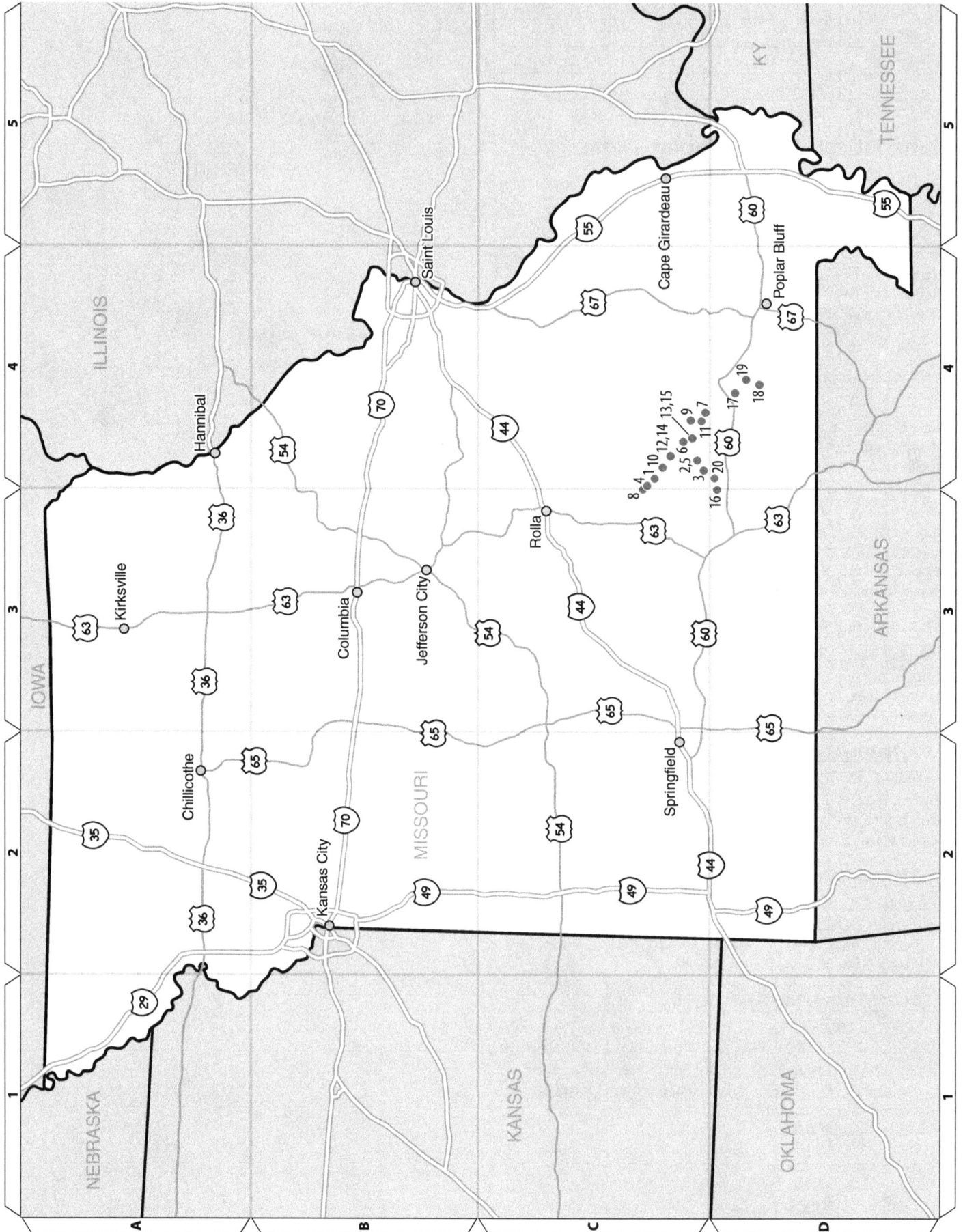

Missouri

ILLINOIS

IOWA

NEBRASKA

KANSAS

OKLAHOMA

ARKANSAS

TENNESSEE

KY

MISSOURI

Saint Louis

Cape Girardeau

Poplar Bluff

Hannibal

Kirksville

Columbia

Jefferson City

Rolla

Chillicothe

Kansas City

Springfield

55

60

67

67

70

54

36

63

63

36

65

65

70

35

35

36

29

49

49

49

44

44

44

54

54

65

65

60

60

63

55

8
4
1 10
12,14 13,15
2,5 6 9
3 11 7
16 20
17 19
18
60

Map	ID	Map	ID
C4	1-15	D4	17-20
D3	16		

Alphabetical List of Camping Areas

Name   **ID**   **Map**

Ozark NSR - Akers Group ....1 .... C4
Ozark NSR - Alley Springs CG ....2 .... C4
Ozark NSR - Bay Creek CG ....3 .... C4
Ozark NSR - Big Spring CG ....17 ....D4
Ozark NSR - Blue Spring ....16 ....D3
Ozark NSR - Cedargrove CG ....4 .... C4
Ozark NSR - Gooseneck CG ....18 ....D4
Ozark NSR - Hickory Landing ....19 ....D4
Ozark NSR - Horse Camp ....5 .... C4
Ozark NSR - Jerktail Landing ....6 .... C4
Ozark NSR - Log Yard CG ....7 .... C4
Ozark NSR - Parker's Ford ....8 .... C4
Ozark NSR - Powder Mill CG ....9 .... C4
Ozark NSR - Pulltite CG ....10 ....C4
Ozark NSR - Roberts Field ....11 ....C4
Ozark NSR - Round Spring CG ....12 ....C4
Ozark NSR - Rymers CG ....20 ....D4
Ozark NSR - Shawnee Creek CG ....13 ....C4
Ozark NSR - Sinking Creek CG ....14 ....C4
Ozark NSR - Two Rivers ....15 ....C4

1 • C4 | Ozark NSR - Akers Group

Total sites: 4, RV sites: 0, Central water, Vault/pit toilet, No showers, No RV dump, Group site: $53, Stay limit: 14 days, Generator hours: 0600-2200, Open Apr-Sep, Reservations accepted, Elev: 866ft/264m, Tel: 573-323-4236, Nearest town: Salem. GPS: 37.376177, -91.561893

2 • C4 | Ozark NSR - Alley Springs CG

Total sites: 162, RV sites: 162, Elec sites: 26, Water at site, RV dump, Tents: $16/RV's: $16-19, Stay limit: 14 days, Generator hours: 0600-2200, Open all year, Reservations not accepted, Elev: 666ft/203m, Tel: 573-323-4236, Nearest town: Eminence. GPS: 37.146471, -91.445361

3 • C4 | Ozark NSR - Bay Creek CG

Dispersed sites, No water, Vault/pit toilet, Tents only: $5, Stay limit: 14 days, Generator hours: 0600-2200, Open all year, Elev: 735ft/224m, Tel: 573-323-4236, Nearest town: Summersville. GPS: 37.121813, -91.503746

4 • C4 | Ozark NSR - Cedargrove CG

Dispersed sites, No water, Vault/pit toilet, Tents only: $5, Stay limit: 14 days, Generator hours: 0600-2200, Open all year, Elev: 866ft/264m, Tel: 573-323-4236. GPS: 37.419339, -91.603251

5 • C4 | Ozark NSR - Horse Camp

Dispersed sites, No water, Tent & RV camping: $5, Stay limit: 14 days, Generator hours: 0600-2200, Open all year, Elev: 679ft/207m, Tel: 573-323-4236, Nearest town: Eminence. GPS: 37.157249, -91.423908

6 • C4 | Ozark NSR - Jerktail Landing

Dispersed sites, No water, Tents only: $5, Stay limit: 14 days, Generator hours: 0600-2200, Open all year, Elev: 663ft/202m, Tel: 573-323-4236, Nearest town: Eminence. GPS: 37.228823, -91.309347

7 • C4 | Ozark NSR - Log Yard CG

Dispersed sites, No water, Vault/pit toilet, Tents only: $5, Stay limit: 14 days, Generator hours: 0600-2200, Open all year, Elev: 630ft/192m, Tel: 573-323-4236. GPS: 37.113091, -91.127042

8 • C4 | Ozark NSR - Parker's Ford

Dispersed sites, No water, No toilets, Tents only: $5, Stay limit: 14 days, Generator hours: 0600-2200, Open all year, Elev: 879ft/268m, Tel: 573-323-4236. GPS: 37.437877, -91.623339

9 • C4 | Ozark NSR - Powder Mill CG

Total sites: 8, RV sites: 8, No water, Tent & RV camping: $12, Stay limit: 14 days, Generator hours: 0600-2200, Open all year, Elev: 594ft/181m, Tel: 573-323-4236. GPS: 37.182437, -91.174816

10 • C4 | Ozark NSR - Pulltite CG

Total sites: 55, RV sites: 55, Central water, Flush toilet, Free showers, No RV dump, Tent & RV camping: $16, Stay limit: 14 days, Generator hours: 0600-2200, Open all year, Reservations accepted, Elev: 748ft/228m, Tel: 573-323-4236, Nearest town: Round Spring. GPS: 37.334049, -91.478526

11 • C4 | Ozark NSR - Roberts Field

Dispersed sites, No water, Tents only: $5, Stay limit: 14 days, Generator hours: 0600-2200, Open all year, Elev: 564ft/172m, Tel: 573-323-4236, Nearest town: Eminence. GPS: 37.127268, -91.173166

12 • C4 | Ozark NSR - Round Spring CG

Total sites: 60, RV sites: 60, Elec sites: 6, Water at site, Flush toilet, Free showers, RV dump, Tents: $16/RV's: $16-19, Stay limit: 14 days, Generator hours: 0600-2200, Open all year, Reservations accepted, Elev: 686ft/209m, Tel: 573-323-4236, Nearest town: Round Spring. GPS: 37.283595, -91.406488

13 • C4 | Ozark NSR - Shawnee Creek CG

Dispersed sites, No water, Vault/pit toilet, Tents only: $5, Stay limit: 14 days, Generator hours: 0600-2200, Open all year, Elev: 607ft/185m, Tel: 573-323-4236, Nearest town: Eminence. GPS: 37.172148, -91.300343

14 • C4 | Ozark NSR - Sinking Creek CG

Dispersed sites, No water, Vault/pit toilet, Tents only: $5, Stay limit: 14 days, Generator hours: 0600-2200, Open all year, Elev: 712ft/217m, Tel: 573-323-4236. GPS: 37.302637, -91.414461

15 • C4 | Ozark NSR - Two Rivers

Total sites: 19, RV sites: 19, Central water, Flush toilet, Free showers, No RV dump, Tent & RV camping: $16, Stay limit: 14 days, Generator hours: 0600-2200, Open all year, Reservations not accepted, Elev: 597ft/182m, Tel: 573-323-4236, Nearest town: Eminence. GPS: 37.189697, -91.276123

16 • D3 | Ozark NSR - Blue Spring

Dispersed sites, No water, Vault/pit toilet, Tents only: $5, Stay limit: 14 days, Generator hours: 0600-2200, Open all year, Elev: 846ft/258m, Tel: 573-323-4236, Nearest town: Mountain View. GPS: 37.053613, -91.636888

17 • D4 | Ozark NSR - Big Spring CG

Total sites: 123, RV sites: 123, Elec sites: 28, Water at site, Flush toilet, Free showers, RV dump, Tents: $16/RV's: $16-19, Stay limit: 14 days, Generator hours: 0600-2200, Open all year, Reservations accepted, Elev: 482ft/147m, Tel: 573-323-4236, Nearest town: Van Buren. GPS: 36.947943, -90.993007

18 • D4 | Ozark NSR - Gooseneck CG

Dispersed sites, No water, Vault/pit toilet, Tents only: $5, Stay limit: 14 days, Generator hours: 0600-2200, Open all year, Elev: 426ft/130m, Tel: 573-323-4236, Nearest town: Eastwood. GPS: 36.820779, -90.946661

19 • D4 | Ozark NSR - Hickory Landing

Dispersed sites, No water, Vault/pit toilet, Tents only: $5, Stay limit: 14 days, Generator hours: 0600-2200, Open all year, Elev: 420ft/128m, Tel: 573-323-4236, Nearest town: Hunter. GPS: 36.891454, -90.910521

20 • D4 | Ozark NSR - Rymers CG

Dispersed sites, No water, Vault/pit toilet, Tents only: $5, Stay limit: 14 days, Generator hours: 0600-2200, Open all year, Elev: 804ft/245m, Tel: 573-323-4236, Nearest town: Mountain View. GPS: 37.060291, -91.559146

Montana

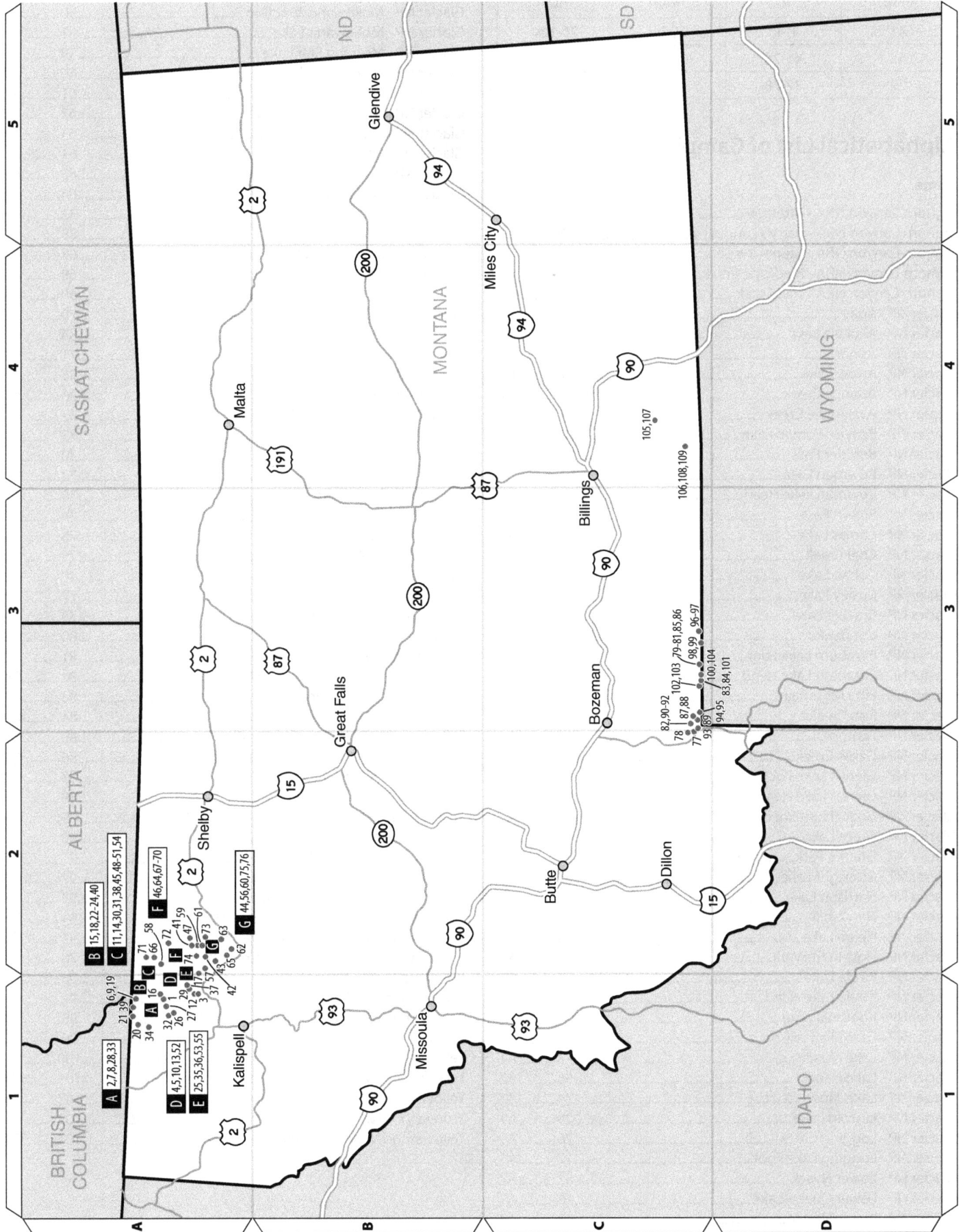

A 2,7,8,28,33

B 15,18,22-24,40

C 11,14,30,31,38,45,48-51,54

D 4,5,10,13,52

E 25,35,36,53,55

F 46,64,67-70

G 44,56,60,75,76

Map	ID	Map	ID
A1	1-40	C3	79-104
A2	41-76	C4	105-109
C2	77-78		

Alphabetical List of Camping Areas

Name	ID	Map
Bighorn Canyon NRA - Afterbay	105	C4
Bighorn Canyon NRA - Barry's Landing CG	106	C4
Bighorn Canyon NRA - Grapevine	107	C4
Bighorn Canyon NRA - Medicine Creek	108	C4
Bighorn Canyon NRA - Trail Creek	109	C4
Glacier NP - Adair	1	A1
Glacier NP - Akokala Lake	2	A1
Glacier NP - Apgar	3	A1
Glacier NP - Arrow Lake	4	A1
Glacier NP - Atlantic Creek	41	A2
Glacier NP - Avalanche Creek	5	A1
Glacier NP - Beaver Woman Lake	42	A2
Glacier NP - Boulder Pass	6	A1
Glacier NP - Bowman Lake	7	A1
Glacier NP - Bowman Lake Head	8	A1
Glacier NP - Brown Pass	9	A1
Glacier NP - Camas Lake	10	A1
Glacier NP - Coal Creek	43	A2
Glacier NP - Cobalt Lake	44	A2
Glacier NP - Cosley Lake	45	A2
Glacier NP - Cracker Lake	46	A2
Glacier NP - Cut Bank	47	A2
Glacier NP - Elizabeth Lake Foot	48	A2
Glacier NP - Elizabeth Lake Head	49	A2
Glacier NP - Fifty Mountain	11	A1
Glacier NP - Fish Creek	12	A1
Glacier NP - Flattop	13	A1
Glacier NP - Gable Creek	50	A2
Glacier NP - Glenns Lake Foot	51	A2
Glacier NP - Glenns Lake Head	14	A1
Glacier NP - Goat Haunt Shelters	15	A1
Glacier NP - Grace Lake	16	A1
Glacier NP - Granite Park	52	A2
Glacier NP - Gunsight Lake	53	A2
Glacier NP - Harrison Lake	17	A1
Glacier NP - Hawksbill	18	A1
Glacier NP - Helen Lake	54	A2
Glacier NP - Hole in the Wall	19	A1
Glacier NP - Kintla Lake	20	A1
Glacier NP - Kintla Lake Head	21	A1
Glacier NP - Kootenai Lake	22	A1
Glacier NP - Lake Ellen Wilson	55	A2
Glacier NP - Lake Francis	23	A1
Glacier NP - Lake Isabel	56	A2
Glacier NP - Lake Janet	24	A1
Glacier NP - Lincoln Lake	25	A1
Glacier NP - Logging Creek	26	A1
Glacier NP - Logging Lake Foot	27	A1
Glacier NP - Lower Nyack	57	A2
Glacier NP - Lower Quartz Lake	28	A1
Glacier NP - Many Glacier	58	A2
Glacier NP - McDonald Lake	29	A1
Glacier NP - Mokowanis Junction	30	A1
Glacier NP - Mokowanis Lake	31	A1
Glacier NP - Morning Star Lake	59	A2
Glacier NP - No Name Lake	60	A2
Glacier NP - Oldman Lake	61	A2
Glacier NP - Ole Creek	62	A2
Glacier NP - Ole Lake	63	A2
Glacier NP - Otokomi Lake	64	A2
Glacier NP - Park Creek	65	A2
Glacier NP - Poia Lake	66	A2
Glacier NP - Quartz Creek	32	A1
Glacier NP - Quartz Lake	33	A1
Glacier NP - Red Eagle Lake Foot	67	A2
Glacier NP - Red Eagle Lake Head	68	A2
Glacier NP - Reynolds Creek	69	A2
Glacier NP - Rising Sun	70	A2
Glacier NP - Round Prairie	34	A1
Glacier NP - Slide Lake	71	A2
Glacier NP - Snyder Lake	35	A1
Glacier NP - Sperry	36	A1
Glacier NP - Sprague Creek	37	A1
Glacier NP - St Mary	72	A2
Glacier NP - Stoney Indian Lake	38	A1
Glacier NP - Two Medicine	73	A2
Glacier NP - Upper Kintla Lake	39	A1
Glacier NP - Upper Nyack Creek	74	A2
Glacier NP - Upper Park Creek	75	A2
Glacier NP - Upper Two Medicine Lake	76	A2
Glacier NP - Waterton River	40	A1
Yellowstone NP - Black Butte Creek (WF1)	77	C2
Yellowstone NP - Coyote Creek (2C1)	79	C3
Yellowstone NP - Coyote Creek (2C2)	80	C3
Yellowstone NP - Coyote Creek Stock (2C3)	81	C3
Yellowstone NP - Crescent Lake (WE6)	82	C3
Yellowstone NP - Crevice Lake (1Y4)	83	C3
Yellowstone NP - East of Blacktail Cabin (1Y6)	84	C3
Yellowstone NP - Hellroaring Creek (2H8)	85	C3
Yellowstone NP - Hellroaring Creek (2H9)	86	C3
Yellowstone NP - High Lake (WD4)	87	C3
Yellowstone NP - High Lake (WD5)	88	C3
Yellowstone NP - High Lake/Sportsman Jct (WD6)	89	C3
Yellowstone NP - Shelf Lake (WE5)	90	C3
Yellowstone NP - Shelf Lake (WE7)	91	C3
Yellowstone NP - Specimen Creek (WE4)	92	C3
Yellowstone NP - Specimen Creek Jct (WE1)	93	C3
Yellowstone NP - Sportsman Lake (WD2)	94	C3
Yellowstone NP - Sportsman Lake (WD3)	95	C3
Yellowstone NP - Upper Dailey Creek (WF2)	78	C2
Yellowstone NP - Upper Pebble Creek (3P4)	96	C3
Yellowstone NP - Upper Pebble Creek (3P5)	97	C3
Yellowstone NP - Upper Slough Creek (2S6)	98	C3
Yellowstone NP - Upper Slough Creek Stock (2S8)	99	C3
Yellowstone NP - West Cottonwood Creek (1R1)	100	C3
Yellowstone NP - Yellowstone River Bridge (1Y5)	101	C3
Yellowstone NP - Yellowstone River Trail (1Y1)	102	C3
Yellowstone NP - Yellowstone River Trail (1Y2)	103	C3
Yellowstone NP - Yellowstone River Trail (1Y9)	104	C3

1 • A1 | Glacier NP - Adair

Dispersed sites, No water, Vault/pit toilet, Tents only: $7, Hike-in, 8 head of stock permitted, Reservations accepted, Elev: 3823ft/1165m, Tel: 406-888-7800. GPS: 48.767639, -114.051713

2 • A1 | Glacier NP - Akokala Lake

Total sites: 3, No water, Vault/pit toilet, Tents only: $7, Hike-in, Reservations accepted, Elev: 4754ft/1449m, Tel: 406-888-7800. GPS: 48.875397, -114.200386

3 • A1 | Glacier NP - Apgar

Total sites: 194, RV sites: 194, Central water, Flush toilet, No showers, RV dump, Tent & RV camping: $23, Group sites (10): $65, Nov-Mar: Free, Generator hours: 0800-1000/1200-1400/1700-1900, Open all year, Max Length: 40ft, Reservations required, Elev: 3186ft/971m, Tel: 406-888-7800, Nearest town: West Glacier. GPS: 48.526611, -113.980957

4 • A1 | Glacier NP - Arrow Lake

Total sites: 2, No water, Vault/pit toilet, Tents only: $7, Hike-in, 8 head of stock permitted, Reservations accepted, Elev: 4092ft/1247m, Tel: 406-888-7800. GPS: 48.702889, -113.886922

5 • A1 | Glacier NP - Avalanche Creek

Total sites: 87, RV sites: 87, Central water, Flush toilet, No showers, No RV dump, Tent & RV camping: $20, Generator hours: 0800-1000/1200-1400/1700-1900, Open Jun-Sep, Max Length: 26ft, Reservations not accepted, Elev: 3445ft/1050m, Tel: 406-888-7800, Nearest town: West Glacier. GPS: 48.678688, -113.818344

6 • A1 | Glacier NP - Boulder Pass

Total sites: 3, No water, Vault/pit toilet, Tents only: $7, Hike-in, Reservations accepted, Elev: 7206ft/2196m, Tel: 406-888-7800. GPS: 48.964437, -114.103151

7 • A1 | Glacier NP - Bowman Lake

Total sites: 48, RV sites: 0, Central water, Vault/pit toilet, No showers, No RV dump, Tents only: $15, No water late season - $10, Generator hours: 0800-1000/1200-1400/1700-1900, Open May-Oct, Reservations not accepted, Elev: 4039ft/1231m, Tel: 406-888-7800, Nearest town: Polebridge. GPS: 48.828705, -114.200931

8 • A1 | Glacier NP - Bowman Lake Head

Total sites: 6, No water, Vault/pit toilet, Tents only: $7, Hike-in, 8 head of stock permitted, Reservations accepted, Elev: 4056ft/1236m, Tel: 406-888-7800. GPS: 48.903801, -114.121739

9 • A1 | Glacier NP - Brown Pass

Total sites: 3, No water, Vault/pit toilet, Tents only: $7, Hike-in, Reservations accepted, Elev: 6169ft/1880m, Tel: 406-888-7800. GPS: 48.952797, -114.041601

10 • A1 | Glacier NP - Camas Lake

Total sites: 2, No water, Vault/pit toilet, Tents only: $7, Hike-in, Reservations accepted, Elev: 5084ft/1550m, Tel: 406-888-7800. GPS: 48.738209, -113.883125

11 • A1 | Glacier NP - Fifty Mountain

Total sites: 5, No water, Vault/pit toilet, Tents only: $7, Hike-in, 8 head of stock permitted, Reservations accepted, Elev: 6695ft/2041m, Tel: 406-888-7800. GPS: 48.852476, -113.861361

12 • A1 | Glacier NP - Fish Creek

Total sites: 178, RV sites: 178, Central water, Flush toilet, Pay showers, RV dump, Tent & RV camping: $23, Hiker/biker: $5, Stay limit: 14 days, Generator hours: 0800-1000/1200-1400/1700-1900 - prohibited in C Loop, Open May-Sep, Max Length: 35ft, Reservations accepted, Elev: 3248ft/990m, Tel: 406-888-7800, Nearest town: West Glacier. GPS: 48.549366, -113.983961

13 • A1 | Glacier NP - Flattop

Total sites: 5, No water, Vault/pit toilet, Tents only: $7, Hike-in, 8 head of stock permitted, Reservations accepted, Elev: 5934ft/1809m, Tel: 406-888-7800. GPS: 48.785718, -113.841891

14 • A1 | Glacier NP - Glenns Lake Head

Total sites: 3, No water, Vault/pit toilet, Tents only: $7, Hike-in, Reservations accepted, Elev: 4877ft/1487m, Tel: 406-888-7800. GPS: 48.891199, -113.807874

15 • A1 | Glacier NP - Goat Haunt Shelters

Total sites: 7, RV sites: 0, Central water, Vault/pit toilet, Hike-to shelter: $7, Reservations accepted, Elev: 4292ft/1308m, Tel: 406-888-7800. GPS: 48.957024, -113.891066

16 • A1 | Glacier NP - Grace Lake

Total sites: 3, No water, Vault/pit toilet, Tents only: $7, Hike-in, Reservations accepted, Elev: 3967ft/1209m, Tel: 406-888-7800. GPS: 48.788994, -114.002796

17 • A1 | Glacier NP - Harrison Lake

Total sites: 3, No water, Vault/pit toilet, Tents only: $7, Hike-in, 8 head of stock permitted, Reservations accepted, Elev: 3717ft/1133m, Tel: 406-888-7800. GPS: 48.527078, -113.756183

18 • A1 | Glacier NP - Hawksbill

Total sites: 2, No water, Vault/pit toilet, Tents only: $7, Hike-in, Reservations accepted, Elev: 5491ft/1674m, Tel: 406-888-7800. GPS: 48.946051, -114.011017

19 • A1 | Glacier NP - Hole in the Wall

Total sites: 5, No water, Vault/pit toilet, Tents only: $7, Hike-in, Reservations accepted, Elev: 6338ft/1932m, Tel: 406-888-7800. GPS: 48.965675, -114.068116

20 • A1 | Glacier NP - Kintla Lake

Total sites: 13, RV sites: 0, Central water, Vault/pit toilet, No showers, No RV dump, Tents only: $15, Generator hours: 0800-1000/1200-1400/1700-1900 , Open Jun-Oct, Max Length: 21ft, Reservations not accepted, Elev: 4058ft/1237m, Tel: 406-888-7800, Nearest town: Polebridge. GPS: 48.935824, -114.346287

21 • A1 | Glacier NP - Kintla Lake Head

Total sites: 6, No water, Vault/pit toilet, Tents only: $7, Hike-in, 8 head of stock permitted, Reservations accepted, Elev: 4021ft/1226m, Tel: 406-888-7800. GPS: 48.975941, -114.253306

22 • A1 | Glacier NP - Kootenai Lake

Total sites: 4, No water, Vault/pit toilet, Tents only: $7, Hike-in, 8 head of stock permitted, Reservations accepted, Elev: 4393ft/1339m, Tel: 406-888-7800. GPS: 48.926438, -113.901978

23 • A1 | Glacier NP - Lake Francis

Total sites: 2, No water, Vault/pit toilet, Tents only: $7, Hike-in, Reservations accepted, Elev: 5312ft/1619m, Tel: 406-888-7800. GPS: 48.941029, -114.004715

24 • A1 | Glacier NP - Lake Janet

Total sites: 2, No water, Vault/pit toilet, Tents only: $7, Hike-in, 8 head of stock permitted, Reservations accepted, Elev: 4988ft/1520m, Tel: 406-888-7800. GPS: 48.945151, -113.946422

25 • A1 | Glacier NP - Lincoln Lake

Total sites: 3, No water, Vault/pit toilet, Tents only: $7, Hike-in, 8 head of stock permitted, Reservations accepted, Elev: 4620ft/1408m, Tel: 406-888-7800. GPS: 48.589207, -113.774956

26 • A1 | Glacier NP - Logging Creek

Total sites: 7, RV sites: 0, No water, Vault/pit toilet, Tents only: $10, Generator hours: 0800-1000/1200-1400/1700-1900 , Open Jun-Sep, Max Length: 21ft, Reservations not accepted, Elev: 3448ft/1051m, Tel: 406-888-7800, Nearest town: Polebridge. GPS: 48.697869, -114.193029

27 • A1 | Glacier NP - Logging Lake Foot

Total sites: 3, No water, Vault/pit toilet, Tents only: $7, Hike-in, Reservations accepted, Elev: 3832ft/1168m, Tel: 406-888-7800. GPS: 48.742631, -114.128224

28 • A1 | Glacier NP - Lower Quartz Lake

Total sites: 4, No water, Vault/pit toilet, Tents only: $7, Hike-in, 8 head of stock permitted, Reservations accepted, Elev: 4204ft/1281m, Tel: 406-888-7800. GPS: 48.798205, -114.173165

29 • A1 | Glacier NP - McDonald Lake

Total sites: 2, No water, Vault/pit toilet, Tents only: $7, Hike-in, Reservations accepted, Elev: 3171ft/967m, Tel: 406-888-7800. GPS: 48.593998, -113.925609

30 • A1 | Glacier NP - Mokowanis Junction

Total sites: 5, No water, Vault/pit toilet, Tents only: $7, Hike-in, 8 head of stock permitted, Reservations accepted, Elev: 4915ft/1498m, Tel: 406-888-7800. GPS: 48.889719, -113.818049

31 • A1 | Glacier NP - Mokowanis Lake

Total sites: 2, No water, Vault/pit toilet, Tents only: $7, Hike-in, Reservations accepted, Elev: 5008ft/1526m, Tel: 406-888-7800. GPS: 48.877246, -113.812335

32 • A1 | Glacier NP - Quartz Creek

Total sites: 7, RV sites: 0, No water, Vault/pit toilet, Tents only: $10, Open Jul-Sep, Max Length: 21ft, Reservations not accepted, Elev: 3534ft/1077m, Tel: 406-888-7800, Nearest town: Polebridge. GPS: 48.721903, -114.224742

33 • A1 | Glacier NP - Quartz Lake

Total sites: 3, No water, Vault/pit toilet, Tents only: $7, Hike-in, Reservations accepted, Elev: 4465ft/1361m, Tel: 406-888-7800. GPS: 48.823622, -114.136997

34 • A1 | Glacier NP - Round Prairie

Total sites: 3, No water, Vault/pit toilet, Tents only: $7, Hike-in, Reservations accepted, Elev: 3687ft/1124m, Tel: 406-888-7800. GPS: 48.857829, -114.366476

35 • A1 | Glacier NP - Snyder Lake

Total sites: 3, No water, Vault/pit toilet, Tents only: $7, Hike-in, 8 head of stock permitted, Reservations accepted, Elev: 5232ft/1595m, Tel: 406-888-7800. GPS: 48.625868, -113.804473

36 • A1 | Glacier NP - Sperry

Total sites: 4, No water, Vault/pit toilet, Tents only: $7, Hike-in, Reservations accepted, Elev: 6714ft/2046m, Tel: 406-888-7800. GPS: 48.601533, -113.786646

37 • A1 | Glacier NP - Sprague Creek

Total sites: 25, RV sites: 0, Central water, No toilets, No showers, No RV dump, Tents only: $20, No towed units, Open May-Sep, Reservations not accepted, Elev: 3209ft/978m, Tel: 406-888-7800, Nearest town: West Glacier. GPS: 48.606193, -113.884713

38 • A1 | Glacier NP - Stoney Indian Lake

Total sites: 3, No water, Vault/pit toilet, Tents only: $7, Hike-in, Reservations accepted, Elev: 6347ft/1935m, Tel: 406-888-7800. GPS: 48.887442, -113.869178

39 • A1 | Glacier NP - Upper Kintla Lake

Total sites: 4, No water, Vault/pit toilet, Tents only: $7, Hike-in, 8 head of stock permitted, Reservations accepted, Elev: 4383ft/1336m, Tel: 406-888-7800. GPS: 48.980246, -114.154427

40 • A1 | Glacier NP - Waterton River

Total sites: 5, No water, Vault/pit toilet, Tents only: $7, Hike-in, 8 head of stock permitted, Reservations accepted, Elev: 4227ft/1288m, Tel: 406-888-7800. GPS: 48.956255, -113.898031

41 • A2 | Glacier NP - Atlantic Creek

Total sites: 4, No water, Vault/pit toilet, Tents only: $7, Hike-in, 8 head of stock permitted, Reservations accepted, Elev: 5440ft/1658m, Tel: 406-888-7800. GPS: 48.575591, -113.453544

42 • A2 | Glacier NP - Beaver Woman Lake

Total sites: 2, No water, Vault/pit toilet, Tents only: $7, Hike-in, 10 head of stock permitted, Reservations accepted, Elev: 5899ft/1798m, Tel: 406-888-7800. GPS: 48.483825, -113.575125

43 • A2 | Glacier NP - Coal Creek

Total sites: 2, No water, Vault/pit toilet, Tents only: $7, Hike-in, 10 head of stock permitted, Reservations accepted, Elev: 3911ft/1192m, Tel: 406-888-7800. GPS: 48.411219, -113.611436

44 • A2 | Glacier NP - Cobalt Lake

Total sites: 2, No water, Vault/pit toilet, Tents only: $7, Hike-in,

Reservations accepted, Elev: 6581ft/2006m, Tel: 406-888-7800. GPS: 48.435466, -113.424779

45 • A2 | Glacier NP - Cosley Lake

Total sites: 4, No water, Vault/pit toilet, Tents only: $7, Hike-in, 8 head of stock permitted, Reservations accepted, Elev: 4855ft/1480m, Tel: 406-888-7800. GPS: 48.925011, -113.757215

46 • A2 | Glacier NP - Cracker Lake

Total sites: 3, No water, Vault/pit toilet, Tents only: $7, Hike-in, Reservations accepted, Elev: 6006ft/1831m, Tel: 406-888-7800. GPS: 48.741616, -113.644151

47 • A2 | Glacier NP - Cut Bank

Total sites: 14, RV sites: 0, No water, Vault/pit toilet, Tents only: $10, No generators, Open Jun-Sep, Reservations not accepted, Elev: 5138ft/1566m, Tel: 406-888-7800, Nearest town: Saint Maryu. GPS: 48.601916, -113.382878

48 • A2 | Glacier NP - Elizabeth Lake Foot

Total sites: 5, No water, Vault/pit toilet, Tents only: $7, Hike-in, 8 head of stock permitted, Reservations accepted, Elev: 4905ft/1495m, Tel: 406-888-7800. GPS: 48.891456, -113.725461

49 • A2 | Glacier NP - Elizabeth Lake Head

Total sites: 4, No water, Vault/pit toilet, Tents only: $7, Hike-in, 8 head of stock permitted, Reservations accepted, Elev: 4923ft/1501m, Tel: 406-888-7800. GPS: 48.872116, -113.727072

50 • A2 | Glacier NP - Gable Creek

Total sites: 4, No water, Vault/pit toilet, Tents only: $7, Hike-in, 8 head of stock permitted, Reservations accepted, Elev: 4662ft/1421m, Tel: 406-888-7800. GPS: 48.934517, -113.713118

51 • A2 | Glacier NP - Glenns Lake Foot

Total sites: 4, No water, Vault/pit toilet, Tents only: $7, Hike-in, 8 head of stock permitted, Reservations accepted, Elev: 4875ft/1486m, Tel: 406-888-7800. GPS: 48.914724, -113.778933

52 • A2 | Glacier NP - Granite Park

Total sites: 4, No water, Vault/pit toilet, Tents only: $7, Hike-in, Reservations accepted, Elev: 6398ft/1950m, Tel: 406-888-7800. GPS: 48.769859, -113.778544

53 • A2 | Glacier NP - Gunsight Lake

Total sites: 7, No water, Vault/pit toilet, Tents only: $7, Hike-in, Reservations accepted, Elev: 5359ft/1633m, Tel: 406-888-7800. GPS: 48.627672, -113.708635

54 • A2 | Glacier NP - Helen Lake

Total sites: 2, No water, Vault/pit toilet, Tents only: $7, Hike-in, Reservations accepted, Elev: 5110ft/1558m, Tel: 406-888-7800. GPS: 48.840981, -113.745321

55 • A2 | Glacier NP - Lake Ellen Wilson

Total sites: 3, No water, Vault/pit toilet, Tents only: $7, Hike-in, 8 head of stock permitted, Reservations accepted, Elev: 5948ft/1813m, Tel: 406-888-7800. GPS: 48.604964, -113.754266

56 • A2 | Glacier NP - Lake Isabel

Total sites: 2, No water, Vault/pit toilet, Tents only: $7, Reservations accepted, Elev: 5735ft/1748m, Tel: 406-888-7800. GPS: 48.424457, -113.491818

57 • A2 | Glacier NP - Lower Nyack

Total sites: 3, No water, Vault/pit toilet, Tents only: $7, Hike-in, 10 head of stock permitted, Reservations accepted, Elev: 3649ft/1112m, Tel: 406-888-7800. GPS: 48.488685, -113.702309

58 • A2 | Glacier NP - Many Glacier

Total sites: 109, RV sites: 13, Central water, Flush toilet, No showers, RV dump, Tent & RV camping: $23, Generator hours: 0800-1000/1200-1400/1700-1900 - prohibited in sites 88-102, Open Jun-Sep, Max Length: 35ft, Reservations accepted, Elev: 4928ft/1502m, Tel: 406-888-7800, Nearest town: Babb. GPS: 48.796553, -113.676712

59 • A2 | Glacier NP - Morning Star Lake

Total sites: 3, No water, Vault/pit toilet, Tents only: $7, Hike-in, Reservations accepted, Elev: 5810ft/1771m, Tel: 406-888-7800. GPS: 48.540816, -113.458011

60 • A2 | Glacier NP - No Name Lake

Total sites: 3, No water, Vault/pit toilet, Tents only: $7, Hike-in, Reservations accepted, Elev: 5944ft/1812m, Tel: 406-888-7800. GPS: 48.479815, -113.448659

61 • A2 | Glacier NP - Oldman Lake

Total sites: 4, No water, Vault/pit toilet, Tents only: $7, Hike-in, 8 head of stock permitted, Reservations accepted, Elev: 6731ft/2052m, Tel: 406-888-7800. GPS: 48.512438, -113.455242

62 • A2 | Glacier NP - Ole Creek

Total sites: 3, No water, Vault/pit toilet, Tents only: $7, Hike-in, 8 head of stock permitted, Reservations accepted, Elev: 4284ft/1306m, Tel: 406-888-7800. GPS: 48.308393, -113.485287

63 • A2 | Glacier NP - Ole Lake

Total sites: 2, No water, Vault/pit toilet, Tents only: $7, Hike-in, 8 head of stock permitted, Reservations accepted, Elev: 5550ft/1692m, Tel: 406-888-7800. GPS: 48.382445, -113.384435

64 • A2 | Glacier NP - Otokomi Lake

Total sites: 3, No water, Vault/pit toilet, Tents only: $7, Hike-in, Reservations accepted, Elev: 6519ft/1987m, Tel: 406-888-7800. GPS: 48.718703, -113.593327

65 • A2 | Glacier NP - Park Creek

Total sites: 3, No water, Vault/pit toilet, Tents only: $7, Hike-in, 8 head of stock permitted, Reservations accepted, Elev: 3986ft/1215m, Tel: 406-888-7800. GPS: 48.336006, -113.545943

66 • A2 | Glacier NP - Poia Lake

Total sites: 4, No water, Vault/pit toilet, Tents only: $7, Hike-in, 8 head of stock permitted, Reservations accepted, Elev: 5797ft/1767m, Tel: 406-888-7800. GPS: 48.850081, -113.606355

67 • A2 | Glacier NP - Red Eagle Lake Foot

Total sites: 4, No water, Vault/pit toilet, Tents only: $7, Hike-in, Reservations accepted, Elev: 4740ft/1445m, Tel: 406-888-7800. GPS: 48.655885, -113.501731

68 • A2 | Glacier NP - Red Eagle Lake Head

Total sites: 4, No water, Vault/pit toilet, Tents only: $7, Hike-in, 8 head of stock permitted, Reservations accepted, Elev: 4746ft/1447m, Tel: 406-888-7800. GPS: 48.645799, -113.510035

69 • A2 | Glacier NP - Reynolds Creek

Total sites: 2, No water, Vault/pit toilet, Tents only: $7, Hike-in, 8 head of stock permitted, Reservations accepted, Elev: 4649ft/1417m, Tel: 406-888-7800. GPS: 48.666769, -113.635419

70 • A2 | Glacier NP - Rising Sun

Total sites: 83, RV sites: 10, Central water, Flush toilet, Pay showers, RV dump, Tent & RV camping: $20, Generator hours: 0800-1000/1200-1400/1700-1900 - prohibited in sites 49-84, Open Jun-Sep, Max Length: 25ft, Reservations not accepted, Elev: 4550ft/1387m, Tel: 406-888-7800, Nearest town: St Mary. GPS: 48.694336, -113.521639

71 • A2 | Glacier NP - Slide Lake

Total sites: 3, No water, Vault/pit toilet, Tents only: $7, Hike-in, 8 head of stock permitted, Reservations accepted, Elev: 6039ft/1841m, Tel: 406-888-7800. GPS: 48.905558, -113.616543

72 • A2 | Glacier NP - St Mary

Total sites: 148, RV sites: 75, Central water, Flush toilet, Pay showers, RV dump, Tent & RV camping: $23, Hiker/biker: $8, Stay limit: 14 days, Generator hours: 0800-1000/1200-1400/1700-1900 - prohibited in A Loop, Open May-Aug, Max Length: 40ft, Reservations accepted, Elev: 4521ft/1378m, Tel: 406-888-7800, Nearest town: St Mary. GPS: 48.752093, -113.442698

73 • A2 | Glacier NP - Two Medicine

Total sites: 99, RV sites: 75, Central water, Flush toilet, No showers, RV dump, Tent & RV camping: $20, No water late season - $10, Generator hours: 0800-1000/1200-1400/1700-1900 - prohibited in sites 1-36, Open May-Oct, Max Length: 35ft, Reservations not accepted, Elev: 5203ft/1586m, Tel: 406-888-7800, Nearest town: East Glacier Park. GPS: 48.491978, -113.363943

74 • A2 | Glacier NP - Upper Nyack Creek

Total sites: 2, No water, Vault/pit toilet, Tents only: $7, Hike-in, 10 head of stock permitted, Reservations accepted, Elev: 4308ft/1313m, Tel: 406-888-7800. GPS: 48.548071, -113.572191

75 • A2 | Glacier NP - Upper Park Creek

Total sites: 3, No water, Vault/pit toilet, Tents only: $7, Hike-in, 8 head of stock permitted, Reservations accepted, Elev: 4762ft/1451m, Tel: 406-888-7800. GPS: 48.414742, -113.460195

76 • A2 | Glacier NP - Upper Two Medicine Lake

Total sites: 4, No water, Vault/pit toilet, Tents only: $7, Hike-in, Reservations accepted, Elev: 5476ft/1669m, Tel: 406-888-7800. GPS: 48.467789, -113.446967

77 • C2 | Yellowstone NP - Black Butte Creek (WF1)

Dispersed sites, Tents only: $5, Hike-in, Permit required, 10 person max, Stock allowed, Reservations accepted, Elev: 7451ft/2271m, Tel: 307-344-2160. GPS: 45.053517, -111.090685

78 • C2 | Yellowstone NP - Upper Dailey Creek (WF2)

Dispersed sites, Tents only: $5, Hike-in, Permit required, 10 person max, Stock allowed, Reservations accepted, Elev: 7535ft/2297m, Tel: 307-344-2160. GPS: 45.090981, -111.106652

79 • C3 | Yellowstone NP - Coyote Creek (2C1)

Dispersed sites, Tents only: $5, Hike-in, Permit required, 8 person max, Reservations accepted, Elev: 6758ft/2060m, Tel: 307-344-2160. GPS: 45.000595, -110.417059

80 • C3 | Yellowstone NP - Coyote Creek (2C2)

Dispersed sites, Tents only: $5, Hike-in, Permit required, 8 person max, Reservations accepted, Elev: 7092ft/2162m, Tel: 307-344-2160. GPS: 45.008936, -110.407961

81 • C3 | Yellowstone NP - Coyote Creek Stock (2C3)

Dispersed sites, Tents only: $5, Hike-in, Permit required, Stock only, 10 person max, Reservations accepted, Elev: 7130ft/2173m, Tel: 307-344-2160. GPS: 45.016067, -110.408693

82 • C3 | Yellowstone NP - Crescent Lake (WE6)

Dispersed sites, Tents only: $5, Hike-in, Permit required, 8 person max, Reservations accepted, Elev: 8595ft/2620m, Tel: 307-344-2160. GPS: 45.061761, -110.995876

83 • C3 | Yellowstone NP - Crevice Lake (1Y4)

Dispersed sites, Tents only: $5, Hike-in, Permit required, 6 person max, Reservations accepted, Elev: 5610ft/1710m, Tel: 307-344-2160. GPS: 45.004111, -110.580858

84 • C3 | Yellowstone NP - East of Blacktail Cabin (1Y6)

Dispersed sites, Tents only: $5, Hike-in, Permit required, 6 person max, No wood fires, Reservations accepted, Elev: 5578ft/1700m, Tel: 307-344-2160. GPS: 44.993897, -110.570833

85 • C3 | Yellowstone NP - Hellroaring Creek (2H8)

Dispersed sites, Tents only: $5, Hike-in, Permit required, 8 person max, No wood fires, Reservations accepted, Elev: 6120ft/1865m, Tel: 307-344-2160. GPS: 44.994348, -110.427902

86 • C3 | Yellowstone NP - Hellroaring Creek (2H9)

Dispersed sites, Tents only: $5, Hike-in, Permit required, 8 person max, Reservations accepted, Elev: 6224ft/1897m, Tel: 307-344-2160. GPS: 45.008787, -110.434038

87 • C3 | Yellowstone NP - High Lake (WD4)

Dispersed sites, Tents only: $5, Hike-in, Permit required, 10 person max, No wood fires, Reservations accepted, Elev: 8799ft/2682m, Tel: 307-344-2160. GPS: 45.055563, -110.937982

88 • C3 | Yellowstone NP - High Lake (WD5)

Dispersed sites, Tents only: $5, Hike-in, Permit required, 10 person max, Stock allowed, No wood fires, Reservations accepted, Elev: 8815ft/2687m, Tel: 307-344-2160. GPS: 45.058041, -110.940159

89 • C3 | Yellowstone NP - High Lake/Sportsman Jct (WD6)

Dispersed sites, Tents only: $5, Hike-in, Permit required, 12 person max, Stock allowed, Reservations accepted, Elev: 8009ft/2441m, Tel: 307-344-2160. GPS: 45.027684, -110.969075

90 • C3 | Yellowstone NP - Shelf Lake (WE5)

Dispersed sites, Tents only: $5, Hike-in, Permit required, 8 person max, No wood fires, Reservations accepted, Elev: 9152ft/2790m, Tel: 307-344-2160. GPS: 45.091835, -111.011876

91 • C3 | Yellowstone NP - Shelf Lake (WE7)

Dispersed sites, Tents only: $5, Hike-in, Permit required, 8 person max, No wood fires, Reservations accepted, Elev: 9191ft/2801m, Tel: 307-344-2160. GPS: 45.091345, -111.014236

92 • C3 | Yellowstone NP - Specimen Creek (WE4)

Dispersed sites, Tents only: $5, Hike-in, Permit required, 12 person max, Reservations accepted, Elev: 7559ft/2304m, Tel: 307-344-2160. GPS: 45.063869, -111.022915

93 • C3 | Yellowstone NP - Specimen Creek Jct (WE1)

Dispersed sites, Tents only: $5, Hike-in, Permit required, 12 person max, Stock allowed, 2 night limit, Reservations accepted, Elev: 7159ft/2182m, Tel: 307-344-2160. GPS: 45.028838, -111.045904

94 • C3 | Yellowstone NP - Sportsman Lake (WD2)

Dispersed sites, Tents only: $5, Hike-in, Permit required, 12 person max, Stock allowed, Reservations accepted, Elev: 7728ft/2355m, Tel: 307-344-2160. GPS: 45.013696, -110.902988

95 • C3 | Yellowstone NP - Sportsman Lake (WD3)

Dispersed sites, Tents only: $5, Hike-in, Permit required, 10 person max, Reservations accepted, Elev: 7730ft/2356m, Tel: 307-344-2160. GPS: 45.015436, -110.900769

96 • C3 | Yellowstone NP - Upper Pebble Creek (3P4)

Dispersed sites, Tents only: $5, Hike-in, Permit required, 12 person max, Reservations accepted, Elev: 7968ft/2429m, Tel: 307-344-2160. GPS: 45.021298, -110.077847

97 • C3 | Yellowstone NP - Upper Pebble Creek (3P5)

Dispersed sites, Tents only: $5, Hike-in, Permit required, 12 person max, Reservations accepted, Elev: 8061ft/2457m, Tel: 307-344-2160. GPS: 45.018989, -110.056492

98 • C3 | Yellowstone NP - Upper Slough Creek (2S6)

Dispersed sites, Tents only: $5, Hike-in, Permit required, 8 person max, Reservations accepted, Elev: 6634ft/2022m, Tel: 307-344-2160. GPS: 45.002733, -110.185242

99 • C3 | Yellowstone NP - Upper Slough Creek Stock (2S8)

Dispersed sites, Tents only: $5, Hike-in, Permit required, Stock only, 12 person max, Reservations accepted, Elev: 6730ft/2051m, Tel: 307-344-2160. GPS: 45.006096, -110.199138

100 • C3 | Yellowstone NP - West Cottonwood Creek (1R1)

Dispersed sites, Tents only: $5, Hike-in, Permit required, 12 person max, Stock allowed - 2 night limit, No wood fires, Reservations accepted, Elev: 5608ft/1709m, Tel: 307-344-2160. GPS: 44.992845, -110.516476

101 • C3 | Yellowstone NP - Yellowstone River Bridge (1Y5)

Dispersed sites, Tents only: $5, Hike-in, Permit required, 6 person max, No wood fires, Reservations accepted, Elev: 5572ft/1698m, Tel: 307-344-2160. GPS: 44.996341, -110.574351

102 • C3 | Yellowstone NP - Yellowstone River Trail (1Y1)

Dispersed sites, Tents only: $5, Hike-in, Permit required, 10 person max, No wood fires, Reservations accepted, Elev: 5404ft/1647m, Tel: 307-344-2160. GPS: 45.013997, -110.626766

103 • C3 | Yellowstone NP - Yellowstone River Trail (1Y2)

Dispersed sites, Tents only: $5, Hike-in, Permit required, 10 person max, No wood fires, Reservations accepted, Elev: 5504ft/1678m, Tel: 307-344-2160. GPS: 45.015752, -110.609829

104 • C3 | Yellowstone NP - Yellowstone River Trail (1Y9)

Dispersed sites, Tents only: $5, Hike-in, Permit required, 8 person max, No wood fires, Reservations accepted, Elev: 5607ft/1709m, Tel: 307-344-2160. GPS: 44.993608, -110.547011

105 • C4 | Bighorn Canyon NRA - Afterbay

Total sites: 27, RV sites: 27, Central water, Vault/pit toilet, No showers, RV dump, Tent & RV camping: $15, Open all year, Reservations not accepted, Elev: 3192ft/973m, Tel: 307-548-5406, Nearest town: Fort Smith. GPS: 45.315277, -107.941664

106 • C4 | Bighorn Canyon NRA - Barry's Landing CG

Total sites: 4, RV sites: 4, No water, Vault/pit toilet, Tent & RV camping: $18, Open all year, Reservations not accepted, Elev: 3724ft/1135m, Tel: 307-548-5406, Nearest town: Lowell. GPS: 45.096033, -108.210146

107 • C4 | Bighorn Canyon NRA - Grapevine

Total sites: 14, RV sites: 8, Central water, Vault/pit toilet, No showers, No RV dump, Tent & RV camping: $15, Open all year, Reservations not accepted, Elev: 3204ft/977m, Tel: 406-666-2412, Nearest town: Fort Smith. GPS: 45.318441, -107.940864

108 • C4 | Bighorn Canyon NRA - Medicine Creek

Total sites: 6, RV sites: 0, No water, Vault/pit toilet, Tents only: Free, Hike-in/boat-in, Bike-in, Open all year, Reservations not accepted, Elev: 3667ft/1118m, Tel: 307-548-5406, Nearest town: Fort Smith. GPS: 45.109891, -108.204218

109 • C4 | Bighorn Canyon NRA - Trail Creek

Total sites: 30, RV sites: 14, No water, Vault/pit toilet, Tent & RV camping: $10, Open all year, Reservations not accepted, Elev: 3727ft/1136m, Tel: 406-657-6200, Nearest town: Lovell. GPS: 45.102892, -108.223862

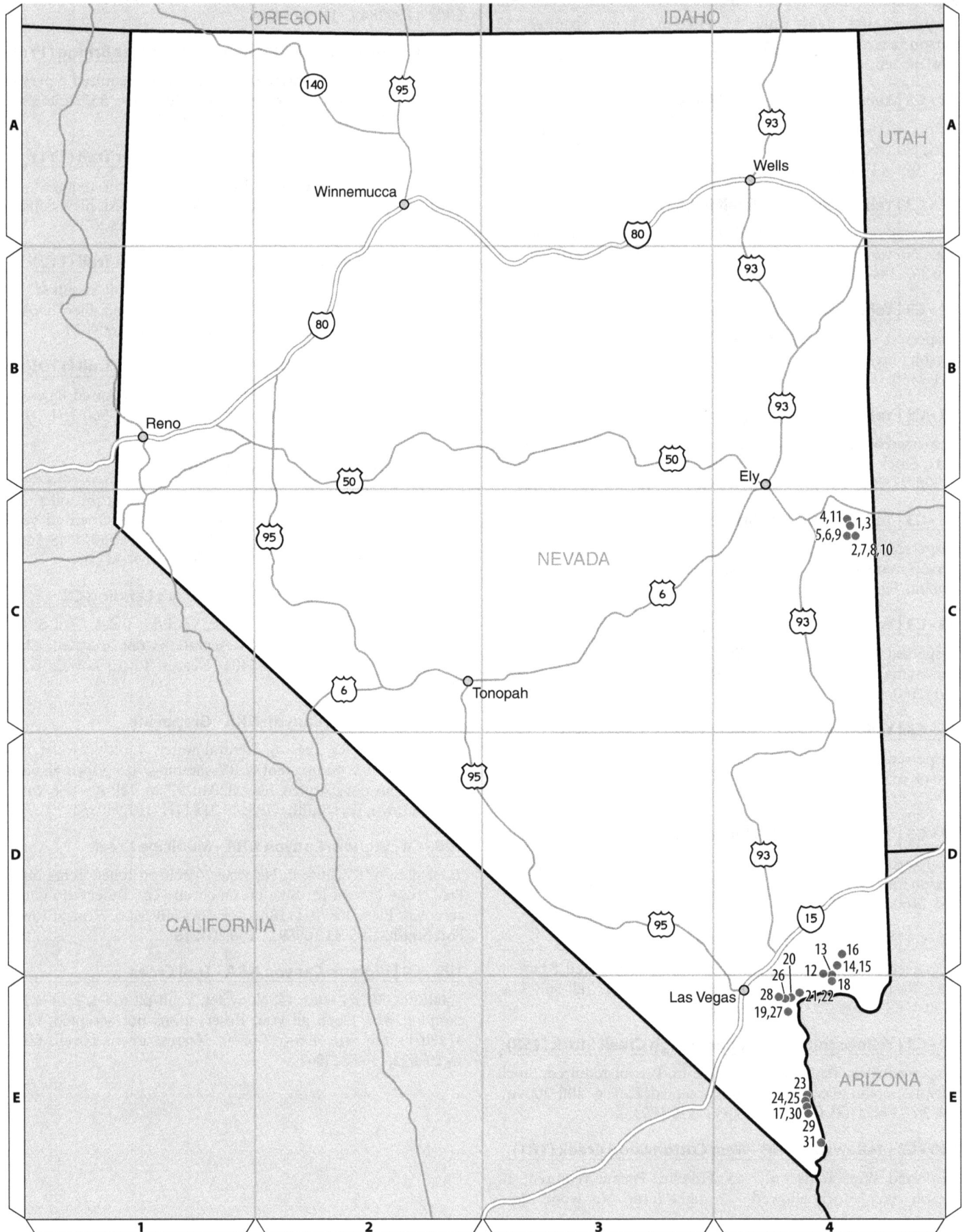

Nevada

OREGON | IDAHO

UTAH

140 | 95

93

Wells

Winnemucca

80

93

80

93

Reno

50

50

Ely

NEVADA

4,11 • 1,3
5,6,9 • 2,7,8,10

95

6

93

6

Tonopah

95

95

93

15

CALIFORNIA

13 • 16
20 | 12 • 14,15
26 | 18
28 • 21,22
Las Vegas | 19,27

ARIZONA

23
24,25
17,30
29
31

1 | 2 | 3 | 4

A | A
B | B
C | C
D | D
E | E

Map	ID	Map	ID
C4	1-11	E4	17-31
D4	12-16		

Alphabetical List of Camping Areas

Name	ID	Map
Great Basin NP - Baker Creek	1	C4
Great Basin NP - Eagle Point	2	C4
Great Basin NP - Grey Cliffs	3	C4
Great Basin NP - Lower Lehman Creek	4	C4
Great Basin NP - Shoshone 1	5	C4
Great Basin NP - Shoshone 2~3	6	C4
Great Basin NP - Snake Creek Dispersed 2	7	C4
Great Basin NP - Snake Creek Dispersed 3	8	C4
Great Basin NP - Snake Creek Dispersed 4	9	C4
Great Basin NP - Squirrel Springs	10	C4
Great Basin NP - Upper Lehman	11	C4
Lake Mead NRA - Area de Playa	17	E4
Lake Mead NRA - Bitter Spring Road	12	D4
Lake Mead NRA - Boathouse Cove Road 1	13	D4
Lake Mead NRA - Boathouse Cove Road 2	18	E4
Lake Mead NRA - Boulder Beach	19	E4
Lake Mead NRA - Boxcar Canyon	20	E4
Lake Mead NRA - Callville Bay	21	E4
Lake Mead NRA - Callville Bay Resort	22	E4
Lake Mead NRA - Copper Mt Cove	23	E4
Lake Mead NRA - Cottonwood Cove Lower	24	E4
Lake Mead NRA - Cottonwood Cove Resort	25	E4
Lake Mead NRA - Echo Bay Lower	14	D4
Lake Mead NRA - Echo Bay Upper	15	D4
Lake Mead NRA - Government Wash Dispersed	26	E4
Lake Mead NRA - Lake Mead RV Village	27	E4
Lake Mead NRA - Las Vegas Bay	28	E4
Lake Mead NRA - Nine Mile Cove	29	E4
Lake Mead NRA - Six Mile Cove	30	E4
Lake Mead NRA - Stewarts Point Dispersed	16	D4
Lake Mead NRA - Telephone Cove	31	E4

1 • C4 | Great Basin NP - Baker Creek

Total sites: 34, RV sites: 34, Central water, Vault/pit toilet, No showers, RV dump, Tent & RV camping: $20, RV dump at Visitors Center, Open May-Oct, Reservations not accepted, Elev: 7625ft/2324m, Tel: 775-234-7331, Nearest town: Baker. GPS: 38.985499, -114.241782

2 • C4 | Great Basin NP - Eagle Point

Total sites: 3, RV sites: 3, No water, Vault/pit toilet, Tent & RV camping: Free, High-clearance vehicles recommended, Stay limit: 14 days, Generator hours: 0800-1800, Open all year, Reservations not accepted, Elev: 7702ft/2348m, Tel: 775-234-7331, Nearest town: Baker. GPS: 38.921637, -114.228186

3 • C4 | Great Basin NP - Grey Cliffs

Total sites: 16, RV sites: 0, No water, Vault/pit toilet, No showers, No RV dump, Tents only: $20, Group site: $30, Open May-Sep, Reservations accepted, Elev: 7120ft/2170m, Tel: 775-234-7500. GPS: 38.989757, -114.221348

4 • C4 | Great Basin NP - Lower Lehman Creek

Total sites: 11, RV sites: 11, Central water, Vault/pit toilet, No showers, RV dump, Tent & RV camping: $20, RV dump at Visitors Center, Open all year, Reservations accepted, Elev: 7284ft/2220m, Tel: 775-234-7331, Nearest town: Baker. GPS: 39.017446, -114.237773

5 • C4 | Great Basin NP - Shoshone 1

Dispersed sites, No water, No toilets, Tents only: Free, Walk-to sites, High-clearance vehicles recommended, Generator hours: 0800-1800, Open all year, Reservations not accepted, Elev: 8288ft/2526m, Tel: 775-234-7331, Nearest town: Baker. GPS: 38.928986, -114.253584

6 • C4 | Great Basin NP - Shoshone 2-3

Dispersed sites, No water, No toilets, Tents only: Free, Walk-to sites, High-clearance vehicles recommended, Generator hours: 0800-1800, Open all year, Reservations not accepted, Elev: 8271ft/2521m, Tel: 775-234-7331, Nearest town: Baker. GPS: 38.925545, -114.255388

7 • C4 | Great Basin NP - Snake Creek Dispersed 2

Dispersed sites, No water, No toilets, Tents only: Free, High-clearance vehicles recommended, Stay limit: 14 days, Generator hours: 0800-1800, Open all year, Reservations not accepted, Elev: 7394ft/2254m, Tel: 775-234-7331, Nearest town: Baker. GPS: 38.920281, -114.208222

8 • C4 | Great Basin NP - Snake Creek Dispersed 3

Dispersed sites, No water, No toilets, Tents only: Free, High-clearance vehicles recommended, Stay limit: 14 days, Generator hours: 0800-1800, Open all year, Reservations not accepted, Elev: 7560ft/2304m, Tel: 775-234-7331, Nearest town: Baker. GPS: 38.920301, -114.219258

9 • C4 | Great Basin NP - Snake Creek Dispersed 4

Dispersed sites, No water, No toilets, Tents only: Free, Walk-to sites, High-clearance vehicles recommended, Stay limit: 14 days, Generator hours: 0800-1800, Open all year, Reservations not accepted, Elev: 8040ft/2451m, Tel: 775-234-7331, Nearest town: Baker. GPS: 38.924972, -114.246423

10 • C4 | Great Basin NP - Squirrel Springs

Total sites: 3, RV sites: 2, No water, Vault/pit toilet, Tent & RV camping: Free, High-clearance vehicles recommended, Stay limit: 14 days, Generator hours: 0800-1800, Open all year, Reservations not accepted, Elev: 7191ft/2192m, Tel: 775-234-7331, Nearest town: Baker. GPS: 38.919288, -114.195961

11 • C4 | Great Basin NP - Upper Lehman

Total sites: 22, RV sites: 22, Central water, Vault/pit toilet, No showers, RV dump, Tent & RV camping: $20, RV dump at Visitors Center, Open Apr-Oct, Reservations accepted, Elev: 7759ft/2365m, Tel: 775-234-7331, Nearest town: Baker. GPS: 39.012887, -114.253532

12 • D4 | Lake Mead NRA - Bitter Spring Road

Dispersed sites, No water, No toilets, Tents only: Free, Also hike-in sites, 4x4 required, Elev: 1960ft/597m, Tel: 702-293-8990, Nearest town: Las Vegas. GPS: 36.257698, -114.532709

13 • D4 | Lake Mead NRA - Boathouse Cove Road 1

Dispersed sites, No water, No toilets, Tents only: Free, Also hike-in sites, 4x4 required, Elev: 2157ft/657m, Tel: 702-293-8990, Nearest town: Las Vegas. GPS: 36.251221, -114.474877

14 • D4 | Lake Mead NRA - Echo Bay Lower

Total sites: 37, RV sites: 37, Central water, Vault/pit toilet, No showers, No RV dump, No tents/RV's: $20, Generator hours: 0600-2200, Open all year, Reservations not accepted, Elev: 1247ft/380m, Nearest town: Kingman. GPS: 36.307894, -114.423717

15 • D4 | Lake Mead NRA - Echo Bay Upper

Total sites: 116, RV sites: 116, Central water, Flush toilet, No showers, RV dump, No tents/RV's: $20, Generator hours: 0600-2200, Open all year, Reservations not accepted, Elev: 1306ft/398m, Nearest town: Kingman. GPS: 36.30881, -114.435308

16 • D4 | Lake Mead NRA - Stewarts Point Dispersed

Dispersed sites, No water, Vault/pit toilet, Tent & RV camping: Free, Elev: 1199ft/365m, Nearest town: Las Vegas. GPS: 36.377354, -114.396517

17 • E4 | Lake Mead NRA - Area de Playa

Dispersed sites, No water, No toilets, Tent & RV camping: Free, Reservations not accepted, Elev: 651ft/198m, Tel: 702-293-8990, Nearest town: Searchlight. GPS: 35.437544, -114.681197

18 • E4 | Lake Mead NRA - Boathouse Cove Road 2

Dispersed sites, No water, No toilets, Tents only: Free, Also hike-in sites, 4x4 required, Elev: 2204ft/672m, Tel: 702-293-8990, Nearest town: Las Vegas. GPS: 36.219792, -114.476712

19 • E4 | Lake Mead NRA - Boulder Beach

Total sites: 146, RV sites: 146, Central water, Flush toilet, No showers, RV dump, Tent & RV camping: $20, Generator hours: 0600-2200, Open all year, Max Length: 30ft, Reservations not accepted, Elev: 1250ft/381m, Tel: 702-293-8990, Nearest town: Boulder City. GPS: 36.037598, -114.802002

20 • E4 | Lake Mead NRA - Boxcar Canyon

Dispersed sites, No water, No toilets, Tent & RV camping: Free, Elev: 1243ft/379m, Tel: 702-293-8990, Nearest town: Henderson. GPS: 36.120912, -114.783143

21 • E4 | Lake Mead NRA - Callville Bay

Total sites: 52, RV sites: 52, Central water, Flush toilet, No showers, RV dump, Tent & RV camping: $20, Open all year, Reservations not accepted, Elev: 1260ft/384m, Tel: 702-293-8906, Nearest town: Callville Bay. GPS: 36.138689, -114.727349

22 • E4 | Lake Mead NRA - Callville Bay Resort

Total sites: 5, RV sites: 5, Elec sites: 5, Water at site, Flush toilet, Free showers, RV dump, No tents/RV's: $20, Concession, Full hookups, Open all year, Elev: 1214ft/370m, Tel: 702-565-8958, Nearest town: Henderson. GPS: 36.142317, -114.723564

23 • E4 | Lake Mead NRA - Copper Mt Cove

Dispersed sites, No water, Vault/pit toilet, Tent & RV camping: Free, Nothing larger than van/PU, Reservations not accepted, Elev: 655ft/200m, Tel: 702-293-8990, Nearest town: Searchlight. GPS: 35.525308, -114.677175

24 • E4 | Lake Mead NRA - Cottonwood Cove Lower

Total sites: 45, RV sites: 45, Central water, Flush toilet, No showers, RV dump, Tent & RV camping: $20, Open all year, Reservations not accepted, Elev: 781ft/238m, Tel: 702-293-8906, Nearest town: Laughlin. GPS: 35.494731, -114.687986

25 • E4 | Lake Mead NRA - Cottonwood Cove Resort

Total sites: 72, RV sites: 72, Elec sites: 72, Water at site, Flush toilet, Free showers, RV dump, No tents/RV's: $41-50, 72 Full hookups, $35-$45 Nov-Mar, Concessionaire, Open all year, Reservations accepted, Elev: 676ft/206m, Tel: 702-297-1464, Nearest town: Laughlin. GPS: 35.490275, -114.687439

26 • E4 | Lake Mead NRA - Government Wash Dispersed

Dispersed sites, No water, No toilets, Tent & RV camping: Free, 4x4 recommended, Park entrance fee, Stay limit: 7 days, Reservations not accepted, Elev: 1202ft/366m, Nearest town: Las Vegas. GPS: 36.119652, -114.819601

27 • E4 | Lake Mead NRA - Lake Mead RV Village

Total sites: 115, RV sites: 115, Elec sites: 115, Water at site, Flush toilet, Free showers, RV dump, No tents/RV's: $45-60, 115 Full hookups, Concession, Open all year, Reservations accepted, Elev: 1270ft/387m, Tel: 702-293-2540, Nearest town: Boulder City. GPS: 36.034818, -114.800297

28 • E4 | Lake Mead NRA - Las Vegas Bay

Total sites: 84, RV sites: 84, Central water, Flush toilet, No showers, RV dump, Tent & RV camping: $20, 1 loop - no generators, Generator hours: 0600-2200, Open all year, Reservations not accepted, Elev: 1247ft/380m, Nearest town: Henderson. GPS: 36.128368, -114.873246

29 • E4 | Lake Mead NRA - Nine Mile Cove

Dispersed sites, No water, Vault/pit toilet, Tent & RV camping: Free, Reservations not accepted, Elev: 653ft/199m, Tel: 702-293-8990, Nearest town: Searchlight. GPS: 35.413748, -114.673394

30 • E4 | Lake Mead NRA - Six Mile Cove

Dispersed sites, No water, Vault/pit toilet, Tent & RV camping: Free, Reservations not accepted, Elev: 658ft/201m, Tel: 702-293-8990, Nearest town: Searchlight. GPS: 35.453316, -114.679244

31 • E4 | Lake Mead NRA - Telephone Cove

Dispersed sites, No water, Vault/pit toilet, Tent & RV camping: Free, Also boat-in sites, Generators allowed/hours unknown, Reservations not accepted, Elev: 649ft/198m, Nearest town: Laughlin. GPS: 35.2305, -114.594

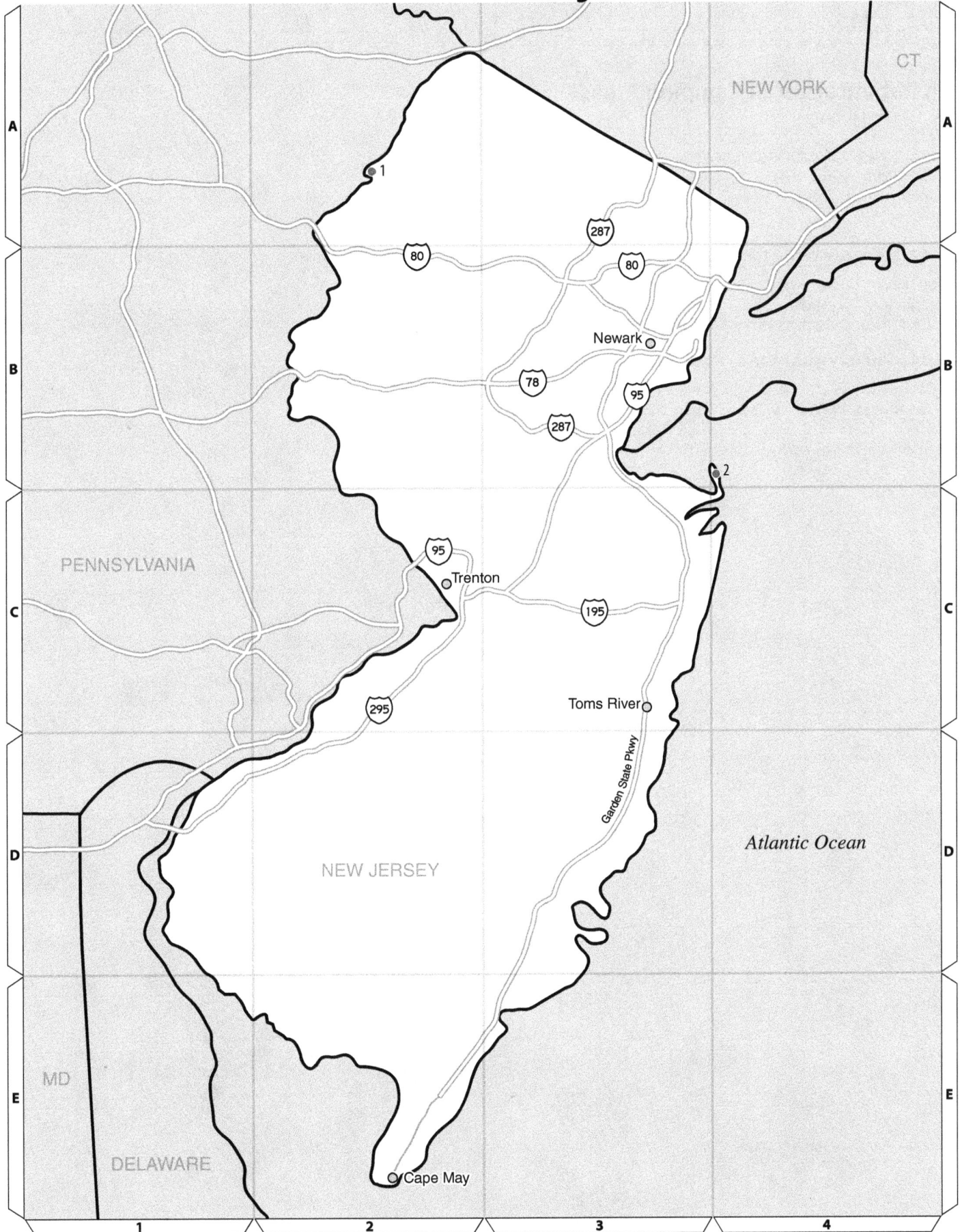

New Jersey

CT

NEW YORK

A

1

287

80

80

Newark

B

78

287

95

2

95

PENNSYLVANIA

Trenton

C

195

295

Toms River

Garden State Pkwy

Atlantic Ocean

D

NEW JERSEY

MD

E

DELAWARE

Cape May

1   2   3   4

Map	ID	Map	ID
A2	1	B4	2

Alphabetical List of Camping Areas

Name	ID	Map
Delaware Water Gap NRA - Rivers Bend Group	1	A2
Gateway NRA - Sandy Hook	2	B4

1 • A2 | Delaware Water Gap NRA - Rivers Bend Group

Total sites: 1, No water, Vault/pit toilet, Group site: $160, Reservations accepted, Elev: 326ft/99m, Tel: 570-828-2253, Nearest town: Dingman's Ferry. GPS: 41.098245, -74.967124

2 • B4 | Gateway NRA - Sandy Hook

Total sites: 20, RV sites: 0, Central water, Flush toilet, No showers, Tents only: $30, Walk-to sites, Open May-Oct, Reservations accepted, Elev: 11ft/3m, Tel: 347-630-1124, Nearest town: Highlands. GPS: 40.449594, -73.996166

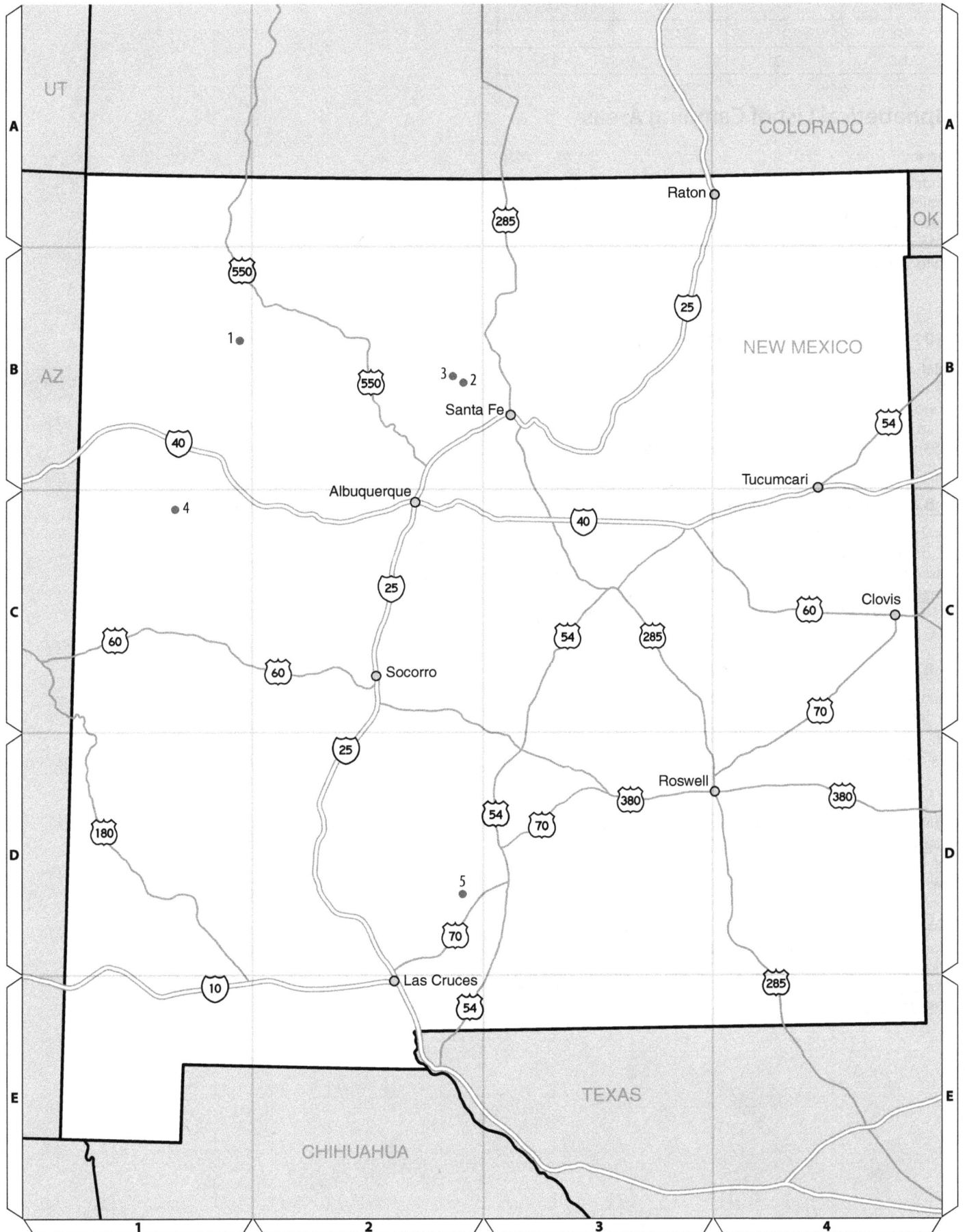

New Mexico

UT

COLORADO

A

OK

Raton

NEW MEXICO

285

25

550

1

3 2

550

Santa Fe

54

AZ

40

Tucumcari

Albuquerque

4

40

60

Clovis

25

60

60

Socorro

54

285

70

180

25

Roswell

380

380

54

70

5

70

10

Las Cruces

285

54

TEXAS

CHIHUAHUA

A

B

C

D

E

1 2 3 4

Map	ID	Map	ID
B1	1	C1	4
B2	2-3	D2	5

Alphabetical List of Camping Areas

Name	ID	Map
Bandelier NM - Juniper CG	2	B2
Bandelier NM - Ponderosa Group	3	B2
Chaco Culture NHP - Gallo CG	1	B1
El Morro NM	4	C1
White Sands NP	5	D2

1 • B1 | Chaco Culture NHP - Gallo CG

Total sites: 49, RV sites: 34, No water, Flush toilet, No showers, RV dump, Tent & RV camping: $15, Non-potable water, 2 group sites $60, Stay limit: 14 days, Generator hours: 0800-2000, Open all year, Max Length: 35ft, Reservations accepted, Elev: 6253ft/1906m, Tel: 505-786-7014, Nearest town: Kimbeto. GPS: 36.036777, -107.890589

2 • B2 | Bandelier NM - Juniper CG

Total sites: 66, RV sites: 50, Central water, Flush toilet, No showers, RV dump, Tent & RV camping: $12, 2 groups sites: $35, RV dump closed in winter, Generator hours: 0800-2000, Open all year, Max Length: 40ft, Reservations not accepted, Elev: 6683ft/2037m, Tel: 505-672-3861 x517, Nearest town: White Rock. GPS: 35.796169, -106.279906

3 • B2 | Bandelier NM - Ponderosa Group

Total sites: 2, No water, Vault/pit toilet, Group site: $35, Only 1 RV allowed per site, Reservations required, Elev: 7594ft/2315m, Tel: 505-672-3861 Ext 517, Nearest town: White Rock. GPS: 35.832849, -106.357024

4 • C1 | El Morro NM

Total sites: 9, RV sites: 9, Central water, Vault/pit toilet, Tent & RV camping: Free, No water in winter, Max Length: 27ft, Reservations not accepted, Elev: 7209ft/2197m, Tel: 505-783-4226, Nearest town: Ramah. GPS: 35.036897, -108.336817

5 • D2 | White Sands NP

Total sites: 10, RV sites: 0, No water, No toilets, Tents only: $3, Hike-in, 1 mi, Permit required: $3/person, Open all year, Elev: 4006ft/1221m, Tel: 575-479-6124, Nearest town: Alamogordo. GPS: 32.806101, -106.277407

New York

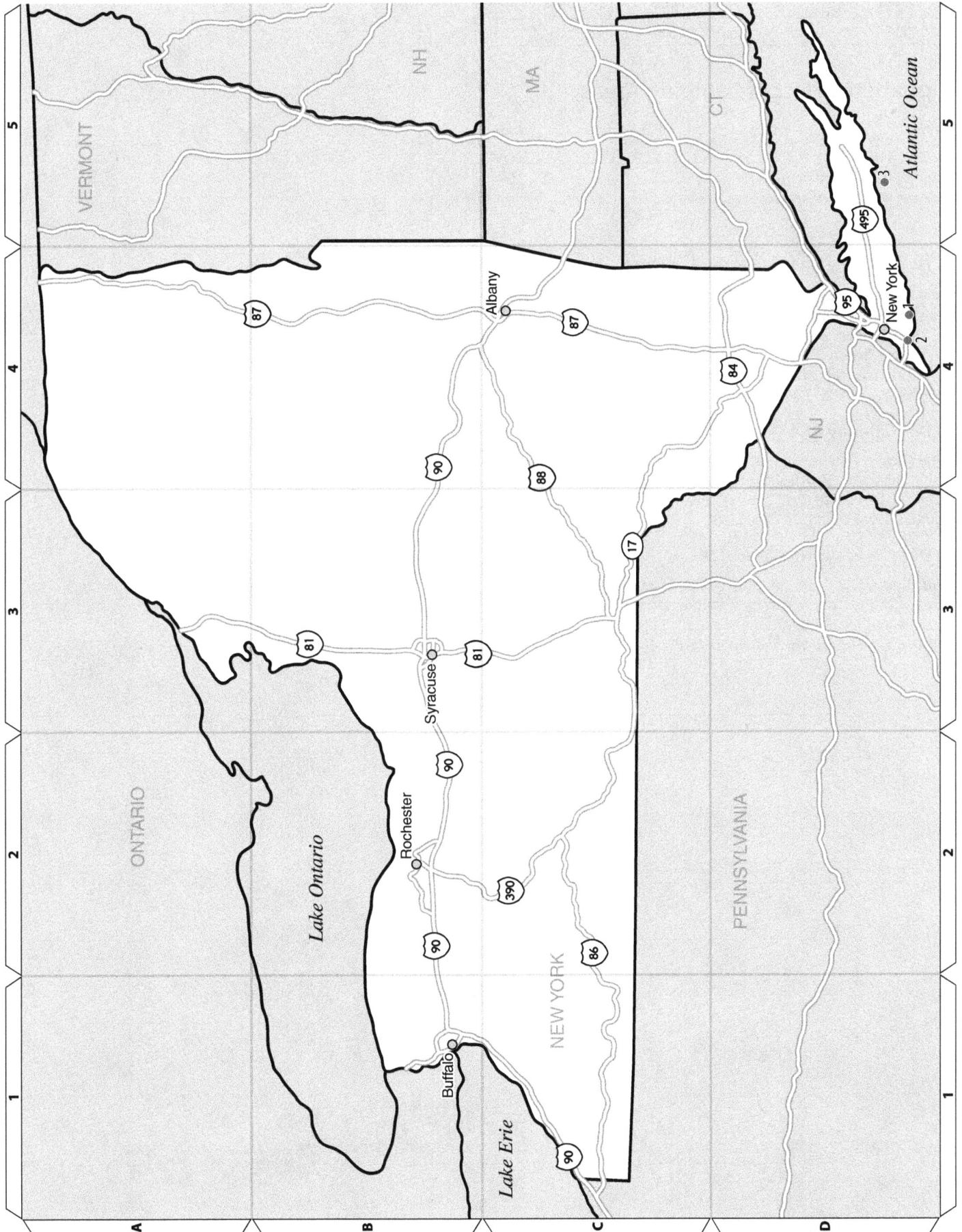

Map	ID	Map	ID
D4	1-2	D5	3

Alphabetical List of Camping Areas

Name	ID	Map
Fire Island NS - Watch Hill	3	D5
Gateway NRA - Floyd Bennett Field	1	D4
Gateway NRA - Fort Wadsworth	2	D4

1 • D4 | Gateway NRA - Floyd Bennett Field

Total sites: 42, RV sites: 12, Central water, Flush toilet, Free showers, RV dump, Tent & RV camping: $30, Do not approach via the Belt Parkway - very Low Bridges - use Flatbush Av or Rockaway Beach Blvd, Open all year, Reservations accepted, Elev: 13ft/4m, Tel: 718-338-3799, Nearest town: Brooklyn. GPS: 40.595867, -73.885737

2 • D4 | Gateway NRA - Fort Wadsworth

Total sites: 7, RV sites: 0, Central water, Flush toilet, Free showers, Tents only: $30, Stay limit: 14 days, Open Jul-Sep, Reservations accepted, Elev: 40ft/12m, Tel: 718-354-4655, Nearest town: Staten Island. GPS: 40.600017, -74.055254

3 • D5 | Fire Island NS - Watch Hill

Total sites: 26, RV sites: 0, Flush toilet, Free showers, RV dump, Tents only: Fee unk, Access by ferry, No open fires, No generators, Open May-Oct, Reservations required, Elev: 12ft/4m, Tel: 631-567-6664, Nearest town: Patchogue. GPS: 40.691425, -72.985814

North Carolina

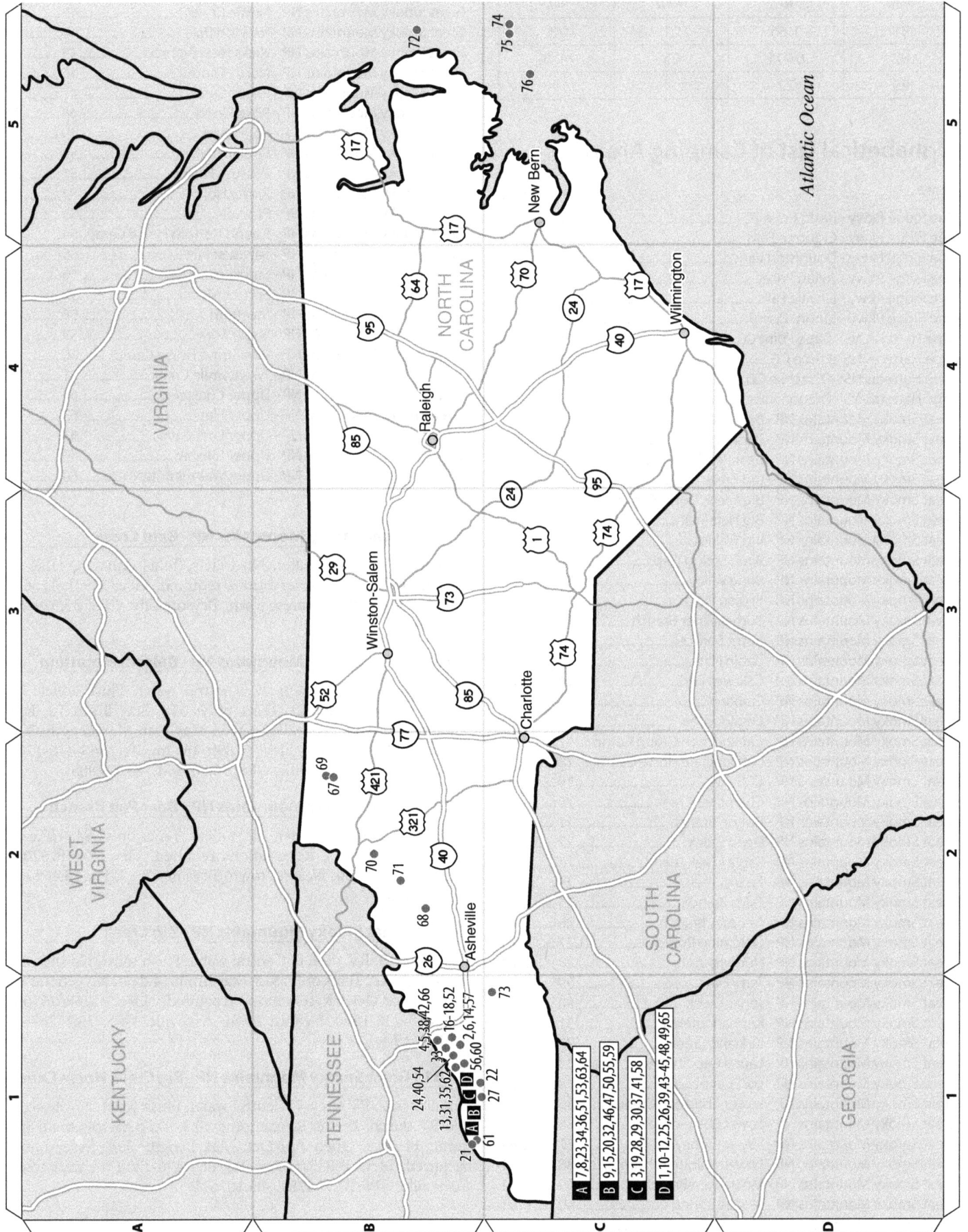

Atlantic Ocean

VIRGINIA

WEST VIRGINIA

KENTUCKY

TENNESSEE

SOUTH CAROLINA

GEORGIA

NORTH CAROLINA

New Bern

Wilmington

Raleigh

Winston-Salem

Charlotte

Asheville

72
74
75
76

17
64
70
24
40
95
85
24
95
1
74
29
73
74
52
85
77
69
67
421
321
40
70
71
68
26
73

24,40,54
4,5,38,42,66
16-18,52
2,6,14,57
13,31,35,62
33
56,60
21
61
27 22

A	7,8,23,34,36,51,53,63,64
B	9,15,20,32,46,47,50,55,59
C	3,19,28,29,30,37,41,58
D	1,10-12,25,26,39,43-45,48,49,65

Map	ID	Map	ID
B1	1-66	C1	73
B2	67-71	C5	74-76
B5	72		

Alphabetical List of Camping Areas

Name	ID	Map
Blue Ridge Pkwy - Basin Cove TC	67	B2
Blue Ridge Pkwy - Crabtree Falls	68	B2
Blue Ridge Pkwy - Doughton Park	69	B2
Blue Ridge Pkwy - Julian Price	70	B2
Blue Ridge Pkwy - Linville Falls	71	B2
Blue Ridge Pkwy - Mount Pisgah	73	C1
Cape Hatteras NS - Cape Point CG	74	C5
Cape Hatteras NS - Frisco CG	75	C5
Cape Hatteras NS - Ocracoke CG	76	C5
Cape Hatteras NS - Oregon Inlet CG	72	B5
Great Smoky Mountains NP - Bald Creek	1	B1
Great Smoky Mountains NP - Balsam Mountain	2	B1
Great Smoky Mountains NP - Bear Pen Branch	3	B1
Great Smoky Mountains NP - Big Creek	4	B1
Great Smoky Mountains NP - Big Creek Horse Camp	5	B1
Great Smoky Mountains NP - Big Hemlock	6	B1
Great Smoky Mountains NP - Big Walnut	7	B1
Great Smoky Mountains NP - Birch Spring Gap	8	B1
Great Smoky Mountains NP - Bone Valley	9	B1
Great Smoky Mountains NP - Bryson Place	10	B1
Great Smoky Mountains NP - Bumgardner Branch	11	B1
Great Smoky Mountains NP - Burnt Spruce	12	B1
Great Smoky Mountains NP - Cabin Flats	13	B1
Great Smoky Mountains NP - Caldwell Fork	14	B1
Great Smoky Mountains NP - Calhoun	15	B1
Great Smoky Mountains NP - Cataloochee	16	B1
Great Smoky Mountains NP - Cataloochee Group Camp	17	B1
Great Smoky Mountains NP - Cataloochee Horse Camp	18	B1
Great Smoky Mountains NP - CCC	19	B1
Great Smoky Mountains NP - Chambers Creek	20	B1
Great Smoky Mountains NP - Dalton Branch	21	B1
Great Smoky Mountains NP - Deep Creek	22	B1
Great Smoky Mountains NP - Eagle Creek Island	23	B1
Great Smoky Mountains NP - Enloe Creek	24	B1
Great Smoky Mountains NP - Estes Branch	25	B1
Great Smoky Mountains NP - Georges Branch	26	B1
Great Smoky Mountains NP - Goldmine Branch	27	B1
Great Smoky Mountains NP - Huggins	28	B1
Great Smoky Mountains NP - Jerry Flats	29	B1
Great Smoky Mountains NP - Jonas Creek	30	B1
Great Smoky Mountains NP - Kephart Shelter	31	B1
Great Smoky Mountains NP - Kirkland Creek	32	B1
Great Smoky Mountains NP - Laurel Gap Shelter	33	B1
Great Smoky Mountains NP - Lost Cove	34	B1
Great Smoky Mountains NP - Lower Chasteen Creek	35	B1
Great Smoky Mountains NP - Lower Ekaneetlee	36	B1
Great Smoky Mountains NP - Lower Forney	37	B1
Great Smoky Mountains NP - Lower Walnut Bottom	38	B1
Great Smoky Mountains NP - McCracken Branch	39	B1
Great Smoky Mountains NP - McGee Spring	40	B1
Great Smoky Mountains NP - Mill Creek	41	B1
Great Smoky Mountains NP - Mt Sterling	42	B1
Great Smoky Mountains NP - Nettle Creek	43	B1
Great Smoky Mountains NP - Newton Bald	44	B1
Great Smoky Mountains NP - Nicks Nest Branch	45	B1
Great Smoky Mountains NP - North Shore	46	B1
Great Smoky Mountains NP - Pilkey Creek	47	B1
Great Smoky Mountains NP - Poke Patch	48	B1
Great Smoky Mountains NP - Pole Road	49	B1
Great Smoky Mountains NP - Poplar Flats	50	B1
Great Smoky Mountains NP - Possum Hollow	51	B1
Great Smoky Mountains NP - Pretty Hollow	52	B1
Great Smoky Mountains NP - Proctor	53	B1
Great Smoky Mountains NP - Round Bottom Horse Camp	54	B1
Great Smoky Mountains NP - Sawdust Pile	55	B1
Great Smoky Mountains NP - Smokemont	56	B1
Great Smoky Mountains NP - Spruce Mt	57	B1
Great Smoky Mountains NP - Steeltrap	58	B1
Great Smoky Mountains NP - Sugar Fork	59	B1
Great Smoky Mountains NP - Tow String Horse Camp	60	B1
Great Smoky Mountains NP - Twentymile Creek	61	B1
Great Smoky Mountains NP - Upper Chasteen	62	B1
Great Smoky Mountains NP - Upper Flats	63	B1
Great Smoky Mountains NP - Upper Lost Cove	64	B1
Great Smoky Mountains NP - Upper Ripshin	65	B1
Great Smoky Mountains NP - Upper Walnut Bottom	66	B1

1 • B1 | Great Smoky Mountains NP - Bald Creek

Dispersed sites, No water, No toilets, Tents only: $4, Hike-in, Stay limit: 14 days, Reservations required, Elev: 3793ft/1156m, Tel: 865-436-1200, Nearest town: Bryson City. GPS: 35.529854, -83.464529

2 • B1 | Great Smoky Mountains NP - Balsam Mountain

Total sites: 43, RV sites: 37, Central water, Flush toilet, No showers, No RV dump, Tents only: $18, Stay limit: 14 days, Generator hours: 0800-2000, Open May-Oct, Max Length: 30ft, Reservations required, Elev: 5289ft/1612m, Tel: 865-436-1200, Nearest town: Waynesville. GPS: 35.565674, -83.174805

3 • B1 | Great Smoky Mountains NP - Bear Pen Branch

Dispersed sites, No water, No toilets, Tents only: $4, Hike-in, Stay limit: 14 days, Reservations required, Elev: 2035ft/620m, Tel: 865-436-1200, Nearest town: Bryson City. GPS: 35.465404, -83.523055

4 • B1 | Great Smoky Mountains NP - Big Creek

Total sites: 5, RV sites: 0, Central water, Flush toilet, No showers, No RV dump, Tents only: $18, Stay limit: 14 days, No generators, Open Apr-Oct, Reservations required, Elev: 1758ft/536m, Tel: 865-436-1200, Nearest town: Asheville. GPS: 35.752686, -83.109619

5 • B1 | Great Smoky Mountains NP - Big Creek Horse Camp

Total sites: 7, RV sites: 7, Central water, Flush toilet, No showers, No RV dump, Tent & RV camping: $23, Steep narrow road, Stay limit: 14 days, Open Apr-Oct, Max Length: 30ft, Reservations required, Elev: 1683ft/513m, Tel: 865-436-1200, Nearest town: Asheville. GPS: 35.754754, -83.107575

6 • B1 | Great Smoky Mountains NP - Big Hemlock

Dispersed sites, No water, No toilets, Tents only: $4, Hike-in, Stay limit: 14 days, Reservations required, Elev: 3398ft/1036m, Tel: 865-436-1200, Nearest town: Maggie Valley. GPS: 35.599445, -83.132498

7 • B1 | Great Smoky Mountains NP - Big Walnut

Dispersed sites, No water, No toilets, Tents only: $4, Hike-in, Stay limit: 14 days, Reservations required, Elev: 2531ft/771m, Tel: 865-436-1200, Nearest town: Fontana Village. GPS: 35.530954, -83.749267

8 • B1 | Great Smoky Mountains NP - Birch Spring Gap

Dispersed sites, No water, No toilets, Tents only: $4, Hike-in, Stay limit: 14 days, Reservations required, Elev: 3760ft/1146m, Tel: 865-436-1200, Nearest town: Fontana Village. GPS: 35.503566, -83.812767

9 • B1 | Great Smoky Mountains NP - Bone Valley

Dispersed sites, No water, No toilets, Tents only: $4, Hike-in, Stay limit: 14 days, Reservations required, Elev: 2269ft/692m, Tel: 865-436-1200, Nearest town: Fontana Village. GPS: 35.499712, -83.680173

10 • B1 | Great Smoky Mountains NP - Bryson Place

Dispersed sites, No water, No toilets, Tents only: $4, Hike-in, Stay limit: 14 days, Reservations required, Elev: 2434ft/742m, Tel: 865-436-1200, Nearest town: Bryson City. GPS: 35.520823, -83.419102

11 • B1 | Great Smoky Mountains NP - Bumgardner Branch

Dispersed sites, No water, No toilets, Tents only: $4, Hike-in, Stay limit: 14 days, Reservations required, Elev: 2019ft/615m, Tel: 865-436-1200, Nearest town: Bryson City. GPS: 35.492709, -83.424766

12 • B1 | Great Smoky Mountains NP - Burnt Spruce

Dispersed sites, No water, No toilets, Tents only: $4, Hike-in, Stay limit: 14 days, Reservations required, Elev: 2436ft/742m, Tel: 865-436-1200, Nearest town: Bryson City. GPS: 35.525287, -83.420305

13 • B1 | Great Smoky Mountains NP - Cabin Flats

Dispersed sites, No water, No toilets, Tents only: $4, Hike-in, Stay limit: 14 days, Reservations required, Elev: 3183ft/970m, Tel: 865-436-1200, Nearest town: Cherokee. GPS: 35.614175, -83.329666

14 • B1 | Great Smoky Mountains NP - Caldwell Fork

Dispersed sites, No water, No toilets, Tents only: $4, Hike-in, Stay limit: 14 days, Reservations required, Elev: 3281ft/1000m, Tel: 865-436-1200, Nearest town: Maggie Valley. GPS: 35.584774, -83.122453

15 • B1 | Great Smoky Mountains NP - Calhoun

Dispersed sites, No water, No toilets, Tents only: $4, Hike-in, Stay limit: 14 days, Reservations required, Elev: 2701ft/823m, Tel: 865-436-1200, Nearest town: Fontana Village. GPS: 35.516953, -83.642001

16 • B1 | Great Smoky Mountains NP - Cataloochee

Total sites: 27, RV sites: 0, Central water, Flush toilet, No showers, No RV dump, Tent & RV camping: $25, Steep narrow road, Stay limit: 14 days, Generator hours: 0800-2000, Open Jun-Oct, Reservations required, Elev: 2687ft/819m, Tel: 865-436-1200, Nearest town: Asheville. GPS: 35.630924, -83.085929

17 • B1 | Great Smoky Mountains NP - Cataloochee Group Camp

Total sites: 1, Central water, Flush toilet, Group site: $40, Stay limit: 14 days, Open Mar-Oct, Reservations accepted, Elev: 2541ft/774m, Tel: 865-436-1200, Nearest town: Bryson City. GPS: 35.650911, -83.073963

18 • B1 | Great Smoky Mountains NP - Cataloochee Horse Camp

Total sites: 7, RV sites: 0, Central water, Flush toilet, No showers, No RV dump, Tents only: $25, Steep narrow road, Stay limit: 14 days, Generator hours: 0800-2000, Open Apr-Oct, Reservations required, Elev: 2854ft/870m, Tel: 865-436-1200, Nearest town: Asheville. GPS: 35.627275, -83.111374

19 • B1 | Great Smoky Mountains NP - CCC

Dispersed sites, No water, No toilets, Tents only: $4, Hike-in, Stay limit: 14 days, Reservations required, Elev: 2210ft/674m, Tel: 865-436-1200, Nearest town: Bryson City. GPS: 35.497393, -83.561092

20 • B1 | Great Smoky Mountains NP - Chambers Creek

Dispersed sites, No water, No toilets, Tents only: $4, Hike-in, Stay limit: 14 days, Reservations required, Elev: 1743ft/531m, Tel: 865-436-1200, Nearest town: Bryson City. GPS: 35.450603, -83.609099

21 • B1 | Great Smoky Mountains NP - Dalton Branch

Dispersed sites, No water, No toilets, Tents only: $4, Hike-in, Stay limit: 14 days, Reservations required, Elev: 2243ft/684m, Tel: 865-436-1200, Nearest town: Fontana Village. GPS: 35.490362, -83.880627

22 • B1 | Great Smoky Mountains NP - Deep Creek

Total sites: 92, RV sites: 50, Central water, Flush toilet, No showers, RV dump, Tent & RV camping: $25, Stay limit: 14 days, Generator hours: 0800-2000, Open Apr-Oct, Max Length: 26ft, Reservations required, Elev: 1857ft/566m, Tel: 865-436-1200, Nearest town: Bryson City. GPS: 35.461182, -83.435547

23 • B1 | Great Smoky Mountains NP - Eagle Creek Island

Dispersed sites, No water, No toilets, Tents only: $4, Hike-in, Stay limit: 14 days, Reservations required, Elev: 2880ft/878m, Tel: 865-436-1200, Nearest town: Fontana Village. GPS: 35.516541, -83.766016

24 • B1 | Great Smoky Mountains NP - Enloe Creek

Dispersed sites, No water, No toilets, Tents only: $4, Hike-in, Stay limit: 14 days, Reservations required, Elev: 3818ft/1164m, Tel: 865-436-1200, Nearest town: Cherokee. GPS: 35.610479, -83.254814

25 • B1 | Great Smoky Mountains NP - Estes Branch

Dispersed sites, No water, No toilets, Tents only: $4, Hike-in, Stay limit: 14 days, Reservations required, Elev: 2582ft/787m, Tel: 865-436-1200, Nearest town: Bryson City. GPS: 35.509081, -83.400721

26 • B1 | Great Smoky Mountains NP - Georges Branch

Dispersed sites, No water, No toilets, Tents only: $4, Hike-in, Stay limit: 14 days, Reservations required, Elev: 2736ft/834m, Tel: 865-436-1200, Nearest town: Bryson City. GPS: 35.503783, -83.394357

27 • B1 | Great Smoky Mountains NP - Goldmine Branch

Dispersed sites, No water, No toilets, Tents only: $4, Hike-in, Stay limit: 14 days, Reservations required, Elev: 1948ft/594m, Tel: 865-436-1200, Nearest town: Bryson City. GPS: 35.455152, -83.551415

28 • B1 | Great Smoky Mountains NP - Huggins

Dispersed sites, No water, No toilets, Tents only: $4, Hike-in, Stay limit: 14 days, Reservations required, Elev: 2785ft/849m, Tel: 865-436-1200, Nearest town: Bryson City. GPS: 35.523791, -83.539567

29 • B1 | Great Smoky Mountains NP - Jerry Flats

Dispersed sites, No water, No toilets, Tents only: $4, Hike-in, Stay limit: 14 days, Reservations required, Elev: 2883ft/879m, Tel: 865-436-1200, Nearest town: Bryson City. GPS: 35.503868, -83.490887

30 • B1 | Great Smoky Mountains NP - Jonas Creek

Dispersed sites, No water, No toilets, Tents only: $4, Hike-in, Stay limit: 14 days, Reservations required, Elev: 2413ft/735m, Tel: 865-436-1200, Nearest town: Bryson City. GPS: 35.513687, -83.557595

31 • B1 | Great Smoky Mountains NP - Kephart Shelter

Dispersed sites, No water, No toilets, Tents only: $4, Hike-in, Stay limit: 14 days, Reservations required, Elev: 3596ft/1096m, Tel: 865-436-1200, Nearest town: Cherokee. GPS: 35.610195, -83.368654

32 • B1 | Great Smoky Mountains NP - Kirkland Creek

Dispersed sites, No water, No toilets, Tents only: $4, Hike-in, Stay limit: 14 days, Reservations required, Elev: 1787ft/545m, Tel: 865-436-1200, Nearest town: Bryson City. GPS: 35.447761, -83.635863

33 • B1 | Great Smoky Mountains NP - Laurel Gap Shelter

Dispersed sites, No water, No toilets, Hike-to shelter: $4, Stay limit: 14 days, Reservations required, Elev: 5462ft/1665m, Tel: 865-436-1200, Nearest town: Waterville. GPS: 35.665498, -83.187727

34 • B1 | Great Smoky Mountains NP - Lost Cove

Dispersed sites, No water, No toilets, Tents only: $4, Hike-in, Stay limit: 14 days, Reservations required, Elev: 1717ft/523m, Tel: 865-436-1200, Nearest town: Fontana Village. GPS: 35.483878, -83.776485

35 • B1 | Great Smoky Mountains NP - Lower Chasteen Creek

Dispersed sites, No water, No toilets, Tents only: $4, Hike-in, Stay limit: 14 days, Reservations required, Elev: 2391ft/729m, Tel: 865-436-1200, Nearest town: Cherokee. GPS: 35.577171, -83.312603

36 • B1 | Great Smoky Mountains NP - Lower Ekaneetlee

Dispersed sites, No water, No toilets, Tents only: $4, Hike-in, Stay limit: 14 days, Reservations required, Elev: 1880ft/573m, Tel: 865-436-1200, Nearest town: Fontana Village. GPS: 35.498654, -83.763803

37 • B1 | Great Smoky Mountains NP - Lower Forney

Dispersed sites, No water, No toilets, Tents only: $4, Hike-in, Stay limit: 14 days, Reservations required, Elev: 1780ft/543m, Tel: 865-436-1200, Nearest town: Bryson City. GPS: 35.467445, -83.563719

38 • B1 | Great Smoky Mountains NP - Lower Walnut Bottom

Dispersed sites, No water, No toilets, Tents only: $4, Hike-in, Stay limit: 14 days, Reservations required, Elev: 3001ft/915m, Tel: 865-436-1200, Nearest town: Waterville. GPS: 35.718042, -83.165932

39 • B1 | Great Smoky Mountains NP - McCracken Branch

Dispersed sites, No water, No toilets, Tents only: $4, Hike-in, Stay limit: 14 days, Reservations required, Elev: 2217ft/676m, Tel: 865-436-1200, Nearest town: Bryson City. GPS: 35.507991, -83.430738

40 • B1 | Great Smoky Mountains NP - McGee Spring

Dispersed sites, No water, No toilets, Tents only: $4, Hike-in, Stay limit: 14 days, Reservations required, Elev: 5032ft/1534m, Tel: 865-436-1200, Nearest town: Maggie Valley. GPS: 35.639545, -83.239816

41 • B1 | Great Smoky Mountains NP - Mill Creek

Dispersed sites, No water, No toilets, Tents only: $4, Hike-in, Stay limit: 14 days, Reservations required, Elev: 2552ft/778m, Tel: 865-436-1200, Nearest town: Bryson City. GPS: 35.497826, -83.501458

42 • B1 | Great Smoky Mountains NP - Mt Sterling

Dispersed sites, No water, No toilets, Tents only: $4, Hike-in, Stay limit: 14 days, Reservations required, Elev: 5820ft/1774m, Tel: 865-436-1200, Nearest town: Waterville. GPS: 35.702203, -83.122473

43 • B1 | Great Smoky Mountains NP - Nettle Creek

Dispersed sites, No water, No toilets, Tents only: $4, Hike-in, Stay limit: 14 days, Reservations required, Elev: 2697ft/822m, Tel: 865-436-1200, Nearest town: Bryson City. GPS: 35.539886, -83.414789

44 • B1 | Great Smoky Mountains NP - Newton Bald

Dispersed sites, No water, No toilets, Tents only: $4, Hike-in, Stay limit: 14 days, Reservations required, Elev: 4867ft/1483m, Tel: 865-436-1200, Nearest town: Bryson City. GPS: 35.543003, -83.366969

45 • B1 | Great Smoky Mountains NP - Nicks Nest Branch

Dispersed sites, No water, No toilets, Tents only: $4, Hike-in, Stay limit: 14 days, Reservations required, Elev: 2331ft/710m, Tel: 865-436-1200, Nearest town: Bryson City. GPS: 35.515161, -83.423935

46 • B1 | Great Smoky Mountains NP - North Shore

Dispersed sites, No water, No toilets, Tents only: $4, Hike-in, Stay limit: 14 days, Reservations required, Elev: 1791ft/546m, Tel: 865-436-1200, Nearest town: Fontana Village. GPS: 35.449905, -83.703143

47 • B1 | Great Smoky Mountains NP - Pilkey Creek

Dispersed sites, No water, No toilets, Tents only: $4, Hike-in, Stay limit: 14 days, Reservations required, Elev: 1831ft/558m, Tel: 865-436-1200, Nearest town: Bryson City. GPS: 35.446206, -83.670431

48 • B1 | Great Smoky Mountains NP - Poke Patch

Dispersed sites, No water, No toilets, Tents only: $4, Hike-in, Stay limit: 14 days, Reservations required, Elev: 3036ft/925m, Tel: 865-436-1200, Nearest town: Bryson City. GPS: 35.561055, -83.420587

49 • B1 | Great Smoky Mountains NP - Pole Road

Dispersed sites, No water, No toilets, Tents only: $4, Hike-in, Stay limit: 14 days, Reservations required, Elev: 2470ft/753m, Tel: 865-436-1200, Nearest town: Bryson City. GPS: 35.530683, -83.421807

50 • B1 | Great Smoky Mountains NP - Poplar Flats

Dispersed sites, No water, No toilets, Tents only: $4, Hike-in, Stay limit: 14 days, Reservations required, Elev: 2954ft/900m, Tel: 865-436-1200, Nearest town: Bryson City. GPS: 35.486712, -83.590572

51 • B1 | Great Smoky Mountains NP - Possum Hollow

Dispersed sites, No water, No toilets, Tents only: $4, Hike-in, Stay limit: 14 days, Reservations required, Elev: 1960ft/597m, Tel: 865-436-1200, Nearest town: Fontana Village. GPS: 35.476172, -83.734689

52 • B1 | Great Smoky Mountains NP - Pretty Hollow

Dispersed sites, No water, No toilets, Tents only: $4, Hike-in, Stay limit: 14 days, Reservations required, Elev: 3025ft/922m, Tel: 865-436-1200, Nearest town: Maggie Valley. GPS: 35.640459, -83.127854

53 • B1 | Great Smoky Mountains NP - Proctor

Dispersed sites, No water, No toilets, Tents only: $4, Hike-in, Stay limit: 14 days, Reservations required, Elev: 1680ft/512m, Tel: 865-436-1200, Nearest town: Fontana Village. GPS: 35.472053, -83.726485

54 • B1 | Great Smoky Mountains NP - Round Bottom Horse Camp

Total sites: 5, RV sites: 5, No water, Vault/pit toilet, Tent & RV camping: $23, Stay limit: 14 days, Generator hours: 0800-2000, Open Apr-Oct, Max Length: 35ft, Reservations required, Elev: 3163ft/964m, Tel: 865-436-1261, Nearest town: Cherokee. GPS: 35.617978, -83.209734

55 • B1 | Great Smoky Mountains NP - Sawdust Pile

Dispersed sites, No water, No toilets, Tents only: $4, Hike-in, Stay limit: 14 days, Reservations required, Elev: 2232ft/680m, Tel: 865-436-1200, Nearest town: Fontana Village. GPS: 35.483717, -83.696417

56 • B1 | Great Smoky Mountains NP - Smokemont

Total sites: 142, RV sites: 142, Water available, Flush toilet, No showers, RV dump, Tent & RV camping: $25, Nov-Dec $17, Stay limit: 14 days, Generator hours: 0800-2000, Open all year, Max Length: Trlrs-35'/RV's-40ft, Reservations required, Elev: 2467ft/752m, Tel: 828-497-9270, Nearest town: Bryson City. GPS: 35.553467, -83.308594

57 • B1 | Great Smoky Mountains NP - Spruce Mt

Dispersed sites, No water, No toilets, Tents only: $4, Hike-in, Stay limit: 14 days, Reservations required, Elev: 5432ft/1656m, Tel: 865-436-1200, Nearest town: Maggie Valley. GPS: 35.606356, -83.179314

58 • B1 | Great Smoky Mountains NP - Steeltrap

Dispersed sites, No water, No toilets, Tents only: $4, Hike-in, Stay limit: 14 days, Reservations required, Elev: 3961ft/1207m, Tel: 865-436-1200, Nearest town: Bryson City. GPS: 35.540608, -83.514781

59 • B1 | Great Smoky Mountains NP - Sugar Fork

Dispersed sites, No water, No toilets, Tents only: $4, Hike-in, Stay limit: 14 days, Reservations required, Elev: 2180ft/664m, Tel: 865-436-1200, Nearest town: Fontana Village. GPS: 35.494704, -83.688334

60 • B1 | Great Smoky Mountains NP - Tow String Horse Camp

Total sites: 2, RV sites: 2, No water, Vault/pit toilet, Tent & RV camping: $23, Must have horse, Stay limit: 14 days, Generator hours: 0800-2000, Open Apr-Oct, Max Length: 35ft, Reservations required, Elev: 2238ft/682m, Tel: 865-436-1261, Nearest town: Cherokee. GPS: 35.540811, -83.297871

61 • B1 | Great Smoky Mountains NP - Twentymile Creek

Dispersed sites, No water, No toilets, Tents only: $4, Hike-in, Stay limit: 14 days, Reservations required, Elev: 2011ft/613m, Tel: 865-436-1200, Nearest town: Fontana Village. GPS: 35.473466, -83.855559

62 • B1 | Great Smoky Mountains NP - Upper Chasteen

Dispersed sites, No water, No toilets, Tents only: $4, Hike-in, Stay limit: 14 days, Reservations required, Elev: 3598ft/1097m, Tel: 865-436-1200, Nearest town: Cherokee. GPS: 35.597882, -83.294858

63 • B1 | Great Smoky Mountains NP - Upper Flats

Dispersed sites, No water, No toilets, Tents only: $4, Hike-in, Stay limit: 14 days, Reservations required, Elev: 2495ft/760m, Tel: 865-436-1200, Nearest town: Fontana Village. GPS: 35.496292, -83.832969

64 • B1 | Great Smoky Mountains NP - Upper Lost Cove

Dispersed sites, No water, No toilets, Tents only: $4, Hike-in, Stay limit: 14 days, Reservations required, Elev: 2269ft/692m, Tel: 865-436-1200, Nearest town: Fontana Village. GPS: 35.491599, -83.795157

65 • B1 | Great Smoky Mountains NP - Upper Ripshin

Dispersed sites, No water, No toilets, Tents only: $4, Hike-in, Stay limit: 14 days, Reservations required, Elev: 3231ft/985m, Tel: 865-436-1200, Nearest town: Bryson City. GPS: 35.514663, -83.464963

66 • B1 | Great Smoky Mountains NP - Upper Walnut Bottom

Dispersed sites, No water, No toilets, Tents only: $4, Hike-in, Stay limit: 14 days, Reservations required, Elev: 3040ft/927m, Tel: 865-436-1200, Nearest town: Waterville. GPS: 35.715886, -83.164435

67 • B2 | Blue Ridge Pkwy - Basin Cove TC

Total sites: 8, Tents only: Free, Hike-in, Permit required, Open all year, Elev: 1549ft/472m, Tel: 336-372-8877. GPS: 36.389053, -81.161468

68 • B2 | Blue Ridge Pkwy - Crabtree Falls

Total sites: 81, RV sites: 22, Central water, Flush toilet, No showers, RV dump, Tent & RV camping: $20, Stay limit: 30 days, Generator hours: 0800-2100, Open May-Oct, Reservations accepted, Elev: 3789ft/1155m, Tel: 828-348-3400, Nearest town: Little Switzerland. GPS: 35.814824, -82.145713

69 • B2 | Blue Ridge Pkwy - Doughton Park

Total sites: 135, RV sites: 25, Central water, Flush toilet, No showers, RV dump, Tent & RV camping: $20, 3 group sites: $35, Stay limit: 30 days, Generator hours: 0800-2100, Open May-Oct, Max Length: 88ft, Reservations accepted, Elev: 3645ft/1111m, Tel: 828-348-3400, Nearest town: Laurel Springs. GPS: 36.429342, -81.155658

70 • B2 | Blue Ridge Pkwy - Julian Price

Total sites: 163, RV sites: 90, Central water, Flush toilet, Free showers, RV dump, Tent & RV camping: $20, Stay limit: 30 days, Generator hours: 0800-2100, Open Apr-Nov, Reservations accepted, Elev: 3468ft/1057m, Tel: 828-963-5911, Nearest town: Blowing Rock. GPS: 36.138968, -81.735816

71 • B2 | Blue Ridge Pkwy - Linville Falls

Total sites: 64, RV sites: 52, Central water, Flush toilet, No showers, RV dump, Tent & RV camping: $20, 2 group sites: $35, Stay limit: 30 days, Generator hours: 0800-2100, Open Apr-Oct, Max Length: 50ft, Reservations accepted, Elev: 3281ft/1000m, Tel: 828-765-7818, Nearest town: Linville Falls. GPS: 35.967205, -81.932857

72 • B5 | Cape Hatteras NS - Oregon Inlet CG

Total sites: 120, RV sites: 120, Elec sites: 47, Water at site, Flush toilet, Free showers, RV dump, Tents: $28/RV's: $28-35, Group site: $70, Solar-heated showers, Generator hours: 0700-2100, Open all year, Max Length: 35ft, Reservations accepted, Elev: 10ft/3m, Tel: 252-441-6246. GPS: 35.79964, -75.54411

73 • C1 | Blue Ridge Pkwy - Mount Pisgah

Total sites: 124, RV sites: 62, Central water, Flush toilet, Free showers, RV dump, Tent & RV camping: $20, Stay limit: 30 days, Generator hours: 0800-2100, Open Apr-Oct, Max Length: 70ft, Reservations accepted, Elev: 4866ft/1483m, Tel: 828-648-2644, Nearest town: Brevard. GPS: 35.403977, -82.757233

74 • C5 | Cape Hatteras NS - Cape Point CG

Total sites: 202, RV sites: 202, Central water, Flush toilet, Free showers, No RV dump, Tent & RV camping: $20, Cold showers, Generator hours: 0700-2100, Open Apr-Nov, Max Length: 35ft, Reservations accepted, Elev: 7ft/2m, Tel: 252-465-9602. GPS: 35.23564, -75.5391

75 • C5 | Cape Hatteras NS - Frisco CG

Total sites: 127, Central water, Flush toilet, Free showers, No RV dump, Tent & RV camping: $28, Cold showers, Generator hours: 0700-2100, Open Apr-Nov, Max Length: 35ft, Reservations accepted, Elev: 33ft/10m, Tel: 252-995-5101. GPS: 35.2367, -75.60414

76 • C5 | Cape Hatteras NS - Ocracoke CG

Total sites: 136, RV sites: 136, Central water, Flush toilet, Free showers, RV dump, Tent & RV camping: $28, Cold showers, Generator hours: 0700-2100, Open all year, Max Length: 35ft, Reservations accepted, Elev: 13ft/4m, Tel: 252-928-6671. GPS: 35.126226, -75.919764

North Dakota

MINNESOTA

MANITOBA

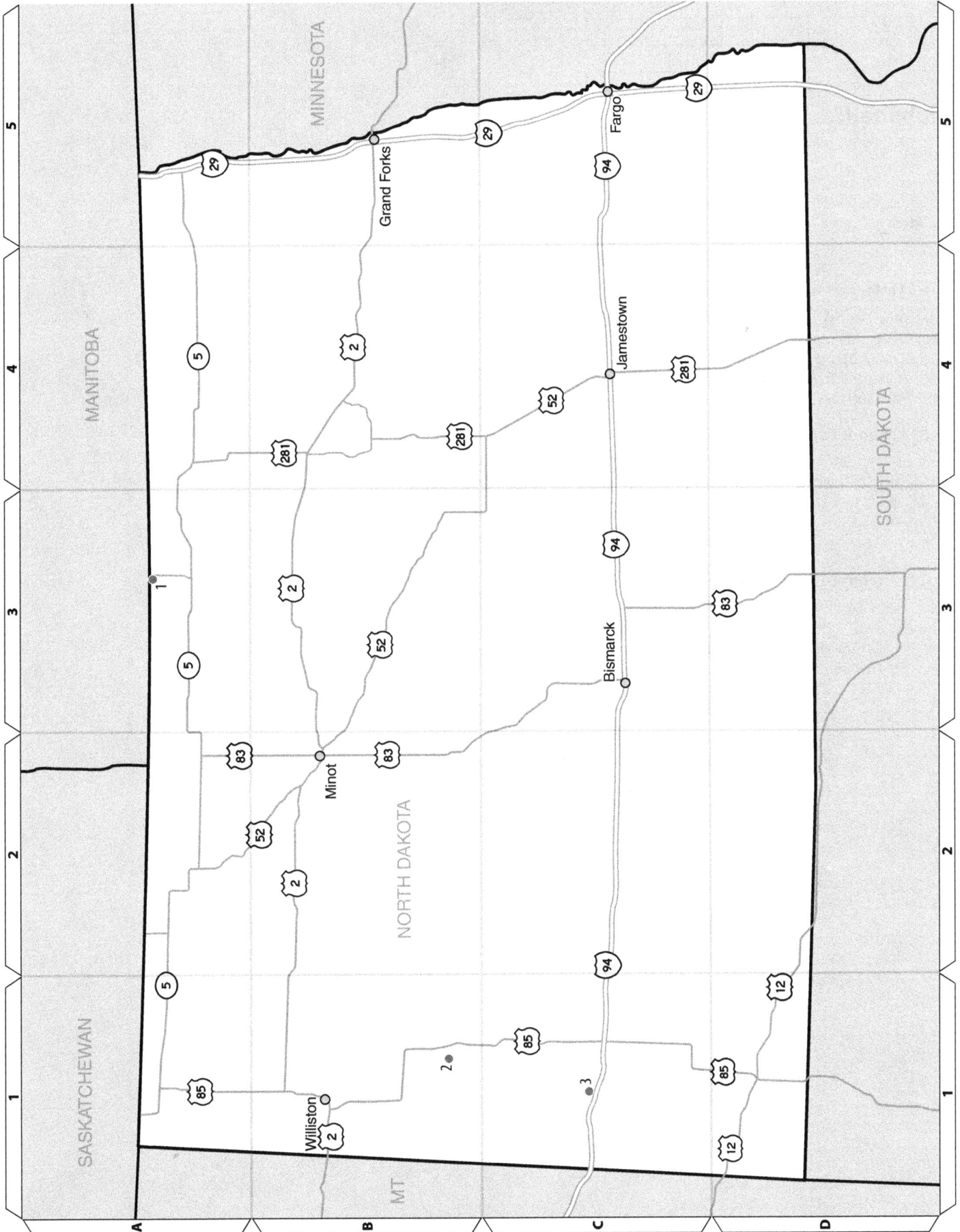

SASKATCHEWAN

SOUTH DAKOTA

NORTH DAKOTA

MT

Grand Forks

Fargo

Jamestown

Bismarck

Minot

Williston

29
29
29
94
5
2
281
52
281
5
2
52
94
83
83
83
5
52
2
94
12
85
85
85
12
2
1
1
2
3

A   B   C   D

Map	ID	Map	ID
A3	1	C1	3
B1	2		

Alphabetical List of Camping Areas

Name	ID	Map
International Peace Garden	1	A3
Theodore Roosevelt NP - Cottonwood CG	3	C1
Theodore Roosevelt NP - Juniper CG	2	B1

1 • A3 | International Peace Garden

Total sites: 36, RV sites: 36, Elec sites: 29, Water at site, Flush toilet, Free showers, RV dump, Tent & RV camping: $25-30, 20 Full hookups, Open May-Sep, Reservations accepted, Elev: 2293ft/699m, Tel: 701-263-4390, Nearest town: Dunseith. GPS: 48.98756, -100.06621

2 • B1 | Theodore Roosevelt NP - Juniper CG

Total sites: 50, RV sites: 50, Central water, No toilets, No showers, RV dump, Tent & RV camping: $14, $7 - no water in winter, Group site $30, Open all year, Reservations not accepted, Elev: 1959ft/597m, Tel: 701-842-6828, Nearest town: Watford City. GPS: 47.59497, -103.33992

3 • C1 | Theodore Roosevelt NP - Cottonwood CG

Total sites: 76, RV sites: 64, Central water, Flush toilet, No showers, No RV dump, Tent & RV camping: $14, $7 - no water Oct-Apr, Group site $30, Open all year, Reservations accepted, Elev: 2251ft/686m, Tel: 701-623-4466, Nearest town: Medora. GPS: 46.950439, -103.53125

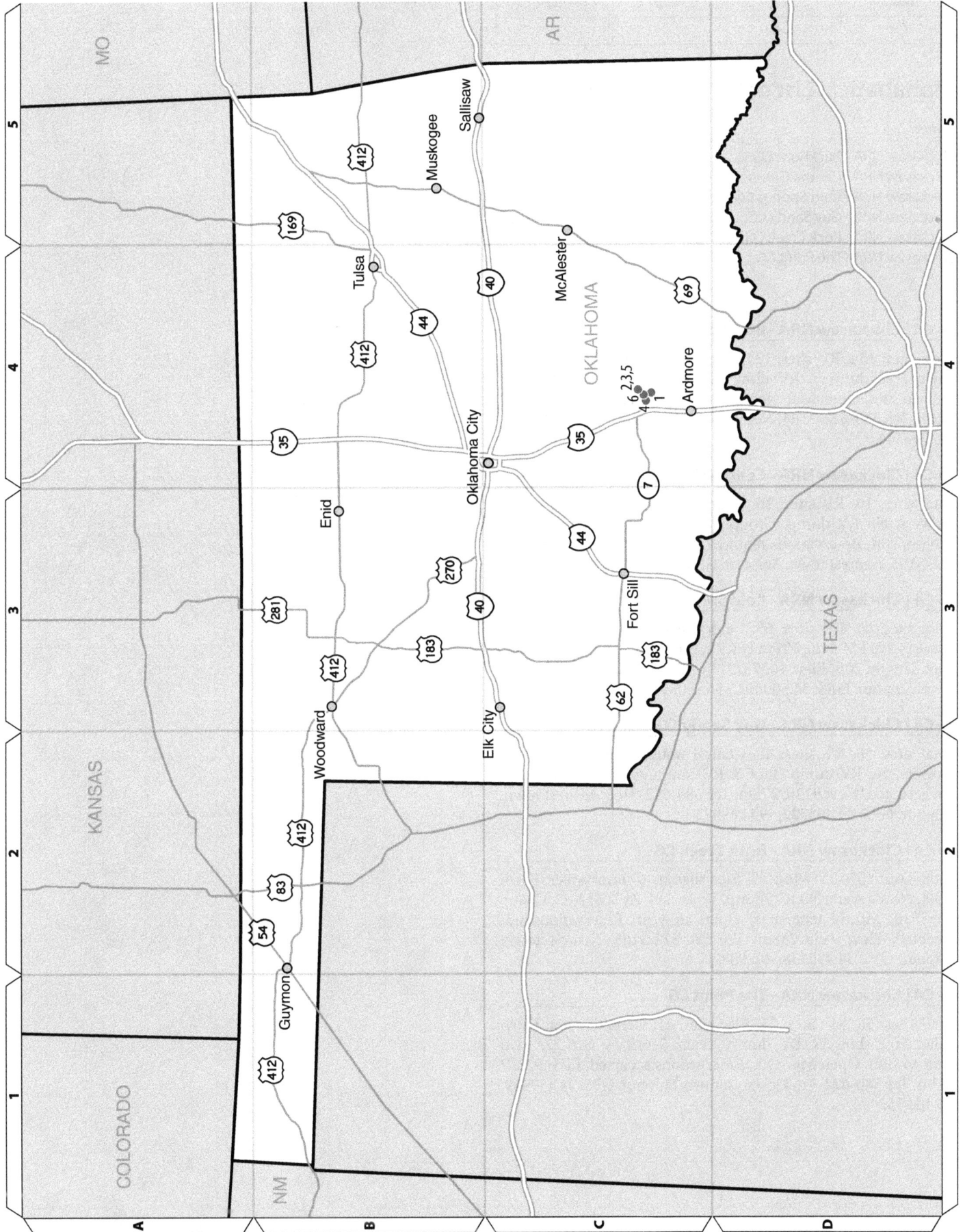

Oklahoma

MO

AR

KANSAS

COLORADO

NM

TEXAS

OKLAHOMA

Sallisaw

Muskogee

McAlester

Tulsa

Oklahoma City

Enid

Ardmore

Fort Sill

Woodward

Elk City

Guymon

412

169

40

44

412

35

35

7

44

270

281

40

183

183

412

62

412

83

54

412

69

6 2,3,5
4 1

A B C D

1 2 3 4 5

Map	ID	Map	ID
C4	1-6		

Alphabetical List of Camping Areas

Name	ID	Map
Chickasaw NRA - Buckhorn CG	1	C4
Chickasaw NRA - Central Group	2	C4
Chickasaw NRA - Cold Springs CG	3	C4
Chickasaw NRA - Guy Sandy CG	4	C4
Chickasaw NRA - Rock Creek CG	5	C4
Chickasaw NRA - The Point CG	6	C4

1 • C4 | Chickasaw NRA - Buckhorn CG

Total sites: 134, RV sites: 134, Elec sites: 41, Water at site, Flush toilet, Free showers, RV dump, Tents: $16/RV's: $16-24, Also walk-to sites, Open Mar-Nov, Reservations accepted, Elev: 958ft/292m, Tel: 580-622-3165, Nearest town: Sulphur. GPS: 34.432389, -96.996744

2 • C4 | Chickasaw NRA - Central Group

Total sites: 10, RV sites: 10, Central water, Vault/pit toilet, No showers, No RV dump, Group site: $30, Open May-Oct, Max Length: 20ft, Reservations required, Elev: 1001ft/305m, Tel: 580-622-3165, Nearest town: Sulphur. GPS: 34.505255, -96.967666

3 • C4 | Chickasaw NRA - Cold Springs CG

Total sites: 65, RV sites: 65, Central water, Vault/pit toilet, No showers, No RV dump, Tent & RV camping: $14, Group site: $30, Max Length: 20ft, Elev: 1027ft/313m, Tel: 580-622-3165, Nearest town: Sulphur. GPS: 34.500852, -96.960391

4 • C4 | Chickasaw NRA - Guy Sandy CG

Total sites: 58, RV sites: 40, Central water, Vault/pit toilet, No showers, No RV dump, Tent & RV camping: $14, Reservations not accepted, Elev: 912ft/278m, Tel: 580-622-3165, Nearest town: Sulphur. GPS: 34.455322, -97.049072

5 • C4 | Chickasaw NRA - Rock Creek CG

Total sites: 105, RV sites: 35, Elec sites: 1, Central water, Flush toilet, No showers, No RV dump, Tents: $14/RV's: $14-22, Group site: $30, Mostly tent sites, Open all year, Reservations not accepted, Elev: 945ft/288m, Tel: 580-622-3165, Nearest town: Sulphur. GPS: 34.496338, -96.98877

6 • C4 | Chickasaw NRA - The Point CG

Total sites: 58, RV sites: 21, Elec sites: 21, Central water, Flush toilet, Free showers, RV dump, Tents: $16/RV's: $16-22, Also walk-to sites, Open Mar-Oct, Reservations accepted, Elev: 928ft/283m, Tel: 580-622-3165, Nearest town: Sulphur. GPS: 34.459969, -97.020353

Oregon

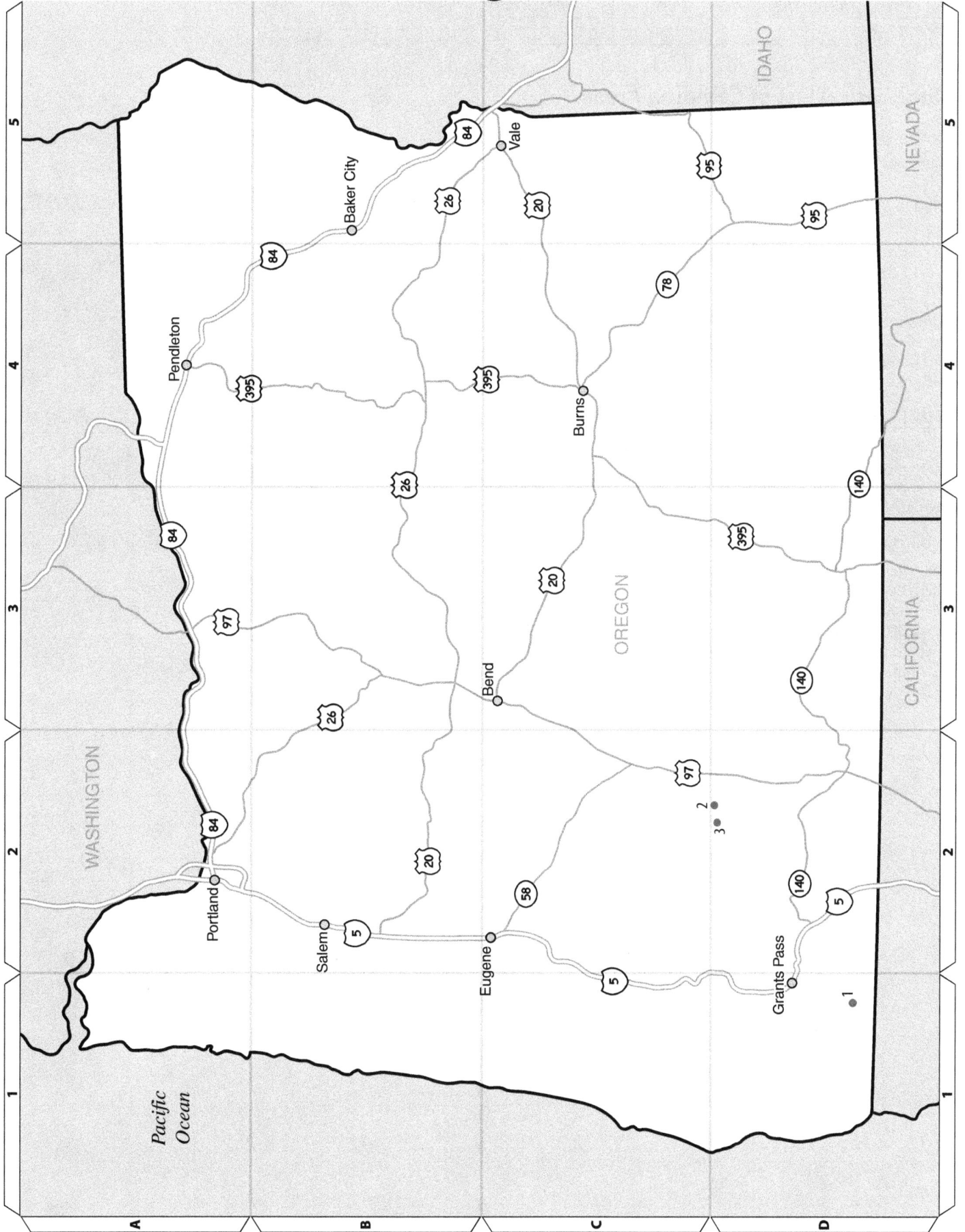

WASHINGTON

IDAHO

NEVADA

CALIFORNIA

OREGON

Pacific Ocean

Vale

Baker City

Pendleton

Burns

Bend

Portland

Salem

Eugene

Grants Pass

84 · 26 · 20 · 95 · 95 · 78 · 84 · 395 · 395 · 140 · 26 · 395 · 20 · 97 · 140 · 84 · 26 · 58 · 20 · 140 · 5 · 5 · 97 · 5

2
3

1

5 4 3 2 1

A B C D

Map	ID	Map	ID
D1	1	D2	2-3

Alphabetical List of Camping Areas

Name	ID	Map
Crater Lake NP - Lost Creek	2	D2
Crater Lake NP - Mazama	3	D2
Oregon Caves NM - Cave Creek	1	D1

1 • D1 | Oregon Caves NM - Cave Creek

Total sites: 17, RV sites: 17, Central water, Vault/pit toilet, No showers, No RV dump, Tent & RV camping: $10, Stay limit: 14 days, Generator hours: 0800-2200, Open May-Sep, Max Length: 16ft, Reservations not accepted, Elev: 3012ft/918m, Tel: 541-592-2100, Nearest town: Cave Junction. GPS: 42.11792, -123.435791

2 • D2 | Crater Lake NP - Lost Creek

Total sites: 16, RV sites: 0, Central water, Flush toilet, No RV dump, Tents only: $5, Stay limit: 14 days, Open Jun-Oct, Reservations not accepted, Elev: 5938ft/1810m, Tel: 541-594-3000, Nearest town: Chemult. GPS: 42.879145, -122.037881

3 • D2 | Crater Lake NP - Mazama

Total sites: 214, RV sites: 214, Elec sites: 15, Water at site, Flush toilet, Pay showers, RV dump, Tents: $21/RV's: $31-43, Some Full hookups, Concessionaire, Stay limit: 14 days, Generator hours: 0800-2000, Open Jun-Sep, Max Length: 50ft, Reservations accepted, Elev: 6050ft/1844m, Tel: 541-594-3000, Nearest town: Chemult. GPS: 42.865508, -122.166149

Pennsylvania

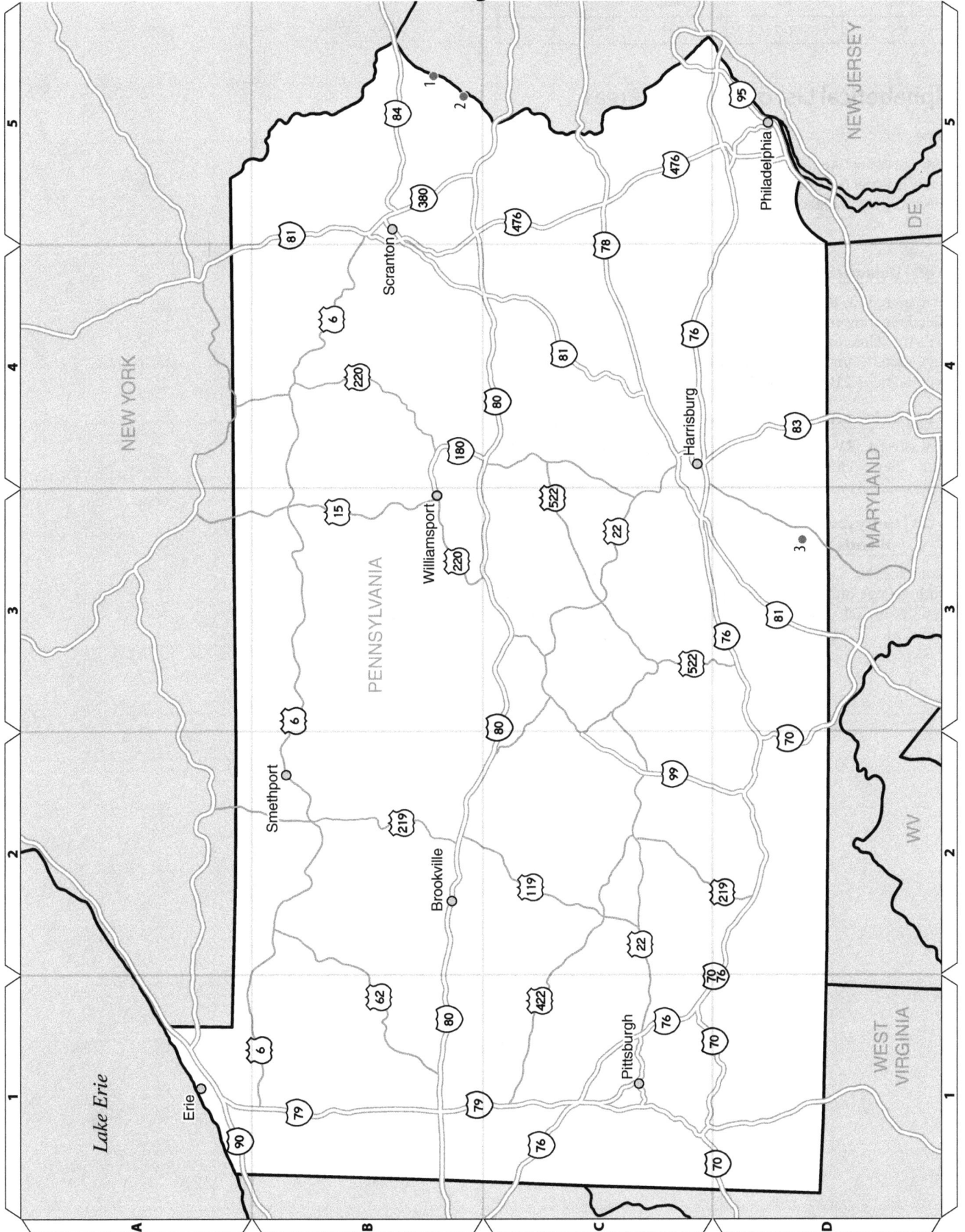

NEW JERSEY

DE

NEW YORK

MARYLAND

WV

WEST VIRGINIA

PENNSYLVANIA

Lake Erie

Philadelphia

Scranton

Harrisburg

Williamsport

Smethport

Brookville

Erie

Pittsburgh

95

84

380

81

476

476

78

76

6

220

81

80

83

180

15

522

22

3

220

81

76

6

522

80

70

219

99

119

219

62

22

80

422

70
76

6

79

80

76

79

76

70

90

Map	ID	Map	ID
B5	1-2	D3	3

Alphabetical List of Camping Areas

Name	ID	Map
Delaware Water Gap NRA - Dingmans CG	1	B5
Delaware Water Gap NRA - Valley View Group	2	B5
Gettysburg Nat'l Military Park - McMillan Woods Youth CG	3	D3

1 • B5 | Delaware Water Gap NRA - Dingmans CG

Total sites: 133, RV sites: 50, Elec sites: 39, Water at site, Flush toilet, Free showers, RV dump, Tents: $40-55/RV's: $42-44, Group site: $160, Concessionaire, Open all year, Reservations accepted, Elev: 436ft/133m, Tel: 570-828-1551, Nearest town: Dingman's Ferry. GPS: 41.210606, -74.871664

2 • B5 | Delaware Water Gap NRA - Valley View Group

Total sites: 1, RV sites: 0, No water, Vault/pit toilet, Group site: $160, Elev: 330ft/101m, Tel: 570-828-2253, Nearest town: Dingman's Ferry. GPS: 41.102986, -74.987434

3 • D3 | Gettysburg National Military Park - McMillan Woods Youth CG

Total sites: 10, Central water, Vault/pit toilet, Group site: Free, Youth groups only, Open Apr-Oct, Reservations required, Elev: 542ft/165m, Tel: 717-334-0909, Nearest town: Gettysburg. GPS: 39.821721, -77.248992

South Carolina

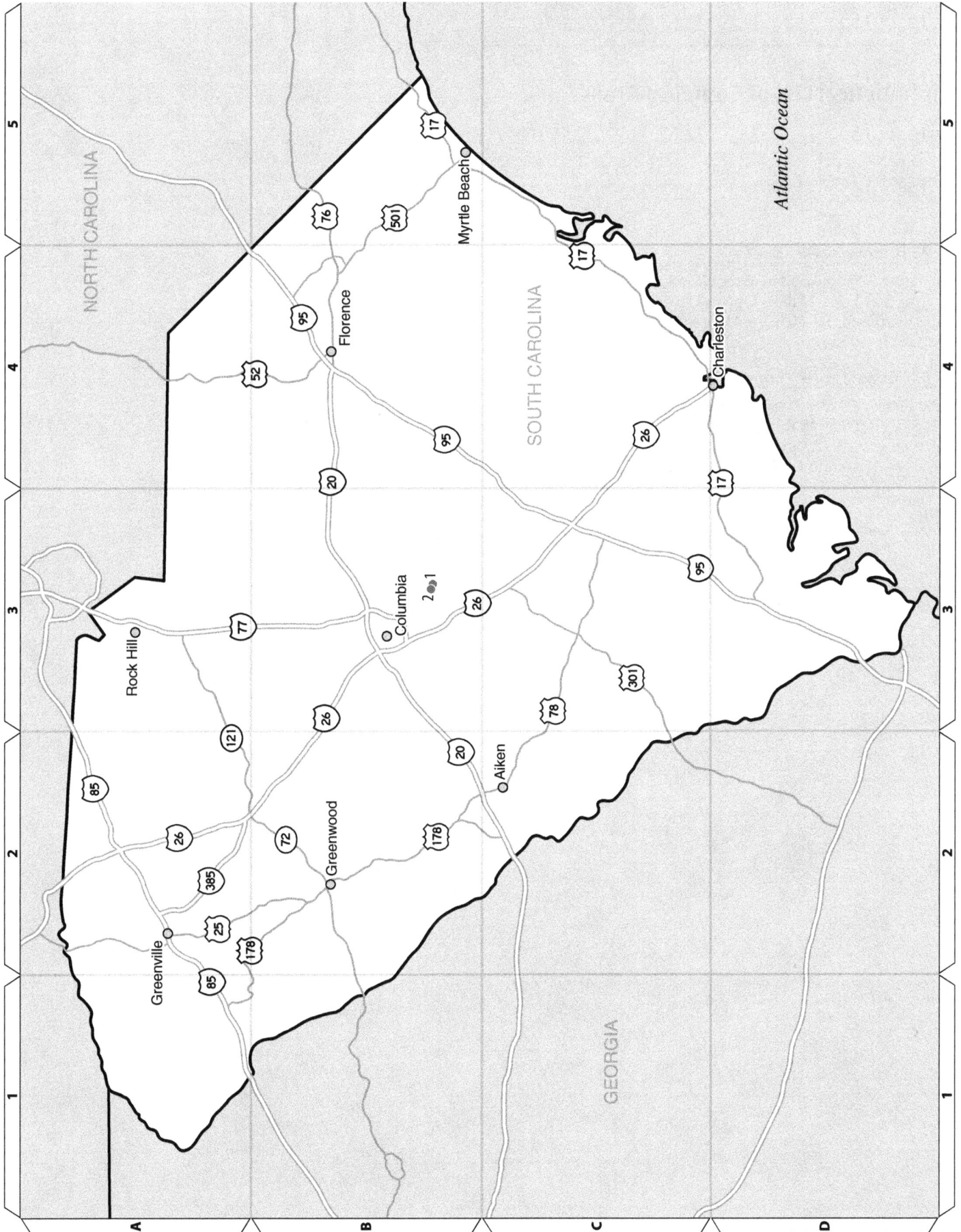

NORTH CAROLINA

Atlantic Ocean

SOUTH CAROLINA

GEORGIA

17

76

501

Myrtle Beach

17

95

Florence

52

95

17

20

26

Charleston

77

26

95

Columbia

2 1

301

Rock Hill

26

78

121

20

85

Aiken

26

72

Greenwood

178

385

25

178

85

Greenville

5 4 3 2 1

A B C D

Map	ID	Map	ID
B3	1-2		

Alphabetical List of Camping Areas

Name	ID	Map
Congaree NP - Bluff	1	B3
Congaree NP - Longleaf	2	B3

1 • B3 | Congaree NP - Bluff

Total sites: 6, RV sites: 0, No water, No toilets, Tents only: $5, Hike-in, 1 mi, Stay limit: 14 days, Open all year, Reservations required, Elev: 192ft/59m, Tel: 803-776-4396, Nearest town: Eastover. GPS: 33.832661, -80.813496

2 • B3 | Congaree NP - Longleaf

Total sites: 8, RV sites: 0, No water, Vault/pit toilet, Tents only: $10, Walk-to sites, Stay limit: 14 days, Generator hours: 0800-2000, Open all year, Reservations required, Elev: 148ft/45m, Tel: 803-776-4396, Nearest town: Eastover. GPS: 33.835951, -80.827945

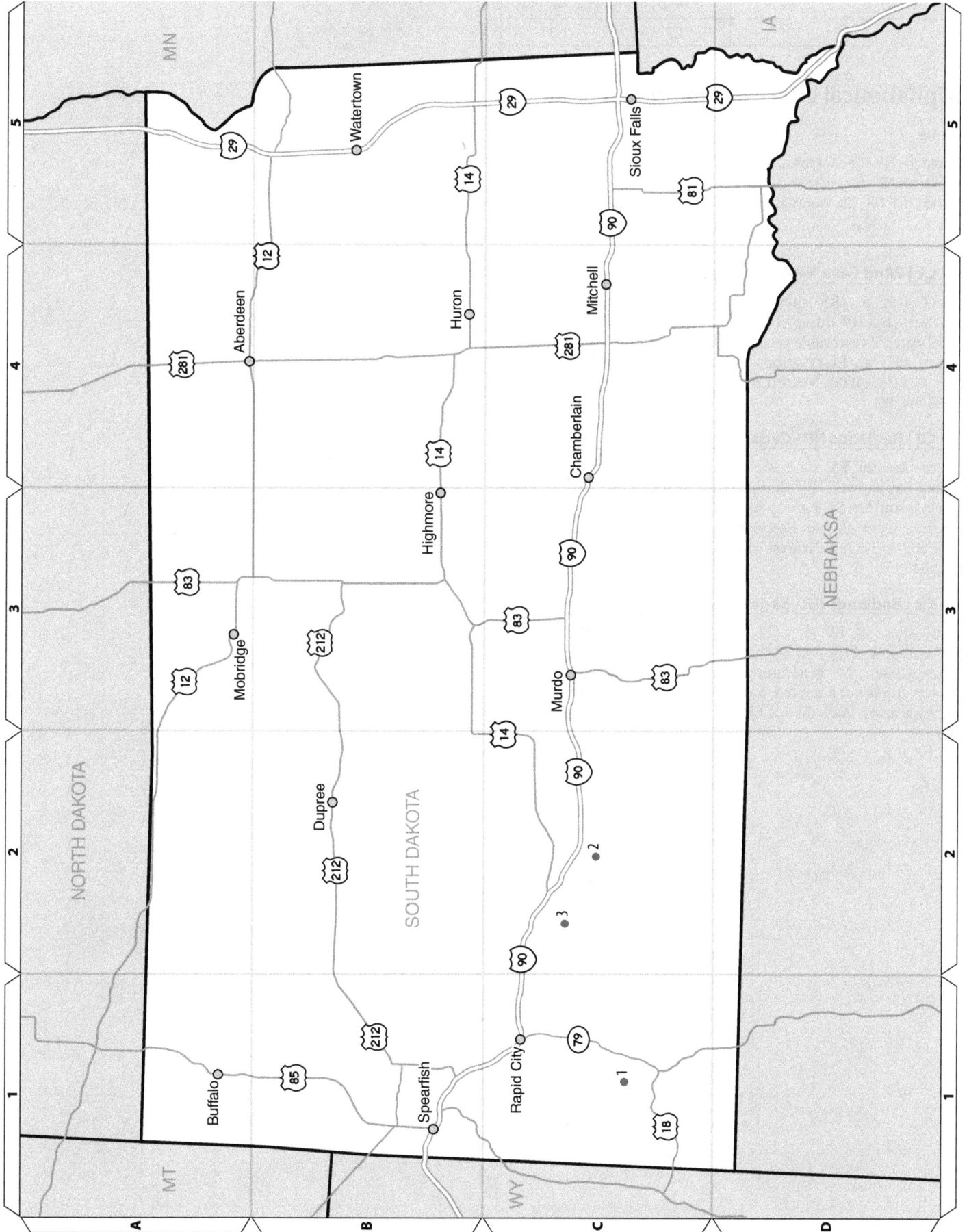

South Dakota

MN

IA

29

Watertown

29

29

Sioux Falls

14

81

90

12

Huron

Mitchell

Aberdeen

281

281

Chamberlain

14

Highmore

NEBRAKSA

83

90

Mobridge

212

83

Murdo

83

12

14

Dupree

90

SOUTH DAKOTA

212

● 2

● 3

NORTH DAKOTA

90

212

79

Buffalo

85

Spearfish

Rapid City

● 1

18

MT

WY

A

B

C

D

Map	ID	Map	ID
C1	1	C2	2-3

Alphabetical List of Camping Areas

Name	ID	Map
Badlands NP - Cedar Pass	2	C2
Badlands NP - Sage Creek	3	C2
Wind Cave NP - Elk Mountain	1	C1

1 • C1 | Wind Cave NP - Elk Mountain

Total sites: 61, RV sites: 48, Central water, Flush toilet, No showers, No RV dump, Tent & RV camping: $18, $9 in winter - no water, 2 reservable group sites, Generator hours: 0800-2000, Open all year, Reservations not accepted, Elev: 4268ft/1301m, Tel: 605-745-4600, Nearest town: Hot Springs. GPS: 43.565467, -103.490381

2 • C2 | Badlands NP - Cedar Pass

Total sites: 96, RV sites: 96, Elec sites: 25, Central water, Flush toilet, Pay showers, RV dump, Tents: $22/RV's: $22-37, No open fires. Dump fee: $1, 4 group sites - $3/person (Min $30), Stay limit: 14 days, Open all year, Reservations accepted, Elev: 2405ft/733m, Tel: 605-433-5361, Nearest town: Cottonwood. GPS: 43.74292, -101.949951

3 • C2 | Badlands NP - Sage Creek

Total sites: 18, RV sites: 11, No water, Vault/pit toilet, Tent & RV camping: Free, No open fires, No RVs or trailers except for horse trailers, No generators, Open all year, Max Length: 18ft, Reservations not accepted, Elev: 2539ft/774m, Tel: 605-433-5361, Nearest town: Wall. GPS: 43.894115, -102.414015

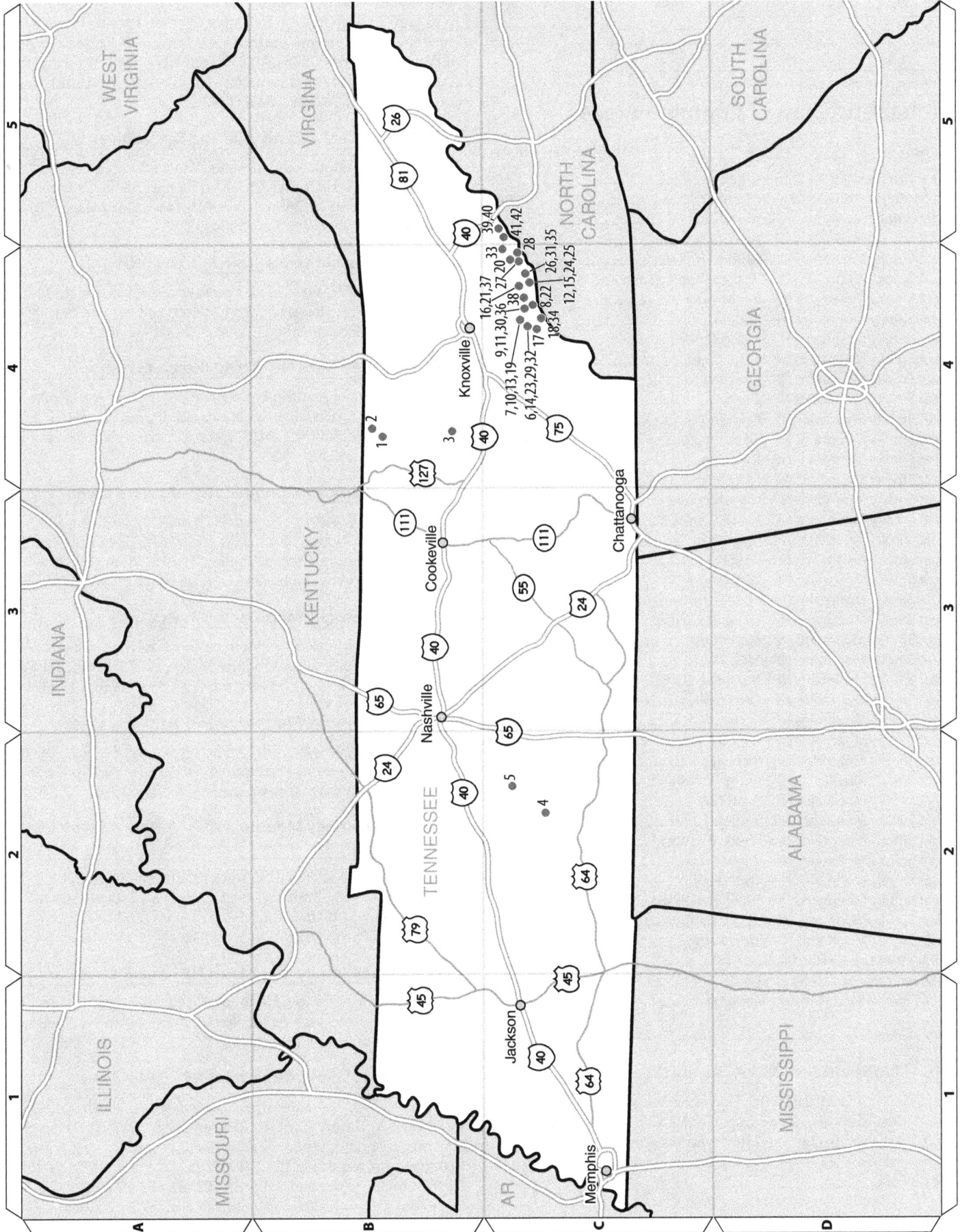

Tennessee

WEST VIRGINIA

VIRGINIA

SOUTH CAROLINA

NORTH CAROLINA

GEORGIA

KENTUCKY

INDIANA

ALABAMA

ILLINOIS

MISSOURI

AR

MISSISSIPPI

TENNESSEE

Knoxville

Cookeville

Chattanooga

Nashville

Jackson

Memphis

26

81

40

40

75

127

111

111

55

24

40

65

65

24

40

79

64

45

45

40

64

39,40
41,42
28
26,31,35
12,15,24,25
33
27,20
16,21,37
38
8,22
18,34
17
9,11,30,36
7,10,13,19
6,14,23,29,32

1 2
3
5
4

Map	ID	Map	ID
B4	1-3	C4	6-38
C2	4-5	C5	39-42

Alphabetical List of Camping Areas

Name	ID	Map
Big South Fork NRRA - Bandy Creek	1	B4
Big South Fork NRRA - Station Camp	2	B4
Great Smoky Mountains NP - Abrams Creek	6	C4
Great Smoky Mountains NP - Ace Gap	7	C4
Great Smoky Mountains NP - Anthony Creek	8	C4
Great Smoky Mountains NP - Anthony Creek Horse Camp	9	C4
Great Smoky Mountains NP - Beard Cane	10	C4
Great Smoky Mountains NP - Cades Cove	11	C4
Great Smoky Mountains NP - Camp Creek	12	C4
Great Smoky Mountains NP - Cane Creek	13	C4
Great Smoky Mountains NP - Cooper Road	14	C4
Great Smoky Mountains NP - Cosby	39	C5
Great Smoky Mountains NP - Dripping Spring Mt	15	C4
Great Smoky Mountains NP - Elkmont	16	C4
Great Smoky Mountains NP - Flint Gap	17	C4
Great Smoky Mountains NP - Forge Creek	18	C4
Great Smoky Mountains NP - Gilliland Creek	40	C5
Great Smoky Mountains NP - Hesse Creek	19	C4
Great Smoky Mountains NP - Injun Creek	20	C4
Great Smoky Mountains NP - King Branch	21	C4
Great Smoky Mountains NP - Ledbetter Ridge	22	C4
Great Smoky Mountains NP - Little Bottoms	23	C4
Great Smoky Mountains NP - Lower Jakes Gap	24	C4
Great Smoky Mountains NP - Marks Cove	25	C4
Great Smoky Mountains NP - Mile 53	26	C4
Great Smoky Mountains NP - Mount Le Conte Shelter	27	C4
Great Smoky Mountains NP - Ottercreek	41	C5
Great Smoky Mountains NP - Porters Flat	28	C4
Great Smoky Mountains NP - Rabbit Creek	29	C4
Great Smoky Mountains NP - Rich Mt	30	C4
Great Smoky Mountains NP - Rough Creek	31	C4
Great Smoky Mountains NP - Scott Gap	32	C4
Great Smoky Mountains NP - Settlers Camp	33	C4
Great Smoky Mountains NP - Sheep Pen Gap	34	C4
Great Smoky Mountains NP - Sugar Cove	42	C5
Great Smoky Mountains NP - Three Forks	35	C4
Great Smoky Mountains NP - Turkeypen Ridge	36	C4
Great Smoky Mountains NP - Upper Henderson	37	C4
Great Smoky Mountains NP - West Prong	38	C4
Meriwether Lewis - Natchez Trace NP	4	C2
Natchez Trace NP - TN 50 Bicycle CG	5	C2
Rock Creek - Obed Wild and Scenic River	3	B4

1 • B4 | Big South Fork NRRA - Bandy Creek

Total sites: 145, RV sites: 96, Elec sites: 96, Water at site, Flush toilet, Free showers, RV dump, Tents: $20/RV's: $25-32, Stay limit: 14 days, Open all year, Reservations accepted, Elev: 1562ft/476m, Tel: 423-286-8368, Nearest town: Oneida. GPS: 36.48885, -84.69556

2 • B4 | Big South Fork NRRA - Station Camp

Total sites: 24, RV sites: 24, Elec sites: 24, Water at site, Flush toilet, Free showers, RV dump, Tent & RV camping: $28, Concessionaire, Generator hours: 0600-2200, Open Apr-Nov, Reservations accepted, Elev: 1476ft/450m, Tel: 931-319-6893, Nearest town: Oneida. GPS: 36.544982, -84.633797

3 • B4 | Rock Creek - Obed Wild and Scenic River

Total sites: 11, RV sites: 0, No water, Vault/pit toilet, No showers, No RV dump, Tents only: $10, Max Length: 20ft, Reservations accepted, Elev: 953ft/290m, Tel: 423-346-6294, Nearest town: Wartburg. GPS: 36.070675, -84.664393

4 • C2 | Meriwether Lewis - Natchez Trace NP

Total sites: 31, RV sites: 31, Central water, Flush toilet, Tent & RV camping: Free, Reservations not accepted, Elev: 928ft/283m, Nearest town: Hohenwald. GPS: 35.522461, -87.455374

5 • C2 | Natchez Trace NP - TN 50 Bicycle CG

Dispersed sites, No water, No toilets, Tents only: Free, Bike-in, Water nearby, Open all year, Reservations not accepted, Elev: 539ft/164m, Tel: 800-305-7417, Nearest town: Duck River. GPS: 35.721742, -87.262383

6 • C4 | Great Smoky Mountains NP - Abrams Creek

Total sites: 16, RV sites: 0, No toilets, Tents only: $18, Stay limit: 14 days, Generator hours: 0800-2000, Open May-Oct, Max Length: 12ft, Reservations not accepted, Elev: 1270ft/387m, Tel: 865-436-1200, Nearest town: Chilhowee. GPS: 35.611632, -83.933863

7 • C4 | Great Smoky Mountains NP - Ace Gap

Dispersed sites, No water, No toilets, Tents only: $4, Hike-in, Stay limit: 14 days, Reservations required, Elev: 1792ft/546m, Tel: 865-436-1200, Nearest town: Townsend. GPS: 35.671916, -83.832546

8 • C4 | Great Smoky Mountains NP - Anthony Creek

Dispersed sites, No water, No toilets, Tents only: $4, Hike-in, Stay limit: 14 days, Reservations required, Elev: 3059ft/932m, Tel: 865-436-1200, Nearest town: Townsend. GPS: 35.581566, -83.744261

9 • C4 | Great Smoky Mountains NP - Anthony Creek Horse Camp

Total sites: 3, RV sites: 3, No water, Vault/pit toilet, Tent & RV camping: $20, Stay limit: 14 days, Open Apr-Nov, Reservations required, Elev: 1961ft/598m, Tel: 865-436-1200, Nearest town: Townsend. GPS: 35.605263, -83.770932

10 • C4 | Great Smoky Mountains NP - Beard Cane

Dispersed sites, No water, No toilets, Tents only: $4, Hike-in, Stay limit: 14 days, Reservations required, Elev: 1624ft/495m, Tel: 865-436-1200, Nearest town: Maryville. GPS: 35.636078, -83.872293

11 • C4 | Great Smoky Mountains NP - Cades Cove

Total sites: 159, RV sites: 159, Central water, Flush toilet, No showers, RV dump, Tent & RV camping: $25, Nov-Dec $17, Stay limit: 14 days, Open all year, Max Length: RV-40'/Trlr-35ft, Reservations required, Elev: 1939ft/591m, Tel: 865-436-1200, Nearest town: Townsend. GPS: 35.602787, -83.775599

12 • C4 | Great Smoky Mountains NP - Camp Creek

Dispersed sites, No water, No toilets, Tents only: $4, Hike-in, Stay limit: 14 days, Reservations required, Elev: 3327ft/1014m, Tel: 865-436-1200, Nearest town: Gatlinburg. GPS: 35.599337, -83.567039

13 • C4 | Great Smoky Mountains NP - Cane Creek

Dispersed sites, No water, No toilets, Tents only: $4, Hike-in, Stay limit: 14 days, Reservations required, Elev: 1409ft/429m, Tel: 865-436-1200, Nearest town: Maryville. GPS: 35.647473, -83.891495

14 • C4 | Great Smoky Mountains NP - Cooper Road

Dispersed sites, No water, No toilets, Tents only: $4, Hike-in, Stay limit: 14 days, Reservations required, Elev: 1258ft/383m, Tel: 865-436-1200, Nearest town: Maryville. GPS: 35.620688, -83.920913

15 • C4 | Great Smoky Mountains NP - Dripping Spring Mt

Dispersed sites, No water, No toilets, Tents only: $4, Hike-in, Stay limit: 14 days, Reservations required, Elev: 4540ft/1384m, Tel: 865-436-1200, Nearest town: Gatlinburg. GPS: 35.609066, -83.591538

16 • C4 | Great Smoky Mountains NP - Elkmont

Total sites: 220, RV sites: 220, Water available, No toilets, No showers, No RV dump, Tent & RV camping: $25-27, Nov $17, Stay limit: 14 days, Generator hours: 0800-2000, Open Mar-Nov, Max Length: RV-35'/Trlr-32ft, Reservations accepted, Elev: 2182ft/665m, Tel: 865-430-5560, Nearest town: Gatlinburg. GPS: 35.657468, -83.582568

17 • C4 | Great Smoky Mountains NP - Flint Gap

Dispersed sites, No water, No toilets, Tents only: $4, Hike-in, Stay limit: 14 days, Reservations required, Elev: 2052ft/625m, Tel: 865-436-1200, Nearest town: Maryville. GPS: 35.566049, -83.925806

18 • C4 | Great Smoky Mountains NP - Forge Creek

Dispersed sites, No water, No toilets, Tents only: $4, Hike-in, Stay limit: 14 days, Reservations required, Elev: 2921ft/890m, Tel: 865-436-1200, Nearest town: Maryville. GPS: 35.543523, -83.836935

19 • C4 | Great Smoky Mountains NP - Hesse Creek

Dispersed sites, No water, No toilets, Tents only: $4, Hike-in, Stay limit: 14 days, Reservations required, Elev: 1706ft/520m, Tel: 865-436-1200, Nearest town: Maryville. GPS: 35.660534, -83.849453

20 • C4 | Great Smoky Mountains NP - Injun Creek

Dispersed sites, No water, No toilets, Tents only: $4, Hike-in, Stay limit: 14 days, Reservations required, Elev: 2293ft/699m, Tel: 865-436-1200, Nearest town: Pittman Center. GPS: 35.705239, -83.419719

21 • C4 | Great Smoky Mountains NP - King Branch

Dispersed sites, No water, No toilets, Tents only: $4, Hike-in, Stay limit: 14 days, Reservations required, Elev: 2493ft/760m, Tel: 865-436-1200, Nearest town: Weare Valley. GPS: 35.648706, -83.608669

22 • C4 | Great Smoky Mountains NP - Ledbetter Ridge

Dispersed sites, No water, No toilets, Tents only: $4, Hike-in, Stay limit: 14 days, Reservations required, Elev: 2783ft/848m, Tel: 865-436-1200, Nearest town: Townsend. GPS: 35.582008, -83.758707

23 • C4 | Great Smoky Mountains NP - Little Bottoms

Dispersed sites, No water, No toilets, Tents only: $4, Hike-in, Stay limit: 14 days, Reservations required, Elev: 1220ft/372m, Tel: 865-436-1200, Nearest town: Maryville. GPS: 35.613369, -83.905913

24 • C4 | Great Smoky Mountains NP - Lower Jakes Gap

Dispersed sites, No water, No toilets, Tents only: $4, Hike-in, Stay limit: 14 days, Reservations required, Elev: 3415ft/1041m, Tel: 865-436-1200, Nearest town: Gatlinburg. GPS: 35.625383, -83.600135

25 • C4 | Great Smoky Mountains NP - Marks Cove

Dispersed sites, No water, No toilets, Tents only: $4, Hike-in, Stay limit: 14 days, Reservations required, Elev: 3476ft/1059m, Tel: 865-436-1200, Nearest town: Gatlinburg. GPS: 35.597665, -83.613849

26 • C4 | Great Smoky Mountains NP - Mile 53

Dispersed sites, No water, No toilets, Tents only: $4, Hike-in, Stay limit: 14 days, Reservations required, Elev: 2636ft/803m, Tel: 865-436-1200, Nearest town: Gatlinburg. GPS: 35.635909, -83.545223

27 • C4 | Great Smoky Mountains NP - Mount Le Conte Shelter

Dispersed sites, No water, Hike-to shelter: $4, 5 mi from AT in GSMNP, No fires, Stay limit: 14 days, Elev: 6464ft/1970m. GPS: 35.653188, -83.438844

28 • C4 | Great Smoky Mountains NP - Porters Flat

Dispersed sites, No water, No toilets, Tents only: $4, Hike-in, Stay limit: 14 days, Reservations required, Elev: 3455ft/1053m, Tel: 865-436-1200, Nearest town: Pittman Center. GPS: 35.657302, -83.378921

29 • C4 | Great Smoky Mountains NP - Rabbit Creek

Dispersed sites, No water, No toilets, Tents only: $4, Hike-in, Stay limit: 14 days, Reservations required, Elev: 1480ft/451m, Tel: 865-436-1200, Nearest town: Maryville. GPS: 35.592402, -83.905619

30 • C4 | Great Smoky Mountains NP - Rich Mt

Dispersed sites, No water, No toilets, Tents only: $4, Hike-in, Stay limit: 14 days, Reservations required, Elev: 3441ft/1049m, Tel: 865-436-1200, Nearest town: Townsend. GPS: 35.628848, -83.789386

31 • C4 | Great Smoky Mountains NP - Rough Creek

Dispersed sites, No water, No toilets, Tents only: $4, Hike-in, Stay limit: 14 days, Reservations required, Elev: 2851ft/869m, Tel: 865-436-1200, Nearest town: Gatlinburg. GPS: 35.615599, -83.530697

32 • C4 | Great Smoky Mountains NP - Scott Gap

Dispersed sites, No water, No toilets, Tents only: $4, Hike-in, Stay limit: 14 days, Reservations required, Elev: 1741ft/531m, Tel: 865-436-1200, Nearest town: Maryville. GPS: 35.594014, -83.918709

33 • C4 | Great Smoky Mountains NP - Settlers Camp

Dispersed sites, No water, No toilets, Tents only: $4, Hike-in, Stay limit: 14 days, Reservations required, Elev: 1968ft/600m, Tel: 865-436-1200, Nearest town: Cosby. GPS: 35.749436, -83.343874

34 • C4 | Great Smoky Mountains NP - Sheep Pen Gap

Dispersed sites, No water, No toilets, Tents only: $4, Hike-in, Stay limit: 14 days, Reservations required, Elev: 4577ft/1395m, Tel: 865-436-1200, Nearest town: Maryville. GPS: 35.521163, -83.872082

35 • C4 | Great Smoky Mountains NP - Three Forks

Dispersed sites, No water, No toilets, Tents only: $4, Hike-in, Stay limit: 14 days, Reservations required, Elev: 3452ft/1052m, Tel: 865-436-1200, Nearest town: Gatlinburg. GPS: 35.593386, -83.513404

36 • C4 | Great Smoky Mountains NP - Turkeypen Ridge

Dispersed sites, No water, No toilets, Tents only: $4, Hike-in, Stay limit: 14 days, Reservations required, Elev: 3129ft/954m, Tel: 865-436-1200, Nearest town: Townsend. GPS: 35.625314, -83.765509

37 • C4 | Great Smoky Mountains NP - Upper Henderson

Dispersed sites, No water, No toilets, Tents only: $4, Hike-in, Stay limit: 14 days, Reservations required, Elev: 2855ft/870m, Tel: 865-436-1200, Nearest town: Weare Valley. GPS: 35.643429, -83.636819

38 • C4 | Great Smoky Mountains NP - West Prong

Dispersed sites, No water, No toilets, Tents only: $4, Hike-in, Stay limit: 14 days, Reservations required, Elev: 1630ft/497m, Tel: 865-436-1200, Nearest town: Townsend. GPS: 35.628735, -83.704345

39 • C5 | Great Smoky Mountains NP - Cosby

Total sites: 157, RV sites: 157, Water available, No toilets, No showers, RV dump, Tent & RV camping: $18, Stay limit: 14 days, Open May-Oct, Max Length: 30ft, Reservations accepted, Elev: 2320ft/707m, Tel: 423-487-2683, Nearest town: Gatlinburg. GPS: 35.753638, -83.207504

40 • C5 | Great Smoky Mountains NP - Gilliland Creek

Dispersed sites, No water, No toilets, Tents only: $4, Hike-in, Stay limit: 14 days, Reservations required, Elev: 2674ft/815m, Tel: 865-436-1200, Nearest town: Cosby. GPS: 35.772137, -83.181549

41 • C5 | Great Smoky Mountains NP - Ottercreek

Dispersed sites, No water, No toilets, Tents only: $4, Hike-in, Stay limit: 14 days, Reservations required, Elev: 4544ft/1385m, Tel: 865-436-1200, Nearest town: Cosby. GPS: 35.730654, -83.254744

42 • C5 | Great Smoky Mountains NP - Sugar Cove

Dispersed sites, No water, No toilets, Tents only: $4, Hike-in, Stay limit: 14 days, Reservations required, Elev: 3238ft/987m, Tel: 865-436-1200, Nearest town: Cosby. GPS: 35.748529, -83.249322

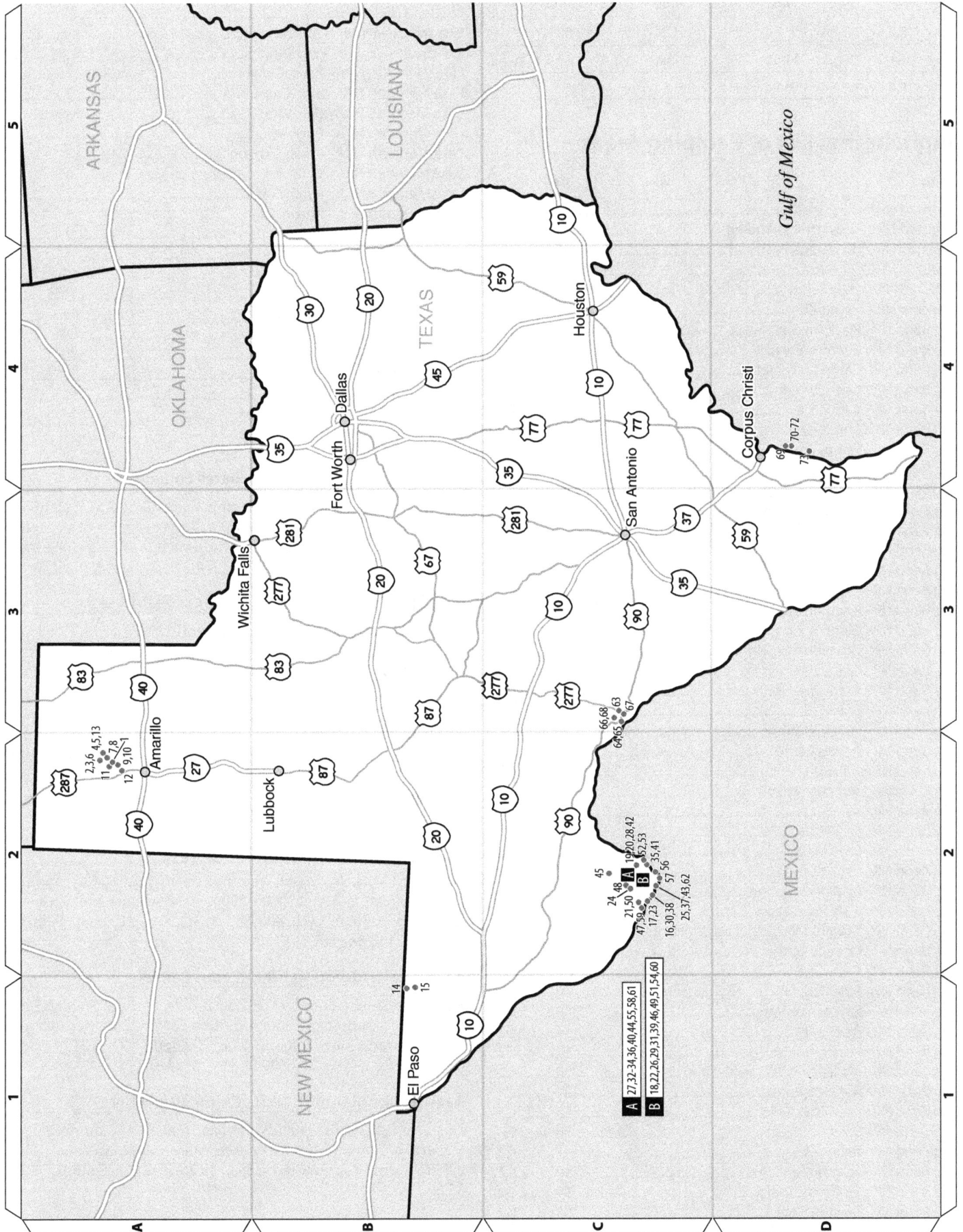

Texas

ARKANSAS

LOUISIANA

OKLAHOMA

NEW MEXICO

TEXAS

MEXICO

Gulf of Mexico

Houston

Dallas

Fort Worth

Wichita Falls

Amarillo

Lubbock

El Paso

San Antonio

Corpus Christi

30
20
59
10
45
10
77
77
35
281
37
59
35
90
10
67
277
83
87
277
277
66,68
64,65 63,67
87
10
90
20
10
40
40
27
287
83
35
281
10

2,3,6 4,5,13
7,8
9,10
11
12
14 15

45
24,48
21,50
47,52
17,23
16,30,38
25,37,43,62
19,20,28,42
52,53
35,41
57,56
A
B

| A | 27,32-34,36,40,44,55,58,61 |
| B | 18,22,26,29,31,39,46,49,51,54,60 |

Map	ID	Map	ID
A2	1-13	C3	63-68
B1	14-15	D4	69-73
C2	16-62		

Alphabetical List of Camping Areas

Name	ID	Map
Amistad NRA - 277 North	63	C3
Amistad NRA - Governor's Landing	64	C3
Amistad NRA - Rock Quarry Group	65	C3
Amistad NRA - Rough Canyon	66	C3
Amistad NRA - San Pedro	67	C3
Amistad NRA - Spur 406	68	C3
Big Bend NP - Black Dike	16	C2
Big Bend NP - Buenos Aires	17	C2
Big Bend NP - Camp Chilicotal	18	C2
Big Bend NP - Camp de Leon	19	C2
Big Bend NP - Candelilla	20	C2
Big Bend NP - Chimneys West	21	C2
Big Bend NP - Chisos Basin	22	C2
Big Bend NP - Cottonwood	23	C2
Big Bend NP - Croton Springs	24	C2
Big Bend NP - Domingues TH	25	C2
Big Bend NP - Elephant Tusk	26	C2
Big Bend NP - Ernst Basin	27	C2
Big Bend NP - Ernst Tinaja	28	C2
Big Bend NP - Fresno	29	C2
Big Bend NP - Gauging Station	30	C2
Big Bend NP - Glenn Springs	31	C2
Big Bend NP - Government Springs	32	C2
Big Bend NP - Grapevine Hills Rd	33	C2
Big Bend NP - Grapevine Spring	34	C2
Big Bend NP - Gravel Pit	35	C2
Big Bend NP - Hannold Draw	36	C2
Big Bend NP - Jewels Camp	37	C2
Big Bend NP - Johnson Ranch	38	C2
Big Bend NP - Juniper Canyon	39	C2
Big Bend NP - K-Bar	40	C2
Big Bend NP - La Clocha	41	C2
Big Bend NP - La Noria	42	C2
Big Bend NP - Loop Camp	43	C2
Big Bend NP - McKinney Spring	44	C2
Big Bend NP - Nine Point Draw	45	C2
Big Bend NP - Nugent Mt	46	C2
Big Bend NP - Ocotillo Grove	47	C2
Big Bend NP - Paint Gap	48	C2
Big Bend NP - Pine Canyon	49	C2
Big Bend NP - Rattlesnake Mt	50	C2
Big Bend NP - Rice Tank	51	C2
Big Bend NP - Rio Grande Village	52	C2
Big Bend NP - Rio Grande Village RV Park	53	C2
Big Bend NP - Robbers Roost	54	C2
Big Bend NP - Roys Peak Vista	55	C2
Big Bend NP - Solis	56	C2
Big Bend NP - Talley	57	C2
Big Bend NP - Telephone Canyon	58	C2
Big Bend NP - Terlingua Abaja	59	C2
Big Bend NP - Twisted Shoe	60	C2
Big Bend NP - Willow Tank	61	C2
Big Bend NP - Woodsons	62	C2
Guadalupe Mts NP - Dog Canyon	14	B1
Guadalupe Mts NP - Pine Springs	15	B1
Lake Meredith NRA - Bates Canyon	1	A2
Lake Meredith NRA - Blue Creek Bridge	2	A2
Lake Meredith NRA - Blue West	3	A2
Lake Meredith NRA - Bugbee	4	A2
Lake Meredith NRA - Cedar Canyon	5	A2
Lake Meredith NRA - Chimney Hollow	6	A2
Lake Meredith NRA - Fritch Fortress	7	A2
Lake Meredith NRA - Harbor Bay	8	A2
Lake Meredith NRA - McBride Canyon	9	A2
Lake Meredith NRA - Mullinaw Creek	10	A2
Lake Meredith NRA - Plum Creek	11	A2
Lake Meredith NRA - Rosita OHV	12	A2
Lake Meredith NRA - Sanford Yake	13	A2
Padre Island NS - Bird Island Basin	69	D4
Padre Island NS - Malaquite	70	D4
Padre Island NS - North Beach	71	D4
Padre Island NS - South Beach	72	D4
Padre Island NS - Yarborough Pass	73	D4

1 • A2 | Lake Meredith NRA - Bates Canyon

Dispersed sites, No water, Vault/pit toilet, Tent & RV camping: Free, Generator hours: 0600-2200, Reservations not accepted, Elev: 2942ft/897m, Nearest town: Fritch. GPS: 35.587504, -101.706219

2 • A2 | Lake Meredith NRA - Blue Creek Bridge

Dispersed sites, No water, Vault/pit toilet, Tent & RV camping: Free, Generator hours: 0600-2200, Reservations not accepted, Elev: 2986ft/910m, Tel: 806-857-3151, Nearest town: Sanford. GPS: 35.721641, -101.663579

3 • A2 | Lake Meredith NRA - Blue West

Total sites: 50, RV sites: 50, No water, Vault/pit toilet, Tent & RV camping: Free, Generator hours: 0600-2200, Reservations not accepted, Elev: 3061ft/933m, Tel: 806-857-3151, Nearest town: Sanford. GPS: 35.685389, -101.629931

4 • A2 | Lake Meredith NRA - Bugbee

Dispersed sites, No water, Vault/pit toilet, Tent & RV camping: Free, Generator hours: 0600-2200, Reservations not accepted, Elev: 2963ft/903m, Tel: 806-857-3151, Nearest town: Sanford. GPS: 35.714899, -101.594138

5 • A2 | Lake Meredith NRA - Cedar Canyon

Dispersed sites, Central water, Flush toilet, Tent & RV camping: Free, Beach camping, Generator hours: 0600-2200, Reservations not accepted, Elev: 2966ft/904m, Tel: 806-857-3151, Nearest town: Sanford. GPS: 35.693944, -101.572953

6 • A2 | Lake Meredith NRA - Chimney Hollow

Dispersed sites, No water, No toilets, Tent & RV camping: Free, Generator hours: 0600-2200, Reservations not accepted, Elev: 2950ft/899m, Tel: 806-857-3151, Nearest town: Sanford. GPS: 35.692061, -101.642041

7 • A2 | Lake Meredith NRA - Fritch Fortress

Total sites: 9, RV sites: 5, Central water, Flush toilet, Free showers, RV dump, Tent & RV camping: Free, Generator hours: 0600-2200, Reservations not accepted, Elev: 3127ft/953m, Tel: 806-857-3151, Nearest town: Sanford. GPS: 35.681674, -101.598428

8 • A2 | Lake Meredith NRA - Harbor Bay

Dispersed sites, No water, Vault/pit toilet, Tent & RV camping: Free, Dispersed, Generator hours: 0600-2200, Reservations not accepted, Elev: 3002ft/915m, Tel: 806-857-3151, Nearest town: Sanford. GPS: 35.648807, -101.629296

9 • A2 | Lake Meredith NRA - McBride Canyon

Dispersed sites, No water, Vault/pit toilet, Tent & RV camping: Free, Generator hours: 0600-2200, Reservations not accepted, Elev: 3071ft/936m, Tel: 806-857-3151, Nearest town: Sanford. GPS: 35.542784, -101.732209

10 • A2 | Lake Meredith NRA - Mullinaw Creek

Dispersed sites, No water, Vault/pit toilet, Tent & RV camping: Free, Generator hours: 0600-2200, Reservations not accepted, Elev: 3058ft/932m, Tel: 806-857-3151, Nearest town: Sanford. GPS: 35.526297, -101.753324

11 • A2 | Lake Meredith NRA - Plum Creek

Dispersed sites, No water, Vault/pit toilet, Tent & RV camping: Free, Horse corrals, Generator hours: 0600-2200, Reservations not accepted, Elev: 3018ft/920m, Tel: 806-857-3151, Nearest town: Sanford. GPS: 35.616004, -101.757741

12 • A2 | Lake Meredith NRA - Rosita OHV

Dispersed sites, No water, No toilets, Tent & RV camping: Free, Generator hours: 0600-2200, Reservations not accepted, Elev: 3048ft/929m, Tel: 806-857-3151, Nearest town: Sanford. GPS: 35.472082, -101.818789

13 • A2 | Lake Meredith NRA - Sanford Yake

Total sites: 51, RV sites: 20, Elec sites: 10, Water at site, Flush toilet, Free showers, RV dump, Tents: Free/RV's: $26, Generator hours: 0600-2200, Reservations not accepted, Elev: 3005ft/916m, Tel: 806-865-3131, Nearest town: Sanford. GPS: 35.706473, -101.560155

14 • B1 | Guadalupe Mts NP - Dog Canyon

Total sites: 13, RV sites: 4, Central water, Flush toilet, No showers, No RV dump, Tent & RV camping: $15, Group site $3/person, Generator hours: 0800-2000, Reservations not accepted, Elev: 6276ft/1913m, Tel: 575-981-2418, Nearest town: Pine Springs. GPS: 31.993408, -104.833984

15 • B1 | Guadalupe Mts NP - Pine Springs

Total sites: 39, RV sites: 19, Central water, Flush toilet, No showers, No RV dump, Tent & RV camping: $15, 2 group sites $3/person, Generator hours: 0800-2000, Reservations not accepted, Elev: 5820ft/1774m, Tel: 915-828-3251, Nearest town: Pine Springs. GPS: 31.896071, -104.827551

16 • C2 | Big Bend NP - Black Dike

Dispersed sites, No water, No toilets, Tents only: $10, High clearance vehicles only, Stay limit: 14 days, No generators, Max Length: 25ft, Elev: 2106ft/642m, Tel: 432-477-2251. GPS: 29.055636, -103.432734

17 • C2 | Big Bend NP - Buenos Aires

Dispersed sites, No water, No toilets, Tents only: $10, High-clearance vehicle required, Stay limit: 14 days, No generators, Elev: 2103ft/641m, Tel: 432-477-2251. GPS: 29.086884, -103.470622

18 • C2 | Big Bend NP - Camp Chilicotal

Dispersed sites, No water, No toilets, Tents only: $10, High clearance vehicles only, Stay limit: 14 days, No generators, Elev: 3258ft/993m, Tel: 432-477-2251. GPS: 29.237771, -103.168694

19 • C2 | Big Bend NP - Camp de Leon

Dispersed sites, No water, No toilets, Tents only: $10, High clearance vehicles only, Stay limit: 14 days, No generators, Elev: 2282ft/696m, Tel: 432-477-2251. GPS: 29.246904, -103.012345

20 • C2 | Big Bend NP - Candelilla

Dispersed sites, No water, No toilets, Tents only: $10, High clearance vehicles only, Stay limit: 14 days, No generators, Elev: 2064ft/629m, Tel: 432-477-2251. GPS: 29.208627, -102.993484

21 • C2 | Big Bend NP - Chimneys West

Dispersed sites, No water, No toilets, Tents: $10/RV's: $12, Stay limit: 14 days, No generators, Elev: 2392ft/729m, Tel: 432-477-2251. GPS: 29.219223, -103.527902

22 • C2 | Big Bend NP - Chisos Basin

Total sites: 60, RV sites: 60, Central water, Flush toilet, No showers, RV dump, Tent & RV camping: $16, 7 group sites: $40-$60, Stay limit: 14 days, Generator hours: 0800-1100/1700-2000, Open all year, Max Length: RV-24'/Trlr-20ft, Reservations accepted, Elev: 5108ft/1557m, Tel: 432-477-2251. GPS: 29.27582, -103.30254

23 • C2 | Big Bend NP - Cottonwood

Total sites: 24, RV sites: 24, Central water, Vault/pit toilet, No showers, No RV dump, Tent & RV camping: $16, Group site: $60, Stay limit: 14 days, No generators, Open all year, Reservations not accepted, Elev: 2142ft/653m, Tel: 432-477-2251. GPS: 29.137207, -103.522705

24 • C2 | Big Bend NP - Croton Springs

Dispersed sites, No water, No toilets, Tent & RV camping: $10, 2 sites, Stay limit: 14 days, No generators, Max Length: 30ft, Elev: 3369ft/1027m, Tel: 432-477-2251. GPS: 29.342949, -103.346156

25 • C2 | Big Bend NP - Domingues TH

Dispersed sites, No water, No toilets, Tents only: $10, High clearance vehicles only, Stay limit: 14 days, No generators, Elev: 2178ft/664m, Tel: 432-477-2251. GPS: 29.044769, -103.279468

26 • C2 | Big Bend NP - Elephant Tusk

Dispersed sites, No water, No toilets, Tents only: $10, High clearance vehicles only, Stay limit: 14 days, No generators, Elev: 2543ft/775m, Tel: 432-477-2251. GPS: 29.129574, -103.206205

27 • C2 | Big Bend NP - Ernst Basin

Dispersed sites, No water, No toilets, Tents only: $10, High clearance vehicles only, Stay limit: 14 days, No generators, Elev: 2546ft/776m, Tel: 432-477-2251. GPS: 29.298796, -103.035537

28 • C2 | Big Bend NP - Ernst Tinaja

Dispersed sites, No water, No toilets, Tents only: $10, Stay limit: 14 days, No generators, Elev: 2474ft/754m, Tel: 432-477-2251. GPS: 29.259439, -103.008114

29 • C2 | Big Bend NP - Fresno

Dispersed sites, No water, No toilets, Tents only: $10, High clearance vehicles only, Stay limit: 14 days, No generators, Elev: 2310ft/704m, Tel: 432-477-2251. GPS: 29.099492, -103.184199

30 • C2 | Big Bend NP - Gauging Station

Dispersed sites, No water, No toilets, Tents only: $10, High clearance vehicles only, Stay limit: 14 days, No generators, Elev: 2126ft/648m, Tel: 432-477-2251. GPS: 29.035035, -103.389898

31 • C2 | Big Bend NP - Glenn Springs

Dispersed sites, No water, No toilets, Tents only: $10, High clearance vehicles only, Stay limit: 14 days, No generators, Elev: 2605ft/794m, Tel: 432-477-2251. GPS: 29.175508, -103.157419

32 • C2 | Big Bend NP - Government Springs

Dispersed sites, No water, No toilets, Tent & RV camping: $10, Stay limit: 14 days, No generators, Reservations not accepted, Elev: 3904ft/1190m, Tel: 432-477-2251. GPS: 29.340626, -103.255386

33 • C2 | Big Bend NP - Grapevine Hills Rd

Dispersed sites, No water, No toilets, Tents only: $10, Stay limit: 14 days, No generators, Elev: 3369ft/1027m, Tel: 432-477-2251. GPS: 29.378153, -103.221135

34 • C2 | Big Bend NP - Grapevine Spring

Dispersed sites, No water, No toilets, Tent & RV camping: $10, Stay limit: 14 days, No generators, Elev: 3071ft/936m, Tel: 432-477-2251. GPS: 29.407612, -103.191921

35 • C2 | Big Bend NP - Gravel Pit

Dispersed sites, No water, No toilets, Tents only: $10, High clearance vehicles only, Stay limit: 14 days, No generators, Elev: 1854ft/565m, Tel: 432-477-2251. GPS: 29.152173, -103.002633

36 • C2 | Big Bend NP - Hannold Draw

Dispersed sites, No water, No toilets, Tent & RV camping: $10, Stay limit: 14 days, No generators, Elev: 3036ft/925m, Tel: 432-477-2251. GPS: 29.375943, -103.153335

37 • C2 | Big Bend NP - Jewels Camp

Dispersed sites, No water, No toilets, Tents only: $10, Stay limit: 14 days, No generators, Elev: 2060ft/628m, Tel: 432-477-2251. GPS: 29.015295, -103.308708

38 • C2 | Big Bend NP - Johnson Ranch

Dispersed sites, No water, No toilets, Tents only: $10, High clearance vehicles only, Stay limit: 14 days, No generators, Elev: 2077ft/633m, Tel: 432-477-2251. GPS: 29.023439, -103.370002

39 • C2 | Big Bend NP - Juniper Canyon

Dispersed sites, No water, No toilets, Tents only: $10, Stay limit: 14 days, No generators, Elev: 3993ft/1217m, Tel: 432-477-2251. GPS: 29.223868, -103.241209

40 • C2 | Big Bend NP - K-Bar

Dispersed sites, No water, No toilets, Tent & RV camping: $10, Stay limit: 14 days, No generators, Elev: 3422ft/1043m, Tel: 432-477-2251. GPS: 29.306817, -103.176681

41 • C2 | Big Bend NP - La Clocha

Dispersed sites, No water, No toilets, Tents only: $10, High clearance vehicles only, Stay limit: 14 days, No generators, Elev: 1867ft/569m, Tel: 432-477-2251. GPS: 29.149096, -103.007776

42 • C2 | Big Bend NP - La Noria

Dispersed sites, No water, No toilets, Tents only: $10, High clearance vehicles only, Stay limit: 14 days, No generators, Elev: 2169ft/661m, Tel: 432-477-2251. GPS: 29.258326, -103.030479

43 • C2 | Big Bend NP - Loop Camp

Dispersed sites, No water, No toilets, Tents only: $10, High clearance vehicles only, Stay limit: 14 days, No generators, Elev: 2060ft/628m, Tel: 432-477-2251. GPS: 29.027593, -103.332641

44 • C2 | Big Bend NP - McKinney Spring

Dispersed sites, No water, No toilets, Tents only: $10, High clearance vehicles only, Stay limit: 14 days, No generators, Elev: 2913ft/888m, Tel: 432-477-2251. GPS: 29.408531, -103.087561

45 • C2 | Big Bend NP - Nine Point Draw

Dispersed sites, No water, No toilets, Tent & RV camping: $10, Stay limit: 14 days, No generators, Elev: 2585ft/788m, Tel: 432-477-2251, Nearest town: Marathon. GPS: 29.612344, -103.138992

46 • C2 | Big Bend NP - Nugent Mt

Dispersed sites, No water, No toilets, Tent & RV camping: $10, Stay limit: 14 days, No generators, Elev: 3127ft/953m, Tel: 432-477-2251. GPS: 29.257202, -103.152477

47 • C2 | Big Bend NP - Ocotillo Grove

Dispersed sites, No water, No toilets, Tent & RV camping: $10, Stay limit: 14 days, No generators, Elev: 2313ft/705m, Tel: 432-477-2251. GPS: 29.203214, -103.594827

48 • C2 | Big Bend NP - Paint Gap

Dispersed sites, No water, No toilets, Tent & RV camping: $10, Stay limit: 14 days, No generators, Elev: 3622ft/1104m, Tel: 432-477-2251. GPS: 29.397406, -103.304247

49 • C2 | Big Bend NP - Pine Canyon

Dispersed sites, No water, No toilets, Tents only: $10, Stay limit: 14 days, No generators, Elev: 4354ft/1327m, Tel: 432-477-2251. GPS: 29.256701, -103.212558

50 • C2 | Big Bend NP - Rattlesnake Mt

Dispersed sites, No water, No toilets, Tents only: $10, High clearance vehicles only, Stay limit: 14 days, No generators, Elev: 2582ft/787m, Tel: 432-477-2251. GPS: 29.254889, -103.532594

51 • C2 | Big Bend NP - Rice Tank

Dispersed sites, No water, No toilets, Tents only: $10, High clearance vehicles only, Stay limit: 14 days, No generators, Elev: 3146ft/959m, Tel: 432-477-2251. GPS: 29.230059, -103.166576

52 • C2 | Big Bend NP - Rio Grande Village

Total sites: 100, RV sites: 100, Central water, Flush toilet, Pay showers, RV dump, Tent & RV camping: $16, Group site: $60-$1000, Stay limit: 14 days, Generator hours: 0800-2000, Open all year, Reservations accepted, Elev: 1841ft/561m, Tel: 432-477-2251. GPS: 29.180396, -102.955946

53 • C2 | Big Bend NP - Rio Grande Village RV Park

Total sites: 25, RV sites: 25, Elec sites: 25, Water at site, Flush toilet, Pay showers, RV dump, No tents/RV's: $36, 25 Full hookups sites, $3/person additional fee, Concessionaire, Stay limit: 14 days, Open all year, Reservations accepted, Elev: 1847ft/563m, Tel: 432-477-22913. GPS: 29.182671, -102.963404

54 • C2 | Big Bend NP - Robbers Roost

Dispersed sites, No water, No toilets, Tents only: $10, High clearance vehicles only, Stay limit: 14 days, No generators, Elev: 3102ft/945m, Tel: 432-477-2251. GPS: 29.191882, -103.192068

55 • C2 | Big Bend NP - Roys Peak Vista

Dispersed sites, No water, No toilets, Tents only: $10, High clearance vehicles only, Stay limit: 14 days, No generators, Elev: 2926ft/892m, Tel: 432-477-2251. GPS: 29.388279, -103.077749

56 • C2 | Big Bend NP - Solis

Dispersed sites, No water, No toilets, Tents only: $10, High clearance vehicles only, Stay limit: 14 days, No generators, Elev: 1913ft/583m, Tel: 432-477-2251. GPS: 29.046247, -103.106724

57 • C2 | Big Bend NP - Talley

Dispersed sites, No water, No toilets, Tents only: $10, High clearance vehicles only, Stay limit: 14 days, No generators, Elev: 1988ft/606m, Tel: 432-477-2251. GPS: 28.988489, -103.184309

58 • C2 | Big Bend NP - Telephone Canyon

Dispersed sites, No water, No toilets, Tents only: $10, High clearance vehicles only, Stay limit: 14 days, No generators, Elev: 3002ft/915m, Tel: 432-477-2251. GPS: 29.364749, -103.040972

59 • C2 | Big Bend NP - Terlingua Abaja

Dispersed sites, No water, No toilets, Tents only: $10, Stay limit: 14 days, No generators, Elev: 2228ft/679m, Tel: 432-477-2251. GPS: 29.199122, -103.603741

60 • C2 | Big Bend NP - Twisted Shoe

Dispersed sites, No water, No toilets, Tent & RV camping: $10, Stay limit: 14 days, No generators, Elev: 3835ft/1169m, Tel: 432-477-2251. GPS: 29.218566, -103.233412

61 • C2 | Big Bend NP - Willow Tank

Dispersed sites, No water, No toilets, Tents only: $10, High clearance vehicles only, Stay limit: 14 days, No generators, Elev: 2572ft/784m, Tel: 432-477-2251. GPS: 29.310639, -103.028157

62 • C2 | Big Bend NP - Woodsons

Dispersed sites, No water, No toilets, Tents only: $10, Stay limit: 14 days, No generators, Elev: 2031ft/619m, Tel: 432-477-2251. GPS: 29.007017, -103.294028

63 • C3 | Amistad NRA - 277 North

Total sites: 17, RV sites: 17, No water, Vault/pit toilet, Tent & RV camping: $6, Reservable group site available, Dump station and potable water near Diablo East boat ramp, Generator hours: 0600-2200, Open all year, Reservations not accepted, Elev: 1116ft/340m, Tel: 830-775-7491, Nearest town: Del Rio. GPS: 29.510255, -100.907455

64 • C3 | Amistad NRA - Governor's Landing

Total sites: 15, RV sites: 15, Central water, Vault/pit toilet, No showers, No RV dump, Tent & RV camping: $10, Dump station near Diablo East boat ramp, Generator hours: 0600-2200, Open all year, Max Length: 28ft, Reservations not accepted, Elev: 1109ft/338m, Tel: 830-775-7491, Nearest town: Del Rio. GPS: 29.478776, -101.028303

65 • C3 | Amistad NRA - Rock Quarry Group

Dispersed sites, No water, Vault/pit toilet, Group site: $30 or $2/person if over 15 people, Dump station and potable water near Diablo East boat ramp, Generator hours: 0600-2200, Open all year, Reservations required, Elev: 1152ft/351m, Tel: 830-775-7491, Nearest town: Del Rio. GPS: 29.493112, -101.037772

66 • C3 | Amistad NRA - Rough Canyon

Total sites: 4, RV sites: 4, No water, Vault/pit toilet, Tent & RV camping: $6, Dump station and potable water near Diablo East boat ramp, Generator hours: 0600-2200, Open all year, Reservations not accepted, Elev: 1138ft/347m, Tel: 830-775-7491, Nearest town: Del Rio. GPS: 29.573395, -100.977144

67 • C3 | Amistad NRA - San Pedro

Total sites: 35, RV sites: 30, No water, Vault/pit toilet, Tent & RV camping: $6, Dump station and potable water near Diablo East boat ramp, Reservable group site available, Generator hours: 0600-2200, Open all year, Reservations not accepted, Elev: 1129ft/344m, Tel: 830-775-7491, Nearest town: Del Rio. GPS: 29.468166, -100.953266

68 • C3 | Amistad NRA - Spur 406

Total sites: 6, RV sites: 6, No water, Vault/pit toilet, Tent & RV camping: $6, Dump station and potable water near Diablo East boat ramp, Generator hours: 0600-2200, Open all year, Reservations not accepted, Elev: 1106ft/337m, Tel: 830-775-7491, Nearest town: Del Rio. GPS: 29.548385, -101.018696

69 • D4 | Padre Island NS - Bird Island Basin

Total sites: 53, RV sites: 53, No water, Vault/pit toilet, Tent & RV camping: $8, $10/year option, Stay limit: 14 days, Generator hours: 0600-2200, Open all year, Reservations not accepted, Elev: 13ft/4m, Tel: 361-949-8068, Nearest town: Corpus Christi. GPS: 27.467339, -97.313462

70 • D4 | Padre Island NS - Malaquite

Total sites: 50, RV sites: 50, Central water, Flush toilet, Free showers, RV dump, Tent & RV camping: $14, Cold showers,

Stay limit: 14 days, Generator hours: 0600-2200, Open all year, Reservations not accepted, Elev: 10ft/3m, Tel: 361-949-8068, Nearest town: Corpus Christi. GPS: 27.431236, -97.295711

71 • D4 | Padre Island NS - North Beach

Dispersed sites, No water, No toilets, Tent & RV camping: Free, Beach camping, Free permit required, Stay limit: 14 days, Generator hours: 0600-2200, Open all year, Reservations not accepted, Elev: 6ft/2m, Tel: 361-949-8068, Nearest town: Corpus Christi. GPS: 27.439768, -97.291089

72 • D4 | Padre Island NS - South Beach

Dispersed sites, No toilets, Tent & RV camping: Free, Beach camping, Free permit required, Stay limit: 14 days, Generator hours: 0600-2200, Open all year, Reservations not accepted, Elev: 13ft/4m, Tel: 361-949-8068, Nearest town: Corpus Christi. GPS: 27.407587, -97.304755

73 • D4 | Padre Island NS - Yarborough Pass

Dispersed sites, No water, No toilets, Tent & RV camping: Free, 4x4 required, Beach camping, Free permit required, Stay limit: 14 days, Generator hours: 0600-2200, Open all year, Reservations not accepted, Elev: 9ft/3m, Tel: 361-949-8068, Nearest town: Corpus Christi. GPS: 27.204149, -97.388122

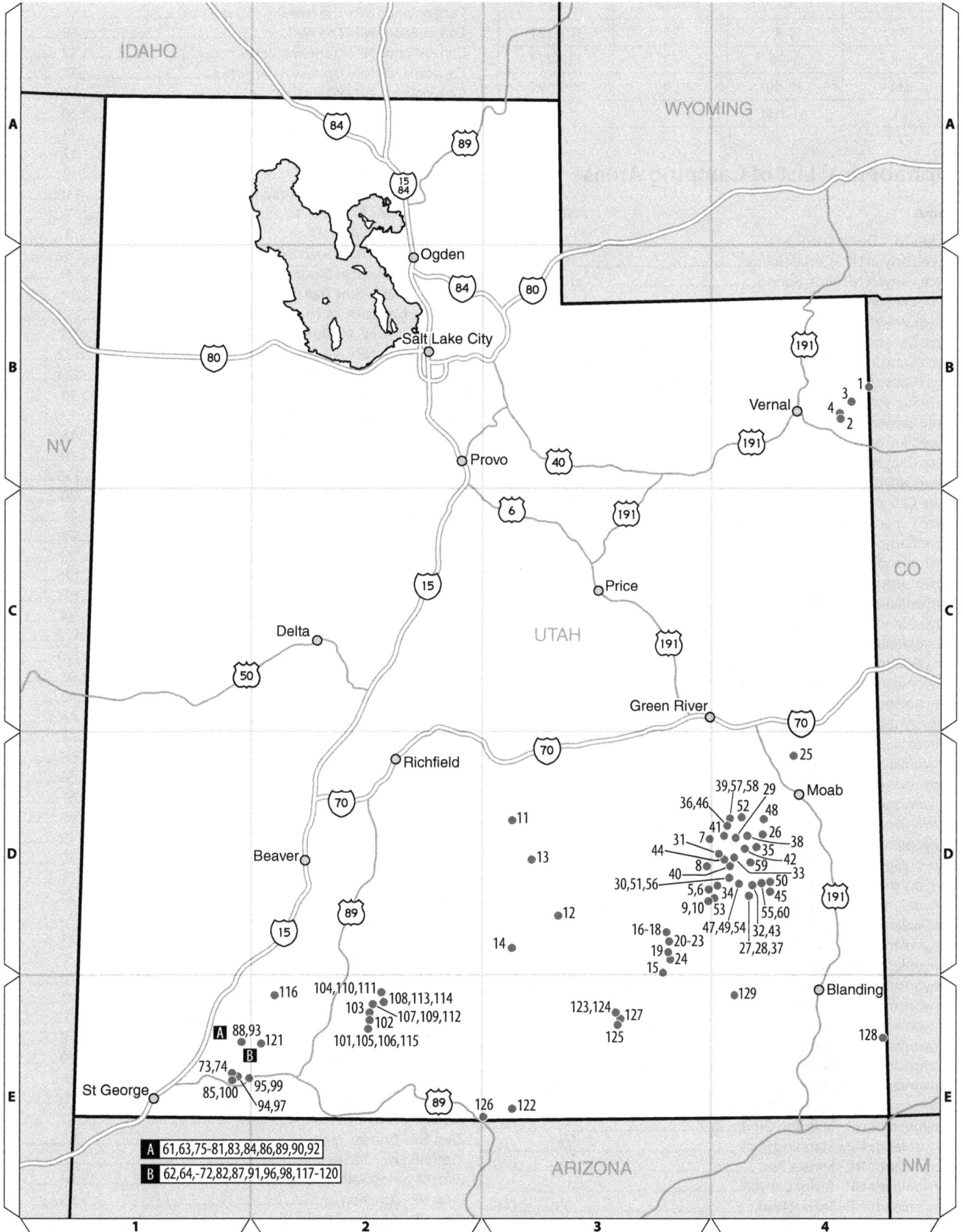

Utah

IDAHO

WYOMING

84

89

15
84

80

Ogden

84

80

Salt Lake City

NV

80

Vernal

1
3
4
2

191

Provo

40

6

191

UTAH

Price

191

Delta

50

Green River

70

CO

70

25

Moab

Richfield

70

39,57,58 29
36,46 52 48
41 26 38
11 31 7 35
44 59 42
13 8 33
40 50
30,51,56 5,6 34 45
9,10 53 55,60
12 47,49,54 32,43
16-18 27,28,37
19 20-23
24
14 15

191

Beaver

89

15

116
104,110,111 108,113,114
103 107,109,112
102
101,105,106,115

129
123,124 127
125

Blanding

128

A 88,93
121
B

73,74
85,100 95,99
94,97

St George

126 122

89

ARIZONA

NM

A 61,63,75-81,83,84,86,89,90,92

B 62,64,-72,82,87,91,96,98,117-120

1   2   3   4

Map	ID	Map	ID
B4	1-4	E2	101-121
D3	5-24	E3	122-127
D4	25-60	E4	128-129
E1	61-100		

Alphabetical List of Camping Areas

Name	ID	Map
Arches NP - Devils Garden CG	25	D4
Bryce Canyon NP - Corral Hollow	101	E2
Bryce Canyon NP - Iron Spring	102	E2
Bryce Canyon NP - Natural Bridge	103	E2
Bryce Canyon NP - North CG	104	E2
Bryce Canyon NP - Riggs Spring	105	E2
Bryce Canyon NP - Riggs Spring Group Site	106	E2
Bryce Canyon NP - Right Fork Swamp Canyon	107	E2
Bryce Canyon NP - Right Fork Yellow Creek	108	E2
Bryce Canyon NP - Sheep Creek	109	E2
Bryce Canyon NP - Sunset CG - Loop A	110	E2
Bryce Canyon NP - Sunset CG - Loops B and C	111	E2
Bryce Canyon NP - Swamp Canyon	112	E2
Bryce Canyon NP - Yellow Creek	113	E2
Bryce Canyon NP - Yellow Creek Group Site	114	E2
Bryce Canyon NP - Yovimpa Pass	115	E2
Canyonlands NP - Airport Tower	26	D4
Canyonlands NP - Bobby Jo	27	D4
Canyonlands NP - Butler Flat	28	D4
Canyonlands NP - Candlestick	29	D4
Canyonlands NP - Chimney Rock	30	D4
Canyonlands NP - Cleopatra's Chair	31	D4
Canyonlands NP - Devils Kitchen	32	D4
Canyonlands NP - Ekker Butte	33	D4
Canyonlands NP - Flint Sheep	5	D3
Canyonlands NP - Golden Stairs	34	D4
Canyonlands NP - Gooseberry	35	D4
Canyonlands NP - Happy Canyon	6	D3
Canyonlands NP - Hardscrabble Bottom	36	D4
Canyonlands NP - High Spur	7	D3
Canyonlands NP - Horsehoof	37	D4
Canyonlands NP - Island in the Sky (Willow Flat)	38	D4
Canyonlands NP - Labyrinth	39	D4
Canyonlands NP - Maze Overlook	40	D4
Canyonlands NP - Millard Canyon	41	D4
Canyonlands NP - Murphy Hogback	42	D4
Canyonlands NP - New Bates Wilson	43	D4
Canyonlands NP - North Point	8	D3
Canyonlands NP - Panorama Point	44	D4
Canyonlands NP - Peekaboo Spring	45	D4
Canyonlands NP - Potato Bottom	46	D4
Canyonlands NP - Rivers Overlook	47	D4
Canyonlands NP - Shafer Canyon	48	D4
Canyonlands NP - Spanish Bottom	49	D4
Canyonlands NP - Split Top Group	50	D4
Canyonlands NP - Standing Rock	51	D4
Canyonlands NP - Sunset Pass	9	D3
Canyonlands NP - Taylor Canyon	52	D4
Canyonlands NP - Teapot Rock	53	D4
Canyonlands NP - The Doll House	54	D4
Canyonlands NP - The Neck	10	D3
Canyonlands NP - The Needles (Squaw Flat)	55	D4
Canyonlands NP - The Wall	56	D4
Canyonlands NP - Upheaval Bottom	57	D4
Canyonlands NP - Upheaval Canyon	58	D4
Canyonlands NP - White Crack	59	D4
Canyonlands NP - Wooden Shoe Group	60	D4
Capitol Reef NP - Cathedral Valley	11	D3
Capitol Reef NP - Cedar Mesa	12	D3
Capitol Reef NP - Fruita CG	13	D3
Cedar Breaks NM - Point Supreme	116	E2
Dinosaur NM - Ely Creek TC	1	B4
Dinosaur NM - Green River	2	B4
Dinosaur NM - Rainbow Park	3	B4
Dinosaur NM - Split Mountain Group	4	B4
Escalante NM - Burr Trail Rd	14	D3
Glen Canyon NRA - Alstrom Point	122	E3
Glen Canyon NRA - Blue Notch Canyon	15	D3
Glen Canyon NRA – Bullfrog	123	E3
Glen Canyon NRA - Bullfrog Main	124	E3
Glen Canyon NRA - Dirty Devil	16	D3
Glen Canyon NRA - Dispersed	17	D3
Glen Canyon NRA - Dispersed	18	D3
Glen Canyon NRA - Farley Canyon	19	D3
Glen Canyon NRA - Halls Crossing FHU	125	E3
Glen Canyon NRA - Hite Developed	20	D3
Glen Canyon NRA - Hite Improved	21	D3
Glen Canyon NRA - Hite Launch Ramp	22	D3
Glen Canyon NRA - Hite RV	23	D3
Glen Canyon NRA - Lone Rock Beach	126	E3
Glen Canyon NRA - Stanton Creek	127	E3
Glen Canyon NRA - White Canyon	24	D3
Hovenweep NM	128	E4
Natural Bridges NM	129	E4
Zion NP - Bear Camp	61	E1
Zion NP - Big Spring	62	E1
Zion NP - Bird Camp	63	E1
Zion NP - Camp 1	64	E1
Zion NP - Camp 2	65	E1
Zion NP - Camp 3	66	E1
Zion NP - Camp 4	67	E1
Zion NP - Camp 5	68	E1
Zion NP - Camp 6	69	E1
Zion NP - Camp 7	70	E1
Zion NP - Camp 7	71	E1
Zion NP - Camp 9	72	E1
Zion NP - Coal Pit Wash	73	E1
Zion NP - Coal Pits Ridge	74	E1
Zion NP - Cottonwood Camp	75	E1
Zion NP - Cougar Camp	76	E1
Zion NP - Cross Creek West Camp	77	E1
Zion NP - Deep Creek	117	E2
Zion NP - Deer Camp	78	E1
Zion NP - Dipper Camp	79	E1
Zion NP - Dry Camp	80	E1
Zion NP - Flat Rock	118	E2
Zion NP - Flat Rock Camp	81	E1
Zion NP - Goose Creek	82	E1
Zion NP - Hop Valley	83	E1
Zion NP - Hop Valley Horse Camp	84	E1
Zion NP - Junction	85	E1
Zion NP - Juniper Camp	86	E1

Zion NP - Kolob Creek.................................87 ....E1
Zion NP - Lava Point ....88 ....E1
Zion NP - Neagle Camp...............................89 ....E1
Zion NP - Oak Point Camp ....90 ....E1
Zion NP - Potato Hollow ....91 ....E1
Zion NP - Right Bench..............................119............E2
Zion NP - Ringtail Camp.............................92 ....E1
Zion NP - River Bend...............................120............E2
Zion NP - Sawmill Springs...........................93 ....E1
Zion NP - Scoggins Wash............................94 ....E1
Zion NP - Simon Gulch.............................121............E2
Zion NP - South CG ....95 ....E1
Zion NP - Spotted Owl ....96 ....E1
Zion NP - Temple View ....97 ....E1
Zion NP - The Grotto ....98 ....E1
Zion NP - Watchman CG ....99 ....E1
Zion NP - Yucca......................................100............E1

1 • B4 | Dinosaur NM - Ely Creek TC

Total sites: 2, RV sites: 0, No water, No toilets, Tents only: Free, Hike-in, Permit required, Elev: 5304ft/1617m, Tel: 435-636-3600, Nearest town: Naples. GPS: 40.565268, -109.057093

2 • B4 | Dinosaur NM - Green River

Total sites: 80, RV sites: 80, Central water, Flush toilet, No showers, No RV dump, Tent & RV camping: $18, Open Apr-Oct, Reservations accepted, Elev: 4793ft/1461m, Tel: 435-781-7700, Nearest town: Jensen. GPS: 40.421143, -109.243408

3 • B4 | Dinosaur NM - Rainbow Park

Total sites: 4, RV sites: 0, No water, Vault/pit toilet, Tents only: $6, Walk-to sites, Road unpassable when wet, Open all year, Reservations not accepted, Elev: 4957ft/1511m, Tel: 435-781-7700, Nearest town: Jensen. GPS: 40.499494, -109.170507

4 • B4 | Dinosaur NM - Split Mountain Group

Total sites: 4, RV sites: 4, Central water, Flush toilet, No showers, No RV dump, Group sites only when Green River CG is open, No water in winter - $6, Open all year, Reservations accepted, Elev: 4862ft/1482m, Tel: 435-781-7700, Nearest town: Jensen. GPS: 40.443784, -109.252894

5 • D3 | Canyonlands NP - Flint Sheep

Total sites: 1, No water, No toilets, Tents only: Free, Back-country, 4x4 needed, Elev: 6810ft/2076m, Tel: 435-719-2100. GPS: 38.130688, -110.134838

6 • D3 | Canyonlands NP - Happy Canyon

Total sites: 1, No water, No toilets, Tents only: Free, Back-country, 4x4 needed, Elev: 6870ft/2094m, Tel: 435-719-2100. GPS: 38.108406, -110.136742

7 • D3 | Canyonlands NP - High Spur

Total sites: 1, No water, No toilets, Tents only: Free, Back-country, 4x4 needed, Elev: 6162ft/1878m, Tel: 435-719-2100. GPS: 38.378964, -110.127159

8 • D3 | Canyonlands NP - North Point

Total sites: 1, No water, No toilets, Tents only: Free, Back-country, 4x4 needed, Elev: 6543ft/1994m, Tel: 435-719-2100. GPS: 38.236415, -110.147373

9 • D3 | Canyonlands NP - Sunset Pass

Total sites: 1, No water, No toilets, Tents only: Free, Back-country, 4x4 needed, Elev: 5629ft/1716m, Tel: 435-719-2100. GPS: 38.061249, -110.147873

10 • D3 | Canyonlands NP - The Neck

Total sites: 1, No water, No toilets, Tents only: Free, Back-country, 4x4 needed, Elev: 6923ft/2110m, Tel: 435-719-2100. GPS: 38.087451, -110.144362

11 • D3 | Capitol Reef NP - Cathedral Valley

Total sites: 6, RV sites: 6, No water, Vault/pit toilet, Tent & RV camping: Free, Open all year, Reservations not accepted, Elev: 6939ft/2115m, Tel: 435-425-3791, Nearest town: Torrey. GPS: 38.474731, -111.367641

12 • D3 | Capitol Reef NP - Cedar Mesa

Total sites: 5, RV sites: 5, No water, Vault/pit toilet, Tent & RV camping: Free, Open all year, Reservations not accepted, Elev: 5610ft/1710m, Tel: 435-425-3791, Nearest town: Torrey. GPS: 38.007, -111.085

13 • D3 | Capitol Reef NP - Fruita CG

Total sites: 71, RV sites: 64, Central water, Flush toilet, No showers, RV dump, Tent & RV camping: $20, First-come/first-served available only Nov-Feb, Generator hours: 0800-1000/1800-2000, Open all year, Reservations required, Elev: 5463ft/1665m, Tel: 435-425-3791, Nearest town: Torrey. GPS: 38.2822, -111.24671

14 • D3 | Escalante NM - Burr Trail Rd

Dispersed sites, No water, No toilets, Tent & RV camping: Free, Free permit required, Elev: 5844ft/1781m. GPS: 37.848684, -111.370475

15 • D3 | Glen Canyon NRA - Blue Notch Canyon

Dispersed sites, No water, No toilets, Tents only: Free, Reservations not accepted, Elev: 3740ft/1140m, Tel: 928-608-6200. GPS: 37.719151, -110.433411

16 • D3 | Glen Canyon NRA - Dirty Devil

Dispersed sites, No water, No toilets, Tent & RV camping: $12, Reservations not accepted, Elev: 3734ft/1138m, Tel: 928-608-6200. GPS: 37.888577, -110.401252

17 • D3 | Glen Canyon NRA - Dispersed

Dispersed sites, No water, No toilets, Tent & RV camping: $6, Open all year, Reservations not accepted, Elev: 3707ft/1130m, Tel: 928-608-6200. GPS: 37.902535, -110.399694

18 • D3 | Glen Canyon NRA - Dispersed

Dispersed sites, No water, No toilets, Tent & RV camping: $6, Open all year, Reservations not accepted, Elev: 3806ft/1160m, Tel: 928-608-6200. GPS: 37.912164, -110.398614

19 • D3 | Glen Canyon NRA - Farley Canyon

Dispersed sites, No water, No toilets, Tent & RV camping: $12,

Open all year, Reservations not accepted, Elev: 3987ft/1215m, Tel: 928-608-6200. GPS: 37.820306, -110.396164

20 • D3 | Glen Canyon NRA - Hite Developed

Total sites: 21, RV sites: 21, Water at site, Flush toilet, Free showers, No RV dump, Tent & RV camping: $24, Stay limit: 14 days, Open all year, Reservations not accepted, Elev: 3762ft/1147m, Tel: 435-233-6822, Nearest town: Hite. GPS: 37.873503, -110.392527

21 • D3 | Glen Canyon NRA - Hite Improved

Dispersed sites, Central water, Flush toilet, Free showers, No RV dump, Tent & RV camping: $18, Stay limit: 14 days, Open all year, Reservations not accepted, Elev: 3704ft/1129m, Tel: 435-233-6822, Nearest town: Hite. GPS: 37.871557, -110.396497

22 • D3 | Glen Canyon NRA - Hite Launch Ramp

Dispersed sites, Central water, Flush toilet, Free showers, No RV dump, Tents only: Fee unk, Stay limit: 14 days, Open all year, Reservations not accepted, Elev: 3676ft/1120m, Tel: 435-233-6822, Nearest town: Hite. GPS: 37.873006, -110.397799

23 • D3 | Glen Canyon NRA - Hite RV

Total sites: 10, RV sites: 10, Water at site, No toilets, No showers, No RV dump, No tents/RV's: $45, 10 Full hookups, Stay limit: 14 days, Open all year, Reservations accepted, Elev: 3776ft/1151m, Tel: 435-233-6822. GPS: 37.875881, -110.380731

24 • D3 | Glen Canyon NRA - White Canyon

Dispersed sites, No water, No toilets, Tents only: Free, Open all year, Reservations not accepted, Elev: 3730ft/1137m, Tel: 928-608-6200. GPS: 37.787897, -110.380381

25 • D4 | Arches NP - Devils Garden CG

Total sites: 50, RV sites: 50, Central water, Flush toilet, No showers, No RV dump, Tent & RV camping: $25, Group sites - $75-$250, Stay limit: 7 days, Generator hours: 0800-1000/1600-2000, Open all year, Max Length: 40ft, Reservations accepted, Elev: 5243ft/1598m, Tel: 518-885-3639, Nearest town: Moab. GPS: 38.775843, -109.588551

26 • D4 | Canyonlands NP - Airport Tower

Total sites: 4, RV sites: 0, No water, No toilets, Tents only: Free, Back-country, 4x4 needed, Reservations accepted, Elev: 4505ft/1373m, Tel: 435-719-2100, Nearest town: Monticello. GPS: 38.391624, -109.793687

27 • D4 | Canyonlands NP - Bobby Jo

Total sites: 2, No water, Vault/pit toilet, Tents only: Free, Back-country, 4x4 needed, Reservations accepted, Elev: 5535ft/1687m, Tel: 435-719-2100, Nearest town: Monticello. GPS: 38.093458, -109.88168

28 • D4 | Canyonlands NP - Butler Flat

Dispersed sites, No water, No toilets, Tents only: Free, Back-country, 4x4 needed, Reservations accepted, Elev: 5436ft/1657m, Tel: 435-719-2100, Nearest town: Monticello. GPS: 38.096811, -109.877703

29 • D4 | Canyonlands NP - Candlestick

Total sites: 1, RV sites: 0, No water, No toilets, Tents only: Free, Back-country, 4x4 needed, Reservations accepted, Elev: 4373ft/1333m, Tel: 435-719-2100, Nearest town: Monticello. GPS: 38.374158, -109.965309

30 • D4 | Canyonlands NP - Chimney Rock

Total sites: 1, No water, No toilets, Tents only: Free, Back-country, 4x4 needed, Reservations accepted, Elev: 5456ft/1663m, Tel: 435-719-2100, Nearest town: Monticello. GPS: 38.185807, -109.975055

31 • D4 | Canyonlands NP - Cleopatra's Chair

Total sites: 1, No water, No toilets, Tents only: Free, Back-country, 4x4 needed, Elev: 6220ft/1896m, Tel: 435-719-2100. GPS: 38.302284, -110.078577

32 • D4 | Canyonlands NP - Devils Kitchen

Total sites: 4, No water, Vault/pit toilet, Tents only: Free, Back-country, 4x4 needed, Reservations accepted, Elev: 5387ft/1642m, Tel: 435-719-2100, Nearest town: Monticello. GPS: 38.136033, -109.859974

33 • D4 | Canyonlands NP - Ekker Butte

Total sites: 1, No water, No toilets, Tents only: Free, Back-country, 4x4 needed, Elev: 4911ft/1497m, Tel: 435-719-2100. GPS: 38.283244, -109.968305

34 • D4 | Canyonlands NP - Golden Stairs

Total sites: 1, No water, No toilets, Tents only: Free, Back-country, 4x4 needed, Elev: 6064ft/1848m, Tel: 435-719-2100. GPS: 38.141893, -110.086956

35 • D4 | Canyonlands NP - Gooseberry

Dispersed sites, No water, No toilets, Tent & RV camping: Free, Back-country, 4x4 needed, Reservations accepted, Elev: 4754ft/1449m, Tel: 435-719-2100, Nearest town: Monticello. GPS: 38.330883, -109.827365

36 • D4 | Canyonlands NP - Hardscrabble Bottom

Total sites: 2, RV sites: 2, No water, No toilets, Tent & RV camping: Free, Back-country, 4x4 needed, Reservations accepted, Elev: 3966ft/1209m, Tel: 435-719-2100, Nearest town: Monticello. GPS: 38.448394, -110.010298

37 • D4 | Canyonlands NP - Horsehoof

Total sites: 1, No water, No toilets, Tents only: Free, Back-country, 4x4 needed, Elev: 5560ft/1695m, Tel: 435-719-2100. GPS: 38.098421, -109.880214

38 • D4 | Canyonlands NP - Island in the Sky (Willow Flat)

Total sites: 12, RV sites: 12, No water, Vault/pit toilet, Tent & RV camping: $15, Generator hours: 0800-1000/1600-1800, Open all year, Max Length: 28ft, Reservations not accepted, Elev: 6079ft/1853m, Tel: 435-719-2100, Nearest town: Monticello. GPS: 38.383182, -109.887874

39 • D4 | Canyonlands NP - Labyrinth

Total sites: 2, RV sites: 2, No water, No toilets, Tent & RV camping: Free, Back-country, 4x4 needed, Reservations accepted, Elev: 4003ft/1220m, Tel: 435-719-2100, Nearest town: Monticello. GPS: 38.474984, -109.999666

40 • D4 | Canyonlands NP - Maze Overlook

Total sites: 2, No water, No toilets, Tents only: Free, Back-country, 4x4 needed, Reservations accepted, Elev: 5171ft/1576m, Tel: 435-719-2100, Nearest town: Monticello. GPS: 38.232845, -110.002958

41 • D4 | Canyonlands NP - Millard Canyon

Total sites: 1, No water, No toilets, Tents only: Free, Back-country, 4x4 needed, Reservations accepted, Elev: 3934ft/1199m, Tel: 435-719-2100, Nearest town: Monticello. GPS: 38.38921, -110.03439

42 • D4 | Canyonlands NP - Murphy Hogback

Dispersed sites, No water, No toilets, Tents only: Free, Back-country, 4x4 needed, Reservations accepted, Elev: 5279ft/1609m, Tel: 435-719-2100, Nearest town: Monticello. GPS: 38.321721, -109.906248

43 • D4 | Canyonlands NP - New Bates Wilson

Total sites: 1, No water, No toilets, Tents only: Free, Back-country, 4x4 needed, Reservations accepted, Elev: 5128ft/1563m, Tel: 435-719-2100. GPS: 38.159576, -109.860513

44 • D4 | Canyonlands NP - Panorama Point

Total sites: 1, No water, No toilets, Tents only: Free, Back-country, 4x4 needed, Elev: 6268ft/1910m, Tel: 435-719-2100. GPS: 38.272203, -110.040375

45 • D4 | Canyonlands NP - Peekaboo Spring

Total sites: 2, No water, Vault/pit toilet, Tents only: Free, Back-country, 4x4 needed, Reservations accepted, Elev: 5066ft/1544m, Tel: 435-719-2100, Nearest town: Monticello. GPS: 38.112238, -109.753435

46 • D4 | Canyonlands NP - Potato Bottom

Total sites: 3, RV sites: 0, No water, No toilets, Tents only: Free, 4x4 needed, Reservations accepted, Elev: 3970ft/1210m, Tel: 435-719-2100, Nearest town: Monticello. GPS: 38.431564, -110.010736

47 • D4 | Canyonlands NP - Rivers Overlook

Dispersed sites, No water, No toilets, Tents only: Free, Back-country, 4x4 needed, Reservations accepted, Elev: 5226ft/1593m, Tel: 435-719-2100, Nearest town: Monticello. GPS: 38.160279, -109.947727

48 • D4 | Canyonlands NP - Shafer Canyon

Total sites: 1, RV sites: 1, No water, No toilets, Tent & RV camping: Free, Back-country, 4x4 needed, Reservations accepted, Elev: 4308ft/1313m, Tel: 435-719-2100, Nearest town: Monticello. GPS: 38.466123, -109.781405

49 • D4 | Canyonlands NP - Spanish Bottom

Dispersed sites, No water, No toilets, Tents only: Free, Back-country, 4x4 needed, Reservations accepted, Elev: 3901ft/1189m, Tel: 435-719-2100, Nearest town: Monticello. GPS: 38.157889, -109.934395

50 • D4 | Canyonlands NP - Split Top Group

Total sites: 1, RV sites: 0, Vault/pit toilet, Group site, Open Mar-Nov, Max Length: 25ft, Reservations accepted, Elev: 4931ft/1503m, Tel: 435-719-2100, Nearest town: Monticello. GPS: 38.155457, -109.755058

51 • D4 | Canyonlands NP - Standing Rock

Total sites: 1, No water, No toilets, Tents only: Free, Back-country, 4x4 needed, Reservations accepted, Elev: 5515ft/1681m, Tel: 435-719-2100, Nearest town: Monticello. GPS: 38.176109, -109.991118

52 • D4 | Canyonlands NP - Taylor Canyon

Total sites: 1, RV sites: 1, No water, No toilets, Tent & RV camping: Free, Back-country, 4x4 needed, Reservations accepted, Elev: 4380ft/1335m, Tel: 435-719-2100, Nearest town: Monticello. GPS: 38.476372, -109.922979

53 • D4 | Canyonlands NP - Teapot Rock

Total sites: 1, No water, No toilets, Tents only: Free, Back-country, 4x4 needed, Elev: 5607ft/1709m, Tel: 435-719-2100. GPS: 38.078496, -110.108916

54 • D4 | Canyonlands NP - The Doll House

Dispersed sites, No water, No toilets, Tents only: Free, Back-country, 4x4 needed, Reservations accepted, Elev: 5112ft/1558m, Tel: 435-719-2100, Nearest town: Monticello. GPS: 38.150597, -109.95213

55 • D4 | Canyonlands NP - The Needles (Squaw Flat)

Total sites: 26, RV sites: 26, Central water, Flush toilet, No showers, No RV dump, Tent & RV camping: $20, Group site available, Generator hours: 0800-1000/1600-1800, Open all year, Max Length: 28ft, Reservations accepted, Elev: 5096ft/1553m, Tel: 435-719-2100, Nearest town: Monticello. GPS: 38.149066, -109.796375

56 • D4 | Canyonlands NP - The Wall

Total sites: 1, No water, No toilets, Tents only: Free, Back-country, 4x4 needed, Reservations accepted, Elev: 5450ft/1661m, Tel: 435-719-2100, Nearest town: Monticello. GPS: 38.170763, -110.019203

57 • D4 | Canyonlands NP - Upheaval Bottom

Dispersed sites, No water, No toilets, Tents only: Free, Back-country, 4x4 needed, Reservations accepted, Elev: 4012ft/1223m, Tel: 435-719-2100, Nearest town: Monticello. GPS: 38.474531, -110.000768

58 • D4 | Canyonlands NP - Upheaval Canyon

Dispersed sites, No water, No toilets, Tents only: Free, Back-country, 4x4 needed, Reservations accepted, Elev: 3960ft/1207m, Tel: 435-719-2100, Nearest town: Monticello. GPS: 38.468208, -109.998715

59 • D4 | Canyonlands NP - White Crack

Total sites: 1, RV sites: 1, No water, No toilets, Tent & RV camping: Free, Back-country, 4x4 needed, Reservations accepted, Elev: 5171ft/1576m, Tel: 435-719-2100, Nearest town: Monticello. GPS: 38.257035, -109.865459

60 • D4 | Canyonlands NP - Wooden Shoe Group

Total sites: 1, RV sites: 0, Vault/pit toilet, Group site, Open Mar-

Nov, Max Length: 25ft, Reservations accepted, Elev: 5046ft/1538m, Tel: 435-719-2100, Nearest town: Monticello. GPS: 38.147711, -109.784506

61 • E1 | Zion NP - Bear Camp

Dispersed sites, Tents only: Fee unk, Hike-in, Permit required - $15-$2, La Verkin Trail, Reservations not accepted, Elev: 5755ft/1754m, Tel: 435-772-0170, Nearest town: Rockville. GPS: 37.431474, -113.126581

62 • E1 | Zion NP - Big Spring

Dispersed sites, Tents only: Fee unk, Hike-in, Permit required - $15-$25, The Narrows, Reservations accepted, Elev: 4731ft/1442m, Tel: 435-772-0170, Nearest town: Rockville. GPS: 37.331159, -112.956794

63 • E1 | Zion NP - Bird Camp

Dispersed sites, Tents only: Fee unk, Hike-in, Permit required - $15-$25, La Verkin Trail, Reservations not accepted, Elev: 5257ft/1602m, Tel: 435-772-0170, Nearest town: Rockville. GPS: 37.415866, -113.150148

64 • E1 | Zion NP - Camp 1

Dispersed sites, Tents only: Fee unk, Hike-in, Permit required - $15-$25, West Rim Trail , Affected by 2007 fire, Reservations not accepted, Elev: 6782ft/2067m, Tel: 435-772-0170, Nearest town: Rockville. GPS: 37.288185, -112.969153

65 • E1 | Zion NP - Camp 2

Dispersed sites, Tents only: Fee unk, Hike-in, Permit required - $15-$25, West Rim Trail , Affected by 2007 fire, Reservations accepted, Elev: 6713ft/2046m, Tel: 435-772-0170, Nearest town: Rockville. GPS: 37.285482, -112.968867

66 • E1 | Zion NP - Camp 3

Dispersed sites, Tents only: Fee unk, Hike-in, Permit required - $15-$25, West Rim Trail , Affected by 2007 fire, Reservations not accepted, Elev: 7018ft/2139m, Tel: 435-772-0170, Nearest town: Rockville. GPS: 37.285429, -112.971137

67 • E1 | Zion NP - Camp 4

Dispersed sites, Tents only: Fee unk, Hike-in, Permit required - $15-$25, West Rim Trail , Affected by 2007 fire, Reservations accepted, Elev: 7290ft/2222m, Tel: 435-772-0170, Nearest town: Rockville. GPS: 37.284534, -112.982731

68 • E1 | Zion NP - Camp 5

Dispersed sites, Tents only: Fee unk, Hike-in, Permit required - $15-$25, West Rim Trail , Affected by 2007 fire, Reservations not accepted, Elev: 7362ft/2244m, Tel: 435-772-0170, Nearest town: Rockville. GPS: 37.292318, -112.987722

69 • E1 | Zion NP - Camp 6

Dispersed sites, Tents only: Fee unk, Hike-in, Permit required - $15-$25, West Rim Trail , Affected by 2007 fire, Reservations accepted, Elev: 7305ft/2227m, Tel: 435-772-0170, Nearest town: Rockville. GPS: 37.304376, -112.987751

70 • E1 | Zion NP - Camp 7

Dispersed sites, Tents only: Fee unk, Hike-in, Permit required

- $15-$25, West Rim Trail , Seasonal water, Reservations not accepted, Elev: 4869ft/1484m, Tel: 435-772-0170, Nearest town: Rockville. GPS: 37.344765, -112.950781

71 • E1 | Zion NP - Camp 7

Dispersed sites, Tents only: Fee unk, Hike-in, Permit required - $15-$25, The Narrows, Reservations not accepted, Elev: 6844ft/2086m, Tel: 435-772-0170, Nearest town: Rockville. GPS: 37.320261, -112.990145

72 • E1 | Zion NP - Camp 9

Dispersed sites, Tents only: Fee unk, Hike-in, Permit required - $15-$25, The Narrows, Reservations not accepted, Elev: 4772ft/1455m, Tel: 435-772-0170, Nearest town: Rockville. GPS: 37.339418, -112.955709

73 • E1 | Zion NP - Coal Pit Wash

Dispersed sites, Tents only: Fee unk, Hike-in, Permit required - $15-$25, Elev: 4106ft/1252m, Tel: 435-772-0170, Nearest town: Rockville. GPS: 37.215841, -113.077799

74 • E1 | Zion NP - Coal Pits Ridge

Dispersed sites, Tents only: Fee unk, Hike-in, Permit required - $15-$25, Elev: 4127ft/1258m, Tel: 435-772-0170, Nearest town: Rockville. GPS: 37.212164, -113.078243

75 • E1 | Zion NP - Cottonwood Camp

Dispersed sites, Tents only: Fee unk, Hike-in, Permit required - $15-$25, La Verkin Trail, Reservations not accepted, Elev: 5360ft/1634m, Tel: 435-772-0170, Nearest town: Rockville. GPS: 37.421443, -113.139605

76 • E1 | Zion NP - Cougar Camp

Dispersed sites, Tents only: Fee unk, Hike-in, Permit required - $15-$25, La Verkin Trail, Reservations accepted, Elev: 5298ft/1615m, Tel: 435-772-0170, Nearest town: Rockville. GPS: 37.417141, -113.143179

77 • E1 | Zion NP - Cross Creek West Camp

Dispersed sites, Tents only: Fee unk, Hike-in, Permit required - $15-$25, La Verkin Trail, Reservations not accepted, Elev: 5226ft/1593m, Tel: 435-772-0170, Nearest town: Rockville. GPS: 37.415106, -113.151404

78 • E1 | Zion NP - Deer Camp

Dispersed sites, Tents only: Fee unk, Hike-in, Permit required - $15-$25, La Verkin Trail, Reservations not accepted, Elev: 5419ft/1652m, Tel: 435-772-0170, Nearest town: Rockville. GPS: 37.422731, -113.195859

79 • E1 | Zion NP - Dipper Camp

Dispersed sites, Tents only: Fee unk, Hike-in, Permit required - $15-$25, La Verkin Trail, Reservations not accepted, Elev: 5107ft/1557m, Tel: 435-772-0170, Nearest town: Rockville. GPS: 37.410847, -113.167479

80 • E1 | Zion NP - Dry Camp

Dispersed sites, Tents only: Fee unk, Hike-in, Permit required - $15-$25, La Verkin Trail, Reservations not accepted, Elev:

5456ft/1663m, Tel: 435-772-0170, Nearest town: Rockville. GPS: 37.407192, -113.196793

81 • E1 | Zion NP - Flat Rock Camp

Dispersed sites, Tents only: Fee unk, Hike-in, Permit required - $15-$25, La Verkin Trail, Reservations accepted, Elev: 5223ft/1592m, Tel: 435-772-0170, Nearest town: Rockville. GPS: 37.415427, -113.152172

82 • E1 | Zion NP - Goose Creek

Dispersed sites, Tents only: Fee unk, Hike-in, Permit required - $15-$25, The Narrows, Reservations accepted, Elev: 4763ft/1452m, Tel: 435-772-0170, Nearest town: Rockville. GPS: 37.338335, -112.957145

83 • E1 | Zion NP - Hop Valley

Dispersed sites, Tents only: Fee unk, Hike-in, Permit required - $15-$25, Hop Valley Trail, Reservations not accepted, Elev: 5730ft/1747m, Tel: 435-772-0170, Nearest town: Rockville. GPS: 37.401512, -113.137898

84 • E1 | Zion NP - Hop Valley Horse Camp

Dispersed sites, Tents only: Fee unk, Hike-in, Permit required - $15-$25, Hop Valley Trail, Reservations not accepted, Elev: 5720ft/1743m, Tel: 435-772-0170, Nearest town: Rockville. GPS: 37.403614, -113.139292

85 • E1 | Zion NP - Junction

Dispersed sites, Tents only: Fee unk, Hike-in, Permit required - $15-$25, Elev: 3805ft/1160m, Tel: 435-772-0170, Nearest town: Rockville. GPS: 37.194164, -113.076181

86 • E1 | Zion NP - Juniper Camp

Dispersed sites, Tents only: Fee unk, Hike-in, Permit required - $15-$25, La Verkin Trail, Reservations accepted, Elev: 5082ft/1549m, Tel: 435-772-0170, Nearest town: Rockville. GPS: 37.407301, -113.175558

87 • E1 | Zion NP - Kolob Creek

Dispersed sites, Tents only: Fee unk, Hike-in, Permit required - $15-$25, The Narrows, Reservations not accepted, Elev: 4895ft/1492m, Tel: 435-772-0170, Nearest town: Rockville. GPS: 37.349505, -112.950747

88 • E1 | Zion NP - Lava Point

Total sites: 6, RV sites: 6, No water, Vault/pit toilet, Tent & RV camping: Free, Open Jun-Oct, Max Length: 19ft, Reservations not accepted, Elev: 7917ft/2413m, Tel: 435-772-3256, Nearest town: Springdale. GPS: 37.383707, -113.032797

89 • E1 | Zion NP - Neagle Camp

Dispersed sites, Tents only: Fee unk, Hike-in, Permit required - $15-$25, La Verkin Trail, Reservations accepted, Elev: 5097ft/1554m, Tel: 435-772-0170, Nearest town: Rockville. GPS: 37.410329, -113.170002

90 • E1 | Zion NP - Oak Point Camp

Dispersed sites, Tents only: Fee unk, Hike-in, Permit required - $15-$25, La Verkin Trail, Reservations accepted, Elev: 5189ft/

1582m, Tel: 435-772-0170, Nearest town: Rockville. GPS: 37.414199, -113.155817

91 • E1 | Zion NP - Potato Hollow

Dispersed sites, Tents only: Fee unk, Hike-in, Permit required - $15-$25, West Rim Trail , Seasonal water, Reservations accepted, Elev: 6777ft/2066m, Tel: 435-772-0170, Nearest town: Rockville. GPS: 37.321642, -112.985398

92 • E1 | Zion NP - Ringtail Camp

Dispersed sites, Tents only: Fee unk, Hike-in, Permit required - $15-$25, La Verkin Trail, Reservations accepted, Elev: 5344ft/1629m, Tel: 435-772-0170, Nearest town: Rockville. GPS: 37.413319, -113.194773

93 • E1 | Zion NP - Sawmill Springs

Dispersed sites, Tents only: Fee unk, Hike-in, Permit required - $15-$25, West Rim Trail, Reservations not accepted, Elev: 7218ft/2200m, Tel: 435-772-0170, Nearest town: Rockville. GPS: 37.370098, -113.016924

94 • E1 | Zion NP - Scoggins Wash

Dispersed sites, Tents only: Fee unk, Hike-in, Permit required - $15-$25, Elev: 4205ft/1282m, Tel: 435-772-0170, Nearest town: Rockville. GPS: 37.210687, -113.050846

95 • E1 | Zion NP - South CG

Total sites: 127, RV sites: 127, Central water, Vault/pit toilet, No showers, RV dump, Tent & RV camping: $20, Group site: $50, Max height 13ft, Generator hours: 0800-1000/1800-2000, Open Mar-Nov, Reservations required, Elev: 3970ft/1210m, Tel: 435-772-3256, Nearest town: Springdale. GPS: 37.203613, -112.981689

96 • E1 | Zion NP - Spotted Owl

Dispersed sites, Tents only: Fee unk, Hike-in, Permit required - $15-$25, The Narrows, Reservations not accepted, Elev: 4761ft/1451m, Tel: 435-772-0170, Nearest town: Rockville. GPS: 37.333899, -112.955681

97 • E1 | Zion NP - Temple View

Dispersed sites, Tents only: Fee unk, Hike-in, Permit required - $15-$25, Elev: 4420ft/1347m, Tel: 435-772-0170, Nearest town: Rockville. GPS: 37.205979, -113.054834

98 • E1 | Zion NP - The Grotto

Dispersed sites, Tents only: Fee unk, Hike-in, Permit required - $15-$25, The Narrows, Reservations not accepted, Elev: 4860ft/1481m, Tel: 435-772-0170, Nearest town: Rockville. GPS: 37.342982, -112.954176

99 • E1 | Zion NP - Watchman CG

Total sites: 164, RV sites: 95, Elec sites: 95, Central water, Vault/pit toilet, No showers, RV dump, Tents: $20/RV's: $30, 6 group sites, No generators, Open all year, Reservations accepted, Elev: 3960ft/1207m, Tel: 435-772-3256, Nearest town: Springdale. GPS: 37.195801, -112.987061

100 • E1 | Zion NP - Yucca

Dispersed sites, Tents only: Fee unk, Hike-in, Permit required -

$15-$25, Elev: 4200ft/1280m, Tel: 435-772-0170, Nearest town: Rockville. GPS: 37.203386, -113.067906

101 • E2 | Bryce Canyon NP - Corral Hollow

Dispersed sites, No water, No toilets, Tents only: $5, Hike-in, No open fires, Permit required, Reservations accepted, Elev: 7932ft/2418m, Tel: 435-834-5322. GPS: 37.465098, -112.234073

102 • E2 | Bryce Canyon NP - Iron Spring

Dispersed sites, No water, No toilets, Tents only: $5, Hike-in, No open fires, Permit required, Reservations accepted, Elev: 7890ft/2405m, Tel: 435-834-5322. GPS: 37.490628, -112.243951

103 • E2 | Bryce Canyon NP - Natural Bridge

Dispersed sites, No water, No toilets, Tents only: $5, Hike-in, No open fires, Permit required, Reservations accepted, Elev: 7549ft/2301m, Tel: 435-834-5322. GPS: 37.526791, -112.241177

104 • E2 | Bryce Canyon NP - North CG

Total sites: 99, RV sites: 99, Central water, Flush toilet, Pay showers, RV dump, Tents: $20/RV's: $30, Only A Loop open all year, $5 dump fee, Generator hours: 0800-2000, Open all year, Reservations not accepted, Elev: 7976ft/2431m, Tel: 435-834-5322, Nearest town: Bryce Canyon. GPS: 37.636153, -112.166055

105 • E2 | Bryce Canyon NP - Riggs Spring

Dispersed sites, No water, No toilets, Tents only: $5, Hike-in, No open fires, Permit required, Reservations accepted, Elev: 7471ft/2277m, Tel: 435-834-5322. GPS: 37.450294, -112.240644

106 • E2 | Bryce Canyon NP - Riggs Spring Group Site

Dispersed sites, No water, No toilets, Tents only: $5, Hike-in, No open fires, Permit required, Reservations accepted, Elev: 7429ft/2264m, Tel: 435-834-5322. GPS: 37.449407, -112.238225

107 • E2 | Bryce Canyon NP - Right Fork Swamp Canyon

Dispersed sites, No water, No toilets, Tents only: $5, Hike-in, No open fires, Permit required, Reservations accepted, Elev: 7473ft/2278m, Tel: 435-834-5322. GPS: 37.576843, -112.212651

108 • E2 | Bryce Canyon NP - Right Fork Yellow Creek

Dispersed sites, No water, No toilets, Tents only: $5, Hike-in, No open fires, Permit required, Reservations accepted, Elev: 7005ft/2135m, Tel: 435-834-5322. GPS: 37.588063, -112.147517

109 • E2 | Bryce Canyon NP - Sheep Creek

Dispersed sites, No water, No toilets, Tents only: $5, Hike-in, No open fires, Permit required, Reservations accepted, Elev: 7256ft/2212m, Tel: 435-834-5322. GPS: 37.571928, -112.199575

110 • E2 | Bryce Canyon NP - Sunset CG - Loop A

Total sites: 52, RV sites: 52, Central water, Flush toilet, No showers, No RV dump, No tents/RV's: $30, Generator hours: 0800-2000, Open Apr-Oct, Max Length: 45ft, Reservations accepted, Elev: 8015ft/2443m, Tel: 435-834-5322, Nearest town: Bryce Canyon. GPS: 37.622924, -112.173958

111 • E2 | Bryce Canyon NP - Sunset CG - Loops B and C

Total sites: 52, Central water, No toilets, No showers, No RV dump, Tents only: $20, No generators, Open Apr-Oct, Reservations accepted, Elev: 8045ft/2452m, Tel: 435-834-5322, Nearest town: Bryce Canyon. GPS: 37.621403, -112.176138

112 • E2 | Bryce Canyon NP - Swamp Canyon

Dispersed sites, No water, No toilets, Tents only: $5, Hike-in, No open fires, Permit required, Reservations accepted, Elev: 8214ft/2504m, Tel: 435-834-5322. GPS: 37.561203, -112.230075

113 • E2 | Bryce Canyon NP - Yellow Creek

Dispersed sites, No water, No toilets, Tents only: $5, Hike-in, No open fires, Permit required, Reservations accepted, Elev: 7135ft/2175m, Tel: 435-834-5322. GPS: 37.584857, -112.162338

114 • E2 | Bryce Canyon NP - Yellow Creek Group Site

Dispersed sites, No water, No toilets, Tents only: $5, Hike-in, No open fires, Permit required, Reservations accepted, Elev: 6822ft/2079m, Tel: 435-834-5322. GPS: 37.575349, -112.147475

115 • E2 | Bryce Canyon NP - Yovimpa Pass

Dispersed sites, No water, No toilets, Tents only: $5, Hike-in, No open fires, Permit required, Reservations accepted, Elev: 8355ft/2547m, Tel: 435-834-5322. GPS: 37.462982, -112.257902

116 • E2 | Cedar Breaks NM - Point Supreme

Total sites: 28, RV sites: 20, Central water, Flush toilet, Free showers, No RV dump, Tent & RV camping: $24, Only credit/debit cards accepted - no cash or checks, Generator hours: 0600-2200, Open Jun-Sep, Max Length: 24ft, Reservations accepted, Elev: 10282ft/3134m, Tel: 435-586-9451, Nearest town: Cedar City. GPS: 37.61036, -112.83038

117 • E2 | Zion NP - Deep Creek

Dispersed sites, Tents only: Fee unk, Hike-in, Permit required - $15-$25, The Narrows, Reservations accepted, Elev: 4972ft/1515m, Tel: 435-772-0170, Nearest town: Rockville. GPS: 37.359395, -112.951557

118 • E2 | Zion NP - Flat Rock

Dispersed sites, Tents only: Fee unk, Hike-in, Permit required - $15-$25, The Narrows, Reservations not accepted, Elev: 4908ft/1496m, Tel: 435-772-0170, Nearest town: Rockville. GPS: 37.350216, -112.949708

119 • E2 | Zion NP - Right Bench

Dispersed sites, Tents only: Fee unk, Hike-in, Permit required - $15-$25, The Narrows, Reservations accepted, Elev: 4923ft/1501m, Tel: 435-772-0170, Nearest town: Rockville. GPS: 37.35327, -112.95133

120 • E2 | Zion NP - River Bend

Dispersed sites, Tents only: Fee unk, Hike-in, Permit required - $15-$25, The Narrows, Reservations not accepted, Elev: 4941ft/1506m, Tel: 435-772-0170, Nearest town: Rockville. GPS: 37.356292, -112.950974

121 • E2 | Zion NP - Simon Gulch

Dispersed sites, Tents only: Fee unk, Hike-in, Permit required - $15-$25, The Narrows, Reservations not accepted, Elev: 5290ft/1612m, Tel: 435-772-0170, Nearest town: Rockville. GPS: 37.371467, -112.912438

122 • E3 | Glen Canyon NRA - Alstrom Point

Dispersed sites, No water, No toilets, Tent & RV camping: Free, Reservations not accepted, Elev: 4690ft/1430m, Nearest town: Big Water. GPS: 37.059277, -111.364684

123 • E3 | Glen Canyon NRA – Bullfrog

Total sites: 24, RV sites: 24, Elec sites: 24, Water at site, Flush toilet, Free showers, RV dump, No tents/RV's: $46, 24 Full hookups, Max Length: 50ft, Reservations accepted, Elev: 3760ft/1146m, Tel: 435-684-3032. GPS: 37.522563, -110.724697

124 • E3 | Glen Canyon NRA - Bullfrog Main

Total sites: 78, RV sites: 78, Central water, Flush toilet, Free showers, RV dump, Tent & RV camping: $20, Reservations not accepted, Elev: 3746ft/1142m, Tel: 928-608-6200. GPS: 37.520477, -110.722579

125 • E3 | Glen Canyon NRA - Halls Crossing FHU

Total sites: 65, RV sites: 24, Elec sites: 24, Water at site, Flush toilet, Free showers, RV dump, Tents: $26/RV's: $45, 24 Full hookups, Max Length: 60ft, Reservations accepted, Elev: 3750ft/1143m, Tel: 435-684-7000. GPS: 37.472263, -110.712501

126 • E3 | Glen Canyon NRA - Lone Rock Beach

Dispersed sites, Central water, Flush toilet, No showers, RV dump, Tent & RV camping: $14, Cold outdoor showers, Generator hours: 0600-2200, Open all year, Reservations not accepted, Elev: 3681ft/1122m, Tel: 928-608-6200, Nearest town: Kanab. GPS: 37.018887, -111.538106

127 • E3 | Glen Canyon NRA - Stanton Creek

Dispersed sites, No water, No toilets, Tent & RV camping: $12, Open all year, Reservations not accepted, Elev: 3705ft/1129m, Tel: 928-608-6200. GPS: 37.499053, -110.699281

128 • E4 | Hovenweep NM

Total sites: 31, RV sites: 7, Central water, Flush toilet, No showers, No RV dump, Tent & RV camping: $15, 5-gallon/person water limit, Nov-Feb: $10, Stay limit: 7 days, Generator hours: 0800-1000/1600-2000, Open all year, Max Length: 36ft, Reservations not accepted, Elev: 5223ft/1592m, Tel: 970-562-4282 x10, Nearest town: Blanding. GPS: 37.383203, -109.071292

129 • E4 | Natural Bridges NM

Total sites: 13, RV sites: 13, No water, Vault/pit toilet, Tent & RV camping: $15, Water available 1/2 mile at Visitor Center - 5 gal/person/day limit, Open all year, Max Length: 26ft, Reservations not accepted, Elev: 6476ft/1974m, Tel: 435-692-1234, Nearest town: Blanding. GPS: 37.60956, -109.98434

Virginia

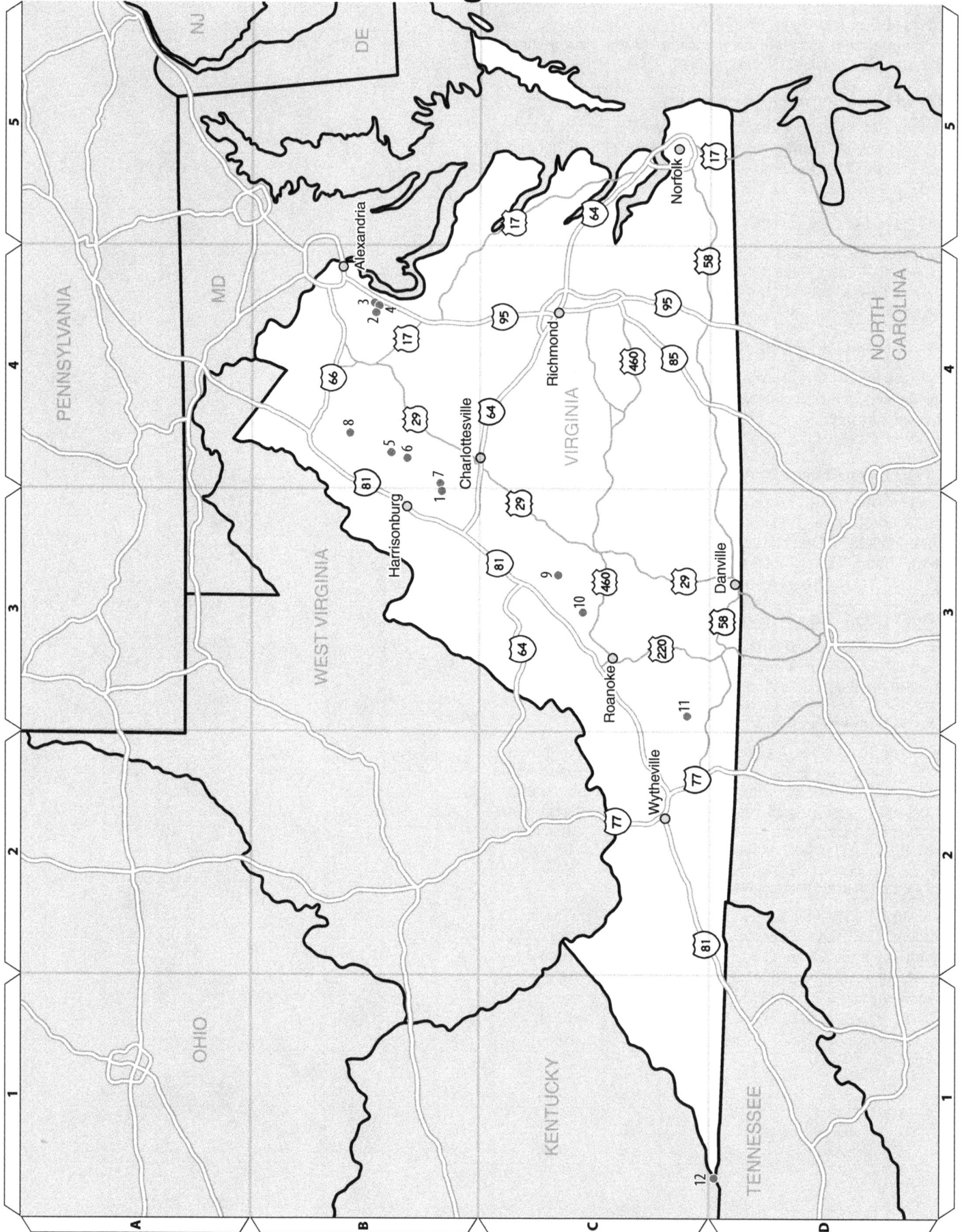

Map	ID	Map	ID
B3	1	C3	9-11
B4	2-8	D1	12

Alphabetical List of Camping Areas

Name   **ID**   **Map**

Blue Ridge Pkwy - Otter Creek...9............C3
Blue Ridge Pkwy - Peaks of Otter..10...........C3
Blue Ridge Pkwy - Rocky Knob..11...........C3
Prince William Forest - Oak Ridge..2............B4
Prince William Forest - Travel Trailer Village.......................3............B4
Prince William Forest - Turkey Run Ridge Group................4............B4
Shenandoah NP - Big Meadows...5............B4
Shenandoah NP - Dundo Group...1............B3
Shenandoah NP - Lewis Mountain...6............B4
Shenandoah NP - Loft Mountain...7............B4
Shenandoah NP - Matthews Arm...8............B4
Wilderness Road - Cumberland Gap....................................12.........D1

1 • B3 | Shenandoah NP - Dundo Group

Total sites: 3, RV sites: 0, No water, Vault/pit toilet, Group sites (tents only): $45, Non-potable water, No generators, Open May-Oct, Reservations accepted, Elev: 2871ft/875m, Tel: 540-999-3132, Nearest town: Charlottesville. GPS: 38.235409, -78.717397

2 • B4 | Prince William Forest - Oak Ridge

Total sites: 100, RV sites: 67, Central water, Flush toilet, Free showers, No RV dump, Tent & RV camping: $26, Reservations required Apr-Oct, Stay limit: 14 days, Generator hours: 0600-2200, Open all year, Max Length: RV-32'/Trlr-26ft, Reservations accepted, Elev: 400ft/122m, Tel: 703-221-7181, Nearest town: Triangle. GPS: 38.599237, -77.417724

3 • B4 | Prince William Forest - Travel Trailer Village

Total sites: 76, RV sites: 76, Elec sites: 76, Water at site, Flush toilet, Free showers, RV dump, No tents/RV's: $37-55, 29 Full hookups, Concessionaire, Generator hours: 0600-2200, Open all year, Max Length: 35ft, Elev: 289ft/88m, Tel: 703-221-2474, Nearest town: Dumfries. GPS: 38.60312, -77.35205

4 • B4 | Prince William Forest - Turkey Run Ridge Group

Total sites: 9, RV sites: 0, Central water, Flush toilet, No showers, No RV dump, Group site: $50-$60, Stay limit: 14 days, Open all year, Reservations accepted, Elev: 282ft/86m, Tel: 703-221-2474, Nearest town: Dumfries. GPS: 38.582795, -77.373646

5 • B4 | Shenandoah NP - Big Meadows

Total sites: 219, RV sites: 168, Central water, Flush toilet, Free showers, RV dump, Tent & RV camping: $20, 2 group sites: $45, Generator-free sites available, Generators allowed/hours unknown, Open Mar-Nov, Reservations accepted, Elev: 3570ft/1088m, Tel: 540-999-3231, Nearest town: Stanley. GPS: 38.526611, -78.438965

6 • B4 | Shenandoah NP - Lewis Mountain

Total sites: 31, RV sites: 31, Central water, Flush toilet, Free showers, No RV dump, Tent & RV camping: $15, Open Apr-Oct, Reservations not accepted, Elev: 3442ft/1049m, Nearest town: Elkton. GPS: 38.43732, -78.47831

7 • B4 | Shenandoah NP - Loft Mountain

Total sites: 199, RV sites: 155, Central water, Flush toilet, Pay showers, RV dump, Tent & RV camping: $15, Generator-free sites available, Generators allowed/hours unknown, Open May-Oct, Reservations accepted, Elev: 3291ft/1003m, Tel: 434-823-4675, Nearest town: Charlottesville. GPS: 38.24824, -78.66998

8 • B4 | Shenandoah NP - Matthews Arm

Total sites: 163, RV sites: 163, Central water, No toilets, No showers, RV dump, Tent & RV camping: $15, Generator-free sites available, Generators allowed/hours unknown, Open May-Oct, Reservations accepted, Elev: 2848ft/868m, Tel: 540-999-3132, Nearest town: Front Royal. GPS: 38.762497, -78.297068

9 • C3 | Blue Ridge Pkwy - Otter Creek

Total sites: 68, RV sites: 26, Central water, Flush toilet, No showers, RV dump, Tent & RV camping: $20, Generator hours: 0800-2100, Open May-Nov, Max Length: 80ft, Reservations not accepted, Elev: 833ft/254m, Tel: 540-377-2377, Nearest town: Lynchburg. GPS: 37.575755, -79.337357

10 • C3 | Blue Ridge Pkwy - Peaks of Otter

Total sites: 139, RV sites: 57, Central water, No toilets, No showers, RV dump, Tent & RV camping: $20, Generator hours: 0800-2100, Open May-Nov, Max Length: 77ft, Reservations accepted, Elev: 2556ft/779m, Tel: 540-586-7321, Nearest town: Bedford. GPS: 37.443047, -79.604307

11 • C3 | Blue Ridge Pkwy - Rocky Knob

Total sites: 110, RV sites: 34, Central water, No toilets, No showers, No RV dump, Tent & RV camping: $20, Group site: $35, Generator hours: 0800-2100, Open May-Nov, Max Length: 55ft, Reservations accepted, Elev: 3090ft/942m, Tel: 540-745-9664, Nearest town: Floyd. GPS: 36.832305, -80.344091

12 • D1 | Wilderness Road - Cumberland Gap

Total sites: 160, Elec sites: 41, Central water, Flush toilet, Free showers, RV dump, Tents: $14/RV's: $20, Open Mar-Nov, Reservations not accepted, Elev: 1362ft/415m, Tel: 606-248-2817, Nearest town: Middlesboro, KY. GPS: 36.602634, -83.631289

Washington

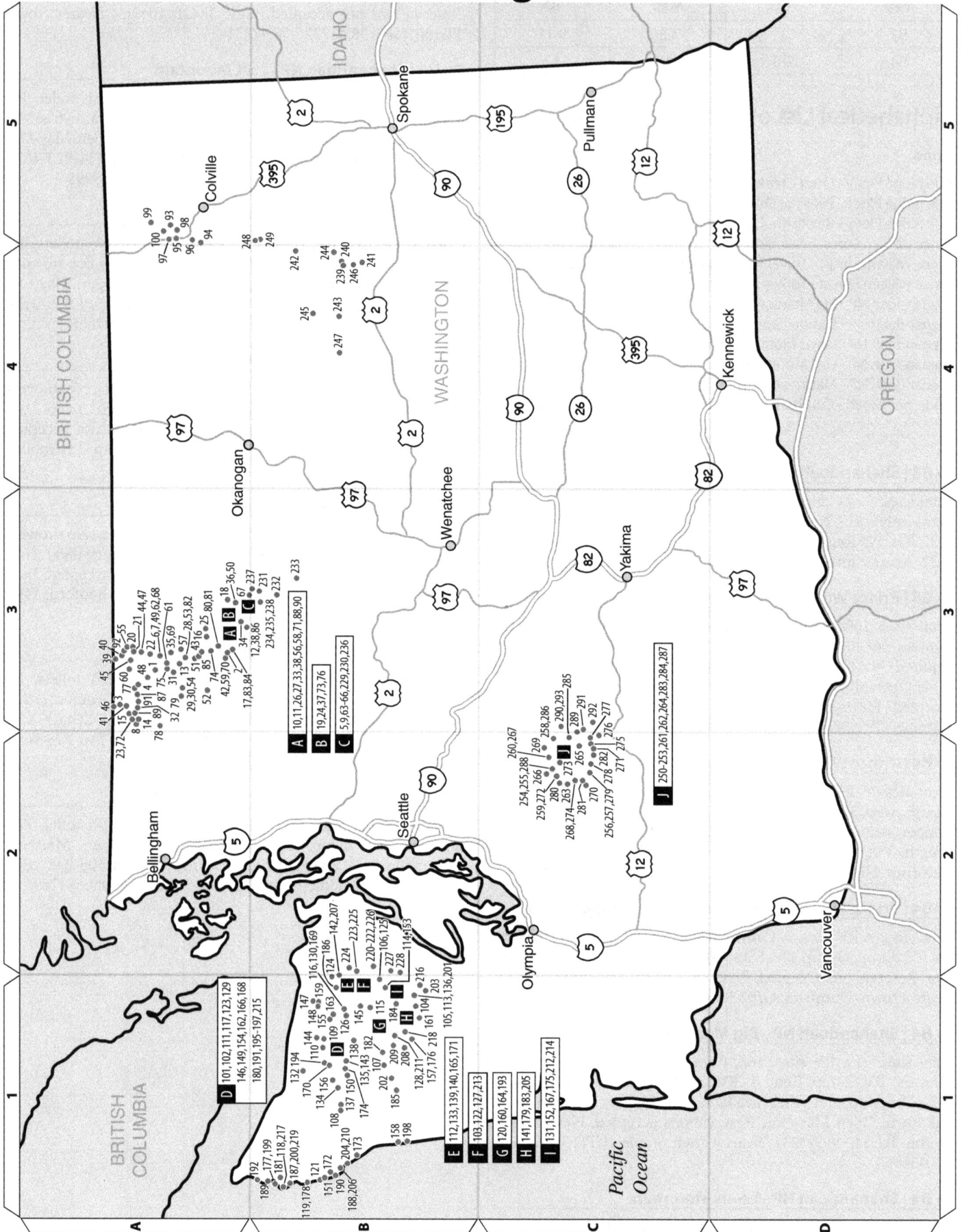

A 10,11,26,27,33,38,56,58,71,88,90
B 19,24,37,73,76
C 5,9,63-66,229,230,236

D 101,102,111,117,123,129
   146,149,154,162,166,168
   180,191,195-197,215

E 112,133,139,140,165,171
F 103,122,127,213
G 120,160,164,193
H 141,179,183,205
I 131,152,167,175,212,214

J 250-253,261,262,264,283,284,287

Map	ID	Map	ID
A3	1-92	B4	239-247
A5	93-100	B5	248-249
B1	101-219	C2	250-288
B2	220-228	C3	289-293
B3	229-238		

Alphabetical List of Camping Areas

Name	ID	Map
Lake Roosevelt NRA - Cloverleaf	248	B5
Lake Roosevelt NRA - Columbia	239	B4
Lake Roosevelt NRA - Evans	93	A5
Lake Roosevelt NRA - Fort Spokane	240	B4
Lake Roosevelt NRA - Gifford	249	B5
Lake Roosevelt NRA - Haag Cove	94	A5
Lake Roosevelt NRA - Hawk Creek	241	B4
Lake Roosevelt NRA - Hunters Park	242	B4
Lake Roosevelt NRA - Kamloops	95	A5
Lake Roosevelt NRA - Keller Ferry	243	B4
Lake Roosevelt NRA - Kettle Falls	96	A5
Lake Roosevelt NRA - Kettle River	97	A5
Lake Roosevelt NRA - Marcus Island	98	A5
Lake Roosevelt NRA - North Gorge	99	A5
Lake Roosevelt NRA - Pierre	244	B4
Lake Roosevelt NRA - Sanpoil	245	B4
Lake Roosevelt NRA - Seven Bays	246	B4
Lake Roosevelt NRA - Snag Cove	100	A5
Lake Roosevelt NRA - Spring Canyon	247	B4
Mt Rainier NP - Berkeley Park TC	250	C2
Mt Rainier NP - Camp Curtis TC	251	C2
Mt Rainier NP - Camp Muir TC/Shelter	252	C2
Mt Rainier NP - Camp Schurman TC	253	C2
Mt Rainier NP - Carbon River TC	254	C2
Mt Rainier NP - Cataract Valley	255	C2
Mt Rainier NP - Cougar Rock	256	C2
Mt Rainier NP - Deer Creek TC	289	C3
Mt Rainier NP - Devil's Dream TC	257	C2
Mt Rainier NP - Dick's Lake TC	258	C2
Mt Rainier NP - Eagle's Roost TC	259	C2
Mt Rainier NP - Fire Creek TC	260	C2
Mt Rainier NP - Forest Lake TC	261	C2
Mt Rainier NP - Glacier Basin TC	262	C2
Mt Rainier NP - Golden Lakes TC	263	C2
Mt Rainier NP - Granite Creek TC	264	C2
Mt Rainier NP - Indian Bar TC/Shelter	265	C2
Mt Rainier NP - Ipsut Creek TC	266	C2
Mt Rainier NP - James Camp TC	267	C2
Mt Rainier NP - Klapatche Park TC	268	C2
Mt Rainier NP - Lake Eleanor TC	269	C2
Mt Rainier NP - Lake George TC/Shelter	270	C2
Mt Rainier NP - Lower Crystal Lake TC	290	C3
Mt Rainier NP - Maple Creek TC	271	C2
Mt Rainier NP - Mowich Lake CG	272	C2
Mt Rainier NP - Mystic TC	273	C2
Mt Rainier NP - N Payallup TC	274	C2
Mt Rainier NP - Nickel Creek TC	275	C2
Mt Rainier NP - Ohanapecosh CG	276	C2
Mt Rainier NP - Olallie Creek TC	277	C2
Mt Rainier NP - Paradise River TC	278	C2
Mt Rainier NP - Pyramid Creek TC	279	C2
Mt Rainier NP - S Mowich River TC/Shelter	280	C2
Mt Rainier NP - S Payallup TC	281	C2
Mt Rainier NP - Shriner Peak TC	291	C3
Mt Rainier NP - Snow Lake TC	282	C2
Mt Rainier NP - Summerland TC/Shelter	283	C2
Mt Rainier NP - Sunrise TC	284	C2
Mt Rainier NP - Tamanos Creek TC	285	C2
Mt Rainier NP - Three Lakes TC	292	C3
Mt Rainier NP - Upper Crystal Lake TC	293	C3
Mt Rainier NP - Upper Palisades Lake TC	286	C2
Mt Rainier NP - White River CG	287	C2
Mt Rainier NP - Yellowstone Cliffs TC	288	C2
North Cascades NP - 39 Mile TC/Stock	1	A3
North Cascades NP - Basin Creek TC	2	A3
North Cascades NP - Bear Creek TC	3	A3
North Cascades NP - Beaver Pass TC	4	A3
North Cascades NP - Bench Creek TC	5	A3
North Cascades NP - Big Beaver	6	A3
North Cascades NP - Big Beaver Stock	7	A3
North Cascades NP - Boundary TC	8	A3
North Cascades NP - Bowan TC	9	A3
North Cascades NP - Bridge Creek Stock	10	A3
North Cascades NP - Bridge Creek TC	11	A3
North Cascades NP - Bullion TC	12	A3
North Cascades NP - Colonial Creek CG	13	A3
North Cascades NP - Copper Creek TC	14	A3
North Cascades NP - Copper Lake TC	15	A3
North Cascades NP - Cosho TC	16	A3
North Cascades NP - Cottonwood TC	17	A3
North Cascades NP - Dagger Lake TC/Stock	18	A3
North Cascades NP - Dan's TC	19	A3
North Cascades NP - Deerlick Stock	20	A3
North Cascades NP - Desolation TC	21	A3
North Cascades NP - Devils Creek TC/Stock	22	A3
North Cascades NP - Egg Lake TC	23	A3
North Cascades NP - Fireweed TC/Stock	24	A3
North Cascades NP - Fisher TC	25	A3
North Cascades NP - Five Mile Stock	26	A3
North Cascades NP - Flat Creek TC	27	A3
North Cascades NP - Fourth of July	28	A3
North Cascades NP - Goodell Creek CG	29	A3
North Cascades NP - Goodell Creek Group	30	A3
North Cascades NP - Gorge Lake CG	31	A3
North Cascades NP - Graybeal TC/Stock	32	A3
North Cascades NP - Grizzly Creek TC	33	A3
North Cascades NP - Harlequin TC	229	B3
North Cascades NP - Heaton Stock	34	A3
North Cascades NP - Hidden Hand Stock	35	A3
North Cascades NP - Hidden Meadows Stock	36	A3
North Cascades NP - Hideaway TC	37	A3
North Cascades NP - High Bridge TC	38	A3
North Cascades NP - Hooter TC	230	B3
North Cascades NP - Hozomeen CG	39	A3
North Cascades NP - Hozomeen Lake TC	40	A3
North Cascades NP - Indian Creek TC	41	A3
North Cascades NP - Johannesburg TC	42	A3
North Cascades NP - Juanita Lake TC/Stock	231	B3
North Cascades NP - Junction TC/Stock	43	A3
North Cascades NP - Lightning Creek Horse Camp	44	A3

North Cascades NP - Little Beaver ....45 ....A3
North Cascades NP - Little Chiliwack TC............46 ....A3
North Cascades NP - Lodgepole ....47 ....A3
North Cascades NP - Luna TC............48 ....A3
North Cascades NP - May Creek Stock............49 ....A3
North Cascades NP - McAlester Lake TC/Stock............50 ....A3
North Cascades NP - McAllister TC/Stock............51 ....A3
North Cascades NP - Monogram Lake TC............52 ....A3
North Cascades NP - Moore Point TC/Boat............232 ....B3
North Cascades NP - Neve TC............53 ....A3
North Cascades NP - Newhalem Creek CG............54 ....A3
North Cascades NP - Nightmare TC............55 ....A3
North Cascades NP - North Fork TC............56 ....A3
North Cascades NP - Panther TC............57 ....A3
North Cascades NP - Park Creek TC............58 ....A3
North Cascades NP - Pelton Basin TC............59 ....A3
North Cascades NP - Perry Creek TC............60 ....A3
North Cascades NP - Pierce Mountain TC............61 ....A3
North Cascades NP - Prince Creek TC/Boat............233 ....B3
North Cascades NP - Pumpkin Mountain TC............62 ....A3
North Cascades NP - Purple Point Overflow............234 ....B3
North Cascades NP - Purple Point TC/Stock............235 ....B3
North Cascades NP - Rainbow Bridge TC............236 ....B3
North Cascades NP - Rainbow Ford TC............63 ....A3
North Cascades NP - Rainbow Lake TC............64 ....A3
North Cascades NP - Rainbow Meadows Group............65 ....A3
North Cascades NP - Rainbow Meadows TC/Stock............66 ....A3
North Cascades NP - Rennie TC............67 ....A3
North Cascades NP - Reynolds TC/Stock............237 ....B3
North Cascades NP - Roland Creek TC............68 ....A3
North Cascades NP - Ruby Pasture TC............69 ....A3
North Cascades NP - Sahale Glacier TC............70 ....A3
North Cascades NP - Shady TC............71 ....A3
North Cascades NP - Silesia TC............72 ....A3
North Cascades NP - Six Mile Group TC............73 ....A3
North Cascades NP - Skagit Queen TC............74 ....A3
North Cascades NP - Sourdough TC............75 ....A3
North Cascades NP - South Fork TC/Stock............76 ....A3
North Cascades NP - Stillwell TC............77 ....A3
North Cascades NP - Sulphide Creek TC............78 ....A3
North Cascades NP - Thornton Lakes TC............79 ....A3
North Cascades NP - Thunder Basin Stock............80 ....A3
North Cascades NP - Thunder Basin TC............81 ....A3
North Cascades NP - Thunder TC............82 ....A3
North Cascades NP - Trapper Lake Inlet - TC............83 ....A3
North Cascades NP - Trapper Lake Outlet TC............84 ....A3
North Cascades NP - Tricouni TC............85 ....A3
North Cascades NP - Tumwater TC............86 ....A3
North Cascades NP - Twin Rocks TC/Stock............87 ....A3
North Cascades NP - Two Mile TC............88 ....A3
North Cascades NP - U.S. Cabin TC/Stock............89 ....A3
North Cascades NP - Walker Park Stock............90 ....A3
North Cascades NP - Weaver Point............238 ....B3
North Cascades NP - Whatcom TC............91 ....A3
North Cascades NP - Willow Lake TC............92 ....A3
Olympic NP - Appleton Jct/Rocky Creek TC............101 ....B1
Olympic NP - Appleton Pass TC............102 ....B1
Olympic NP - Bear Camp TC............103 ....B1
Olympic NP - Belview TC............104 ....B1
Olympic NP - Big Log TC............105 ....B1
Olympic NP - Big Timber TC............106 ....B1
Olympic NP - Bob Creek TC............107 ....B1
Olympic NP - Bogachiel TC............108 ....B1
Olympic NP - Boulder Creek TC............109 ....B1
Olympic NP - Boulder Lake TC............110 ....B1
Olympic NP - C. B. Flats Group............111 ....B1
Olympic NP - Camp Ellis TC............112 ....B1
Olympic NP - Camp Pleasant TC............113 ....B1
Olympic NP - Camp Siberia TC............114 ....B1
Olympic NP - Camp Wilder TC............115 ....B1
Olympic NP - Canyon Camp TC............116 ....B1
Olympic NP - Canyon Creek TC............117 ....B1
Olympic NP - Cape Alava............118 ....B1
Olympic NP - Cedar Creek............119 ....B1
Olympic NP - Chicago Camp TC............120 ....B1
Olympic NP - Chilean Memorial............121 ....B1
Olympic NP - Deception Creek TC............122 ....B1
Olympic NP - Deer Lake TC............123 ....B1
Olympic NP - Deer Park............124 ....B1
Olympic NP - Diamond Meadow TC............125 ....B1
Olympic NP - Dodger Point TC............126 ....B1
Olympic NP - Dose Forks TC............220 ....B2
Olympic NP - Dose Meadows TC............127 ....B1
Olympic NP - Elip Creek TC............128 ....B1
Olympic NP - Elk Lake TC............129 ....B1
Olympic NP - Elkhorn TC............130 ....B1
Olympic NP - Enchanted Valley TC............131 ....B1
Olympic NP - Fairholme............132 ....B1
Olympic NP - Falls Camp TC............133 ....B1
Olympic NP - Fifteen Mile TC............134 ....B1
Olympic NP - Five Mile Island............135 ....B1
Olympic NP - Flapjack Lakes TC............136 ....B1
Olympic NP - Flapjack TC............137 ....B1
Olympic NP - Glacier Meadows TC............138 ....B1
Olympic NP - Gladys Lake TC............139 ....B1
Olympic NP - Grand Lake TC............140 ....B1
Olympic NP - Graves Creek............141 ....B1
Olympic NP - Gray Wolf TC............142 ....B1
Olympic NP - Happy Four TC............143 ....B1
Olympic NP - Happy Lake TC............144 ....B1
Olympic NP - Hayes River TC............145 ....B1
Olympic NP - Heart Lake TC............146 ....B1
Olympic NP - Heart O'The Hills............147 ....B1
Olympic NP - Heather Park TC............148 ....B1
Olympic NP - Hoh Lake TC............149 ....B1
Olympic NP - Hoh Rain Forest............150 ....B1
Olympic NP - Hole-in-the-Wall............151 ....B1
Olympic NP - Home Lake TC............221 ....B2
Olympic NP - Home Sweet Home TC............152 ....B1
Olympic NP - Honeymoon Meadows TC............153 ....B1
Olympic NP - Horsehead Stock Camp............154 ....B1
Olympic NP - Humes Ranch TC............155 ....B1
Olympic NP - Hyak TC............156 ....B1
Olympic NP - Irely Lake............157 ....B1
Olympic NP - Kalaloch............158 ....B1
Olympic NP - Lake Angeles TC............159 ....B1
Olympic NP - Lake Beauty TC............160 ....B1
Olympic NP - Lake Constance TC............222 ....B2
Olympic NP - Lake Sundown TC............161 ....B1
Olympic NP - Lewis Meadow TC............162 ....B1
Olympic NP - Lillian River TC............163 ....B1
Olympic NP - Low Divide TC............164 ....B1
Olympic NP - Lower Cameron TC............165 ....B1
Olympic NP - Lower Royal Meadow TC............223 ....B2

Olympic NP - Lunch Lake TC ....166 .... B1
Olympic NP - Marmot Lake TC ....167 .... B1
Olympic NP - Martin Creek Stock ....168 .... B1
Olympic NP - Mary's Falls TC ....169 .... B1
Olympic NP - Mink Lake TC ....170 .... B1
Olympic NP - Moose Lake TC ....171 .... B1
Olympic NP - Mora ....172 .... B1
Olympic NP - Mosquito Creek ....173 .... B1
Olympic NP - Mt. Tom Creek TC ....174 .... B1
Olympic NP - Nine Stream TC ....175 .... B1
Olympic NP - North Fork ....176 .... B1
Olympic NP - North Ozette River ....177 .... B1
Olympic NP - Norwegian Memorial ....178 .... B1
Olympic NP - O'Neil Creek TC ....179 .... B1
Olympic NP - Olympus Ranger Station ....180 .... B1
Olympic NP - Ozette ....181 .... B1
Olympic NP - Pelton Creek TC ....182 .... B1
Olympic NP - Pony Bridge TC ....183 .... B1
Olympic NP - Pyrites Creek TC ....184 .... B1
Olympic NP - Queets ....185 .... B1
Olympic NP - Roaring Winds TC ....186 .... B1
Olympic NP - Royal Creek TC ....224 .... B2
Olympic NP - Royal Lake TC ....225 .... B2
Olympic NP - Sand Point ....187 .... B1
Olympic NP - Scott Creek ....188 .... B1
Olympic NP - Seafield Creek ....189 .... B1
Olympic NP - Second Beach ....190 .... B1
Olympic NP - Seven Mile Group ....191 .... B1
Olympic NP - Shi Shi Beach ....192 .... B1
Olympic NP - Sixteen Mile TC ....193 .... B1
Olympic NP - Sol Duc ....194 .... B1
Olympic NP - Sol Duc Falls TC ....195 .... B1
Olympic NP - Sol Duc Park TC ....196 .... B1
Olympic NP - Sol Duc River TC's 1-4 ....197 .... B1
Olympic NP - South Beach ....198 .... B1
Olympic NP - South Ozette River ....199 .... B1
Olympic NP - South Sand Point ....200 .... B1
Olympic NP - Spike Camp TC ....201 .... B1
Olympic NP - Spruce Bottom TC ....202 .... B1
Olympic NP - Staircase ....203 .... B1
Olympic NP - Strawberry Point ....204 .... B1
Olympic NP - Success Creek TC ....205 .... B1
Olympic NP - Sunnybrook Meadows TC ....226 .... B2
Olympic NP - Ten Mile TC ....227 .... B2
Olympic NP - Third Beach ....206 .... B1
Olympic NP - Three Forks TC ....207 .... B1
Olympic NP - Three Lakes ....208 .... B1
Olympic NP - Three Prune TC ....209 .... B1
Olympic NP - Toleak Point ....210 .... B1
Olympic NP - Trapper TC ....211 .... B1
Olympic NP - Two Bear TC ....212 .... B1
Olympic NP - Upper Cameron TC ....213 .... B1
Olympic NP - Upper Duckabush TC ....214 .... B1
Olympic NP - Upper Lena Lake TC ....228 .... B2
Olympic NP - Upper Sol Duc Bridge TC ....215 .... B1
Olympic NP - Wagonwheel Lake TC ....216 .... B1
Olympic NP - Wedding Rocks ....217 .... B1
Olympic NP - Wolf Bar TC ....218 .... B1
Olympic NP - Yellow Banks ....219 .... B1

1 • A3 | North Cascades NP - 39 Mile TC/Stock

Total sites: 4, No water, Vault/pit toilet, Tents only: Free, Hike-in, $20 non-refundable reservation fee, Permit required, Reservations accepted, Elev: 1715ft/523m, Tel: 360-854-7200. GPS: 48.803367, -121.143958

2 • A3 | North Cascades NP - Basin Creek TC

Total sites: 3, No water, Vault/pit toilet, Tents only: Free, Hike-in, $20 non-refundable reservation fee, Permit required, No fires, Shared cooking area, Reservations accepted, Elev: 3110ft/948m, Tel: 360-854-7200. GPS: 48.462973, -121.017776

3 • A3 | North Cascades NP - Bear Creek TC

Total sites: 1, No water, Vault/pit toilet, Tents only: Free, Hike-in, $20 non-refundable reservation fee, Permit required, Reservations accepted, Elev: 2260ft/689m, Tel: 360-854-7200. GPS: 48.964836, -121.387066

4 • A3 | North Cascades NP - Beaver Pass TC

Total sites: 1, No water, Vault/pit toilet, Tents only: Free, Hike-in, $20 non-refundable reservation fee, Permit required, Reservations accepted, Elev: 3654ft/1114m, Tel: 360-854-7200. GPS: 48.878672, -121.250775

5 • A3 | North Cascades NP - Bench Creek TC

Total sites: 1, No water, Vault/pit toilet, Tents only: Free, Hike-in, $20 non-refundable reservation fee, Permit required, Also 1 group site, Reservations accepted, Elev: 3766ft/1148m, Tel: 360-854-7200. GPS: 48.376392, -120.685955

6 • A3 | North Cascades NP - Big Beaver

Total sites: 7, No water, Vault/pit toilet, Tents only: Free, Hike-in/boat-in, $20 non-refundable reservation fee, Permit required, Reservations accepted, Elev: 1762ft/537m, Tel: 360-854-7200. GPS: 48.775568, -121.058188

7 • A3 | North Cascades NP - Big Beaver Stock

Total sites: 1, No water, Vault/pit toilet, Tents only: Free, Hike-in, $20 non-refundable reservation fee, Permit required, Reservations accepted, Elev: 1604ft/489m, Tel: 360-854-7200. GPS: 48.776021, -121.062852

8 • A3 | North Cascades NP - Boundary TC

Total sites: 3, No water, Vault/pit toilet, Tents only: Free, Hike-in, No fires, $20 non-refundable reservation fee, Permit required, Reservations accepted, Elev: 4445ft/1355m, Tel: 360-854-7200. GPS: 48.887985, -121.522761

9 • A3 | North Cascades NP - Bowan TC

Total sites: 2, No water, Vault/pit toilet, Tents only: Free, Hike-in, $20 non-refundable reservation fee, Permit required, Reservations accepted, Elev: 4383ft/1336m, Tel: 360-854-7200. GPS: 48.395689, -120.686015

10 • A3 | North Cascades NP - Bridge Creek Stock

Total sites: 3, No water, Vault/pit toilet, Tents only: Free, Hike-in, $20 non-refundable reservation fee, Permit required, Also 1 group site, Reservations accepted, Elev: 2112ft/644m, Tel: 360-854-7200. GPS: 48.431471, -120.870102

11 • A3 | North Cascades NP - Bridge Creek TC

Total sites: 3, No water, Vault/pit toilet, Tents only: Free, Hike-in, $20 non-refundable reservation fee, Permit required, Reservations accepted, Elev: 2112ft/644m, Tel: 360-854-7200. GPS: 48.430163, -120.868347

12 • A3 | North Cascades NP - Bullion TC

Dispersed sites, No water, Vault/pit toilet, Tents only: Free, Hike-in, Permit required, Reservations accepted, Elev: 1616ft/493m, Tel: 360-854-7200. GPS: 48.378955, -120.824923

13 • A3 | North Cascades NP - Colonial Creek CG

Total sites: 142, RV sites: 142, Central water, Flush toilet, No showers, RV dump, Tent & RV camping: $16, 10 sites open in winter - no services or fees, 1 group site - $30, Open all year, Max Length: 22ft, Reservations not accepted, Elev: 1227ft/374m, Tel: 360-854-7200, Nearest town: Newhalem. GPS: 48.686768, -121.094482

14 • A3 | North Cascades NP - Copper Creek TC

Total sites: 5, No water, Vault/pit toilet, Tents only: Free, Hike-in, $20 non-refundable reservation fee, Permit required, Reservations accepted, Elev: 3123ft/952m, Tel: 360-854-7200. GPS: 48.880833, -121.488913

15 • A3 | North Cascades NP - Copper Lake TC

Total sites: 3, No water, Vault/pit toilet, Tents only: Free, Hike-in, No fires, $20 non-refundable reservation fee, Permit required, Reservations accepted, Elev: 5265ft/1605m, Tel: 360-854-7200. GPS: 48.918144, -121.447993

16 • A3 | North Cascades NP - Cosho TC

Total sites: 3, No water, Vault/pit toilet, Tents only: Free, Hike-in, $20 non-refundable reservation fee, Permit required, Reservations accepted, Elev: 3988ft/1216m, Tel: 360-854-7200. GPS: 48.561618, -120.910084

17 • A3 | North Cascades NP - Cottonwood TC

Total sites: 3, No water, Vault/pit toilet, Tents only: Free, Hike-in, $20 non-refundable reservation fee, Permit required, Also 1 group site, Reservations accepted, Elev: 2752ft/839m, Tel: 360-854-7200. GPS: 48.451542, -120.991387

18 • A3 | North Cascades NP - Dagger Lake TC/Stock

Total sites: 2, No water, Vault/pit toilet, Tents only: Free, Hike-in, $20 non-refundable reservation fee, Permit required, Reservations accepted, Elev: 5508ft/1679m, Tel: 360-854-7200. GPS: 48.468725, -120.656531

19 • A3 | North Cascades NP - Dan's TC

Total sites: 1, No water, Vault/pit toilet, Tents only: Free, Hike-in, Small site - 2 tents, $20 non-refundable reservation fee, Permit required, Reservations accepted, Elev: 3971ft/1210m, Tel: 360-854-7200. GPS: 48.432388, -120.758976

20 • A3 | North Cascades NP - Deerlick Stock

Total sites: 2, No water, Vault/pit toilet, Tents only: Free, Hike-in, $20 non-refundable reservation fee, Permit required, Reservations accepted, Elev: 1932ft/589m, Tel: 360-854-7200. GPS: 48.905707, -120.978988

21 • A3 | North Cascades NP - Desolation TC

Total sites: 1, No water, Vault/pit toilet, Tents only: Free, Hike-in, $20 non-refundable reservation fee, Permit required, Reservations accepted, Elev: 5564ft/1696m, Tel: 360-854-7200. GPS: 48.903292, -121.010416

22 • A3 | North Cascades NP - Devils Creek TC/Stock

Total sites: 1, No water, Vault/pit toilet, Tents only: Free, Hike-in, $20 non-refundable reservation fee, Permit required, Reservations accepted, Elev: 1807ft/551m, Tel: 360-854-7200. GPS: 48.826043, -121.030989

23 • A3 | North Cascades NP - Egg Lake TC

Total sites: 3, No water, Vault/pit toilet, Tents only: Free, Hike-in, No fires, $20 non-refundable reservation fee, Permit required, Reservations accepted, Elev: 5173ft/1577m, Tel: 360-854-7200. GPS: 48.899549, -121.483879

24 • A3 | North Cascades NP - Fireweed TC/Stock

Total sites: 4, No water, Vault/pit toilet, Tents only: Free, Hike-in, Cook area separate from tent pads, $20 non-refundable reservation fee, Permit required, Reservations accepted, Elev: 3635ft/1108m, Tel: 360-854-7200. GPS: 48.467723, -120.718752

25 • A3 | North Cascades NP - Fisher TC

Total sites: 3, No water, Vault/pit toilet, Tents only: Free, Hike-in, No fires, $20 non-refundable reservation fee, Permit required, Reservations accepted, Elev: 5252ft/1601m, Tel: 360-854-7200. GPS: 48.567275, -120.854421

26 • A3 | North Cascades NP - Five Mile Stock

Total sites: 2, No water, Vault/pit toilet, Tents only: Free, Hike-in, $20 non-refundable reservation fee, Permit required, Reservations accepted, Elev: 3940ft/1201m, Tel: 360-854-7200. GPS: 48.464794, -120.939331

27 • A3 | North Cascades NP - Flat Creek TC

Total sites: 2, No water, Vault/pit toilet, Tents only: Free, Hike-in, $20 non-refundable reservation fee, Permit required, Reservations accepted, Elev: 2290ft/698m, Tel: 360-854-7200. GPS: 48.430239, -120.923178

28 • A3 | North Cascades NP - Fourth of July

Total sites: 3, No water, Vault/pit toilet, Tents only: Free, Hike-in, No fires, $20 non-refundable reservation fee, Permit required, Reservations accepted, Elev: 3438ft/1048m, Tel: 360-854-7200. GPS: 48.659446, -121.038806

29 • A3 | North Cascades NP - Goodell Creek CG

Total sites: 21, RV sites: 21, Central water, Vault/pit toilet, No showers, No RV dump, Tent & RV camping: $16, No services or fees in winter, Open all year, Max Length: 22ft, Reservations not accepted, Elev: 518ft/158m, Tel: 360-854-7200, Nearest town: Newhalem. GPS: 48.67334, -121.26709

30 • A3 | North Cascades NP - Goodell Creek Group

Total sites: 3, Central water, Vault/pit toilet, No showers, No RV dump, Group site: $25-$34, No services or fees in winter, Open all year, Reservations not accepted, Elev: 518ft/158m, Tel: 360-854-7200, Nearest town: Newhalem. GPS: 48.676747, -121.271232

31 • A3 | North Cascades NP - Gorge Lake CG

Total sites: 6, RV sites: 0, No water, Vault/pit toilet, Tents only: Free, Open all year, Reservations not accepted, Elev: 1198ft/365m, Tel: 360-854-7200. GPS: 48.715515, -121.155252

32 • A3 | North Cascades NP - Graybeal TC/Stock

Total sites: 4, No water, Vault/pit toilet, Tents only: Free, Hike-in, $20 non-refundable reservation fee, Permit required, Reservations accepted, Elev: 3123ft/952m, Tel: 360-854-7200. GPS: 48.880891, -121.412446

33 • A3 | North Cascades NP - Grizzly Creek TC

Total sites: 3, No water, Vault/pit toilet, Tents only: Free, Hike-in, $20 non-refundable reservation fee, Permit required, Reservations accepted, Elev: 3133ft/955m, Tel: 360-854-7200. GPS: 48.493157, -120.861869

34 • A3 | North Cascades NP - Heaton Stock

Total sites: 1, No water, Vault/pit toilet, Tents only: Free, Hike-in, $20 non-refundable reservation fee, Permit required, Reservations accepted, Elev: 7000ft/2134m, Tel: 360-854-7200. GPS: 48.403505, -120.807427

35 • A3 | North Cascades NP - Hidden Hand Stock

Total sites: 1, No water, Vault/pit toilet, Tents only: Free, Hike-in, $20 non-refundable reservation fee, Permit required, Also 1 group site, Reservations accepted, Elev: 2276ft/694m, Tel: 360-854-7200. GPS: 48.730885, -121.020629

36 • A3 | North Cascades NP - Hidden Meadows Stock

Total sites: 1, No water, Vault/pit toilet, Tents only: Free, Hike-in, $20 non-refundable reservation fee, Permit required, Reservations accepted, Elev: 6498ft/1981m, Tel: 360-854-7200. GPS: 48.434789, -120.665368

37 • A3 | North Cascades NP - Hideaway TC

Total sites: 1, No water, Vault/pit toilet, Tents only: Free, Hike-in, $20 non-refundable reservation fee, Permit required, Reservations accepted, Elev: 3585ft/1093m, Tel: 360-854-7200. GPS: 48.465525, -120.735705

38 • A3 | North Cascades NP - High Bridge TC

Total sites: 2, No water, Vault/pit toilet, Tents only: Free, Hike-in, $20 non-refundable reservation fee, Permit required, Reservations accepted, Elev: 1653ft/504m, Tel: 360-854-7200. GPS: 48.380331, -120.839533

39 • A3 | North Cascades NP - Hozomeen CG

Total sites: 75, RV sites: Unk, Central water, Vault/pit toilet, No showers, No RV dump, Tent & RV camping: Free, Only accessible from Canada, Rough road, Open all year, Max Length: 25ft, Reservations not accepted, Elev: 1703ft/519m, Tel: 360-854-7200, Nearest town: Newhalem. GPS: 48.985726, -121.071609

40 • A3 | North Cascades NP - Hozomeen Lake TC

Dispersed sites, No water, No toilets, Tents only: Free, Hike-in, $20 non-refundable reservation fee, Permit required, Reservations accepted, Elev: 2894ft/882m, Tel: 360-854-7200. GPS: 48.955656, -121.037633

41 • A3 | North Cascades NP - Indian Creek TC

Total sites: 3, No water, Vault/pit toilet, Tents only: Free, Hike-in, $20 non-refundable reservation fee, Permit required, Reservations accepted, Elev: 2352ft/717m, Tel: 360-854-7200. GPS: 48.935613, -121.394705

42 • A3 | North Cascades NP - Johannesburg TC

Total sites: 3, No water, Vault/pit toilet, Tents only: Free, Hike-in, No fires, $20 non-refundable reservation fee, Permit required, Reservations accepted, Elev: 3648ft/1112m, Tel: 360-854-7200. GPS: 48.476072, -121.074958

43 • A3 | North Cascades NP - Junction TC/Stock

Total sites: 3, No water, Vault/pit toilet, Tents only: Free, Hike-in, $20 non-refundable reservation fee, Permit required, Reservations accepted, Elev: 3129ft/954m, Tel: 360-854-7200. GPS: 48.584319, -121.017628

44 • A3 | North Cascades NP - Lightning Creek Horse Camp

Total sites: 3, No water, No toilets, Tents only: Free, Hike-in, $20 non-refundable reservation fee, Permit required, Pack-in, Elev: 1736ft/529m, Tel: 360-854-7200, Nearest town: Marblemount. GPS: 48.873098, -121.017628

45 • A3 | North Cascades NP - Little Beaver

Total sites: 5, No water, Vault/pit toilet, Tents only: Free, Hike-in/boat-in, $20 non-refundable reservation fee, Permit required, Elev: 1854ft/565m, Tel: 360-854-7200. GPS: 48.915877, -121.075715

46 • A3 | North Cascades NP - Little Chiliwack TC

Total sites: 3, No water, Vault/pit toilet, Tents only: Free, Hike-in, Camp washed out - not maintained, $20 non-refundable reservation fee, Permit required, Reservations accepted, Elev: 2070ft/631m, Tel: 360-854-7200. GPS: 48.991455, -121.408385

47 • A3 | North Cascades NP - Lodgepole

Total sites: 3, No water, Vault/pit toilet, Tents only: Free, Hike-in/boat-in, $20 non-refundable reservation fee, Permit required, Elev: 1814ft/553m, Tel: 360-854-7200. GPS: 48.866069, -121.016964

48 • A3 | North Cascades NP - Luna TC

Total sites: 2, No water, Vault/pit toilet, Tents only: Free, Hike-in, $20 non-refundable reservation fee, Permit required, Reservations accepted, Elev: 2518ft/767m, Tel: 360-854-7200. GPS: 48.833719, -121.200618

49 • A3 | North Cascades NP - May Creek Stock

Total sites: 1, No water, Vault/pit toilet, Tents only: Free, Hike-in, $20 non-refundable reservation fee, Permit required, Reservations accepted, Elev: 1640ft/500m, Tel: 360-854-7200. GPS: 48.788166, -121.028629

50 • A3 | North Cascades NP - McAlester Lake TC/Stock

Total sites: 3, No water, Vault/pit toilet, Tents only: Free, Hike-in, $20 non-refundable reservation fee, Permit required, Reservations accepted, Elev: 5547ft/1691m, Tel: 360-854-7200. GPS: 48.429548, -120.678469

51 • A3 | North Cascades NP - McAllister TC/Stock

Total sites: 6, No water, Vault/pit toilet, Tents only: Free, Hike-in, $20 non-refundable reservation fee, Permit required, Reservations accepted, Elev: 1900ft/579m, Tel: 360-854-7200. GPS: 48.621539, -121.058384

52 • A3 | North Cascades NP - Monogram Lake TC

Total sites: 2, No water, Vault/pit toilet, Tents only: Free, Hike-in, No fires, $20 non-refundable reservation fee, Permit required, Reservations accepted, Elev: 4872ft/1485m, Tel: 360-854-7200. GPS: 48.557091, -121.283419

53 • A3 | North Cascades NP - Neve TC

Total sites: 3, No water, Vault/pit toilet, Tents only: Free, Hike-in, Cooking area separated from tent pads, Eroding stream bank, $20 non-refundable reservation fee, Permit required, Reservations accepted, Elev: 1381ft/421m, Tel: 360-854-7200. GPS: 48.666782, -121.068083

54 • A3 | North Cascades NP - Newhalem Creek CG

Total sites: 111, RV sites: 111, Central water, Flush toilet, No showers, RV dump, Tent & RV camping: $16, Reservations accepted, Elev: 535ft/163m, Tel: 360-854-7200, Nearest town: Newhalem. GPS: 48.670682, -121.260705

55 • A3 | North Cascades NP - Nightmare TC

Dispersed sites, No water, No toilets, Tents only: Free, Hike-in, Reservations accepted, Elev: 2639ft/804m, Tel: 360-854-7200. GPS: 48.929602, -120.983086

56 • A3 | North Cascades NP - North Fork TC

Total sites: 2, No water, Vault/pit toilet, Tents only: Free, Hike-in, Reservations accepted, Elev: 2559ft/780m. GPS: 48.456538, -120.843735

57 • A3 | North Cascades NP - Panther TC

Total sites: 2, No water, Vault/pit toilet, Tents only: Free, Hike-in, $20 non-refundable reservation fee, Permit required, Reservations accepted, Elev: 2460ft/750m, Tel: 360-854-7200. GPS: 48.684562, -120.996492

58 • A3 | North Cascades NP - Park Creek TC

Total sites: 2, No water, Vault/pit toilet, Tents only: Free, Hike-in, $20 non-refundable reservation fee, Permit required, Reservations accepted, Elev: 2332ft/711m, Tel: 360-854-7200. GPS: 48.425871, -120.912166

59 • A3 | North Cascades NP - Pelton Basin TC

Total sites: 4, No water, Vault/pit toilet, Tents only: Free, Hike-in, No fires, $20 non-refundable reservation fee, Permit required, Also 1 group site, Reservations accepted, Elev: 4849ft/1478m, Tel: 360-854-7200. GPS: 48.464878, -121.050494

60 • A3 | North Cascades NP - Perry Creek TC

Total sites: 3, No water, Vault/pit toilet, Tents only: Free, Hike-in, $20 non-refundable reservation fee, Permit required, Also 1 group site, Reservations accepted, Elev: 2080ft/634m, Tel: 360-854-7200. GPS: 48.919717, -121.143408

61 • A3 | North Cascades NP - Pierce Mountain TC

Total sites: 4, No water, Vault/pit toilet, Tents only: Free, Hike-in, No fires, $20 non-refundable reservation fee, Permit required, Small site, Reservations accepted, Elev: 5400ft/1646m, Tel: 360-854-7200. GPS: 48.744121, -121.098826

62 • A3 | North Cascades NP - Pumpkin Mountain TC

Total sites: 2, No water, Vault/pit toilet, Tents only: Free, Hike-in, $20 non-refundable reservation fee, Permit required, Reservations accepted, Elev: 1614ft/492m, Tel: 360-854-7200. GPS: 48.774048, -121.065346

63 • A3 | North Cascades NP - Rainbow Ford TC

Total sites: 1, No water, Vault/pit toilet, Tents only: Free, Hike-in, Small site, $20 non-refundable reservation fee, Permit required, Reservations accepted, Elev: 3179ft/969m, Tel: 360-854-7200. GPS: 48.368308, -120.688603

64 • A3 | North Cascades NP - Rainbow Lake TC

Total sites: 2, No water, Vault/pit toilet, Tents only: Free, Hike-in, $20 non-refundable reservation fee, Permit required, Reservations accepted, Elev: 5630ft/1716m, Tel: 360-854-7200. GPS: 48.401237, -120.736901

65 • A3 | North Cascades NP - Rainbow Meadows Group

Total sites: 1, No water, Vault/pit toilet, Group site: $20 non-refundable reservation fee, Permit required, Reservations accepted, Elev: 4960ft/1512m, Tel: 360-854-7200. GPS: 48.395001, -120.733041

66 • A3 | North Cascades NP - Rainbow Meadows TC/Stock

Total sites: 2, No water, Vault/pit toilet, Tents only: Free, Hike-in, $20 non-refundable reservation fee, Permit required, Reservations accepted, Elev: 4960ft/1512m, Tel: 360-854-7200. GPS: 48.389954, -120.725684

67 • A3 | North Cascades NP - Rennie TC

Total sites: 1, No water, Vault/pit toilet, Tents only: Free, Hike-in, $20 non-refundable reservation fee, Permit required, Burned in 2014, Reservations accepted, Elev: 4081ft/1244m, Tel: 360-854-7200. GPS: 48.360734, -120.617181

68 • A3 | North Cascades NP - Roland Creek TC

Total sites: 3, No water, Vault/pit toilet, Tents only: Free, Hike-in, $20 non-refundable reservation fee, Permit required, Also 1 group site, Reservations accepted, Elev: 1761ft/537m, Tel: 360-854-7200. GPS: 48.772068, -121.021387

69 • A3 | North Cascades NP - Ruby Pasture TC

Total sites: 1, No water, Vault/pit toilet, Tents only: Free, Hike-in, $20 non-refundable reservation fee, Permit required, Reservations accepted, Elev: 2053ft/626m, Tel: 360-854-7200. GPS: 48.730177, -121.015819

70 • A3 | North Cascades NP - Sahale Glacier TC

Total sites: 6, No water, Vault/pit toilet, Tents only: Free, Hike-in, No fires, $20 non-refundable reservation fee, Permit required, Reservations accepted, Elev: 7686ft/2343m, Tel: 360-854-7200. GPS: 48.485187, -121.046003

71 • A3 | North Cascades NP - Shady TC

Total sites: 1, No water, Vault/pit toilet, Tents only: Free, Hike-in, $20 non-refundable reservation fee, Permit required, Reservations accepted, Elev: 1942ft/592m, Tel: 360-854-7200. GPS: 48.416646, -120.864074

72 • A3 | North Cascades NP - Silesia TC

Total sites: 2, No water, Vault/pit toilet, Tents only: Free, Hike-in, No fires, $20 non-refundable reservation fee, Permit required, Reservations accepted, Elev: 5649ft/1722m, Tel: 360-854-7200. GPS: 48.894055, -121.482617

73 • A3 | North Cascades NP - Six Mile Group TC

Total sites: 1, No water, Vault/pit toilet, Hike-in group site(s), Cooking area separated from tent pads, $20 non-refundable reservation fee, Permit required, Reservations accepted, Elev: 2946ft/898m, Tel: 360-854-7200. GPS: 48.461897, -120.791144

74 • A3 | North Cascades NP - Skagit Queen TC

Total sites: 3, No water, Vault/pit toilet, Tents only: Free, Hike-in, $20 non-refundable reservation fee, Permit required, Reservations accepted, Elev: 2772ft/845m, Tel: 360-854-7200. GPS: 48.541634, -121.010479

75 • A3 | North Cascades NP - Sourdough TC

Total sites: 1, No water, Vault/pit toilet, Tents only: Free, Hike-in, Small site - 2 tents, $20 non-refundable reservation fee, Permit required, Reservations accepted, Elev: 5055ft/1541m, Tel: 360-854-7200. GPS: 48.743173, -121.128286

76 • A3 | North Cascades NP - South Fork TC/Stock

Total sites: 3, No water, Vault/pit toilet, Tents only: Free, Hike-in, Cook area separate from tent pads, $20 non-refundable reservation fee, Permit required, Reservations accepted, Elev: 3208ft/978m, Tel: 360-854-7200. GPS: 48.462575, -120.771293

77 • A3 | North Cascades NP - Stillwell TC

Total sites: 4, No water, Vault/pit toilet, Tents only: Free, Hike-in, $20 non-refundable reservation fee, Permit required, Reservations accepted, Elev: 2486ft/758m, Tel: 360-854-7200. GPS: 48.891968, -121.269184

78 • A3 | North Cascades NP - Sulphide Creek TC

Total sites: 2, No water, Vault/pit toilet, Tents only: Free, Hike-in, $20 non-refundable reservation fee, Permit required, Reservations accepted, Elev: 905ft/276m, Tel: 360-854-7200. GPS: 48.776796, -121.533878

79 • A3 | North Cascades NP - Thornton Lakes TC

Total sites: 3, No water, Vault/pit toilet, Tents only: Free, Hike-in, $20 non-refundable reservation fee, Permit required, Reservations accepted, Elev: 4504ft/1373m, Tel: 360-854-7200. GPS: 48.681263, -121.330166

80 • A3 | North Cascades NP - Thunder Basin Stock

Total sites: 2, No water, Vault/pit toilet, Tents only: Free, Hike-in, $20 non-refundable reservation fee, Permit required, Reservations accepted, Elev: 4900ft/1494m, Tel: 360-854-7200. GPS: 48.515837, -120.983348

81 • A3 | North Cascades NP - Thunder Basin TC

Total sites: 2, No water, Vault/pit toilet, Tents only: Free, Hike-in, $20 non-refundable reservation fee, Permit required, Reservations accepted, Elev: 4900ft/1494m, Tel: 360-854-7200. GPS: 48.507307, -120.975911

82 • A3 | North Cascades NP - Thunder TC

Total sites: 3, No water, Vault/pit toilet, Tents only: Free, Hike-in, $20 non-refundable reservation fee, Permit required, Also 1 group site, Reservations accepted, Elev: 1354ft/413m, Tel: 360-854-7200. GPS: 48.673317, -121.070401

83 • A3 | North Cascades NP - Trapper Lake Inlet - TC

Total sites: 1, No water, No toilets, Tents only: Free, Hike-in, No trail, Dig cathole, $20 non-refundable reservation fee, Permit required, Reservations accepted, Elev: 4163ft/1269m, Tel: 360-854-7200. GPS: 48.442122, -121.011517

84 • A3 | North Cascades NP - Trapper Lake Outlet TC

Total sites: 2, No water, Vault/pit toilet, Tents only: Free, Hike-in, No trail, Dig cathole, $20 non-refundable reservation fee, Permit required, Reservations accepted, Elev: 4284ft/1306m, Tel: 360-854-7200. GPS: 48.440574, -120.992855

85 • A3 | North Cascades NP - Tricouni TC

Total sites: 2, No water, Vault/pit toilet, Tents only: Free, Hike-in, Small sites, $20 non-refundable reservation fee, Permit required, Reservations accepted, Elev: 1971ft/601m, Tel: 360-854-7200. GPS: 48.602705, -121.048331

86 • A3 | North Cascades NP - Tumwater TC

Total sites: 2, No water, Vault/pit toilet, Tents only: Free, Hike-in, $20 non-refundable reservation fee, Permit required, Reservations accepted, Elev: 1742ft/531m, Tel: 360-854-7200. GPS: 48.389873, -120.843831

87 • A3 | North Cascades NP - Twin Rocks TC/Stock

Total sites: 3, No water, Vault/pit toilet, Tents only: Free, Hike-in, $20 non-refundable reservation fee, Permit required, Reservations accepted, Elev: 2703ft/824m, Tel: 360-854-7200. GPS: 48.880222, -121.319248

88 • A3 | North Cascades NP - Two Mile TC

Total sites: 1, No water, Vault/pit toilet, Tents only: Free, Hike-in, $20 non-refundable reservation fee, Permit required, Reservations accepted, Elev: 3412ft/1040m, Tel: 360-854-7200. GPS: 48.444922, -120.906814

89 • A3 | North Cascades NP - U.S. Cabin TC/Stock

Total sites: 5, No water, Vault/pit toilet, Tents only: Free, Hike-in, $20 non-refundable reservation fee, Permit required, Reservations accepted, Elev: 2595ft/791m, Tel: 360-854-7200. GPS: 48.898553, -121.446862

90 • A3 | North Cascades NP - Walker Park Stock

Total sites: 1, No water, Vault/pit toilet, Tents only: Free, Hike-in, $20 non-refundable reservation fee, Permit required, Reservations accepted, Elev: 3051ft/930m, Tel: 360-854-7200. GPS: 48.476284, -120.842264

91 • A3 | North Cascades NP - Whatcom TC

Total sites: 3, No water, Vault/pit toilet, Tents only: Free, Hike-in, $20 non-refundable reservation fee, Permit required, Reservations accepted, Elev: 5055ft/1541m, Tel: 360-854-7200. GPS: 48.875284, -121.369558

92 • A3 | North Cascades NP - Willow Lake TC

Total sites: 1, No water, Vault/pit toilet, Tents only: Free, Hike-in, $20 non-refundable reservation fee, Permit required, Reservations accepted, Elev: 2854ft/870m, Tel: 360-854-7200. GPS: 48.943682, -121.013964

93 • A5 | Lake Roosevelt NRA - Evans

Total sites: 43, RV sites: 43, Central water, Vault/pit toilet, No showers, RV dump, Tent & RV camping: $18, 1 group site, $9 Oct-Apr, Generator hours: 0600-2200, Open all year, Max Length: 30ft, Reservations not accepted, Elev: 1312ft/400m, Tel: 509-633-3830, Nearest town: Evans. GPS: 48.697998, -118.017578

94 • A5 | Lake Roosevelt NRA - Haag Cove

Total sites: 16, RV sites: 16, Central water, Vault/pit toilet, No showers, No RV dump, Tent & RV camping: $18, $9 Oct-Apr, Generator hours: 0600-2200, Open all year, Reservations not accepted, Elev: 1388ft/423m, Tel: 509-633-3830, Nearest town: Kettle Falls. GPS: 48.561976, -118.151729

95 • A5 | Lake Roosevelt NRA - Kamloops

Total sites: 12, RV sites: 8, Central water, Vault/pit toilet, No showers, No RV dump, Tent & RV camping: $18, $9 Oct-Apr, 4 walk-to sites, Generator hours: 0600-2200, Open all year, Reservations not accepted, Elev: 1250ft/381m, Tel: 509-633-3830, Nearest town: Coulee Dam. GPS: 48.679056, -118.117441

96 • A5 | Lake Roosevelt NRA - Kettle Falls

Total sites: 76, RV sites: 76, Central water, Flush toilet, No showers, RV dump, Tent & RV camping: $18, 2 group sites, $9 Oct-Apr, Generator hours: 0600-2200, Open all year, Max Length: 30ft, Reservations accepted, Elev: 1332ft/406m, Tel: 509-633-3830, Nearest town: Kettle Falls. GPS: 48.600916, -118.122333

97 • A5 | Lake Roosevelt NRA - Kettle River

Total sites: 13, RV sites: 13, Central water, Vault/pit toilet, No showers, No RV dump, Tent & RV camping: $18, $9 Oct-Apr, Generator hours: 0600-2200, Open all year, Reservations not accepted, Elev: 1286ft/392m, Tel: 509-633-3830, Nearest town: Coulee Dam. GPS: 48.707021, -118.121009

98 • A5 | Lake Roosevelt NRA - Marcus Island

Total sites: 27, RV sites: 27, Central water, Vault/pit toilet, No showers, No RV dump, Tent & RV camping: $18, $9 Oct-Apr, Generator hours: 0600-2200, Open all year, Reservations not accepted, Elev: 1316ft/401m, Tel: 509-633-3830, Nearest town: Kettle Falls. GPS: 48.6687, -118.05682

99 • A5 | Lake Roosevelt NRA - North Gorge

Total sites: 12, RV sites: 12, Central water, Vault/pit toilet, No showers, No RV dump, Tent & RV camping: $18, $9 Oct-Apr, Generator hours: 0600-2200, Open all year, Reservations not accepted, Elev: 1266ft/386m, Tel: 509-633-3830, Nearest town: Coulee Dam. GPS: 48.786372, -118.002391

100 • A5 | Lake Roosevelt NRA - Snag Cove

Total sites: 9, RV sites: 9, Central water, Vault/pit toilet, No showers, No RV dump, Tent & RV camping: $18, $9 Oct-Apr, Generator hours: 0600-2200, Open all year, Reservations not accepted, Elev: 1263ft/385m, Tel: 509-633-3830, Nearest town: Coulee Dam. GPS: 48.733274, -118.059715

101 • B1 | Olympic NP - Appleton Jct/Rocky Creek TC

Dispersed sites, No water, No toilets, Tents only: $5, Hike-in, Permit required, Reservations accepted, Elev: 3135ft/956m, Tel: 360-565-3130. GPS: 47.932481, -123.749419

102 • B1 | Olympic NP - Appleton Pass TC

Dispersed sites, No water, No toilets, Tents only: $5, Hike-in, No fires, Permit required, Reservations not accepted, Elev: 5377ft/1639m, Tel: 360-565-3130. GPS: 47.937321, -123.710847

103 • B1 | Olympic NP - Bear Camp TC

Dispersed sites, No water, Vault/pit toilet, Tents only: $5, Hike-in, No fires, Permit required, Also stock camp, Reservations not accepted, Elev: 3877ft/1182m, Tel: 360-565-3130. GPS: 47.809215, -123.314448

104 • B1 | Olympic NP - Belview TC

Dispersed sites, No water, No toilets, Tents only: $5, Hike-in, No fires, Permit required, Reservations not accepted, Elev: 4505ft/1373m, Tel: 360-565-3130. GPS: 47.557481, -123.443014

105 • B1 | Olympic NP - Big Log TC

Dispersed sites, No water, Vault/pit toilet, Tents only: $5, Hike-in, Permit required, Reservations not accepted, Elev: 1491ft/454m, Tel: 360-565-3130. GPS: 47.568605, -123.376804

106 • B1 | Olympic NP - Big Timber TC

Dispersed sites, No water, Vault/pit toilet, Tents only: $5, Hike-in, Permit required, Also stock camp, Reservations not accepted, Elev: 2329ft/710m, Tel: 360-565-3130. GPS: 47.733055, -123.235798

107 • B1 | Olympic NP - Bob Creek TC

Dispersed sites, No water, No toilets, Tents only: $5, Hike-in, Permit required, Reservations not accepted, Elev: 623ft/190m, Tel: 360-565-3130. GPS: 47.691725, -123.852933

108 • B1 | Olympic NP - Bogachiel TC

Dispersed sites, No water, No toilets, Tents only: $5, Hike-in, Permit required, Reservations not accepted, Elev: 494ft/151m, Tel: 360-565-3130. GPS: 47.883587, -124.168306

109 • B1 | Olympic NP - Boulder Creek TC

Dispersed sites, No water, Vault/pit toilet, Tents only: $5, Hike-in, No fires, Permit required, Reservations not accepted, Elev: 2216ft/675m, Tel: 360-565-3130. GPS: 47.978093, -123.693789

110 • B1 | Olympic NP - Boulder Lake TC

Dispersed sites, No water, Vault/pit toilet, Tents only: $5, Hike-in, No fires, Permit required, Reservations not accepted, Elev: 4341ft/1323m, Tel: 360-565-3130. GPS: 47.977925, -123.749959

111 • B1 | Olympic NP - C. B. Flats Group

Dispersed sites, No water, Vault/pit toilet, Tents only: $5, Hike-in, No fires, Permit required, Reservations accepted, Elev: 4054ft/1236m, Tel: 360-565-3130. GPS: 47.894197, -123.789834

112 • B1 | Olympic NP - Camp Ellis TC

Dispersed sites, No water, No toilets, Tents only: $5, Hike-in, Permit required, Reservations not accepted, Elev: 3025ft/922m, Tel: 360-565-3130. GPS: 47.882676, -123.248769

113 • B1 | Olympic NP - Camp Pleasant TC

Dispersed sites, No water, Vault/pit toilet, Tents only: $5, Hike-in, Permit required, Also stock camp, Reservations not accepted, Elev: 1573ft/479m, Tel: 360-565-3130. GPS: 47.580517, -123.366017

114 • B1 | Olympic NP - Camp Siberia TC

Dispersed sites, No water, Vault/pit toilet, Tents only: $5, Hike-in, No fires, Permit required, Reservations not accepted, Elev: 4225ft/1288m, Tel: 360-565-3130. GPS: 47.698892, -123.321382

115 • B1 | Olympic NP - Camp Wilder TC

Dispersed sites, No water, No toilets, Tents only: $5, Hike-in, Permit required, Reservations not accepted, Elev: 1928ft/588m, Tel: 360-565-3130. GPS: 47.765267, -123.459377

116 • B1 | Olympic NP - Canyon Camp TC

Dispersed sites, No water, No toilets, Tents only: $5, Hike-in, Permit required, Reservations not accepted, Elev: 1399ft/426m, Tel: 360-565-3130. GPS: 47.886271, -123.478491

117 • B1 | Olympic NP - Canyon Creek TC

Dispersed sites, No water, No toilets, Tents only: $5, Hike-in, 3 sites about 1/2 mile apart, Permit required, Reservations accepted, Elev: 2882ft/878m, Tel: 360-565-3130. GPS: 47.936651, -123.820368

118 • B1 | Olympic NP - Cape Alava

Dispersed sites, No water, No toilets, Tents only: $5, Hike-in, Reservations accepted, Elev: 30ft/9m, Tel: 360-565-3130. GPS: 48.161951, -124.732387

119 • B1 | Olympic NP - Cedar Creek

Dispersed sites, No water, No toilets, Tents only: $5, Hike-in, Reservations not accepted, Elev: 84ft/26m, Tel: 360-565-3130. GPS: 48.021216, -124.681698

120 • B1 | Olympic NP - Chicago Camp TC

Dispersed sites, No water, Vault/pit toilet, Tents only: $5, Hike-in, Permit required, Reservations not accepted, Elev: 2191ft/668m, Tel: 360-565-3130. GPS: 47.735586, -123.528207

121 • B1 | Olympic NP - Chilean Memorial

Dispersed sites, No water, No toilets, Tents only: $5, Hike-in, Reservations not accepted, Elev: 47ft/14m, Tel: 360-565-3130. GPS: 47.963025, -124.663619

122 • B1 | Olympic NP - Deception Creek TC

Dispersed sites, No water, Vault/pit toilet, Tents only: $5, Hike-in, Permit required, Also stock camp, Reservations not accepted, Elev: 3109ft/948m, Tel: 360-565-3130. GPS: 47.795826, -123.264517

123 • B1 | Olympic NP - Deer Lake TC

Dispersed sites, No water, Vault/pit toilet, Tents only: $5, Hike-in, No fires, Permit required, Also group site, Reservations accepted, Elev: 3508ft/1069m, Tel: 360-565-3130. GPS: 47.925563, -123.822827

124 • B1 | Olympic NP - Deer Park

Total sites: 14, RV sites: 0, No water, Vault/pit toilet, Tents only: $15, Open Jun-Oct, Reservations not accepted, Elev: 5400ft/1646m, Tel: 360-565-3130, Nearest town: Sequim. GPS: 47.948304, -123.258872

125 • B1 | Olympic NP - Diamond Meadow TC

Dispersed sites, No water, Vault/pit toilet, Tents only: $5, Hike-in, Permit required, Also stock camp, Reservations not accepted, Elev: 2723ft/830m, Tel: 360-565-3130. GPS: 47.721431, -123.275272

126 • B1 | Olympic NP - Dodger Point TC

Dispersed sites, No water, No toilets, Tents only: $5, Hike-in, No fires, Permit required, Reservations not accepted, Elev: 5058ft/1542m, Tel: 360-565-3130. GPS: 47.875129, -123.518803

127 • B1 | Olympic NP - Dose Meadows TC

Dispersed sites, No water, Vault/pit toilet, Tents only: $5, Hike-in, No fires, Permit required, Reservations not accepted, Elev: 4459ft/1359m, Tel: 360-565-3130. GPS: 47.797368, -123.343792

128 • B1 | Olympic NP - Elip Creek TC

Dispersed sites, No water, Vault/pit toilet, Tents only: $5, Hike-in, Permit required, Reservations not accepted, Elev: 981ft/299m, Tel: 360-565-3130. GPS: 47.639259, -123.651423

129 • B1 | Olympic NP - Elk Lake TC

Dispersed sites, No water, Tents only: $5, Hike-in, No fires, Permit required, Also group site, Reservations accepted, Elev: 2592ft/790m, Tel: 360-565-3130, Nearest town: `. GPS: 47.857212, -123.692403

130 • B1 | Olympic NP - Elkhorn TC

Dispersed sites, No water, Vault/pit toilet, Tents only: $5, Hike-in, Permit required, Reservations not accepted, Elev: 1412ft/430m, Tel: 360-565-3130. GPS: 47.872144, -123.469926

131 • B1 | Olympic NP - Enchanted Valley TC

Dispersed sites, No water, Vault/pit toilet, Tents only: $5, Hike-in, Permit required, Reservations not accepted, Elev: 2044ft/623m, Tel: 360-565-3130. GPS: 47.671941, -123.388047

132 • B1 | Olympic NP - Fairholme

Total sites: 88, RV sites: 88, Central water, Flush toilet, No showers, RV dump, Tent & RV camping: $20, Dump fee - $10, Open May-Oct, Max Length: 21ft, Reservations not accepted, Elev: 659ft/201m, Tel: 360-565-3130, Nearest town: Port Angeles. GPS: 48.068604, -123.916992

133 • B1 | Olympic NP - Falls Camp TC

Dispersed sites, No water, No toilets, Tents only: $5, Hike-in,

Permit required, Reservations not accepted, Elev: 3961ft/1207m, Tel: 360-565-3130. GPS: 47.856997, -123.279421

134 • B1 | Olympic NP - Fifteen Mile TC

Dispersed sites, No water, No toilets, Tents only: $5, Hike-in, Permit required, Reservations not accepted, Elev: 1271ft/387m, Tel: 360-565-3130. GPS: 47.902275, -124.023017

135 • B1 | Olympic NP - Five Mile Island

Dispersed sites, No water, Vault/pit toilet, Tents only: $5, Hike-in, Permit required, Also stock and group sites, Reservations not accepted, Elev: 859ft/262m, Tel: 360-565-3130. GPS: 47.868396, -123.839761

136 • B1 | Olympic NP - Flapjack Lakes TC

Dispersed sites, No water, Vault/pit toilet, Tents only: $5, Hike-in, No fires, Permit required, Also group site, Reservations accepted, Elev: 3862ft/1177m, Tel: 360-565-3130. GPS: 47.562043, -123.342187

137 • B1 | Olympic NP - Flapjack TC

Dispersed sites, No water, No toilets, Tents only: $5, Hike-in, Permit required, Reservations not accepted, Elev: 641ft/195m, Tel: 360-565-3130. GPS: 47.881618, -124.132875

138 • B1 | Olympic NP - Glacier Meadows TC

Dispersed sites, No water, Tents only: $5, Hike-in, No fires, Permit required, Also group site, Reservations accepted, Elev: 4231ft/1290m, Tel: 360-565-3130. GPS: 47.832258, -123.690951

139 • B1 | Olympic NP - Gladys Lake TC

Dispersed sites, No water, No toilets, Tents only: $5, Hike-in, No fires, Permit required, Reservations accepted, Elev: 5415ft/1650m, Tel: 360-565-3130. GPS: 47.878247, -123.359055

140 • B1 | Olympic NP - Grand Lake TC

Dispersed sites, No water, Vault/pit toilet, Tents only: $5, Hike-in, No fires, Permit required, Reservations accepted, Elev: 4765ft/1452m, Tel: 360-565-3130. GPS: 47.889091, -123.345724

141 • B1 | Olympic NP - Graves Creek

Total sites: 30, RV sites: 0, No water, Vault/pit toilet, Tents only: $20, No water in winter, Open all year, Max Length: 21ft, Reservations not accepted, Elev: 666ft/203m, Tel: 360-565-3130, Nearest town: Amanda Park. GPS: 47.573148, -123.578806

142 • B1 | Olympic NP - Gray Wolf TC

Dispersed sites, No water, Vault/pit toilet, Tents only: $5, Hike-in, Permit required, Reservations not accepted, Elev: 2093ft/638m, Tel: 360-565-3130. GPS: 47.915829, -123.242188

143 • B1 | Olympic NP - Happy Four TC

Dispersed sites, No water, No toilets, Tents only: $5, Hike-in, Permit required, Reservations not accepted, Elev: 882ft/269m, Tel: 360-565-3130. GPS: 47.869411, -123.817046

144 • B1 | Olympic NP - Happy Lake TC

Dispersed sites, No water, No toilets, Tents only: $5, Hike-in, No fires, Permit required, Reservations not accepted, Elev: 4895ft/1492m, Tel: 360-565-3130. GPS: 48.008554, -123.686657

145 • B1 | Olympic NP - Hayes River TC

Dispersed sites, No water, Vault/pit toilet, Tents only: $5, Hike-in, Permit required, Reservations not accepted, Elev: 1686ft/514m, Tel: 360-565-3130. GPS: 47.809359, -123.453925

146 • B1 | Olympic NP - Heart Lake TC

Dispersed sites, No water, Vault/pit toilet, Tents only: $5, Hike-in, No fires, Permit required, Reservations accepted, Elev: 4779ft/1457m, Tel: 360-565-3130. GPS: 47.910538, -123.732984

147 • B1 | Olympic NP - Heart O' The Hills

Total sites: 102, RV sites: 102, Central water, Vault/pit toilet, No showers, No RV dump, Tent & RV camping: $20, Walk-in only during heavy snowfall, Open all year, Max Length: 20ft, Reservations not accepted, Elev: 1834ft/559m, Tel: 360-565-3130, Nearest town: Port Angeles. GPS: 48.036267, -123.427612

148 • B1 | Olympic NP - Heather Park TC

Dispersed sites, No water, No toilets, Tents only: $5, Hike-in, No fires, Permit required, Reservations not accepted, Elev: 5627ft/1715m, Tel: 360-565-3130. GPS: 48.009373, -123.460499

149 • B1 | Olympic NP - Hoh Lake TC

Dispersed sites, No water, Vault/pit toilet, Tents only: $5, Hike-in, No fires, Permit required, Reservations accepted, Elev: 4525ft/1379m, Tel: 360-565-3130. GPS: 47.897591, -123.788005

150 • B1 | Olympic NP - Hoh Rain Forest

Total sites: 88, RV sites: 88, Central water, Flush toilet, No showers, No RV dump, Tent & RV camping: $20, Dump fee $10, Open all year, Max Length: 21ft, Reservations not accepted, Elev: 633ft/193m, Tel: 360-565-3130, Nearest town: Forks. GPS: 47.85964, -123.93576

151 • B1 | Olympic NP - Hole-in-the-Wall

Dispersed sites, No water, No toilets, Tents only: $5, Hike-in, Reservations not accepted, Elev: 41ft/12m, Tel: 360-565-3130. GPS: 47.941417, -124.649062

152 • B1 | Olympic NP - Home Sweet Home TC

Dispersed sites, No water, Vault/pit toilet, Tents only: $5, Hike-in, No fires, Permit required, Reservations not accepted, Elev: 4175ft/1273m, Tel: 360-565-3130. GPS: 47.638425, -123.308031

153 • B1 | Olympic NP - Honeymoon Meadows TC

Dispersed sites, No water, Vault/pit toilet, Tents only: $5, Hike-in, No fires, Permit required, Reservations not accepted, Elev: 3630ft/1106m, Tel: 360-565-3130. GPS: 47.703655, -123.314049

154 • B1 | Olympic NP - Horsehead Stock Camp

Dispersed sites, No water, No toilets, Tents only: $5, Hike-in, Permit required, Reservations accepted, Elev: 3243ft/988m, Tel: 360-565-3130. GPS: 47.929973, -123.739511

155 • B1 | Olympic NP - Humes Ranch TC

Dispersed sites, No water, No toilets, Tents only: $5, Hike-in, Permit required, Reservations not accepted, Elev: 800ft/244m, Tel: 360-565-3130. GPS: 47.947841, -123.545184

156 • B1 | Olympic NP - Hyak TC

Dispersed sites, No water, No toilets, Tents only: $5, Hike-in, Permit required, Reservations not accepted, Elev: 1802ft/549m, Tel: 360-565-3130. GPS: 47.924159, -123.970788

157 • B1 | Olympic NP - Irely Lake

Dispersed sites, No water, No toilets, Tents only: $5, Hike-in, Elev: 758ft/231m, Nearest town: Port Angeles. GPS: 47.568188, -123.673361

158 • B1 | Olympic NP - Kalaloch

Total sites: 170, RV sites: 170, Central water, Flush toilet, No showers, RV dump, Tent & RV camping: $22, Dump fee $10, Open all year, Max Length: 35ft, Reservations accepted, Elev: 76ft/23m, Tel: 360-565-3130, Nearest town: Quetts. GPS: 47.612739, -124.375244

159 • B1 | Olympic NP - Lake Angeles TC

Dispersed sites, No water, No toilets, Tents only: $5, Hike-in, No fires, Permit required, Reservations not accepted, Elev: 4260ft/1298m, Tel: 360-565-3130. GPS: 48.008747, -123.433617

160 • B1 | Olympic NP - Lake Beauty TC

Dispersed sites, No water, No toilets, Tents only: $5, Hike-in, No fires, Permit required, Reservations not accepted, Elev: 4734ft/1443m, Tel: 360-565-3130, Nearest town: Port Angeles. GPS: 47.716789, -123.640765

161 • B1 | Olympic NP - Lake Sundown TC

Dispersed sites, No water, No toilets, Tents only: $5, Hike-in, No fires, Permit required, Reservations not accepted, Elev: 3833ft/1168m, Tel: 360-565-3130. GPS: 47.536332, -123.511635

162 • B1 | Olympic NP - Lewis Meadow TC

Dispersed sites, No water, Vault/pit toilet, Tents only: $5, Hike-in, Permit required, Also stock and group sites, Reservations not accepted, Elev: 1010ft/308m, Tel: 360-565-3130. GPS: 47.879203, -123.738388

163 • B1 | Olympic NP - Lillian River TC

Dispersed sites, No water, Vault/pit toilet, Tents only: $5, Hike-in, Permit required, Reservations not accepted, Elev: 1310ft/399m, Tel: 360-565-3130. GPS: 47.937377, -123.518488

164 • B1 | Olympic NP - Low Divide TC

Dispersed sites, No water, Vault/pit toilet, Tents only: $5, Hike-in, Permit required, Reservations not accepted, Elev: 3621ft/1104m, Tel: 360-565-3130. GPS: 47.724133, -123.558924

165 • B1 | Olympic NP - Lower Cameron TC

Dispersed sites, No water, No toilets, Tents only: $5, Hike-in, No fires, Permit required, Reservations not accepted, Elev: 3665ft/1117m, Tel: 360-565-3130. GPS: 47.876372, -123.317124

166 • B1 | Olympic NP - Lunch Lake TC

Dispersed sites, No water, Vault/pit toilet, Tents only: $5, Hike-in, No fires, Permit required, Reservations accepted, Elev: 4524ft/1379m, Tel: 360-565-3130. GPS: 47.915625, -123.785558

167 • B1 | Olympic NP - Marmot Lake TC

Dispersed sites, No water, Vault/pit toilet, Tents only: $5, Hike-in, No fires, Permit required, Also group site, Reservations not accepted, Elev: 4396ft/1340m, Tel: 360-565-3130. GPS: 47.649384, -123.363044

168 • B1 | Olympic NP - Martin Creek Stock

Dispersed sites, No water, No toilets, Tents only: $5, Hike-in, Permit required, Reservations accepted, Elev: 2244ft/684m, Tel: 360-565-3130. GPS: 47.864704, -123.691437

169 • B1 | Olympic NP - Mary's Falls TC

Dispersed sites, No water, Vault/pit toilet, Tents only: $5, Hike-in, Permit required, Reservations not accepted, Elev: 1273ft/388m, Tel: 360-565-3130. GPS: 47.901618, -123.490009

170 • B1 | Olympic NP - Mink Lake TC

Dispersed sites, No water, No toilets, Tents only: $5, Hike-in, Permit required, Reservations accepted, Elev: 3105ft/946m, Tel: 360-565-3130. GPS: 47.948538, -123.869628

171 • B1 | Olympic NP - Moose Lake TC

Dispersed sites, No water, Vault/pit toilet, Tents only: $5, Hike-in, No fires, Permit required, Also group site, Reservations accepted, Elev: 5072ft/1546m, Tel: 360-565-3130. GPS: 47.882834, -123.351237

172 • B1 | Olympic NP - Mora

Total sites: 94, RV sites: 94, Central water, Flush toilet, No showers, RV dump, Tent & RV camping: $20, Dump fee $10, Open all year, Max Length: 35ft, Reservations accepted, Elev: 105ft/32m, Tel: 360-565-3130, Nearest town: Forks. GPS: 47.917579, -124.605111

173 • B1 | Olympic NP - Mosquito Creek

Dispersed sites, No water, No toilets, Tents only: $5, Hike-in, Reservations not accepted, Elev: 75ft/23m, Tel: 360-565-3130. GPS: 47.798494, -124.480676

174 • B1 | Olympic NP - Mt. Tom Creek TC

Dispersed sites, No water, No toilets, Tents only: $5, Hike-in, Permit required, Also group site, Reservations not accepted, Elev: 877ft/267m, Tel: 360-565-3130. GPS: 47.869424, -123.886561

175 • B1 | Olympic NP - Nine Stream TC

Dispersed sites, No water, Vault/pit toilet, Tents only: $5, Hike-in, Permit required, Also stock camp, Reservations not accepted, Elev: 2010ft/613m, Tel: 360-565-3130. GPS: 47.613092, -123.343262

176 • B1 | Olympic NP - North Fork

Total sites: 9, RV sites: 9, No water, Vault/pit toilet, Tent & RV camping: $15, Not recommended for RV's, Open all year, Max Length: 21ft, Reservations not accepted, Elev: 574ft/175m, Tel: 360-565-3130. GPS: 47.56799, -123.6522

177 • B1 | Olympic NP - North Ozette River

Dispersed sites, No water, No toilets, Tents only: $5, Hike-in, Reservations accepted, Elev: 5ft/2m, Tel: 360-565-3130. GPS: 48.18145, -124.708639

178 • B1 | Olympic NP - Norwegian Memorial

Dispersed sites, No water, No toilets, Tents only: $5, Hike-in, Reservations not accepted, Elev: 30ft/9m, Tel: 360-565-3130. GPS: 48.036844, -124.681233

179 • B1 | Olympic NP - O'Neil Creek TC

Dispersed sites, No water, Vault/pit toilet, Tents only: $5, Hike-in, Permit required, Reservations not accepted, Elev: 1210ft/369m, Tel: 360-565-3130. GPS: 47.615998, -123.473248

180 • B1 | Olympic NP - Olympus Ranger Station

Dispersed sites, No water, Vault/pit toilet, Tents only: $5, Hike-in, Permit required, Also group site, Reservations not accepted, Elev: 946ft/288m, Tel: 360-565-3130. GPS: 47.878196, -123.765729

181 • B1 | Olympic NP - Ozette

Total sites: 15, RV sites: 15, No water, Vault/pit toilet, No showers, No RV dump, Tent & RV camping: $20, Open all year, Max Length: 21ft, Reservations not accepted, Elev: 89ft/27m, Tel: 360-565-3130, Nearest town: Beaver. GPS: 48.152708, -124.666723

182 • B1 | Olympic NP - Pelton Creek TC

Dispersed sites, No water, No toilets, Tents only: $5, Hike-in, Permit required, Reservations not accepted, Elev: 796ft/243m, Tel: 360-565-3130. GPS: 47.700193, -123.767707

183 • B1 | Olympic NP - Pony Bridge TC

Dispersed sites, No water, No toilets, Tents only: $5, Hike-in, Permit required, Reservations not accepted, Elev: 938ft/286m, Tel: 360-565-3130. GPS: 47.596535, -123.541533

184 • B1 | Olympic NP - Pyrites Creek TC

Dispersed sites, No water, No toilets, Tents only: $5, Hike-in, Permit required, Reservations not accepted, Elev: 1489ft/454m, Tel: 360-565-3130. GPS: 47.640727, -123.432274

185 • B1 | Olympic NP - Queets

Total sites: 20, No water, Vault/pit toilet, Tents only: $15, Open all year, Reservations not accepted, Elev: 354ft/108m, Tel: 360-565-3130. GPS: 47.62635, -124.0179

186 • B1 | Olympic NP - Roaring Winds TC

Dispersed sites, No water, No toilets, Tents only: $5, Hike-in, No fires, Permit required, Reservations required, Elev: 6003ft/1830m, Tel: 360-565-3130. GPS: 47.927147, -123.328789

187 • B1 | Olympic NP - Sand Point

Dispersed sites, No water, No toilets, Tents only: $5, Hike-in, Reservations accepted, Elev: 17ft/5m, Tel: 360-565-3130. GPS: 48.125893, -124.709306

188 • B1 | Olympic NP - Scott Creek

Dispersed sites, No water, No toilets, Tents only: $5, Hike-in, Reservations not accepted, Elev: 50ft/15m, Tel: 360-565-3130. GPS: 47.861692, -124.557912

189 • B1 | Olympic NP - Seafield Creek

Dispersed sites, No water, No toilets, Tents only: $5, Hike-in, Reservations accepted, Elev: 20ft/6m, Tel: 360-565-3130. GPS: 48.209271, -124.692354

190 • B1 | Olympic NP - Second Beach

Dispersed sites, No water, No toilets, Tents only: $5, Hike-in, Reservations not accepted, Elev: 70ft/21m, Tel: 360-565-3130. GPS: 47.891577, -124.626775

191 • B1 | Olympic NP - Seven Mile Group

Dispersed sites, No water, No toilets, Tents only: $5, Hike-in, Permit required, Reservations accepted, Elev: 3203ft/976m, Tel: 360-565-3130. GPS: 47.930652, -123.739402

192 • B1 | Olympic NP - Shi Shi Beach

Dispersed sites, No water, No toilets, Tents only: $5, Hike-in, TH parking fee on Makah Reservation, Reservations not accepted, Elev: 15ft/5m, Tel: 360-565-3130. GPS: 48.257233, -124.683426

193 • B1 | Olympic NP - Sixteen Mile TC

Dispersed sites, No water, No toilets, Tents only: $5, Hike-in, Permit required, Reservations not accepted, Elev: 2048ft/624m, Tel: 360-565-3130. GPS: 47.689115, -123.591057

194 • B1 | Olympic NP - Sol Duc

Total sites: 82, RV sites: 82, Central water, No toilets, No showers, RV dump, Tent & RV camping: $21-24, Dump fee $10, No services in winter, Open all year, Max Length: 35ft, Reservations accepted, Elev: 1827ft/557m, Tel: 360-565-3130, Nearest town: Port Angeles. GPS: 47.964844, -123.85498

195 • B1 | Olympic NP - Sol Duc Falls TC

Dispersed sites, No water, No toilets, Tents only: $5, Hike-in, Permit required, Reservations accepted, Elev: 2118ft/646m, Tel: 360-565-3130. GPS: 47.951297, -123.819908

196 • B1 | Olympic NP - Sol Duc Park TC

Dispersed sites, No water, Vault/pit toilet, Tents only: $5, Hike-in, No fires, Permit required, Also group site, Reservations accepted, Elev: 4294ft/1309m, Tel: 360-565-3130. GPS: 47.916341, -123.728192

197 • B1 | Olympic NP - Sol Duc River TC's 1-4

Dispersed sites, No water, No toilets, Tents only: $5, Hike-in, 4 sites along 3 miles of river, Permit required, Reservations accepted, Elev: 2204ft/672m, Tel: 360-565-3130. GPS: 47.943846, -123.791307

198 • B1 | Olympic NP - South Beach

Total sites: 55, RV sites: 55, No water, Flush toilet, No showers, No RV dump, Tent & RV camping: $15, Open May-Sep, Max Length: 35ft, Reservations not accepted, Elev: 76ft/23m, Tel: 360-565-3130, Nearest town: Kalaloch Beach. GPS: 47.567571, -124.361393

199 • B1 | Olympic NP - South Ozette River

Dispersed sites, No water, No toilets, Tents only: $5, Hike-in, Reservations accepted, Elev: 10ft/3m, Tel: 360-565-3130. GPS: 48.181667, -124.710056

200 • B1 | Olympic NP - South Sand Point

Dispersed sites, No water, No toilets, Tents only: $5, Hike-in, Reservations accepted, Elev: 26ft/8m, Tel: 360-565-3130. GPS: 48.115001, -124.694195

201 • B1 | Olympic NP - Spike Camp TC

Dispersed sites, No water, Vault/pit toilet, Tents only: $5, Hike-in, Permit required, Reservations not accepted, Elev: 1469ft/448m, Tel: 360-565-3130. GPS: 47.544984, -123.376023

202 • B1 | Olympic NP - Spruce Bottom TC

Dispersed sites, No water, No toilets, Tents only: $5, Hike-in, Permit required, Reservations not accepted, Elev: 538ft/164m, Tel: 360-565-3130. GPS: 47.652855, -123.942286

203 • B1 | Olympic NP - Staircase

Total sites: 49, RV sites: 49, Central water, No toilets, No showers, No RV dump, Tent & RV camping: $20, No services in winter, Open all year, Max Length: 35ft, Reservations not accepted, Elev: 948ft/289m, Tel: 360-565-3130, Nearest town: Hoodsport. GPS: 47.515171, -123.328255

204 • B1 | Olympic NP - Strawberry Point

Dispersed sites, No water, No toilets, Tents only: $5, Hike-in, Reservations not accepted, Elev: 55ft/17m, Tel: 360-565-3130. GPS: 47.846555, -124.549657

205 • B1 | Olympic NP - Success Creek TC

Dispersed sites, No water, No toilets, Tents only: $5, Hike-in, Permit required, Reservations not accepted, Elev: 1874ft/571m, Tel: 360-565-3130. GPS: 47.566724, -123.508636

206 • B1 | Olympic NP - Third Beach

Dispersed sites, No water, No toilets, Tents only: $5, Hike-in, Reservations not accepted, Elev: 30ft/9m, Tel: 360-565-3130. GPS: 47.878768, -124.588032

207 • B1 | Olympic NP - Three Forks TC

Dispersed sites, No water, Vault/pit toilet, Tents only: $5, Hike-in, Permit required, Reservations not accepted, Elev: 2127ft/648m, Tel: 360-565-3130. GPS: 47.915297, -123.247237

208 • B1 | Olympic NP - Three Lakes

Dispersed sites, No water, Vault/pit toilet, Tents only: $5, Hike-in, No fires, Permit required, Reservations not accepted, Elev: 3159ft/963m, Tel: 360-565-3130. GPS: 47.601168, -123.723207

209 • B1 | Olympic NP - Three Prune TC

Dispersed sites, No water, No toilets, Tents only: $5, Hike-in, No fires, Permit required, Reservations not accepted, Elev: 3621ft/1104m, Tel: 360-565-3130. GPS: 47.647837, -123.717507

210 • B1 | Olympic NP - Toleak Point

Dispersed sites, No water, No toilets, Tents only: $5, Hike-in, Reservations not accepted, Elev: 96ft/29m, Tel: 360-565-3130. GPS: 47.835596, -124.538541

211 • B1 | Olympic NP - Trapper TC

Dispersed sites, No water, Vault/pit toilet, Tents only: $5, Hike-in, Permit required, Reservations not accepted, Elev: 1230ft/375m, Tel: 360-565-3130. GPS: 47.657952, -123.642708

212 • B1 | Olympic NP - Two Bear TC

Dispersed sites, No water, No toilets, Tents only: $5, Hike-in, No fires, Permit required, Reservations not accepted, Elev: 3732ft/1138m, Tel: 360-565-3130. GPS: 47.627298, -123.319143

213 • B1 | Olympic NP - Upper Cameron TC

Dispersed sites, No water, No toilets, Tents only: $5, Hike-in, No fires, Permit required, Reservations not accepted, Elev: 5422ft/1653m, Tel: 360-565-3130. GPS: 47.816804, -123.344444

214 • B1 | Olympic NP - Upper Duckabush TC

Dispersed sites, No water, Vault/pit toilet, Tents only: $5, Hike-in, Permit required, Also stock camp, Reservations not accepted, Elev: 2731ft/832m, Tel: 360-565-3130. GPS: 47.654485, -123.319406

215 • B1 | Olympic NP - Upper Sol Duc Bridge TC

Dispersed sites, No water, No toilets, Tents only: $5, Hike-in, Permit required, Reservations accepted, Elev: 3315ft/1010m, Tel: 360-565-3130. GPS: 47.930337, -123.737581

216 • B1 | Olympic NP - Wagonwheel Lake TC

Dispersed sites, No water, No toilets, Tents only: $5, Hike-in, Reservations not accepted, Elev: 4051ft/1235m, Tel: 360-565-3130. GPS: 47.533378, -123.299824

217 • B1 | Olympic NP - Wedding Rocks

Dispersed sites, No water, No toilets, Tents only: $5, Hike-in, Reservations accepted, Elev: 48ft/15m, Tel: 360-565-3130. GPS: 48.149144, -124.719574

218 • B1 | Olympic NP - Wolf Bar TC

Dispersed sites, No water, No toilets, Tents only: $5, Hike-in, Permit required, Reservations not accepted, Elev: 644ft/196m, Tel: 360-565-3130. GPS: 47.599391, -123.618855

219 • B1 | Olympic NP - Yellow Banks

Dispersed sites, No water, No toilets, Tents only: $5, Hike-in, Reservations accepted, Elev: 34ft/10m, Tel: 360-565-3130. GPS: 48.097437, -124.686507

220 • B2 | Olympic NP - Dose Forks TC

Dispersed sites, No water, Vault/pit toilet, Tents only: $5, Hike-in, Permit required, Reservations not accepted, Elev: 1766ft/538m, Tel: 360-565-3130. GPS: 47.742619, -123.194007

221 • B2 | Olympic NP - Home Lake TC

Dispersed sites, No water, No toilets, Tents only: $5, Hike-in, No fires, Permit required, Reservations not accepted, Elev: 5333ft/1625m, Tel: 360-565-3130. GPS: 47.771033, -123.164627

222 • B2 | Olympic NP - Lake Constance TC

Dispersed sites, No water, Vault/pit toilet, Tents only: $5, Hike-in, No fires, Permit required, Also group site, Reservations required, Elev: 4714ft/1437m, Tel: 360-565-3130. GPS: 47.750375, -123.141214

223 • B2 | Olympic NP - Lower Royal Meadow TC

Dispersed sites, No water, No toilets, Tents only: $5, Hike-in, No fires, Permit required, Reservations required, Elev: 4717ft/1438m, Tel: 360-565-3130. GPS: 47.839074, -123.211544

224 • B2 | Olympic NP - Royal Creek TC

Dispersed sites, No water, No toilets, Tents only: $5, Hike-in, Permit required, Reservations required, Elev: 3591ft/1095m, Tel: 360-565-3130. GPS: 47.865825, -123.193217

225 • B2 | Olympic NP - Royal Lake TC

Dispersed sites, No water, Vault/pit toilet, Tents only: $5, Hike-in, No fires, Permit required, Also group site, Reservations required, Elev: 5132ft/1564m, Tel: 360-565-3130. GPS: 47.831289, -123.211039

226 • B2 | Olympic NP - Sunnybrook Meadows TC

Dispersed sites, No water, No toilets, Tents only: $5, Hike-in, No fires, Permit required, Reservations not accepted, Elev: 5517ft/1682m, Tel: 360-565-3130. GPS: 47.768394, -123.193285

227 • B2 | Olympic NP - Ten Mile TC

Dispersed sites, No water, Vault/pit toilet, Tents only: $5, Hike-in, Permit required, Also stock camp, Reservations not accepted, Elev: 1506ft/459m, Tel: 360-565-3130. GPS: 47.676724, -123.202146

228 • B2 | Olympic NP - Upper Lena Lake TC

Dispersed sites, No water, Vault/pit toilet, Tents only: $5, Hike-in, No fires, Permit required, Also group site, Reservations accepted, Elev: 4568ft/1392m, Tel: 360-565-3130. GPS: 47.633947, -123.209611

229 • B3 | North Cascades NP - Harlequin TC

Total sites: 7, No water, Vault/pit toilet, Tents only: Free, Hike-in, $20 non-refundable reservation fee, Permit required, Also 1 group site, Reservations accepted, Elev: 1210ft/369m, Tel: 360-854-7200. GPS: 48.348333, -120.714287

230 • B3 | North Cascades NP - Hooter TC

Total sites: 1, No water, Vault/pit toilet, Tents only: Free, Hike-in, No fires, $20 non-refundable reservation fee, Permit required, Reservations accepted, Elev: 2677ft/816m, Tel: 360-854-7200. GPS: 48.352256, -120.641457

231 • B3 | North Cascades NP - Juanita Lake TC/Stock

Total sites: 2, No water, Vault/pit toilet, Tents only: Free, Also hike-in sites, No fires, $20 non-refundable reservation fee, Permit required, Reservations accepted, Elev: 6676ft/2035m, Tel: 360-854-7200. GPS: 48.320474, -120.588525

232 • B3 | North Cascades NP - Moore Point TC/Boat

Total sites: 4, No water, Vault/pit toilet, Tents only: Free, Hike-in/boat-in, $20 non-refundable reservation fee, Permit required, USFS dock permit required for boaters, Reservations accepted, Elev: 1100ft/335m, Tel: 360-854-7200. GPS: 48.236, -120.616

233 • B3 | North Cascades NP - Prince Creek TC/Boat

Total sites: 6, No water, Vault/pit toilet, Tents only: Free, Hike-in, $20 non-refundable reservation fee, Permit required, USFS dock permit required for boaters, Reservations accepted, Elev: 1100ft/335m, Tel: 360-854-7200. GPS: 48.145658, -120.494451

234 • B3 | North Cascades NP - Purple Point Overflow

Total sites: 4, No water, Vault/pit toilet, Tents only: Free, Hike-in, No fires, $20 non-refundable reservation fee, Permit required, Also 1 group site, Reservations accepted, Elev: 1167ft/356m, Tel: 360-854-7200. GPS: 48.307619, -120.654501

235 • B3 | North Cascades NP - Purple Point TC/Stock

Total sites: 6, No water, Vault/pit toilet, Tents only: Free, Hike-in, $20 non-refundable reservation fee, Permit required, Also 1 group site, Reservations accepted, Elev: 1167ft/356m, Tel: 360-854-7200. GPS: 48.316271, -120.661945

236 • B3 | North Cascades NP - Rainbow Bridge TC

Total sites: 2, No water, Vault/pit toilet, Tents only: Free, Hike-in, $20 non-refundable reservation fee, Permit required, Reservations accepted, Elev: 2040ft/622m, Tel: 360-854-7200. GPS: 48.347243, -120.694469

237 • B3 | North Cascades NP - Reynolds TC/Stock

Total sites: 2, No water, Vault/pit toilet, Tents only: Free, Hike-in, $20 non-refundable reservation fee, Permit required, Reservations accepted, Elev: 5663ft/1726m, Tel: 360-854-7200. GPS: 48.353163, -120.581424

238 • B3 | North Cascades NP - Weaver Point

Total sites: 16, No water, Flush toilet, Tents only: Free, Hike-in/boat-in, USFS dock permit required, Elev: 1092ft/333m, Tel: 360-854-7200. GPS: 48.314931, -120.674283

239 • B4 | Lake Roosevelt NRA - Columbia

Dispersed sites, No toilets, Tent & RV camping: $10, $9 Oct-Apr, Generator hours: 0600-2200, Open all year, Reservations not accepted, Elev: 1601ft/488m, Tel: 509-633-3830, Nearest town: Coulee Dam. GPS: 47.906404, -118.334884

240 • B4 | Lake Roosevelt NRA - Fort Spokane

Total sites: 67, RV sites: 67, Central water, Flush toilet, No showers, RV dump, Tent & RV camping: $18, 2 group sites, $9 Oct-Apr, Generator hours: 0600-2200, Open all year, Max Length: 30ft, Reservations accepted, Elev: 1322ft/403m, Tel: 509-633-3830, Nearest town: Davenport. GPS: 47.90772, -118.31311

241 • B4 | Lake Roosevelt NRA - Hawk Creek

Total sites: 21, RV sites: 21, Central water, Vault/pit toilet, No showers, No RV dump, Tent & RV camping: $18, $9 Oct-Apr, Generator hours: 0600-2200, Open all year, Reservations not accepted, Elev: 1345ft/410m, Tel: 509-633-3830, Nearest town: Coulee Dam. GPS: 47.815143, -118.324621

242 • B4 | Lake Roosevelt NRA - Hunters Park

Total sites: 39, RV sites: 39, Central water, Flush toilet, No showers, RV dump, Tent & RV camping: $18, 3 group sites, $9 Oct-Apr, Generator hours: 0600-2200, Open all year, Max Length: 30ft, Reservations not accepted, Elev: 1319ft/402m, Tel: 509-633-3830, Nearest town: Hunters. GPS: 48.124894, -118.232224

243 • B4 | Lake Roosevelt NRA - Keller Ferry

Total sites: 55, RV sites: 55, Central water, Flush toilet, No showers, RV dump, Tent & RV camping: $20, 2 group sites, $9 Oct-Apr, Concessionaire, Generator hours: 0600-2200, Open May-Sep, Max Length: 30ft, Reservations not accepted, Elev: 1286ft/392m, Tel: 509-633-3830, Nearest town: Wilbur. GPS: 47.928711, -118.692139

244 • B4 | Lake Roosevelt NRA - Pierre

Dispersed sites, No water, Vault/pit toilet, Tent & RV camping: Free, Generator hours: 0600-2200, Reservations not accepted, Elev: 1339ft/408m, Tel: 509-633-3830, Nearest town: Seven Bays. GPS: 47.946948, -118.243883

245 • B4 | Lake Roosevelt NRA - Sanpoil

Dispersed sites, No water, No toilets, Tent & RV camping: $18, $9 Oct-Apr, Generator hours: 0600-2200, Open all year, Reservations not accepted, Elev: 1348ft/411m, Tel: 509-633-3830, Nearest town: Coulee Dam. GPS: 48.051091, -118.666854

246 • B4 | Lake Roosevelt NRA - Seven Bays

Total sites: 33, RV sites: 33, Vault/pit toilet, Tent & RV camping: $18, $9 Oct-Apr, Generator hours: 0600-2200, Open all year, Reservations not accepted, Elev: 1405ft/428m, Tel: 509-633-3830, Nearest town: Coulee Dam. GPS: 47.855853, -118.337851

247 • B4 | Lake Roosevelt NRA - Spring Canyon

Total sites: 87, RV sites: 87, Central water, Flush toilet, No showers, RV dump, Tent & RV camping: $18, $9 Oct-Apr, Generator hours: 0600-2200, Open all year, Reservations not accepted, Elev: 1322ft/403m, Tel: 509-633-3830, Nearest town: Coulee Dam. GPS: 47.934157, -118.939411

248 • B5 | Lake Roosevelt NRA - Cloverleaf

Total sites: 9, Central water, Vault/pit toilet, Tents only: $18, Generator hours: 0600-2200, Reservations not accepted, Elev: 1283ft/391m, Tel: 509-633-3830, Nearest town: Gifford. GPS: 48.305242, -118.151433

249 • B5 | Lake Roosevelt NRA - Gifford

Total sites: 42, RV sites: 42, Central water, Vault/pit toilet, No showers, RV dump, Tent & RV camping: $18, 1 group site, $9 Oct-Apr, Generator hours: 0600-2200, Open all year, Reservations not accepted, Elev: 1368ft/417m, Tel: 509-633-3830, Nearest town: Gifford. GPS: 48.286621, -118.141602

250 • C2 | Mt Rainier NP - Berkeley Park TC

Dispersed sites, No water, Vault/pit toilet, Tents only: $6, Hike-in, 5.1 mi, 2 sites, Permit required, Reservation fee: $26, Reservations accepted, Elev: 5621ft/1713m, Tel: 360-569-6650. GPS: 46.929483, -121.686723

251 • C2 | Mt Rainier NP - Camp Curtis TC

Dispersed sites, No water, Vault/pit toilet, Tents only: $6, Hike-in, 5.0 mi, 2 sites, Permit required, Reservation fee: $26, Reservations accepted, Elev: 8973ft/2735m, Tel: 360-569-6650. GPS: 46.873095, -121.724055

252 • C2 | Mt Rainier NP - Camp Muir TC/Shelter

Dispersed sites, No water, Vault/pit toilet, Tents only: $6, Hike-in, Permit required, Reservation fee: $26, Reservations accepted, Elev: 10046ft/3062m, Tel: 360-569-6650. GPS: 46.835425, -121.732507

253 • C2 | Mt Rainier NP - Camp Schurman TC

Dispersed sites, No water, Vault/pit toilet, Tents only: $6, Hike-in, 5.8 mi, 35 people, Permit required, Reservation fee: $26, Reservations accepted, Elev: 9528ft/2904m, Tel: 360-569-6650. GPS: 46.870435, -121.732757

254 • C2 | Mt Rainier NP - Carbon River TC

Dispersed sites, No water, Vault/pit toilet, Tents only: $6, Hike-in, 8.1 mi, 4 sites, Permit required, Reservation fee: $26, Reservations accepted, Elev: 3385ft/1032m, Tel: 360-569-6650. GPS: 46.959581, -121.799474

255 • C2 | Mt Rainier NP - Cataract Valley

Dispersed sites, No water, Vault/pit toilet, Tents only: $6, Hike-in, 6.5 mi, 6 sites, Permit required, Reservation fee: $26, Reservations accepted, Elev: 5107ft/1557m, Tel: 360-569-6650. GPS: 46.938164, -121.806779

256 • C2 | Mt Rainier NP - Cougar Rock

Total sites: 173, RV sites: 173, Central water, No toilets, No showers, RV dump, Tent & RV camping: $20, 5 group sites $60, Generator hours: 0800-1000/1200-1400/1700-1900, Open May-Oct, Max Length: RV:35'/Trlr:27ft, Reservations accepted, Elev: 3225ft/983m, Tel: 360-569-2211, Nearest town: Enumclaw. GPS: 46.767511, -121.792613

257 • C2 | Mt Rainier NP - Devil's Dream TC

Dispersed sites, No water, Vault/pit toilet, Tents only: $6, Hike-in, 5.0 mi, 7 sites, 1 group site, Permit required, Reservation fee: $26, Reservations accepted, Elev: 4852ft/1479m, Tel: 360-569-6650, Nearest town: Enumclaw. GPS: 46.782343, -121.832161

258 • C2 | Mt Rainier NP - Dick's Lake TC

Dispersed sites, No water, Vault/pit toilet, Tents only: $6, Hike-in, 3.0 mi, 2 sites, Permit required, Reservation fee: $26, Reservations accepted, Elev: 5657ft/1724m, Tel: 360-569-6650. GPS: 46.940225, -121.594181

259 • C2 | Mt Rainier NP - Eagle's Roost TC

Dispersed sites, No water, Vault/pit toilet, Tents only: $6, Hike-in, 1.8 mi, 7 sites, Permit required, Reservation fee: $26, Reservations accepted, Elev: 4739ft/1444m, Tel: 360-569-6650. GPS: 46.914791, -121.846791

260 • C2 | Mt Rainier NP - Fire Creek TC

Dispersed sites, No water, Vault/pit toilet, Tents only: $6, Hike-in, 7.7 mi, 3 sites, Permit required, Reservation fee: $26, Reservations accepted, Elev: 4716ft/1437m, Tel: 360-569-6650. GPS: 46.967461, -121.695827

261 • C2 | Mt Rainier NP - Forest Lake TC

Dispersed sites, No water, Vault/pit toilet, Tents only: $6, Hike-in, 2.0 mi, 1 site, Permit required, Reservation fee: $26, Reservations accepted, Elev: 5672ft/1729m, Tel: 360-569-6650. GPS: 46.932621, -121.652048

262 • C2 | Mt Rainier NP - Glacier Basin TC

Dispersed sites, No water, Vault/pit toilet, Tents only: $6, Hike-in, 3.0 mi, 5 sites, 1 group site, Permit required, Reservation fee: $26, Reservations accepted, Elev: 5975ft/1821m, Tel: 360-569-6650. GPS: 46.888911, -121.701118

263 • C2 | Mt Rainier NP - Golden Lakes TC

Dispersed sites, No water, Vault/pit toilet, Tents only: $6, Hike-in, 10.2 mi, 5 sites, Permit required, Reservation fee: $26, Reservations accepted, Elev: 4930ft/1503m, Tel: 360-569-6650. GPS: 46.883401, -121.898764

264 • C2 | Mt Rainier NP - Granite Creek TC

Dispersed sites, No water, Vault/pit toilet, Tents only: $6, Hike-in, 7.2 mi, 3 sites/1 group site, Permit required, Reservation fee: $26, Reservations accepted, Elev: 5760ft/1756m, Tel: 360-569-6650. GPS: 46.920541, -121.711538

265 • C2 | Mt Rainier NP - Indian Bar TC/Shelter

Dispersed sites, No water, Vault/pit toilet, Hike-to shelter: $6, 8.7 mi, 4 sites/1 group site, Permit required, Reservation fee: $26, Reservations accepted, Elev: 5116ft/1559m, Tel: 360-569-6650. GPS: 46.825916, -121.639708

266 • C2 | Mt Rainier NP - Ipsut Creek TC

Dispersed sites, No water, Vault/pit toilet, Tents only: $6, Hike-in, Permit required, Reservation fee: $26, Reservations accepted, Elev: 2361ft/720m, Tel: 360-569-6650. GPS: 46.976091, -121.830654

267 • C2 | Mt Rainier NP - James Camp TC

Dispersed sites, No water, Vault/pit toilet, Tents only: $6, Hike-in, 11.9 mi, 3 sites/1 group site, Permit required, Reservation fee: $26, Reservations accepted, Elev: 4475ft/1364m, Tel: 360-569-6650. GPS: 46.965639, -121.732751

268 • C2 | Mt Rainier NP - Klapatche Park TC

Dispersed sites, No water, Vault/pit toilet, Tents only: $6, Hike-in, 14.8 mi, 4 sites, Permit required, Reservation fee: $26, Reservations accepted, Elev: 5484ft/1672m, Tel: 360-569-6650. GPS: 46.836754, -121.875182

269 • C2 | Mt Rainier NP - Lake Eleanor TC

Dispersed sites, No water, Vault/pit toilet, Tents only: $6, Hike-in, 9.2 mi, 3 sites/1 group site, Permit required, Reservation fee: $26, Reservations accepted, Elev: 5019ft/1530m, Tel: 360-569-6650. GPS: 46.990055, -121.654895

270 • C2 | Mt Rainier NP - Lake George TC/Shelter

Dispersed sites, No water, Vault/pit toilet, Hike-to shelter: $6, 7.2 mi, 5 sites/1 group site, Permit required, Reservation fee: $26, Reservations accepted, Elev: 4355ft/1327m, Tel: 360-569-6650, Nearest town: Enumclaw. GPS: 46.792599, -121.901948

271 • C2 | Mt Rainier NP - Maple Creek TC

Dispersed sites, No water, Vault/pit toilet, Tents only: $6, Hike-in, 2.4 mi, Permit required, Reservation fee: $26, Reservations accepted, Elev: 2811ft/857m, Tel: 360-569-6650. GPS: 46.757447, -121.656789

272 • C2 | Mt Rainier NP - Mowich Lake CG

Total sites: 10, RV sites: 0, No water, Vault/pit toilet, Tents only: Free, Walk-to sites, fires prohibited, Generator hours: 0800-1000/1200-1400/1700-1900, Open Jul-Oct, Reservations not accepted, Elev: 4934ft/1504m, Tel: 360-569-2211, Nearest town: Enumclaw. GPS: 46.933646, -121.863958

273 • C2 | Mt Rainier NP - Mystic TC

Dispersed sites, No water, Vault/pit toilet, Tents only: $6, Hike-in, 13.2 mi, 7 sites/1 group site, Permit required, Reservation fee: $26, Reservations accepted, Elev: 5806ft/1770m, Tel: 360-569-6650. GPS: 46.914922, -121.754821

274 • C2 | Mt Rainier NP - N Payallup TC

Dispersed sites, No water, Vault/pit toilet, Tents only: $6, Hike-in, 17.6 mi, 3 sites/1 group site, Permit required, Reservation fee: $26, Reservations accepted, Elev: 3714ft/1132m, Tel: 360-569-6650. GPS: 46.846256, -121.869924

275 • C2 | Mt Rainier NP - Nickel Creek TC

Dispersed sites, No water, Vault/pit toilet, Tents only: $6, Hike-in, 1.2 mi, Permit required, Reservation fee: $26, Reservations accepted, Elev: 3388ft/1033m, Tel: 360-569-6650. GPS: 46.771858, -121.624715

276 • C2 | Mt Rainier NP - Ohanapecosh CG

Total sites: 188, RV sites: 188, Central water, Flush toilet, No showers, RV dump, Tent & RV camping: $20, 2 group sites $60, No generators, Open May-Oct, Max Length: RV: 32'/Trlr: 27ft, Reservations accepted, Elev: 2014ft/614m, Tel: 360-569-2211, Nearest town: Enumclaw. GPS: 46.734481, -121.567995

277 • C2 | Mt Rainier NP - Olallie Creek TC

Dispersed sites, No water, Vault/pit toilet, Tents only: $6, Hike-in, 2.8 mi, Permit required, Reservation fee: $26, Reservations accepted, Elev: 3949ft/1204m, Tel: 360-569-6650. GPS: 46.775876, -121.588094

278 • C2 | Mt Rainier NP - Paradise River TC

Dispersed sites, No water, Vault/pit toilet, Tents only: $6, Hike-in, 2.0 mi, Permit required, Reservation fee: $26, Reservations accepted, Elev: 3935ft/1199m, Tel: 360-569-6650. GPS: 46.770489, -121.759135

279 • C2 | Mt Rainier NP - Pyramid Creek TC

Dispersed sites, No water, Vault/pit toilet, Tents only: $6, Hike-in, 3.0 mi, 3 sites, Permit required, Reservation fee: $26, Reservations accepted, Elev: 4159ft/1268m, Tel: 360-569-6650, Nearest town: Enumclaw. GPS: 46.783427, -121.812234

280 • C2 | Mt Rainier NP - S Mowich River TC/Shelter

Dispersed sites, No water, Vault/pit toilet, Hike-to shelter: $6, 3.0 mi, 3 sites/1 group site, Permit required, Reservation fee: $26, Reservations accepted, Elev: 2658ft/810m, Tel: 360-569-6650. GPS: 46.913367, -121.892999

281 • C2 | Mt Rainier NP - S Payallup TC

Dispersed sites, No water, Vault/pit toilet, Tents only: $6, Hike-in, 11.1 mi, 4 sites/1 group site, Permit required, Reservation fee:

$26, Reservations accepted, Elev: 4013ft/1223m, Tel: 360-569-6650, Nearest town: Enumclaw. GPS: 46.8118, -121.8706

282 • C2 | Mt Rainier NP - Snow Lake TC

Dispersed sites, No water, Vault/pit toilet, Tents only: $6, Hike-in, 1.3 mi, Permit required, Reservation fee: $26, Reservations accepted, Elev: 4687ft/1429m, Tel: 360-569-6650. GPS: 46.758463, -121.697425

283 • C2 | Mt Rainier NP - Summerland TC/Shelter

Dispersed sites, No water, Vault/pit toilet, Hike-to shelter: $6, 4.2 mi, 5 sites/1 group site, Permit required, Reservation fee: $26, Reservations accepted, Elev: 6003ft/1830m, Tel: 360-569-6650. GPS: 46.866375, -121.658304

284 • C2 | Mt Rainier NP - Sunrise TC

Dispersed sites, No water, Vault/pit toilet, Tents only: $6, Hike-in, 2.7 mi, 8 sites/2 group sites, Permit required, Reservation fee: $26, Reservations accepted, Elev: 6265ft/1910m, Tel: 360-569-6650. GPS: 46.910934, -121.659936

285 • C2 | Mt Rainier NP - Tamanos Creek TC

Dispersed sites, No water, Vault/pit toilet, Tents only: $6, Hike-in, 3.0 mi, 4 sites/1 group site, Permit required, Reservation fee: $26, Reservations accepted, Elev: 5353ft/1632m, Tel: 360-569-6650. GPS: 46.874236, -121.585906

286 • C2 | Mt Rainier NP - Upper Palisades Lake TC

Dispersed sites, No water, Vault/pit toilet, Tents only: $6, Hike-in, 3.8 mi, 2 sites, Permit required, Reservation fee: $26, Reservations accepted, Elev: 5880ft/1792m, Tel: 360-569-6650. GPS: 46.949608, -121.592973

287 • C2 | Mt Rainier NP - White River CG

Total sites: 112, RV sites: 112, Central water, Flush toilet, No showers, No RV dump, Tent & RV camping: $20, Generator hours: 0800-1000/1200-1400/1700-1900, Open Jun-Sep, Max Length: RV: 27'/Trlr: 18ft, Reservations not accepted, Elev: 4354ft/1327m, Tel: 360-569-2211, Nearest town: Enumclaw. GPS: 46.902013, -121.644016

288 • C2 | Mt Rainier NP - Yellowstone Cliffs TC

Dispersed sites, No water, Vault/pit toilet, Tents only: $6, Hike-in, 10.5 mi, 2 sites, Permit required, Reservation fee: $26, Reservations accepted, Elev: 5182ft/1579m, Tel: 360-569-6650. GPS: 46.959429, -121.765192

289 • C3 | Mt Rainier NP - Deer Creek TC

Dispersed sites, No water, Vault/pit toilet, Tents only: $6, Hike-in, .5 mi, 2 sites, Permit required, Reservation fee: $26, Reservations accepted, Elev: 2932ft/894m, Tel: 360-569-6650. GPS: 46.835808, -121.540137

290 • C3 | Mt Rainier NP - Lower Crystal Lake TC

Dispersed sites, No water, Vault/pit toilet, Tents only: $6, Hike-in, 2.4 mi, 2 sites, Permit required, Reservation fee: $26, Reservations accepted, Elev: 5467ft/1666m, Tel: 360-569-6650. GPS: 46.911472, -121.513649

291 • C3 | Mt Rainier NP - Shriner Peak TC

Dispersed sites, No water, Vault/pit toilet, Tents only: $6, Hike-in, 4.2 mi, Permit required, Reservation fee: $26, Reservations accepted, Elev: 5806ft/1770m, Tel: 360-569-6650. GPS: 46.812362, -121.529786

292 • C3 | Mt Rainier NP - Three Lakes TC

Dispersed sites, No water, Vault/pit toilet, Tents only: $6, Hike-in, 5.8 mi, Permit required, Reservation fee: $26, Reservations accepted, Elev: 4711ft/1436m, Tel: 360-569-6650. GPS: 46.762697, -121.473467

293 • C3 | Mt Rainier NP - Upper Crystal Lake TC

Dispersed sites, No water, Vault/pit toilet, Tents only: $6, Hike-in, 3.0 mi, 2 sites, Permit required, Reservation fee: $26, Reservations accepted, Elev: 5848ft/1782m, Tel: 360-569-6650. GPS: 46.905973, -121.508907

West Virginia

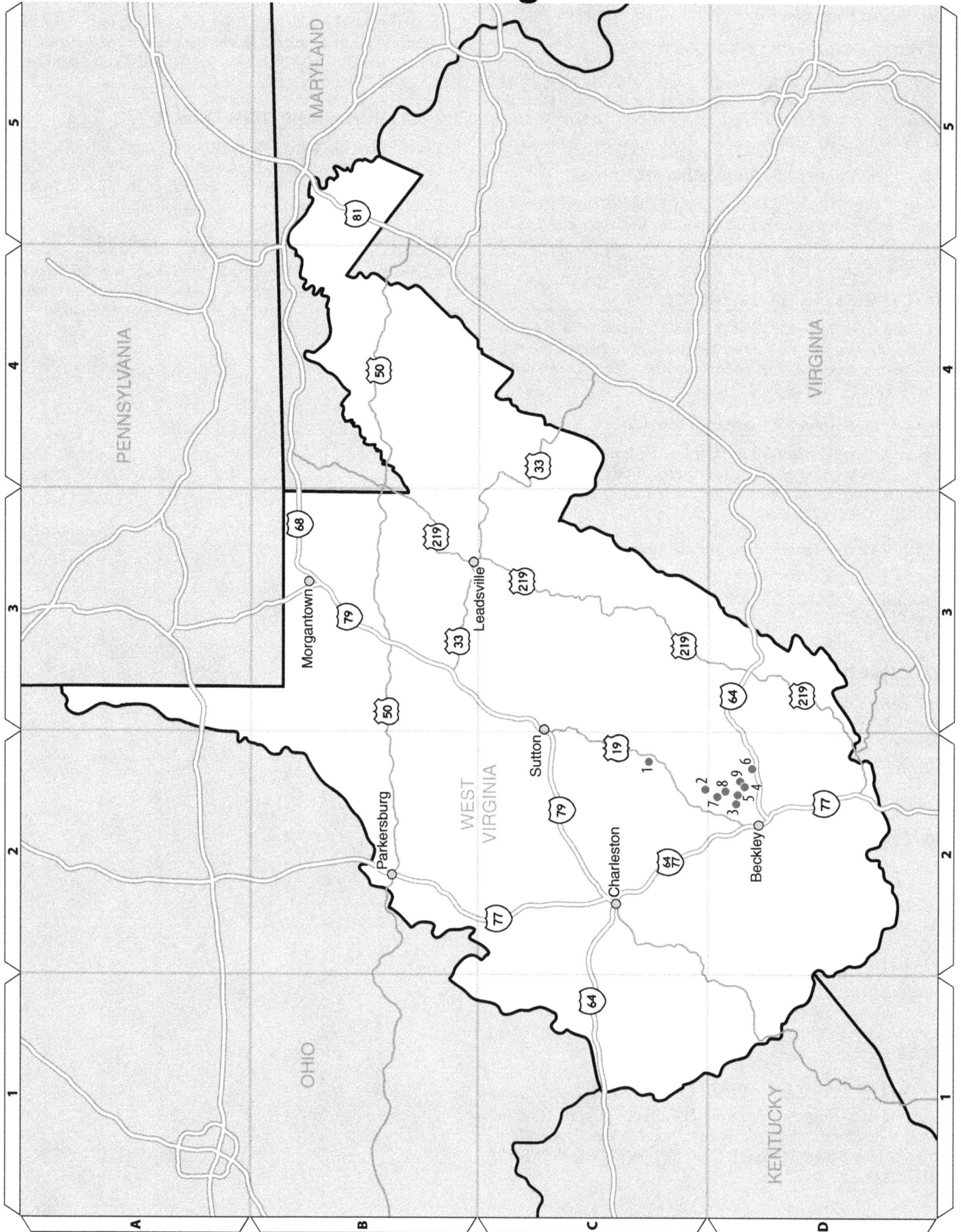

Map	ID	Map	ID
C2	1-2	D2	3-9

Alphabetical List of Camping Areas

Name	ID	Map
Gauley River NRA - Gauley Tailwaters	1	C2
New River Gorge NR - Army Camp	3	D2
New River Gorge NR - Brooklyn	2	C2
New River Gorge NR - Glade Creek	4	D2
New River Gorge NR - Grandview Sandbar	5	D2
New River Gorge NR - Meadow Creek	6	D2
New River Gorge NR - Stone Cliff Beach	7	D2
New River Gorge NR - Thayer	8	D2
New River Gorge NR - War Ridge	9	D2

1 • C2 | Gauley River NRA - Gauley Tailwaters

Total sites: 18, RV sites: 18, Tent & RV camping: Free, Reservations not accepted, Elev: 1391ft/424m, Tel: 304-465-0508, Nearest town: Fayetteville. GPS: 38.214447, -80.888834

2 • C2 | New River Gorge NR - Brooklyn

Total sites: 5, RV sites: 0, No water, Vault/pit toilet, No showers, No RV dump, Tents only: Free, Also walk-to sites, 4, Stay limit: 14 days, Reservations not accepted, Elev: 980ft/299m, Tel: 304-465-0508. GPS: 37.984498, -81.027765

3 • D2 | New River Gorge NR - Army Camp

Total sites: 11, RV sites: 11, No water, Vault/pit toilet, Tent & RV camping: Free, Stay limit: 14 days, Reservations not accepted, Elev: 1184ft/361m, Tel: 304-465-0508, Nearest town: Prince. GPS: 37.858373, -81.098429

4 • D2 | New River Gorge NR - Glade Creek

Total sites: 11, RV sites: 5, No water, Vault/pit toilet, Tent & RV camping: Free, Stay limit: 14 days, Max Length: 22ft, Reservations not accepted, Elev: 1266ft/386m, Tel: 304-465-0508, Nearest town: Prince. GPS: 37.827201, -81.010669

5 • D2 | New River Gorge NR - Grandview Sandbar

Total sites: 18, RV sites: 10, No water, Vault/pit toilet, Tent & RV camping: Free, Also walk-to sites, Stay limit: 14 days, Max Length: 22ft, Reservations not accepted, Elev: 1247ft/380m, Tel: 304-465-0508, Nearest town: Prince. GPS: 37.855056, -81.053299

6 • D2 | New River Gorge NR - Meadow Creek

Total sites: 19, RV sites: 19, No water, Vault/pit toilet, Tent & RV camping: Free, Stay limit: 14 days, Reservations not accepted, Elev: 1275ft/389m, Tel: 304-465-0508, Nearest town: Meadow Creek. GPS: 37.797536, -80.920395

7 • D2 | New River Gorge NR - Stone Cliff Beach

Total sites: 7, RV sites: 1, No water, Vault/pit toilet, Tent & RV camping: Free, Stay limit: 14 days, Reservations not accepted, Elev: 1063ft/324m, Tel: 304-465-0508, Nearest town: Thurmond. GPS: 37.933751, -81.063704

8 • D2 | New River Gorge NR - Thayer

Dispersed sites, No water, Vault/pit toilet, Tent & RV camping: Fee unk, Stay limit: 14 days, Reservations not accepted, Elev: 1086ft/331m, Tel: 304-465-0508, Nearest town: Prince. GPS: 37.901911, -81.032239

9 • D2 | New River Gorge NR - War Ridge

Total sites: 8, RV sites: 8, No water, Vault/pit toilet, No showers, No RV dump, Tent & RV camping: Free, Stay limit: 14 days, Max Length: 22ft, Reservations not accepted, Elev: 2539ft/774m, Tel: 304-465-0508, Nearest town: Prince. GPS: 37.845225, -80.985195

Wisconsin

Lake Superior

MINNESOTA

Superior

MICHIGAN

2

53

51

2

1

8

53

8

8

141

63

53

94

29

Wausau

51

29

Eau Claire

WISCONSIN

Green Bay

94

41

39

43

21

21

90

Lake
Michigan

90
94

151

61

41

18

Madison

94

Milwaukee

61

151

39
90

43

94

IOWA

ILLINOIS

Map	ID	Map	ID
B1	1-2		

Alphabetical List of Camping Areas

Name	ID	Map
St Croix NSR - Sandrock Cliffs	1	B1
St. Croix NSR - Riverside Landing	2	B1

1 • B1 | St Croix NSR - Sandrock Cliffs

Dispersed sites, No water, Vault/pit toilet, Tents only: Free, Walk-to sites, Elev: 770ft/235m, Tel: 715-483-2274, Nearest town: Grantsburg. GPS: 45.793924, -92.769574

2 • B1 | St. Croix NSR - Riverside Landing

Dispersed sites, Central water, Vault/pit toilet, Tents only: Free, Walk-to sites, Elev: 899ft/274m, Tel: 715-483-2274, Nearest town: Danbury. GPS: 46.077117, -92.246754

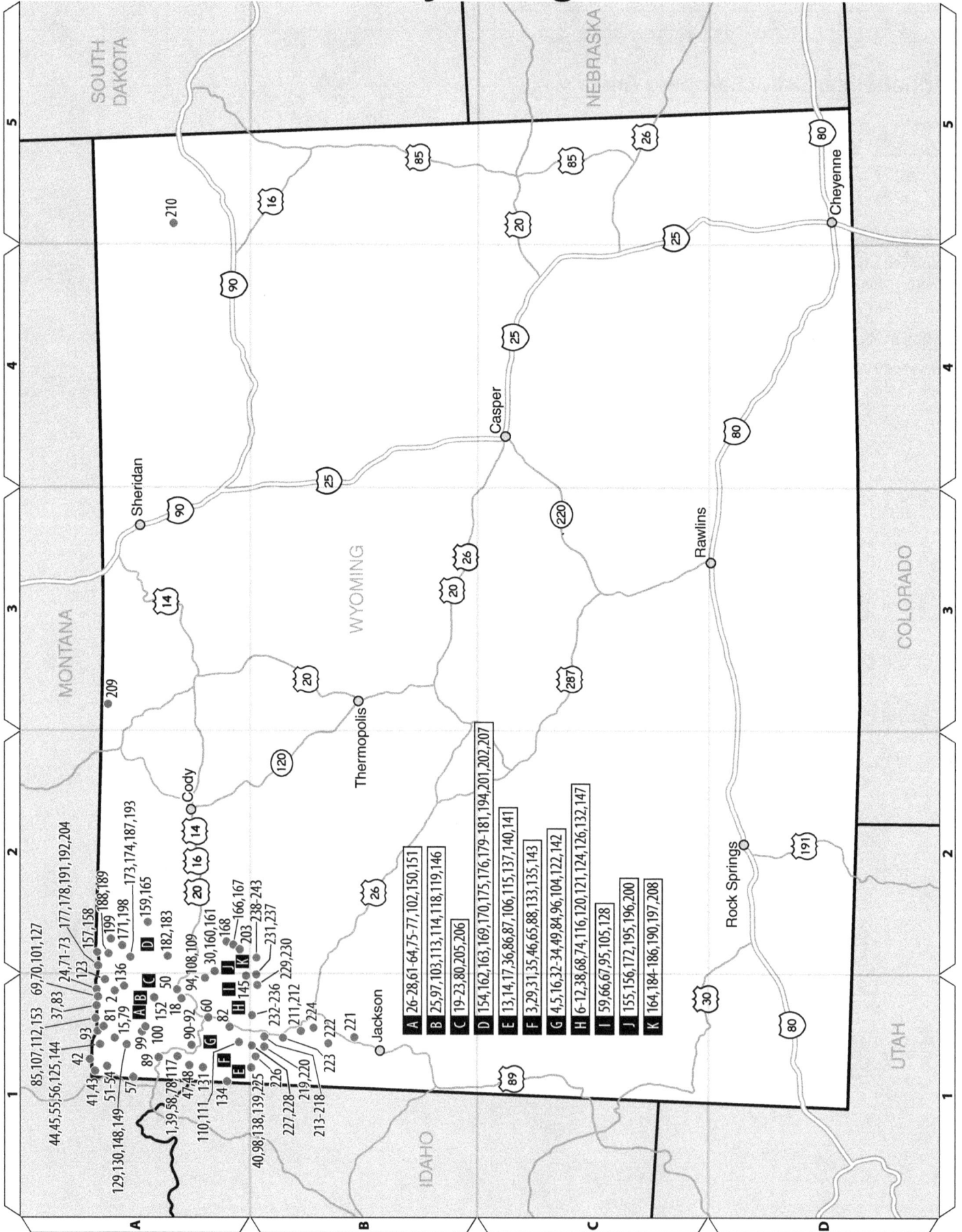

Wyoming

SOUTH DAKOTA

NEBRASKA

MONTANA

WYOMING

COLORADO

UTAH

IDAHO

Sheridan

Cody

Thermopolis

Casper

Rawlins

Rock Springs

Cheyenne

Jackson

• 210

• 209

A 26-28,61-64,75-77,102,150,151
B 25,97,103,113,114,118,119,146
C 19-23,80,205,206
D 154,162,163,169,170,175,176,179-181,194,201,202,207
E 13,14,17,36,86,87,106,115,137,140,141
F 3,29,31,35,46,65,88,133,135,143
G 4,5,16,32-34,49,84,96,104,122,142
H 6-12,38,68,74,116,120,121,124,126,132,147
I 59,66,67,95,105,128
J 155,156,172,195,196,200
K 164,184-186,190,197,208

85,107,112,153   69,70,101,127
44,45,55,56,125,144
177,178,191,192,204
173,174,187,193
24,71-73,
157,158
199 188,189
171,198 159,165
123   182,183
136   30,160,161
37,83   50   166,167
81 2   94,108,109 168
15,79 A B C 145 238-243
99   18   231,237
100 152   229,230
89   90-92 60   232-236
47,48   82   211,212
51-54   G   224
57   E   219,220   222
134   226   223   221
40,98,138,139,225   213-218
110,111,131
1,39,58,78,117
129,130,148,149
42
93
41,43

Map	ID	Map	ID
A1	1-153	A5	210
A2	154-208	B1	211-237
A3	209	B2	238-243

Alphabetical List of Camping Areas

Name	ID	Map
Bighorn Canyon NRA - Horseshoe Bend	209	A3
Devils Tower NM - Belle Fourche CG	210	A5
Grand Teton NP - Colter Bay CG	211	B1
Grand Teton NP - Colter Bay RV Park	212	B1
Grand Teton NP - Flagg Ranch Headwaters	213	B1
Grand Teton NP - Flagg Ranch Rd Site #1	214	B1
Grand Teton NP - Flagg Ranch Rd Site #2	215	B1
Grand Teton NP - Flagg Ranch Rd Site #3	216	B1
Grand Teton NP - Flagg Ranch Rd Site #4	217	B1
Grand Teton NP - Flagg Ranch Rd Site #5	218	B1
Grand Teton NP - Flagg Ranch Rd Site #6	219	B1
Grand Teton NP - Flagg Ranch Rd Site #8	220	B1
Grand Teton NP - Gros Ventre CG	221	B1
Grand Teton NP - Jenny Lake CG	222	B1
Grand Teton NP - Lizard Creek CG	223	B1
Grand Teton NP - Signal Mountain CG	224	B1
Yellowstone NP - (9C6)	225	B1
Yellowstone NP - (OG2)	1	A1
Yellowstone NP - Cascade River (9U6)	226	B1
Yellowstone NP - Agate Creek (2Y1)	2	A1
Yellowstone NP - Albright Falls (9B9)	3	A1
Yellowstone NP - Appaloosa Meadows (3M1)	154	A2
Yellowstone NP - Basin Bay Point (8R5)	4	A1
Yellowstone NP - Basin Beach (8T1)	5	A1
Yellowstone NP - Basin Creek (8B1)	6	A1
Yellowstone NP - Basin Creek (8B5)	7	A1
Yellowstone NP - Basin Creek Lake (8B2)	8	A1
Yellowstone NP - Basin Creek Stock (8B3)	9	A1
Yellowstone NP - Basin Creek Stock (8B4)	10	A1
Yellowstone NP - Beaver Creek (8J1)	11	A1
Yellowstone NP - Beaver Creek Meadow Stock (8J2)	12	A1
Yellowstone NP - Beaverdam Meadow (6B4)	155	A2
Yellowstone NP - Beaverdam Trail (5E1)	156	A2
Yellowstone NP - Bechler Ford North (9B2)	13	A1
Yellowstone NP - Bechler Ford South (9B2)	14	A1
Yellowstone NP - Beula Lake (8A1)	227	B1
Yellowstone NP - Beula Lake (8A2)	228	B1
Yellowstone NP - Big Horn Pass (1B1)	15	A1
Yellowstone NP - Bliss Pass Jct (3P2)	157	A2
Yellowstone NP - Bliss Pass Jct (3P3)	158	A2
Yellowstone NP - Bluff Top (8R2)	16	A1
Yellowstone NP - Boundary (3M7)	159	A2
Yellowstone NP - Boundary Creek Meadows (9A1)	17	A1
Yellowstone NP - Bridge Bay	18	A1
Yellowstone NP - Brimstone Bay (5E4)	160	A2
Yellowstone NP - Brimstone Point (5E3)	161	A2
Yellowstone NP - Broad Creek (4B2)	19	A1
Yellowstone NP - Broad Creek (4B3)	20	A1
Yellowstone NP - Broad Creek (4B4)	21	A1
Yellowstone NP - Broad Creek (5B1)	22	A1
Yellowstone NP - Broad View (5B2)	23	A1
Yellowstone NP - Buffalo Plateau (2B1)	24	A1
Yellowstone NP - Canyon	25	A1
Yellowstone NP - Cascade Lake (4E2)	26	A1
Yellowstone NP - Cascade Lake (4E3)	27	A1
Yellowstone NP - Cascade Lake (4E4)	28	A1
Yellowstone NP - Cliff Creek (6Y5)	238	B2
Yellowstone NP - Cold Creek (3F1)	162	A2
Yellowstone NP - Cold Creek Jct Stock (3U4)	163	A2
Yellowstone NP - Colonnade Fall (9B5)	29	A1
Yellowstone NP - Colter Meadows (6C1)	164	A2
Yellowstone NP - Columbine Meadow (5E6)	30	A1
Yellowstone NP - Continental Divide (9D4)	31	A1
Yellowstone NP - Cove (8R3)	32	A1
Yellowstone NP - Coyote (8S3)	33	A1
Yellowstone NP - Crooked Creek (8C9)	229	B1
Yellowstone NP - DeLacy Creek (8S2)	34	A1
Yellowstone NP - Douglas Knob Meadow (9D3)	35	A1
Yellowstone NP - Dunanda Falls (9A3)	36	A1
Yellowstone NP - East Confluence (6Y4)	239	B2
Yellowstone NP - East Cottonwood Creek (1R2)	37	A1
Yellowstone NP - East Shore (8J6)	38	A1
Yellowstone NP - Fairy Meadows (0D1)	39	A1
Yellowstone NP - Falls River Cutoff (9U1)	40	A1
Yellowstone NP - Fan Creek (WC2)	41	A1
Yellowstone NP - Fan Creek Northeast Stock (WC4)	42	A1
Yellowstone NP - Fan Creek Stock (WC3)	43	A1
Yellowstone NP - Fawn Creek/Gardners Hole (1F1)	44	A1
Yellowstone NP - Fawn Lake (1F2)	45	A1
Yellowstone NP - Ferris Fork (9D1)	46	A1
Yellowstone NP - Firehole Falls (0D3)	47	A1
Yellowstone NP - Firehole Meadows (0D2)	48	A1
Yellowstone NP - Firehole Springs (0A3)	49	A1
Yellowstone NP - Fishing Bridge	50	A1
Yellowstone NP - Fox Creek (6M7)	230	B1
Yellowstone NP - Gallatin River (WB1)	51	A1
Yellowstone NP - Gallatin River (WB6)	52	A1
Yellowstone NP - Gallatin River Stock (WB3)	53	A1
Yellowstone NP - Gallatin River Stock (WB4)	54	A1
Yellowstone NP - Gardner River (1G3)	55	A1
Yellowstone NP - Gardners Hole (1G2)	56	A1
Yellowstone NP - Gneiss Creek (WA1)	57	A1
Yellowstone NP - Goose Lake (0D5)	58	A1
Yellowstone NP - Gowdy Camp (7N2)	59	A1
Yellowstone NP - Grant Village	60	A1
Yellowstone NP - Grebe lake (4G2)	61	A1
Yellowstone NP - Grebe lake (4G3)	62	A1
Yellowstone NP - Grebe lake (4G4)	63	A1
Yellowstone NP - Grebe lake (4G5)	64	A1
Yellowstone NP - Gregg Fork (9D2)	65	A1
Yellowstone NP - Grouse Creek (7G1)	66	A1
Yellowstone NP - Grouse Creek (7G2)	67	A1
Yellowstone NP - Heart River (8J4)	68	A1
Yellowstone NP - Hellroaring Creek (2H3)	69	A1
Yellowstone NP - Hellroaring Creek (2H4)	70	A1
Yellowstone NP - Hellroaring Creek (2H5)	71	A1
Yellowstone NP - Hellroaring Creek (2H6)	72	A1
Yellowstone NP - Hellroaring Creek (2H7)	73	A1
Yellowstone NP - Hideaway (8H3)	74	A1
Yellowstone NP - Hoodoo Basin (3M6)	165	A2
Yellowstone NP - Howell Creek (6D6)	166	A2
Yellowstone NP - Howell Creek (6D7)	167	A2
Yellowstone NP - Howell Creek (6D8)	168	A2

Yellowstone NP - Ice Lake East (4D2)........................75.........A1
Yellowstone NP - Ice Lake North (4D1)......................76.........A1
Yellowstone NP - Ice Lake South (4D3)......................77.........A1
Yellowstone NP - Imperial Meadows (0D4)..................78.........A1
Yellowstone NP - Indian Creek CG.............................79.........A1
Yellowstone NP - Joseph's Coat Spring (4B1)...............80.........A1
Yellowstone NP - Lava Creek (1A3)............................81.........A1
Yellowstone NP - Lemon City (3F2)...........................169.........A2
Yellowstone NP - Lewis Lake CG................................82.........A1
Yellowstone NP - Little Cottonwood Creek (1R3)..........83.........A1
Yellowstone NP - Little Saddle Creek (3U3)................170.........A2
Yellowstone NP - Lone Star (0A1)...............................84.........A1
Yellowstone NP - Lower Blacktail Creek (1A1)..............85.........A1
Yellowstone NP - Lower Boundary Creek (9B1A)..........86.........A1
Yellowstone NP - Lower Boundary Creek (9B1B)...........87.........A1
Yellowstone NP - Lower Cache Creek (3C2).................171.........A2
Yellowstone NP - Lower Ford (6B1).............................172.........A2
Yellowstone NP - Lower Ford (9B6).............................88.........A1
Yellowstone NP - Lower Lamar (3L3)..........................173.........A2
Yellowstone NP - Lower Lamar (3L4)..........................174.........A2
Yellowstone NP - Lower Miller Creek (3M2)................175.........A2
Yellowstone NP - Lower Miller Creek (3M3)................176.........A2
Yellowstone NP - Lower Slough Creek (2S1)................177.........A2
Yellowstone NP - Lower Slough Creek (2S2)................178.........A2
Yellowstone NP - Lower Willow Creek (3U2)................179.........A2
Yellowstone NP - Madison.......................................89.........A1
Yellowstone NP - Mallard Lake East (0B3)..................90.........A1
Yellowstone NP - Mallard Lake Outlet (0B4)................91.........A1
Yellowstone NP - Mallard Lake Southeast (0B2)...........92.........A1
Yellowstone NP - Mammoth CG................................93.........A1
Yellowstone NP - Mariposa Lake (6M3).....................231.........B1
Yellowstone NP - Meadow Creek (5E7).......................94.........A1
Yellowstone NP - Middle Lamar (3L7)........................180.........A2
Yellowstone NP - Middle Lamar Stock (3L6)...............181.........A2
Yellowstone NP - Mist Creek Meadows (3T2)..............182.........A2
Yellowstone NP - Mist Creek Pass (3T3).....................183.........A2
Yellowstone NP - Monument Camp (5L2)....................95.........A1
Yellowstone NP - Moose Creek (8M1)........................96.........A1
Yellowstone NP - Moss Creek (4M2)..........................97.........A1
Yellowstone NP - Mountain Ash Creek (9U2)...............98.........A1
Yellowstone NP - Mountain Creek (6D1)...................184.........A2
Yellowstone NP - Mountain Creek Ford (6D2).............185.........A2
Yellowstone NP - Mountain Creek Stock (6D3)............186.........A2
Yellowstone NP - Norris CG.....................................99.........A1
Yellowstone NP - Norris Meadows (4F1)...................100.........A1
Yellowstone NP - North Lower Cache Creek Stock (3L1).....187.........A2
Yellowstone NP - North Thorofare (6T2)....................240.........B2
Yellowstone NP - North Yell/Hell Confluence (2H1).....101.........A1
Yellowstone NP - Observation Peak (4P1)..................102.........A1
Yellowstone NP - Old Seven Mile Hole (4C1)..............103.........A1
Yellowstone NP - Outlet (8S1)..................................104.........A1
Yellowstone NP - Outlet Creek (8O2)........................105.........A1
Yellowstone NP - Ouzel Falls (9B4)...........................106.........A1
Yellowstone NP - Oxbow Creek (1Y8)........................107.........A1
Yellowstone NP - Park Point North (5E9)...................108.........A1
Yellowstone NP - Park Point South (5E8)...................109.........A1
Yellowstone NP - Pebble Creek (3P1)........................188.........A2
Yellowstone NP - Pebble Creek CG...........................189.........A2
Yellowstone NP - Phantom Campsite (8P1).................110.........A1
Yellowstone NP - Phantom Campsite (8P2).................111.........A1
Yellowstone NP - Rescue Creek (1A2)........................112.........A1
Yellowstone NP - Ribbon Lake (4R1).........................113.........A1

Yellowstone NP - Ribbon Lake (4R2).........................114.........A1
Yellowstone NP - Rivers Edge (6C2)..........................190.........A2
Yellowstone NP - Rocky Ford (9C1)...........................115.........A1
Yellowstone NP - Rustic (8H6)..................................116.........A1
Yellowstone NP - Sentinel Meadows East (0G1)..........117.........A1
Yellowstone NP - Seven Mile Hole (4C2)....................118.........A1
Yellowstone NP - Seven Mile Hole (4C3)....................119.........A1
Yellowstone NP - Sheridan Creek (8H2).....................120.........A1
Yellowstone NP - Sheridan Trail (8H5).......................121.........A1
Yellowstone NP - Shoshone Meadows (8G1)...............122.........A1
Yellowstone NP - Slough Creek (2S3).........................191.........A2
Yellowstone NP - Slough Creek (2S4).........................192.........A2
Yellowstone NP - Slough Creek CG............................123.........A1
Yellowstone NP - Snake River (8C1)..........................232.........B1
Yellowstone NP - Snake River (8C2)..........................233.........B1
Yellowstone NP - Snake River (8C4)..........................234.........B1
Yellowstone NP - Snake River (8C5)..........................124.........A1
Yellowstone NP - Snake River Ford (8C6)...................235.........B1
Yellowstone NP - Snake River Stock (8C7)..................236.........B1
Yellowstone NP - Soldiers Corral Stock (1G5)..............125.........A1
Yellowstone NP - South Bay (8H1)............................126.........A1
Yellowstone NP - South Lower Cache Creek (3L2).........193.........A2
Yellowstone NP - South Thorofare (6T1)....................241.........B2
Yellowstone NP - South Yell/Hell Confluence (2H2).....127.........A1
Yellowstone NP - South Yellowstone River (6Y2).........242.........B2
Yellowstone NP - Southwest Bay (7N4)......................128.........A1
Yellowstone NP - Straight Creek North (1C2)..............129.........A1
Yellowstone NP - Straight Creek South (1C1)..............130.........A1
Yellowstone NP - Summit Lake.................................131.........A1
Yellowstone NP - Surprise Creek (8J3).......................132.........A1
Yellowstone NP - Talus Spring (9B7)..........................133.........A1
Yellowstone NP - Talus Terrace (9A4)........................134.........A1
Yellowstone NP - Three Mile Bend (6Y6)....................243.........B2
Yellowstone NP - Three Rivers Meadow (9B0)..............135.........A1
Yellowstone NP - Timothy Creek (3L8).......................194.........A2
Yellowstone NP - Tower Fall....................................136.........A1
Yellowstone NP - Trail Bay (6A4)..............................195.........A2
Yellowstone NP - Trail Point (6A3)............................196.........A2
Yellowstone NP - Trail Spring Stock (9B3)..................137.........A1
Yellowstone NP - Turret View (6C3)..........................197.........A2
Yellowstone NP - Two Ocean Trail Jct (6M4)..............237.........B1
Yellowstone NP - Union Falls (9U4)...........................138.........A1
Yellowstone NP - Union Falls (9U5)...........................139.........A1
Yellowstone NP - Upper Boundary Creek North (9A2).....140.........A1
Yellowstone NP - Upper Boundary Creek South (9A2).....141.........A1
Yellowstone NP - Upper Cache Creek (3C3).................198.........A2
Yellowstone NP - Upper Cache Creek (3C4).................199.........A2
Yellowstone NP - Upper Firehole (0A2)......................142.........A1
Yellowstone NP - Upper Ford (6B2)...........................200.........A2
Yellowstone NP - Upper Ford (9B8)...........................143.........A1
Yellowstone NP - Upper Gardner River (1G4)..............144.........A1
Yellowstone NP - Upper Miller Creek (3M4)................201.........A2
Yellowstone NP - Upper Miller Creek (3M5)................202.........A2
Yellowstone NP - Upper Mountain Creek (6D5)............203.........A2
Yellowstone NP - Upper Passage Creek (6M5)..............145.........A1
Yellowstone NP - Upper Slough Creek Stock (2S7).........204.........A2
Yellowstone NP - Wapiti Lake (4W2).........................205.........A2
Yellowstone NP - Wapiti Lake (4W3).........................206.........A2
Yellowstone NP - Warm Spring Meadow (3L9)..............207.........A2
Yellowstone NP - Washburn Meadow (4E1).................146.........A1
Yellowstone NP - West Shore (8H4)...........................147.........A1
Yellowstone NP - Winter Creek (1C4)........................148.........A1

Yellowstone NP - Winter Creek SW (1C5) ....149..........A1
Yellowstone NP - Wolf Lake (4G6) ....150..........A1
Yellowstone NP - Wolf Lake (4G7) ....151..........A1
Yellowstone NP - Wrangler Lake (4W1)..152..........A1
Yellowstone NP - Yellowstone Meadows Stock (6Y7) ....208..........A2
Yellowstone NP - Yellowstone River Trail (1Y7)........................153..........A1

1 • A1 | Yellowstone NP - (OG2)

Dispersed sites, Tents only: $3, Hike-in, Permit required, 8 person max, No wood fires, Reservations accepted, Elev: 7241ft/2207m, Tel: 307-344-2160. GPS: 44.570705, -110.887787

2 • A1 | Yellowstone NP - Agate Creek (2Y1)

Dispersed sites, Tents only: $3, Hike-in, Permit required, 8 person max, Reservations accepted, Elev: 6460ft/1969m, Tel: 307-344-2160. GPS: 44.851988, -110.358435

3 • A1 | Yellowstone NP - Albright Falls (9B9)

Dispersed sites, Tents only: $3, Hike-in, Permit required, 12 person max, No wood fires, Stay limit: 2 days, Reservations accepted, Elev: 7232ft/2204m, Tel: 307-344-2160. GPS: 44.278931, -110.905191

4 • A1 | Yellowstone NP - Basin Bay Point (8R5)

Dispersed sites, Vault/pit toilet, Tents only: $3, Hike-in, Permit required, No fires, 8 person max, Reservations accepted, Elev: 7819ft/2383m, Tel: 307-344-2160. GPS: 44.355885, -110.787707

5 • A1 | Yellowstone NP - Basin Beach (8T1)

Total sites: 1, Vault/pit toilet, Tents only: $3, Hike-in, Permit required, No fires, 4 person max, Reservations accepted, Elev: 7814ft/2382m, Tel: 307-344-2160. GPS: 44.342496, -110.786589

6 • A1 | Yellowstone NP - Basin Creek (8B1)

Dispersed sites, Tents only: $3, Hike-in, Permit required, 4 person max, Reservations accepted, Elev: 7375ft/2248m, Tel: 307-344-2160. GPS: 44.229624, -110.511156

7 • A1 | Yellowstone NP - Basin Creek (8B5)

Dispersed sites, Tents only: $3, Hike-in, Permit required, 8 person max, Reservations accepted, Elev: 7262ft/2213m, Tel: 307-344-2160. GPS: 44.206426, -110.501034

8 • A1 | Yellowstone NP - Basin Creek Lake (8B2)

Dispersed sites, Tents only: $3-5, Hike-in, Permit required, 12 person max, Stock allowed, Reservations accepted, Elev: 7427ft/2264m, Tel: 307-344-2160. GPS: 44.210293, -110.524833

9 • A1 | Yellowstone NP - Basin Creek Stock (8B3)

Dispersed sites, Tents only: $3, Hike-in, Permit required, 12 person max, Reservations accepted, Elev: 7285ft/2220m, Tel: 307-344-2160. GPS: 44.217034, -110.510064

10 • A1 | Yellowstone NP - Basin Creek Stock (8B4)

Dispersed sites, Tents only: $3, Hike-in, Permit required, 12 person max, Reservations accepted, Elev: 7270ft/2216m, Tel: 307-344-2160. GPS: 44.209583, -110.502771

11 • A1 | Yellowstone NP - Beaver Creek (8J1)

Dispersed sites, Tents only: $3, Hike-in, Permit required, 8 person max, Reservations accepted, Elev: 7486ft/2282m, Tel: 307-344-2160. GPS: 44.277109, -110.474762

12 • A1 | Yellowstone NP - Beaver Creek Meadow Stock (8J2)

Dispersed sites, Tents only: $3, Hike-in, Permit required, 12 person max, Stay limit: 2 days, Reservations accepted, Elev: 7483ft/2281m, Tel: 307-344-2160. GPS: 44.279144, -110.466067

13 • A1 | Yellowstone NP - Bechler Ford North (9B2)

Dispersed sites, Tents only: $3, Hike-in, Permit required, 12 person max, No wood fires, Stay limit: 2 days, Reservations accepted, Elev: 6418ft/1956m, Tel: 307-344-2160. GPS: 44.211291, -110.991201

14 • A1 | Yellowstone NP - Bechler Ford South (9B2)

Dispersed sites, Tents only: $3, Hike-in, Permit required, 12 person max, No wood fires, Stay limit: 2 days, Reservations accepted, Elev: 6402ft/1951m, Tel: 307-344-2160. GPS: 44.209926, -110.990955

15 • A1 | Yellowstone NP - Big Horn Pass (1B1)

Dispersed sites, Tents only: $3, Hike-in, Permit required, 10 person max, Reservations accepted, Elev: 7396ft/2254m, Tel: 307-344-2160. GPS: 44.887442, -110.750611

16 • A1 | Yellowstone NP - Bluff Top (8R2)

Dispersed sites, Vault/pit toilet, Tents only: $3, Hike-in/boat-in, Permit required, No fires, 8 person max, Reservations accepted, Elev: 7825ft/2385m, Tel: 307-344-2160. GPS: 44.368516, -110.744815

17 • A1 | Yellowstone NP - Boundary Creek Meadows (9A1)

Dispersed sites, Tents only: $3-5, Hike-in, Permit required, 12 person max, Stock allowed, Reservations accepted, Elev: 6402ft/1951m, Tel: 307-344-2160. GPS: 44.207371, -111.013491

18 • A1 | Yellowstone NP - Bridge Bay

Total sites: 432, RV sites: 432, Central water, Flush toilet, No showers, RV dump, Tent & RV camping: $27, Hiker/biker: $9, Group site: $136-$399, Concession-operated, Generator hours: 0800-2000, Open May-Sep, Reservations accepted, Elev: 7835ft/2388m, Tel: Info: 307-344-7381/Res: 307-344-7311, Nearest town: Tower Junction. GPS: 44.538266, -110.433318

19 • A1 | Yellowstone NP - Broad Creek (4B2)

Dispersed sites, Tents only: $3, Hike-in, Permit required, 6 person max, Off-trail travel required, Reservations accepted, Elev: 8085ft/2464m, Tel: 307-344-2160. GPS: 44.730255, -110.303062

20 • A1 | Yellowstone NP - Broad Creek (4B3)

Dispersed sites, Tents only: $3-5, Hike-in, Permit required, 12 person max, Off-trail travel required, Stock allowed, Reservations accepted, Elev: 8172ft/2491m, Tel: 307-344-2160. GPS: 44.710979, -110.282072

21 • A1 | Yellowstone NP - Broad Creek (4B4)

Dispersed sites, Tents only: $3-5, Hike-in, Permit required, 12 person max, Stock allowed, Reservations accepted, Elev: 8258ft/2517m, Tel: 307-344-2160. GPS: 44.711691, -110.273068

22 • A1 | Yellowstone NP - Broad Creek (5B1)

Dispersed sites, Tents only: $3-5, Hike-in, Permit required, 20 person max, Stock allowed, Reservations accepted, Elev: 8254ft/2516m, Tel: 307-344-2160. GPS: 44.686455, -110.266002

23 • A1 | Yellowstone NP - Broad View (5B2)

Dispersed sites, Tents only: $3, Hike-in, Permit required, Reservations accepted, Elev: 8238ft/2511m, Tel: 307-344-2160. GPS: 44.697729, -110.261176

24 • A1 | Yellowstone NP - Buffalo Plateau (2B1)

Dispersed sites, Tents only: $3-5, Hike-in, Permit required, 10 person max, Stock allowed, Reservations accepted, Elev: 8437ft/2572m, Tel: 307-344-2160. GPS: 45.016763, -110.377928

25 • A1 | Yellowstone NP - Canyon

Total sites: 272, RV sites: 272, Central water, Flush toilet, Pay showers, RV dump, Tent & RV camping: $32, Shower Fee, Hiker/biker: $9, Concession-operated, Generator hours: 0800-2000, Open May-Sep, Reservations accepted, Elev: 8045ft/2452m, Tel: Info: 307-344-7381/Res: 307-344-7311, Nearest town: Tower Junction. GPS: 44.737553, -110.482769

26 • A1 | Yellowstone NP - Cascade Lake (4E2)

Dispersed sites, Tents only: $3, Hike-in, Permit required, 4 person max, Reservations accepted, Elev: 8049ft/2453m, Tel: 307-344-2160. GPS: 44.749811, -110.527897

27 • A1 | Yellowstone NP - Cascade Lake (4E3)

Dispersed sites, Tents only: $3, Hike-in, Permit required, 8 person max, Reservations accepted, Elev: 8078ft/2462m, Tel: 307-344-2160. GPS: 44.756222, -110.524266

28 • A1 | Yellowstone NP - Cascade Lake (4E4)

Dispersed sites, Tents only: $3-5, Hike-in, Permit required, 8 person max, Stock allowed, Reservations accepted, Elev: 8005ft/2440m, Tel: 307-344-2160. GPS: 44.755112, -110.517109

29 • A1 | Yellowstone NP - Colonnade Fall (9B5)

Dispersed sites, Tents only: $3, Hike-in, Permit required, 12 person max, Stay limit: 1 day, Reservations accepted, Elev: 6611ft/2015m, Tel: 307-344-2160. GPS: 44.239031, -110.946069

30 • A1 | Yellowstone NP - Columbine Meadow (5E6)

Dispersed sites, Tents only: $3, Hike-in/boat-in, Permit required, 12 person max, Stay limit: 1 day, Reservations accepted, Elev: 7747ft/2361m, Tel: 307-344-2160. GPS: 44.405805, -110.255609

31 • A1 | Yellowstone NP - Continental Divide (9D4)

Dispersed sites, Tents only: $3, Hike-in, Permit required, 12 person max, No wood fires, Stay limit: 1 day, Reservations accepted, Elev: 8508ft/2593m, Tel: 307-344-2160. GPS: 44.339717, -110.841849

32 • A1 | Yellowstone NP - Cove (8R3)

Dispersed sites, Vault/pit toilet, Tents only: $3, Hike-in, Permit required, No fires, 8 person max, Reservations accepted, Elev: 7824ft/2385m, Tel: 307-344-2160. GPS: 44.367889, -110.748188

33 • A1 | Yellowstone NP - Coyote (8S3)

Dispersed sites, Vault/pit toilet, Tents only: $3, Hike-in, Permit required, No fires, 8 person max, Reservations accepted, Elev: 7820ft/2384m, Tel: 307-344-2160. GPS: 44.404303, -110.712418

34 • A1 | Yellowstone NP - DeLacy Creek (8S2)

Dispersed sites, Vault/pit toilet, Tents only: $3, Hike-in/boat-in, Permit required, No fires, 8 person max, Reservations accepted, Elev: 7820ft/2384m, Tel: 307-344-2160. GPS: 44.409563, -110.706599

35 • A1 | Yellowstone NP - Douglas Knob Meadow (9D3)

Dispersed sites, Tents only: $3-5, Hike-in, Permit required, 12 person max, Stock allowed, No wood fires, Stay limit: 1 day, Reservations accepted, Elev: 8376ft/2553m, Tel: 307-344-2160. GPS: 44.321034, -110.849864

36 • A1 | Yellowstone NP - Dunanda Falls (9A3)

Dispersed sites, Tents only: $3, Hike-in, Permit required, 12 person max, Reservations accepted, Elev: 6621ft/2018m, Tel: 307-344-2160. GPS: 44.245665, -111.026052

37 • A1 | Yellowstone NP - East Cottonwood Creek (1R2)

Dispersed sites, Tents only: $3, Hike-in, Permit required, 6 person max, No wood fires, Reservations accepted, Elev: 5596ft/1706m, Tel: 307-344-2160. GPS: 44.992055, -110.513781

38 • A1 | Yellowstone NP - East Shore (8J6)

Dispersed sites, Tents only: $3, Hike-in, Permit required, 4 person max, Reservations accepted, Elev: 7470ft/2277m, Tel: 307-344-2160. GPS: 44.250933, -110.449882

39 • A1 | Yellowstone NP - Fairy Meadows (0D1)

Dispersed sites, Tents only: $3, Hike-in, Permit required, 6 person max, No wood fires, Reservations accepted, Elev: 7275ft/2217m, Tel: 307-344-2160. GPS: 44.525944, -110.855687

40 • A1 | Yellowstone NP - Falls River Cutoff (9U1)

Dispersed sites, Tents only: $3-5, Hike-in, Permit required, 12 person max, Stock allowed, Reservations accepted, Elev: 6450ft/1966m, Tel: 307-344-2160. GPS: 44.160178, -110.939129

41 • A1 | Yellowstone NP - Fan Creek (WC2)

Dispersed sites, Tents only: $3, Hike-in, Permit required, 10 person max, Reservations accepted, Elev: 7335ft/2236m, Tel: 307-344-2160. GPS: 44.969997, -111.012973

42 • A1 | Yellowstone NP - Fan Creek Northeast Stock (WC4)

Dispersed sites, Tents only: $5, Hike-in, Permit required, 12 person max, Reservations accepted, Elev: 7557ft/2303m, Tel: 307-344-2160. GPS: 44.993036, -110.966932

43 • A1 | Yellowstone NP - Fan Creek Stock (WC3)

Dispersed sites, Tents only: $5, Hike-in, Permit required, 12 person max, Reservations accepted, Elev: 7432ft/2265m, Tel: 307-344-2160. GPS: 44.986538, -110.993229

44 • A1 | Yellowstone NP - Fawn Creek/Gardners Hole (1F1)

Dispersed sites, Tents only: $5, Hike-in, Permit required, Stock only, 12 person max, Reservations accepted, Elev: 7735ft/2358m, Tel: 307-344-2160. GPS: 44.954904, -110.790988

45 • A1 | Yellowstone NP - Fawn Lake (1F2)

Dispersed sites, Tents only: $3, Hike-in, Permit required, 10 person max, Reservations accepted, Elev: 7809ft/2380m, Tel: 307-344-2160. GPS: 44.957139, -110.798644

46 • A1 | Yellowstone NP - Ferris Fork (9D1)

Dispersed sites, Tents only: $3, Hike-in, Permit required, 12 person max, No wood fires, Stay limit: 1 day, Reservations accepted, Elev: 7319ft/2231m, Tel: 307-344-2160. GPS: 44.289732, -110.891752

47 • A1 | Yellowstone NP - Firehole Falls (0D3)

Dispersed sites, Tents only: $3, Hike-in, Permit required, 6 person max, Reservations accepted, Elev: 7876ft/2401m, Tel: 307-344-2160. GPS: 44.486011, -110.918046

48 • A1 | Yellowstone NP - Firehole Meadows (0D2)

Dispersed sites, Tents only: $3, Hike-in, Permit required, 10 person max, Reservations accepted, Elev: 7907ft/2410m, Tel: 307-344-2160. GPS: 44.484896, -110.928409

49 • A1 | Yellowstone NP - Firehole Springs (0A3)

Dispersed sites, Tents only: $3, Hike-in, Permit required, 6 person max, Reservations accepted, Elev: 7706ft/2349m, Tel: 307-344-2160. GPS: 44.405365, -110.826246

50 • A1 | Yellowstone NP - Fishing Bridge

Total sites: 346, RV sites: 346, Elec sites: 346, Water available, Flush toilet, Pay showers, RV dump, No tents/RV's: $79, Full hookups sites, No campfires, Concession-operated, Generator hours: 0800-2000, Open May-Sep, Reservations accepted, Elev: 7812ft/2381m, Tel: Info: 307-344-7381/Res: 307-344-7311, Nearest town: Tower Junction. GPS: 44.564819, -110.368844

51 • A1 | Yellowstone NP - Gallatin River (WB1)

Dispersed sites, Tents only: $3, Hike-in, Permit required, 10 person max, Reservations accepted, Elev: 7433ft/2266m, Tel: 307-344-2160. GPS: 44.923779, -110.969658

52 • A1 | Yellowstone NP - Gallatin River (WB6)

Dispersed sites, Tents only: $3, Hike-in, Permit required, 10 person max, Reservations accepted, Elev: 7600ft/2316m, Tel: 307-344-2160. GPS: 44.915376, -110.933775

53 • A1 | Yellowstone NP - Gallatin River Stock (WB3)

Dispersed sites, Tents only: $5, Hike-in, Permit required, 12 person max, Reservations accepted, Elev: 7486ft/2282m, Tel: 307-344-2160. GPS: 44.924503, -110.956769

54 • A1 | Yellowstone NP - Gallatin River Stock (WB4)

Dispersed sites, Tents only: $3, Hike-in, Permit required, 12 person max, Reservations accepted, Elev: 7522ft/2293m, Tel: 307-344-2160. GPS: 44.923355, -110.945127

55 • A1 | Yellowstone NP - Gardner River (1G3)

Dispersed sites, Tents only: $3, Hike-in, Permit required, 10 person max, Reservations accepted, Elev: 8005ft/2440m, Tel: 307-344-2160. GPS: 44.972248, -110.808926

56 • A1 | Yellowstone NP - Gardners Hole (1G2)

Dispersed sites, Tents only: $3, Hike-in, Permit required, 10 person max, Reservations accepted, Elev: 7731ft/2356m, Tel: 307-344-2160. GPS: 44.952255, -110.781569

57 • A1 | Yellowstone NP - Gneiss Creek (WA1)

Dispersed sites, Tents only: $3-5, Hike-in, Permit required, 10 person max, Stock allowed, Reservations accepted, Elev: 6636ft/2023m, Tel: 307-344-2160. GPS: 44.777412, -111.032535

58 • A1 | Yellowstone NP - Goose Lake (0D5)

Dispersed sites, Tents only: $3, Hike-in, Permit required, 6 person max, Special needs or bicyclists only, Reservations accepted, Elev: 7229ft/2203m, Tel: 307-344-2160. GPS: 44.544756, -110.844147

59 • A1 | Yellowstone NP - Gowdy Camp (7N2)

Dispersed sites, Vault/pit toilet, Tents only: $3, Hike-in/boat-in, Permit required, No fires, 12 person max, Non-motorized boats only, Reservations accepted, Elev: 7752ft/2363m, Tel: 307-344-2160. GPS: 44.296663, -110.343054

60 • A1 | Yellowstone NP - Grant Village

Total sites: 425, RV sites: 425, Central water, Flush toilet, Pay showers, RV dump, Tent & RV camping: $32, Hiker/biker: $9, Group sites: $136-$399, Concession-operated, Generator hours: 0800-2000, Open Jun-Sep, Reservations accepted, Elev: 7782ft/2372m, Tel: Info: 307-344-7381/Res: 307-344-7311, Nearest town: Tower Junction. GPS: 44.399976, -110.565437

61 • A1 | Yellowstone NP - Grebe lake (4G2)

Dispersed sites, Tents only: $3, Hike-in, Permit required, 8 person max, Reservations accepted, Elev: 8042ft/2451m, Tel: 307-344-2160. GPS: 44.749326, -110.555744

62 • A1 | Yellowstone NP - Grebe lake (4G3)

Dispersed sites, Tents only: $3-5, Hike-in, Permit required, 8 person max, No wood fires, Stock allowed, Reservations accepted, Elev: 8068ft/2459m, Tel: 307-344-2160. GPS: 44.754216, -110.551877

63 • A1 | Yellowstone NP - Grebe lake (4G4)

Dispersed sites, Tents only: $3-5, Hike-in, Permit required, 8 person max, Stock allowed, Reservations accepted, Elev: 8042ft/2451m, Tel: 307-344-2160. GPS: 44.755333, -110.559953

64 • A1 | Yellowstone NP - Grebe lake (4G5)

Dispersed sites, Tents only: $3-5, Hike-in, Permit required, 8 person max, Stock allowed, Reservations accepted, Elev: 8043ft/2452m, Tel: 307-344-2160. GPS: 44.753735, -110.564256

65 • A1 | Yellowstone NP - Gregg Fork (9D2)

Dispersed sites, Tents only: $3, Hike-in, Permit required, 12 person max, Stay limit: 1 day, Reservations accepted, Elev: 7983ft/2433m, Tel: 307-344-2160. GPS: 44.297437, -110.864977

66 • A1 | Yellowstone NP - Grouse Creek (7G1)

Dispersed sites, Tents only: $3-5, Hike-in, Permit required, 12 person max, Stock allowed, Reservations accepted, Elev: 7799ft/2377m, Tel: 307-344-2160. GPS: 44.273748, -110.347619

67 • A1 | Yellowstone NP - Grouse Creek (7G2)

Dispersed sites, Tents only: $3-5, Hike-in, Permit required, 12 person max, Stock allowed, Reservations accepted, Elev: 7773ft/2369m, Tel: 307-344-2160. GPS: 44.279316, -110.343323

68 • A1 | Yellowstone NP - Heart River (8J4)

Dispersed sites, Tents only: $3, Hike-in, Permit required, 8 person max, Reservations accepted, Elev: 7478ft/2279m, Tel: 307-344-2160. GPS: 44.247944, -110.445518

69 • A1 | Yellowstone NP - Hellroaring Creek (2H3)

Dispersed sites, Tents only: $3, Hike-in, Permit required, 10 person max, No wood fires, Reservations accepted, Elev: 5815ft/1772m, Tel: 307-344-2160. GPS: 44.972207, -110.458709

70 • A1 | Yellowstone NP - Hellroaring Creek (2H4)

Dispersed sites, Tents only: $3, Hike-in, Permit required, 6 person max, No wood fires, Reservations accepted, Elev: 5801ft/1768m, Tel: 307-344-2160. GPS: 44.975052, -110.464769

71 • A1 | Yellowstone NP - Hellroaring Creek (2H5)

Dispersed sites, Tents only: $3, Hike-in, Permit required, 8 person max, No wood fires, Reservations accepted, Elev: 5927ft/1807m, Tel: 307-344-2160. GPS: 44.977759, -110.442844

72 • A1 | Yellowstone NP - Hellroaring Creek (2H6)

Dispersed sites, Tents only: $3, Hike-in, Permit required, 8 person max, No wood fires, Reservations accepted, Elev: 5887ft/1794m, Tel: 307-344-2160. GPS: 44.976696, -110.443726

73 • A1 | Yellowstone NP - Hellroaring Creek (2H7)

Dispersed sites, Tents only: $3, Hike-in, Permit required, 10 person max, No wood fires, Reservations accepted, Elev: 5978ft/1822m, Tel: 307-344-2160. GPS: 44.983527, -110.433017

74 • A1 | Yellowstone NP - Hideaway (8H3)

Dispersed sites, Tents only: $3, Hike-in, Permit required, 4 person max, Reservations accepted, Elev: 7482ft/2281m, Tel: 307-344-2160. GPS: 44.271167, -110.502077

75 • A1 | Yellowstone NP - Ice Lake East (4D2)

Dispersed sites, Tents only: $3, Hike-in, Permit required, 8 person max, Reservations accepted, Elev: 7907ft/2410m, Tel: 307-344-2160. GPS: 44.722073, -110.620193

76 • A1 | Yellowstone NP - Ice Lake North (4D1)

Dispersed sites, Tents only: $3, Hike-in, Permit required, 6 person max, Reservations accepted, Elev: 7905ft/2409m, Tel: 307-344-2160. GPS: 44.722614, -110.631986

77 • A1 | Yellowstone NP - Ice Lake South (4D3)

Dispersed sites, Tents only: $3, Hike-in, Permit required, 4 person max, For special needs campers, Reservations accepted, Elev: 7909ft/2411m, Tel: 307-344-2160. GPS: 44.720095, -110.633036

78 • A1 | Yellowstone NP - Imperial Meadows (0D4)

Dispersed sites, Tents only: $3, Hike-in, Permit required, 12 person max, Reservations accepted, Elev: 7270ft/2216m, Tel: 307-344-2160. GPS: 44.530662, -110.868912

79 • A1 | Yellowstone NP - Indian Creek CG

Total sites: 70, RV sites: 70, Central water, Vault/pit toilet, No showers, No RV dump, Tent & RV camping: $15, Biker/hiker: $5, No generators, Open Jun-Sep, Max Length: 35ft, Reservations not accepted, Elev: 7303ft/2226m, Tel: 307-344-7381, Nearest town: Mammoth Springs Junction. GPS: 44.88623, -110.736084

80 • A1 | Yellowstone NP - Joseph's Coat Spring (4B1)

Dispersed sites, Tents only: $3, Hike-in, Permit required, 6 person max, Off-trail travel required, Reservations accepted, Elev: 8030ft/2448m, Tel: 307-344-2160. GPS: 44.738224, -110.325091

81 • A1 | Yellowstone NP - Lava Creek (1A3)

Dispersed sites, Tents only: $3, Hike-in, Permit required, 6 person max, No wood fires, Reservations accepted, Elev: 6097ft/1858m, Tel: 307-344-2160. GPS: 44.950253, -110.655754

82 • A1 | Yellowstone NP - Lewis Lake CG

Total sites: 85, RV sites: 85, Central water, Vault/pit toilet, No showers, No RV dump, Tent & RV camping: $15, Biker/hiker: $5, No generators, Open Jul-Oct, Max Length: 25ft, Reservations not accepted, Elev: 7828ft/2386m, Tel: 307-344-7381, Nearest town: West Thumb Junction. GPS: 44.281333, -110.627352

83 • A1 | Yellowstone NP - Little Cottonwood Creek (1R3)

Dispersed sites, Tents only: $3-5, Hike-in, Permit required, 10 person max, Stock allowed, No wood fires, Stay limit: 2 days, Reservations accepted, Elev: 6181ft/1884m, Tel: 307-344-2160. GPS: 44.990358, -110.483849

84 • A1 | Yellowstone NP - Lone Star (0A1)

Dispersed sites, Tents only: $3, Hike-in, Permit required, 12 person max, Stock allowed, Reservations accepted, Elev: 7667ft/2337m, Tel: 307-344-2160. GPS: 44.418036, -110.812934

85 • A1 | Yellowstone NP - Lower Blacktail Creek (1A1)

Dispersed sites, Tents only: $3-5, Hike-in, Permit required, 10 person max, Stock allowed, Reservations accepted, Elev: 6345ft/1934m, Tel: 307-344-2160. GPS: 44.979862, -110.593445

86 • A1 | Yellowstone NP - Lower Boundary Creek (9B1A)

Dispersed sites, Tents only: $3, Hike-in, Permit required, 12 person max, No wood fires, Stay limit: 2 days, Reservations accepted, Elev: 6399ft/1950m, Tel: 307-344-2160. GPS: 44.186551, -111.003877

87 • A1 | Yellowstone NP - Lower Boundary Creek (9B1B)

Dispersed sites, Tents only: $3, Hike-in, Permit required, 12 person max, No wood fires, Stay limit: 2 days, Reservations accepted, Elev: 6399ft/1950m, Tel: 307-344-2160. GPS: 44.185454, -111.005073

88 • A1 | Yellowstone NP - Lower Ford (9B6)

Dispersed sites, Tents only: $3, Hike-in, Permit required, 12 person max, Stay limit: 1 day, Reservations accepted, Elev: 6903ft/2104m, Tel: 307-344-2160. GPS: 44.251001, -110.932652

89 • A1 | Yellowstone NP - Madison

Total sites: 275, RV sites: 275, Central water, Flush toilet, No showers, RV dump, Tent & RV camping: $27, Group sites: $136-$399, Concession-operated, Generator hours: 0800-2000, Open May-Oct, Reservations accepted, Elev: 6860ft/2091m, Tel: Info: 307-344-7381/Res: 307-344-7311. GPS: 44.644424, -110.865443

90 • A1 | Yellowstone NP - Mallard Lake East (0B3)

Dispersed sites, Tents only: $3, Hike-in, Permit required, 6 person max, Reservations accepted, Elev: 8050ft/2454m, Tel: 307-344-2160. GPS: 44.477595, -110.773658

91 • A1 | Yellowstone NP - Mallard Lake Outlet (0B4)

Dispersed sites, Tents only: $3, Hike-in, Permit required, 6 person max, No wood fires, Reservations accepted, Elev: 8084ft/2464m, Tel: 307-344-2160. GPS: 44.475548, -110.777177

92 • A1 | Yellowstone NP - Mallard Lake Southeast (0B2)

Dispersed sites, Tents only: $3, Hike-in, Permit required, 6 person max, Reservations accepted, Elev: 8051ft/2454m, Tel: 307-344-2160. GPS: 44.476646, -110.774067

93 • A1 | Yellowstone NP - Mammoth CG

Total sites: 85, RV sites: 85, Central water, Flush toilet, No showers, No RV dump, Tent & RV camping: $20, Biker/hiker: $5, Generator hours: 0800-2000, Open all year, Max Length: 30ft, Reservations not accepted, Elev: 6040ft/1841m, Tel: 307-344-7381, Nearest town: Mammoth Springs Junction. GPS: 44.974196, -110.693582

94 • A1 | Yellowstone NP - Meadow Creek (5E7)

Dispersed sites, Tents only: $3-5, Hike-in, Permit required, 12 person max, Stock allowed, Reservations accepted, Elev: 7760ft/2365m, Tel: 307-344-2160. GPS: 44.427069, -110.286168

95 • A1 | Yellowstone NP - Monument Camp (5L2)

Dispersed sites, Tents only: $3-5, Hike-in/boat-in, Permit required, 8 person max, Stock allowed, Reservations accepted, Elev: 7775ft/2370m, Tel: 307-344-2160. GPS: 44.276514, -110.308114

96 • A1 | Yellowstone NP - Moose Creek (8M1)

Dispersed sites, Vault/pit toilet, Tents only: $3-5, Hike-in, Permit required, No fires, 8 person max, Stock allowed, No wood fires, Reservations accepted, Elev: 7826ft/2385m, Tel: 307-344-2160. GPS: 44.345079, -110.703898

97 • A1 | Yellowstone NP - Moss Creek (4M2)

Dispersed sites, Tents only: $3-5, Hike-in, Permit required, 12 person max, Stock allowed, Reservations accepted, Elev: 8503ft/2592m, Tel: 307-344-2160. GPS: 44.726808, -110.362808

98 • A1 | Yellowstone NP - Mountain Ash Creek (9U2)

Dispersed sites, Tents only: $3, Hike-in, Permit required, 12 person max, No wood fires, Reservations accepted, Elev: 6481ft/1975m, Tel: 307-344-2160. GPS: 44.171482, -110.924205

99 • A1 | Yellowstone NP - Norris CG

Total sites: 111, RV sites: 50, Central water, Flush toilet, No showers, No RV dump, Tent & RV camping: $20, Biker/hiker: $5, Generator hours: 0800-2000, Open May-Sep, Max Length: 50ft, Reservations not accepted, Elev: 7576ft/2309m, Tel: 307-344-7381, Nearest town: Norris Junction. GPS: 44.737955, -110.693528

100 • A1 | Yellowstone NP - Norris Meadows (4F1)

Dispersed sites, Tents only: $3, Hike-in, Permit required, 8 person max, Reservations accepted, Elev: 7572ft/2308m, Tel: 307-344-2160. GPS: 44.730107, -110.663998

101 • A1 | Yellowstone NP - North Yell/Hell Confluence (2H1)

Dispersed sites, Tents only: $3, Hike-in, Permit required, 8 person max, No wood fires, Reservations accepted, Elev: 5748ft/1752m, Tel: 307-344-2160. GPS: 44.974564, -110.475288

102 • A1 | Yellowstone NP - Observation Peak (4P1)

Dispersed sites, Tents only: $3, Hike-in, Permit required, 8 person max, No wood fires, Reservations accepted, Elev: 9374ft/2857m, Tel: 307-344-2160. GPS: 44.771503, -110.546156

103 • A1 | Yellowstone NP - Old Seven Mile Hole (4C1)

Dispersed sites, Tents only: $3, Hike-in, Permit required, 8 person max, No wood fires, Reservations accepted, Elev: 6812ft/2076m, Tel: 307-344-2160. GPS: 44.748371, -110.413813

104 • A1 | Yellowstone NP - Outlet (8S1)

Dispersed sites, Vault/pit toilet, Tents only: $3, Hike-in/boat-in, Permit required, No fires, 8 person max, Reservations accepted, Elev: 7820ft/2384m, Tel: 307-344-2160. GPS: 44.359947, -110.662715

105 • A1 | Yellowstone NP - Outlet Creek (8O2)

Dispersed sites, Tents only: $3, Hike-in, Permit required, 6 person max, Reservations accepted, Elev: 7794ft/2376m, Tel: 307-344-2160. GPS: 44.269609, -110.393344

106 • A1 | Yellowstone NP - Ouzel Falls (9B4)

Dispersed sites, Tents only: $3, Hike-in, Permit required, 12 person max, Stay limit: 1 day, Reservations accepted, Elev: 6432ft/1960m, Tel: 307-344-2160. GPS: 44.226437, -110.974921

107 • A1 | Yellowstone NP - Oxbow Creek (1Y8)

Dispersed sites, Tents only: $3, Hike-in, Permit required, 6 person max, No wood fires, Reservations accepted, Elev: 5577ft/1700m, Tel: 307-344-2160. GPS: 44.992035, -110.565018

108 • A1 | Yellowstone NP - Park Point North (5E9)

Dispersed sites, Tents only: $3, Hike-in, Permit required, 12 person max, Reservations accepted, Elev: 7758ft/2365m, Tel: 307-344-2160. GPS: 44.428489, -110.293606

109 • A1 | Yellowstone NP - Park Point South (5E8)

Dispersed sites, Tents only: $3, Hike-in, Permit required, 12 person max, Reservations accepted, Elev: 7750ft/2362m, Tel: 307-344-2160. GPS: 44.424383, -110.288733

110 • A1 | Yellowstone NP - Phantom Campsite (8P1)

Dispersed sites, Tents only: $3-5, Hike-in, Permit required, 8 person max, Stock use not recommended, Reservations accepted, Elev: 8540ft/2603m, Tel: 307-344-2160. GPS: 44.229461, -110.739021

111 • A1 | Yellowstone NP - Phantom Campsite (8P2)

Dispersed sites, Tents only: $3, Hike-in, Permit required, 8 person max, Reservations accepted, Elev: 8547ft/2605m, Tel: 307-344-2160. GPS: 44.230232, -110.739964

112 • A1 | Yellowstone NP - Rescue Creek (1A2)

Dispersed sites, Tents only: $3, Hike-in, Permit required, 10 person max, Reservations accepted, Elev: 6711ft/2046m, Tel: 307-344-2160. GPS: 44.982468, -110.623814

113 • A1 | Yellowstone NP - Ribbon Lake (4R1)

Dispersed sites, Tents only: $3, Hike-in, Permit required, 8 person max, Reservations accepted, Elev: 7830ft/2387m, Tel: 307-344-2160. GPS: 44.724411, -110.449885

114 • A1 | Yellowstone NP - Ribbon Lake (4R2)

Dispersed sites, Tents only: $3, Hike-in, Permit required, 8 person max, Reservations accepted, Elev: 7839ft/2389m, Tel: 307-344-2160. GPS: 44.726225, -110.447622

115 • A1 | Yellowstone NP - Rocky Ford (9C1)

Dispersed sites, Tents only: $3, Hike-in, Permit required, 12 person max, Stay limit: 2 days, Reservations accepted, Elev: 6404ft/1952m, Tel: 307-344-2160. GPS: 44.177251, -111.000908

116 • A1 | Yellowstone NP - Rustic (8H6)

Dispersed sites, Tents only: $3, Hike-in, Permit required, 6 person max, No wood fires, Reservations accepted, Elev: 7476ft/2279m, Tel: 307-344-2160. GPS: 44.280928, -110.502241

117 • A1 | Yellowstone NP - Sentinel Meadows East (0G1)

Dispersed sites, Tents only: $3, Hike-in, Permit required, 8 person max, Reservations accepted, Elev: 7205ft/2196m, Tel: 307-344-2160. GPS: 44.564897, -110.853222

118 • A1 | Yellowstone NP - Seven Mile Hole (4C2)

Dispersed sites, Tents only: $3, Hike-in, Permit required, 8 person max, No wood fires, Reservations accepted, Elev: 6784ft/2068m, Tel: 307-344-2160. GPS: 44.753377, -110.405043

119 • A1 | Yellowstone NP - Seven Mile Hole (4C3)

Dispersed sites, Tents only: $3, Hike-in, Permit required, 8 person max, No wood fires, Reservations accepted, Elev: 6729ft/2051m, Tel: 307-344-2160. GPS: 44.755081, -110.401291

120 • A1 | Yellowstone NP - Sheridan Creek (8H2)

Dispersed sites, Tents only: $3, Hike-in, Permit required, 6 person max, Reservations accepted, Elev: 7481ft/2280m, Tel: 307-344-2160. GPS: 44.270579, -110.501885

121 • A1 | Yellowstone NP - Sheridan Trail (8H5)

Dispersed sites, Tents only: $3, Hike-in, Permit required, 6 person max, No wood fires, Reservations accepted, Elev: 7480ft/2280m, Tel: 307-344-2160. GPS: 44.280006, -110.501958

122 • A1 | Yellowstone NP - Shoshone Meadows (8G1)

Dispersed sites, Tents only: $5, Hike-in, Permit required, 12 person max, llamas only, No wood fires, Stay limit: 1 day, Reservations accepted, Elev: 7910ft/2411m, Tel: 307-344-2160. GPS: 44.373738, -110.817251

123 • A1 | Yellowstone NP - Slough Creek CG

Total sites: 23, RV sites: 23, Central water, Vault/pit toilet, No showers, No RV dump, Tent & RV camping: $15, No generators, Open Jun-Oct, Max Length: 30ft, Reservations not accepted, Elev: 6266ft/1910m, Tel: 307-344-7381, Nearest town: Tower Junction. GPS: 44.948293, -110.308719

124 • A1 | Yellowstone NP - Snake River (8C5)

Dispersed sites, Tents only: $3-5, Hike-in, Permit required, 12 person max, Stock allowed, Reservations accepted, Elev: 7317ft/2230m, Tel: 307-344-2160. GPS: 44.214874, -110.461311

125 • A1 | Yellowstone NP - Soldiers Corral Stock (1G5)

Dispersed sites, Tents only: $5, Hike-in, Permit required, Stock only, 12 person max, Reservations accepted, Elev: 7692ft/2345m, Tel: 307-344-2160. GPS: 44.946703, -110.782717

126 • A1 | Yellowstone NP - South Bay (8H1)

Dispersed sites, Tents only: $3, Hike-in, Permit required, 8 person max, No wood fires, Reservations accepted, Elev: 7493ft/2284m, Tel: 307-344-2160. GPS: 44.256484, -110.502849

127 • A1 | Yellowstone NP - South Yell/Hell Confluence (2H2)

Dispersed sites, Tents only: $3, Hike-in, Permit required, 6 person max, No wood fires, Reservations accepted, Elev: 5738ft/1749m, Tel: 307-344-2160. GPS: 44.973657, -110.475257

128 • A1 | Yellowstone NP - Southwest Bay (7N4)

Dispersed sites, Vault/pit toilet, Tents only: $3, Hike-in/boat-in, Permit required, No fires, 12 person max, Non-motorized boats only, Reservations accepted, Elev: 7750ft/2362m, Tel: 307-344-2160. GPS: 44.288643, -110.343962

129 • A1 | Yellowstone NP - Straight Creek North (1C2)

Dispersed sites, Tents only: $5, Hike-in, Permit required, Stock/llama only, 10 person max, Reservations accepted, Elev: 7463ft/2275m, Tel: 307-344-2160. GPS: 44.834489, -110.766016

130 • A1 | Yellowstone NP - Straight Creek South (1C1)

Dispersed sites, Tents only: $3, Hike-in, Permit required, 10 person max, Reservations accepted, Elev: 7485ft/2281m, Tel: 307-344-2160. GPS: 44.825882, -110.769695

131 • A1 | Yellowstone NP - Summit Lake

Dispersed sites, No water, No toilets, Tents only: Free, Hike-in, Elev: 8576ft/2614m. GPS: 44.415434, -110.937202

132 • A1 | Yellowstone NP - Surprise Creek (8J3)

Dispersed sites, Tents only: $3, Hike-in, Permit required, 8 person max, Reservations accepted, Elev: 7493ft/2284m, Tel: 307-344-2160. GPS: 44.252266, -110.439643

133 • A1 | Yellowstone NP - Talus Spring (9B7)

Dispersed sites, Tents only: $3, Hike-in, Permit required, 12 person max, Stay limit: 1 day, Reservations accepted, Elev: 6994ft/2132m, Tel: 307-344-2160. GPS: 44.259423, -110.927853

134 • A1 | Yellowstone NP - Talus Terrace (9A4)

Dispersed sites, Tents only: $3-5, Hike-in, Permit required, 12 person max, Stock allowed, Reservations accepted, Elev: 7364ft/2245m, Tel: 307-344-2160. GPS: 44.281735, -111.039842

135 • A1 | Yellowstone NP - Three Rivers Meadow (9B0)

Dispersed sites, Tents only: $3-5, Hike-in, Permit required, 12 person max, Stock allowed, No wood fires, Stay limit: 2 days, Reservations accepted, Elev: 7208ft/2197m, Tel: 307-344-2160. GPS: 44.282975, -110.905771

136 • A1 | Yellowstone NP - Tower Fall

Total sites: 31, RV sites: 31, Vault/pit toilet, Tent & RV camping: $15, Biker/hiker: $5, No generators, Open May-Sep, Max Length: 30ft, Reservations not accepted, Elev: 6594ft/2010m, Tel: 307-344-7381. GPS: 44.889348, -110.390427

137 • A1 | Yellowstone NP - Trail Spring Stock (9B3)

Dispersed sites, Tents only: $5, Hike-in, Permit required, 20 person max, Stay limit: 2 days, Reservations accepted, Elev: 6428ft/1959m, Tel: 307-344-2160. GPS: 44.216784, -110.980267

138 • A1 | Yellowstone NP - Union Falls (9U4)

Dispersed sites, Tents only: $3, Hike-in, Permit required, 12 person max, Stay limit: 2 days, Reservations accepted, Elev: 6565ft/2001m, Tel: 307-344-2160. GPS: 44.180244, -110.886836

139 • A1 | Yellowstone NP - Union Falls (9U5)

Dispersed sites, Tents only: $3-5, Hike-in, Permit required, 12 person max, Stock allowed, No wood fires, Stay limit: 2 days, Reservations accepted, Elev: 6484ft/1976m, Tel: 307-344-2160. GPS: 44.172961, -110.922837

140 • A1 | Yellowstone NP - Upper Boundary Crk North (9A2)

Dispersed sites, Tents only: $3, Hike-in, Permit required, 12 person max, Reservations accepted, Elev: 6420ft/1957m, Tel: 307-344-2160. GPS: 44.231001, -111.017975

141 • A1 | Yellowstone NP - Upper Boundary Crk South (9A2)

Dispersed sites, Tents only: $3, Hike-in, Permit required, 12 person max, Reservations accepted, Elev: 6416ft/1956m, Tel: 307-344-2160. GPS: 44.228344, -111.018035

142 • A1 | Yellowstone NP - Upper Firehole (0A2)

Dispersed sites, Tents only: $3, Hike-in, Permit required, 6 person max, Reservations accepted, Elev: 7663ft/2336m, Tel: 307-344-2160. GPS: 44.413885, -110.819059

143 • A1 | Yellowstone NP - Upper Ford (9B8)

Dispersed sites, Tents only: $3, Hike-in, Permit required, 12 person max, Stay limit: 1 day, Reservations accepted, Elev: 7014ft/2138m, Tel: 307-344-2160. GPS: 44.270865, -110.918278

144 • A1 | Yellowstone NP - Upper Gardner River (1G4)

Dispersed sites, Tents only: $3, Hike-in, Permit required, 10 person max, Reservations accepted, Elev: 8023ft/2445m, Tel: 307-344-2160. GPS: 44.974549, -110.811355

145 • A1 | Yellowstone NP - Upper Passage Creek (6M5)

Dispersed sites, Tents only: $3-5, Hike-in, Permit required, 12 person max, Stock allowed after 7/20, Reservations accepted, Elev: 8680ft/2646m, Tel: 307-344-2160. GPS: 44.203393, -110.260082

146 • A1 | Yellowstone NP - Washburn Meadow (4E1)

Dispersed sites, Tents only: $3, Hike-in, Permit required, 8 person max, Reservations accepted, Elev: 8195ft/2498m, Tel: 307-344-2160. GPS: 44.777647, -110.411084

147 • A1 | Yellowstone NP - West Shore (8H4)

Dispersed sites, Tents only: $3, Hike-in, Permit required, 8 person max, No wood fires, Reservations accepted, Elev: 7486ft/2282m, Tel: 307-344-2160. GPS: 44.278014, -110.502669

148 • A1 | Yellowstone NP - Winter Creek (1C4)

Dispersed sites, Tents only: $3-5, Hike-in, Permit required, 10 person max, Stock allowed, Reservations accepted, Elev: 7670ft/2338m, Tel: 307-344-2160. GPS: 44.812188, -110.796945

149 • A1 | Yellowstone NP - Winter Creek SW (1C5)

Dispersed sites, Tents only: $3-5, Hike-in, Permit required, 10 person max, Stock allowed, Reservations accepted, Elev: 7679ft/2341m, Tel: 307-344-2160. GPS: 44.808558, -110.798562

150 • A1 | Yellowstone NP - Wolf Lake (4G6)

Dispersed sites, Tents only: $3-5, Hike-in, Permit required, 8 person max, Stock allowed, Reservations accepted, Elev: 8019ft/2444m, Tel: 307-344-2160. GPS: 44.745561, -110.580889

151 • A1 | Yellowstone NP - Wolf Lake (4G7)

Dispersed sites, Tents only: $3, Hike-in, Permit required, 8 person max, Reservations accepted, Elev: 8009ft/2441m, Tel: 307-344-2160. GPS: 44.743433, -110.585954

152 • A1 | Yellowstone NP - Wrangler Lake (4W1)

Dispersed sites, Tents only: $3-5, Hike-in, Permit required, 12 person max, Stock allowed, Reservations accepted, Elev: 7875ft/2400m, Tel: 307-344-2160. GPS: 44.685248, -110.436277

153 • A1 | Yellowstone NP - Yellowstone River Trail (1Y7)

Dispersed sites, Tents only: $3-5, Hike-in, Permit required, 10 person max, Stock allowed, No wood fires, Reservations accepted, Elev: 5602ft/1707m, Tel: 307-344-2160. GPS: 44.992085, -110.557069

154 • A2 | Yellowstone NP - Appaloosa Meadows (3M1)

Dispersed sites, Tents only: $3-5, Hike-in, Permit required, 12 person max, 2 night limit for stock, Reservations accepted, Elev: 7104ft/2165m, Tel: 307-344-2160. GPS: 44.761659, -110.074734

155 • A2 | Yellowstone NP - Beaverdam Meadow (6B4)

Dispersed sites, Tents only: $3-5, Hike-in, Permit required, 20 person max, Stock allowed, Reservations accepted, Elev: 7816ft/2382m, Tel: 307-344-2160. GPS: 44.323918, -110.177974

156 • A2 | Yellowstone NP - Beaverdam Trail (5E1)

Dispersed sites, Tents only: $3, Hike-in, Permit required, 12 person max, Reservations accepted, Elev: 7836ft/2388m, Tel: 307-344-2160. GPS: 44.324883, -110.181151

157 • A2 | Yellowstone NP - Bliss Pass Jct (3P2)

Dispersed sites, No water, No toilets, Tents only: $3, Hike-in,

Permit required, 12 person max, Reservations accepted, Elev: 7742ft/2360m, Tel: 307-344-2160. GPS: 44.994848, -110.110116

158 • A2 | Yellowstone NP - Bliss Pass Jct (3P3)

Dispersed sites, Tents only: $3, Hike-in, Permit required, 6 person max, Reservations accepted, Elev: 7816ft/2382m, Tel: 307-344-2160. GPS: 45.001282, -110.106834

159 • A2 | Yellowstone NP - Boundary (3M7)

Dispersed sites, Tents only: $3-5, Hike-in, Permit required, 12 person max, 1 night stock limit, No stock before 1 Aug, Reservations accepted, Elev: 9717ft/2962m, Tel: 307-344-2160. GPS: 44.727531, -109.866223

160 • A2 | Yellowstone NP - Brimstone Bay (5E4)

Dispersed sites, Tents only: $3, Hike-in/boat-in, Permit required, 12 person max, Reservations accepted, Elev: 7753ft/2363m, Tel: 307-344-2160. GPS: 44.374354, -110.228245

161 • A2 | Yellowstone NP - Brimstone Point (5E3)

Dispersed sites, Tents only: $3, Hike-in/boat-in, Permit required, 12 person max, Reservations accepted, Elev: 7748ft/2362m, Tel: 307-344-2160. GPS: 44.351972, -110.226548

162 • A2 | Yellowstone NP - Cold Creek (3F1)

Dispersed sites, Tents only: $3, Hike-in, Permit required, 6 person max, Reservations accepted, Elev: 7331ft/2234m, Tel: 307-344-2160. GPS: 44.679324, -110.052392

163 • A2 | Yellowstone NP - Cold Creek Jct Stock (3U4)

Dispersed sites, Tents only: $5, Hike-in, Permit required, 12 person max, Stock only, Reservations accepted, Elev: 7297ft/2224m, Tel: 307-344-2160. GPS: 44.679114, -110.057773

164 • A2 | Yellowstone NP - Colter Meadows (6C1)

Dispersed sites, Tents only: $3-5, Hike-in, Permit required, 20 person max, Stock allowed, Reservations accepted, Elev: 7846ft/2391m, Tel: 307-344-2160. GPS: 44.269777, -110.128519

165 • A2 | Yellowstone NP - Hoodoo Basin (3M6)

Dispersed sites, Tents only: $3, Hike-in, Permit required, 12 person max, Reservations accepted, Elev: 9376ft/2858m, Tel: 307-344-2160. GPS: 44.727669, -109.884572

166 • A2 | Yellowstone NP - Howell Creek (6D6)

Dispersed sites, Tents only: $3-5, Hike-in, Permit required, 20 person max, Stock allowed, Reservations accepted, Elev: 8267ft/2520m, Tel: 307-344-2160. GPS: 44.267168, -110.025946

167 • A2 | Yellowstone NP - Howell Creek (6D7)

Dispersed sites, Tents only: $3, Hike-in, Permit required, 20 person max, Reservations accepted, Elev: 8327ft/2538m, Tel: 307-344-2160. GPS: 44.277156, -110.018634

168 • A2 | Yellowstone NP - Howell Creek (6D8)

Dispersed sites, Tents only: $3-5, Hike-in, Permit required, 20 person max, Stock allowed, Reservations accepted, Elev: 8560ft/2609m, Tel: 307-344-2160. GPS: 44.304354, -110.003012

169 • A2 | Yellowstone NP - Lemon City (3F2)

Dispersed sites, Tents only: $3-5, Hike-in, Permit required, 12 person max, Stock allowed, Reservations accepted, Elev: 7361ft/2244m, Tel: 307-344-2160. GPS: 44.669557, -110.041792

170 • A2 | Yellowstone NP - Little Saddle Creek (3U3)

Dispersed sites, Tents only: $3, Hike-in, Permit required, 12 person max, Reservations accepted, Elev: 7257ft/2212m, Tel: 307-344-2160. GPS: 44.689992, -110.068173

171 • A2 | Yellowstone NP - Lower Cache Creek (3C2)

Dispersed sites, Tents only: $3-5, Hike-in, Permit required, 12 person max, 2 night limit for stock, Reservations accepted, Elev: 7115ft/2169m, Tel: 307-344-2160. GPS: 44.854191, -110.066955

172 • A2 | Yellowstone NP - Lower Ford (6B1)

Dispersed sites, Tents only: $3-5, Hike-in, Permit required, 20 person max, Stock allowed, Reservations accepted, Elev: 7777ft/2370m, Tel: 307-344-2160. GPS: 44.296671, -110.155396

173 • A2 | Yellowstone NP - Lower Lamar (3L3)

Dispersed sites, Tents only: $3, Hike-in, Permit required, 12 person max, Reservations accepted, Elev: 6795ft/2071m, Tel: 307-344-2160. GPS: 44.813513, -110.142629

174 • A2 | Yellowstone NP - Lower Lamar (3L4)

Dispersed sites, Tents only: $3, Hike-in, Permit required, 12 person max, Reservations accepted, Elev: 6798ft/2072m, Tel: 307-344-2160. GPS: 44.807638, -110.135176

175 • A2 | Yellowstone NP - Lower Miller Creek (3M2)

Dispersed sites, Tents only: $3, Hike-in, Permit required, 12 person max, Reservations accepted, Elev: 7190ft/2192m, Tel: 307-344-2160. GPS: 44.755736, -110.044421

176 • A2 | Yellowstone NP - Lower Miller Creek (3M3)

Dispersed sites, Tents only: $3-5, Hike-in, Permit required, 12 person max, Stock allowed, Reservations accepted, Elev: 7259ft/2213m, Tel: 307-344-2160. GPS: 44.751704, -110.031267

177 • A2 | Yellowstone NP - Lower Slough Creek (2S1)

Dispersed sites, Tents only: $3-5, Hike-in, Permit required, 8 person max, Stock allowed, Reservations accepted, Elev: 6589ft/2008m, Tel: 307-344-2160. GPS: 44.970079, -110.236334

178 • A2 | Yellowstone NP - Lower Slough Creek (2S2)

Dispersed sites, Tents only: $3, Hike-in, Permit required, 6 person max, Reservations accepted, Elev: 6652ft/2028m, Tel: 307-344-2160. GPS: 44.965924, -110.228106

179 • A2 | Yellowstone NP - Lower Willow Creek (3U2)

Dispersed sites, Tents only: $3, Hike-in, Permit required, 12 person max, Reservations accepted, Elev: 7176ft/2187m, Tel: 307-344-2160. GPS: 44.702438, -110.080146

180 • A2 | Yellowstone NP - Middle Lamar (3L7)

Dispersed sites, Tents only: $3, Hike-in, Permit required, 12 person max, Reservations accepted, Elev: 6996ft/2132m, Tel: 307-344-2160. GPS: 44.753512, -110.097012

181 • A2 | Yellowstone NP - Middle Lamar Stock (3L6)

Dispersed sites, Tents only: $5, Hike-in, Permit required, 12 person max, Stay limit: 2 days, Reservations accepted, Elev: 7007ft/2136m, Tel: 307-344-2160. GPS: 44.755651, -110.097936

182 • A2 | Yellowstone NP - Mist Creek Meadows (3T2)

Dispersed sites, Tents only: $3-5, Hike-in, Permit required, 12 person max, Stock allowed, Stay limit: 2 days, Reservations accepted, Elev: 8119ft/2475m, Tel: 307-344-2160. GPS: 44.622071, -110.118791

183 • A2 | Yellowstone NP - Mist Creek Pass (3T3)

Dispersed sites, Tents only: $3-5, Hike-in, Permit required, 12 person max, Stock allowed, Stay limit: 2 days, Reservations accepted, Elev: 8132ft/2479m, Tel: 307-344-2160. GPS: 44.613693, -110.134016

184 • A2 | Yellowstone NP - Mountain Creek (6D1)

Dispersed sites, Tents only: $3-5, Hike-in, Permit required, 20 person max, Stock allowed, Reservations accepted, Elev: 7830ft/2387m, Tel: 307-344-2160. GPS: 44.224403, -110.128865

185 • A2 | Yellowstone NP - Mountain Creek Ford (6D2)

Dispersed sites, Tents only: $3, Hike-in, Permit required, 20 person max, Reservations accepted, Elev: 7875ft/2400m, Tel: 307-344-2160. GPS: 44.230466, -110.106821

186 • A2 | Yellowstone NP - Mountain Creek Stock (6D3)

Dispersed sites, Tents only: $5, Hike-in, Permit required, 20 person max, Reservations accepted, Elev: 7884ft/2403m, Tel: 307-344-2160. GPS: 44.231012, -110.101862

187 • A2 | Yellowstone NP - North Lower Cache Creek Stock (3L1)

Dispersed sites, Tents only: $5, Hike-in, Permit required, 12 person max, Reservations accepted, Elev: 6745ft/2056m, Tel: 307-344-2160. GPS: 44.831438, -110.143259

188 • A2 | Yellowstone NP - Pebble Creek (3P1)

Dispersed sites, No water, No toilets, Tents only: $3, Hike-in, Permit required, 12 person max, Reservations accepted, Elev: 7500ft/2286m, Tel: 307-344-2160. GPS: 44.959062, -110.118662

189 • A2 | Yellowstone NP - Pebble Creek CG

Total sites: 27, RV sites: 27, Central water, Vault/pit toilet, No showers, No RV dump, Tent & RV camping: $15, Biker/hiker: $5, No generators, Open Jun-Sep, Max Length: 24ft, Reservations not accepted, Elev: 6906ft/2105m, Tel: 307-344-7381, Nearest town: Tower Junction. GPS: 44.917557, -110.113719

190 • A2 | Yellowstone NP - Rivers Edge (6C2)

Dispersed sites, Tents only: $3-5, Hike-in, Permit required, 20 person max, Stock allowed, 1.5 miles west of main trail, Reservations accepted, Elev: 7795ft/2376m, Tel: 307-344-2160. GPS: 44.251308, -110.133816

191 • A2 | Yellowstone NP - Slough Creek (2S3)

Dispersed sites, Tents only: $3, Hike-in, Permit required, 8 person max, Reservations accepted, Elev: 6658ft/2029m, Tel: 307-344-2160. GPS: 44.976362, -110.212517

192 • A2 | Yellowstone NP - Slough Creek (2S4)

Dispersed sites, Tents only: $3, Hike-in, Permit required, 8 person max, Reservations accepted, Elev: 6614ft/2016m, Tel: 307-344-2160. GPS: 44.990125, -110.203939

193 • A2 | Yellowstone NP - South Lower Cache Creek (3L2)

Dispersed sites, Tents only: $3, Hike-in, Permit required, 12 person max, Reservations accepted, Elev: 6736ft/2053m, Tel: 307-344-2160. GPS: 44.831168, -110.149099

194 • A2 | Yellowstone NP - Timothy Creek (3L8)

Dispersed sites, Tents only: $3, Hike-in, Permit required, 12 person max, Reservations accepted, Elev: 7065ft/2153m, Tel: 307-344-2160. GPS: 44.729954, -110.087816

195 • A2 | Yellowstone NP - Trail Bay (6A4)

Dispersed sites, Tents only: $3, Hike-in/boat-in, Permit required, 12 person max, Non-motorized boats only, Reservations accepted, Elev: 7760ft/2365m, Tel: 307-344-2160. GPS: 44.294522, -110.221656

196 • A2 | Yellowstone NP - Trail Point (6A3)

Dispersed sites, Tents only: $3, Hike-in/boat-in, Permit required, 12 person max, Non-motorized boats only, Reservations accepted, Elev: 7746ft/2361m, Tel: 307-344-2160. GPS: 44.303125, -110.233363

197 • A2 | Yellowstone NP - Turret View (6C3)

Dispersed sites, Tents only: $3, Hike-in, Permit required, 10 person max, Reservations accepted, Elev: 7849ft/2392m, Tel: 307-344-2160. GPS: 44.259413, -110.114966

198 • A2 | Yellowstone NP - Upper Cache Creek (3C3)

Dispersed sites, Tents only: $3-5, Hike-in, Permit required, 12 person max, Stock allowed, Reservations accepted, Elev: 7330ft/2234m, Tel: 307-344-2160. GPS: 44.874421, -110.047944

199 • A2 | Yellowstone NP - Upper Cache Creek (3C4)

Dispersed sites, Tents only: $3, Hike-in, Permit required, 12 person max, Reservations accepted, Elev: 7866ft/2398m, Tel: 307-344-2160. GPS: 44.923241, -110.005303

200 • A2 | Yellowstone NP - Upper Ford (6B2)

Dispersed sites, Tents only: $3, Hike-in, Permit required, 8 person max, Reservations accepted, Elev: 7770ft/2368m, Tel: 307-344-2160. GPS: 44.290052, -110.150689

201 • A2 | Yellowstone NP - Upper Miller Creek (3M4)

Dispersed sites, Tents only: $3, Hike-in, Permit required, 6 person max, Reservations accepted, Elev: 7495ft/2284m, Tel: 307-344-2160. GPS: 44.751145, -109.978079

202 • A2 | Yellowstone NP - Upper Miller Creek (3M5)

Dispersed sites, Tents only: $3, Hike-in, Permit required, 12 person max, Reservations accepted, Elev: 7545ft/2300m, Tel: 307-344-2160. GPS: 44.750189, -109.970735

203 • A2 | Yellowstone NP - Upper Mountain Creek (6D5)

Dispersed sites, Tents only: $3-5, Hike-in, Permit required, 20 person max, Stock allowed, Reservations accepted, Elev: 8035ft/2449m, Tel: 307-344-2160. GPS: 44.243732, -110.058382

204 • A2 | Yellowstone NP - Upper Slough Creek Stock (2S7)

Dispersed sites, Tents only: $5, Hike-in, Permit required, Stock only, 12 person max, Reservations accepted, Elev: 6719ft/2048m, Tel: 307-344-2160. GPS: 44.993345, -110.213973

205 • A2 | Yellowstone NP - Wapiti Lake (4W2)

Dispersed sites, Tents only: $3, Hike-in, Permit required, 8 person max, Reservations accepted, Elev: 8443ft/2573m, Tel: 307-344-2160. GPS: 44.720213, -110.255832

206 • A2 | Yellowstone NP - Wapiti Lake (4W3)

Dispersed sites, Tents only: $3, Hike-in, Permit required, 8 person max, Reservations accepted, Elev: 8447ft/2575m, Tel: 307-344-2160. GPS: 44.721218, -110.254905

207 • A2 | Yellowstone NP - Warm Spring Meadow (3L9)

Dispersed sites, Tents only: $3-5, Hike-in, Permit required, 12 person max, Stock allowed, Reservations accepted, Elev: 7108ft/2167m, Tel: 307-344-2160. GPS: 44.718103, -110.085977

208 • A2 | Yellowstone NP - Yellowstone Meadows Stock (6Y7)

Dispersed sites, Tents only: $5, Hike-in, Permit required, 20 person max, Reservations accepted, Elev: 7833ft/2387m, Tel: 307-344-2160. GPS: 44.211886, -110.110111

209 • A3 | Bighorn Canyon NRA - Horseshoe Bend

Total sites: 48, RV sites: 48, Elec sites: 19, Water at site, No toilets, No showers, RV dump, Tents: $10/RV's: $20, No utilities in winter, Open all year, Reservations not accepted, Elev: 3743ft/1141m, Tel: 307-548-5406, Nearest town: Lowell. GPS: 44.962897, -108.262301

210 • A5 | Devils Tower NM - Belle Fourche CG

Total sites: 50, RV sites: 50, Central water, Flush toilet, No showers, No RV dump, Tent & RV camping: $20, 3 group sites: $30, Stay limit: 14 days, Reservations not accepted, Elev: 3858ft/1176m, Tel: 307-467-5283, Nearest town: Devils Tower. GPS: 44.581543, -104.706299

211 • B1 | Grand Teton NP - Colter Bay CG

Total sites: 324, RV sites: 277, Elec sites: 13, Central water, Flush toilet, Pay showers, RV dump, Tents: $38-60/RV's: $42, Dump fee: $10, $12/person hikers/bicyclists, Reservable group site: $31 + $12/person, Stay limit: 14 days, Open May-Sep, Max Length: 38ft, Reservations required, Elev: 6834ft/2083m, Tel: 307-543-3100, Nearest town: Jackson. GPS: 43.909455, -110.641665

212 • B1 | Grand Teton NP - Colter Bay RV Park

Total sites: 112, RV sites: 112, Elec sites: 112, Water at site, Flush toilet, Pay showers, RV dump, No tents/RV's: $74-98, 112 Full hookups, No campfires, Stay limit: 14 days, No generators, Open May-Oct, Max Length: 45ft, Reservations required, Elev: 6820ft/2079m, Tel: 307-543-3100, Nearest town: Jackson. GPS: 43.905188, -110.642195

213 • B1 | Grand Teton NP - Flagg Ranch Headwaters

Total sites: 131, RV sites: 97, Elec sites: 97, Water at site, Flush toilet, Pay showers, RV dump, Tents: $49/RV's: $92, 97 Full hookups, $25/$68 w/ Access card, Concession, Stay limit: 14 days, Open May-Sep, Reservations required, Elev: 6847ft/2087m, Tel: 307-543-2861, Nearest town: Jackson. GPS: 44.104802, -110.668965

214 • B1 | Grand Teton NP - Flagg Ranch Rd Site #1

Total sites: 4, RV sites: 4, No water, Vault/pit toilet, Tent & RV camping: Fee unk, Stay limit: 14 days, Max Length: 45ft, Elev: 6808ft/2075m, Nearest town: Jackson. GPS: 44.103405, -110.686234

215 • B1 | Grand Teton NP - Flagg Ranch Rd Site #2

Total sites: 2, RV sites: 2, No water, Vault/pit toilet, Tent & RV camping: Fee unk, Stay limit: 14 days, Max Length: 40ft, Elev: 6812ft/2076m, Nearest town: Jackson. GPS: 44.097132, -110.689357

216 • B1 | Grand Teton NP - Flagg Ranch Rd Site #3

Total sites: 2, RV sites: 2, No water, Vault/pit toilet, Tent & RV camping: Fee unk, Stay limit: 14 days, Max Length: 30ft, Elev: 6826ft/2081m, Nearest town: Jackson. GPS: 44.088708, -110.69578

217 • B1 | Grand Teton NP - Flagg Ranch Rd Site #4

Total sites: 2, RV sites: 2, No water, Vault/pit toilet, Tent & RV camping: Free, Stay limit: 14 days, Max Length: 18ft, Elev: 6866ft/2093m, Nearest town: Jackson. GPS: 44.086294, -110.699272

218 • B1 | Grand Teton NP - Flagg Ranch Rd Site #5

Total sites: 1, RV sites: 1, No water, Vault/pit toilet, Tent & RV camping: Fee unk, Stay limit: 14 days, Max Length: 18ft, Elev: 6877ft/2096m, Nearest town: Jackson. GPS: 44.08686, -110.70973

219 • B1 | Grand Teton NP - Flagg Ranch Rd Site #6

Total sites: 1, RV sites: 1, No water, Vault/pit toilet, Tent & RV camping: Fee unk, Stay limit: 14 days, Max Length: 20ft, Elev: 7131ft/2174m, Nearest town: Jackson. GPS: 44.100444, -110.760252

220 • B1 | Grand Teton NP - Flagg Ranch Rd Site #8

Total sites: 1, RV sites: 1, No water, Vault/pit toilet, Tent & RV camping: Fee unk, Stay limit: 14 days, Max Length: 16ft, Elev: 7161ft/2183m, Nearest town: Jackson. GPS: 44.105228, -110.768701

221 • B1 | Grand Teton NP - Gros Ventre CG

Total sites: 305, RV sites: 268, Elec sites: 35, Central water, Flush toilet, No showers, RV dump, Tents: $38/RV's: $38-60, 4 group sites - $33 + $14/person, Stay limit: 14 days, Generator hours: 0800-2200, Open May-Oct, Max Length: 45ft, Reservations required, Elev: 6578ft/2005m, Tel: 307-543-3100, Nearest town: Jackson. GPS: 43.616211, -110.666748

222 • B1 | Grand Teton NP - Jenny Lake CG

Total sites: 51, RV sites: 0, Central water, Flush toilet, Tents only: $12-36, Also 10 hiker/biker sites: $13/person, Stay limit: 7 days, No generators, Open May-Sep, Reservations required, Elev:

6821ft/2079m, Tel: 307-543-3100, Nearest town: Jackson. GPS: 43.75415, -110.720459

223 • B1 | Grand Teton NP - Lizard Creek CG

Total sites: 60, RV sites: 60, Central water, Flush toilet, No showers, No RV dump, Tent & RV camping: $37, Stay limit: 14 days, Open Jun-Sep, Max Length: RV-30'/Tlr-20ft, Reservations required, Elev: 6834ft/2083m, Tel: 307-543-2831, Nearest town: Jackson. GPS: 44.001552, -110.689701

224 • B1 | Grand Teton NP - Signal Mountain CG

Total sites: 81, RV sites: 77, Elec sites: 25, Central water, Flush toilet, Free showers, RV dump, Tents: $40/RV's: $40-62, Stay limit: 14 days, Open May-Oct, Max Length: 30ft, Reservations required, Elev: 6821ft/2079m, Tel: 307-543-2831, Nearest town: Jackson. GPS: 43.84082, -110.615234

225 • B1 | Yellowstone NP - (9C6)

Dispersed sites, Tents only: $3, Hike-in, Permit required, 8 person max, No wood fires, Reservations accepted, Elev: 6462ft/1970m, Tel: 307-344-2160. GPS: 44.137982, -110.933955

226 • B1 | Yellowstone NP - Cascade River (9U6)

Dispersed sites, Tents only: $3, Hike-in, Permit required, 8 person max, No wood fires, Reservations accepted, Elev: 7065ft/2153m, Tel: 307-344-2160. GPS: 44.139977, -110.837282

227 • B1 | Yellowstone NP - Beula Lake (8A1)

Dispersed sites, Tents only: $3, Hike-in, Permit required, 8 person max, Reservations accepted, Elev: 7423ft/2263m, Tel: 307-344-2160. GPS: 44.155566, -110.767708

228 • B1 | Yellowstone NP - Beula Lake (8A2)

Dispersed sites, Tents only: $3, Hike-in, Permit required, 6 person max, Reservations accepted, Elev: 7418ft/2261m, Tel: 307-344-2160. GPS: 44.156889, -110.767769

229 • B1 | Yellowstone NP - Crooked Creek (8C9)

Dispersed sites, Tents only: $3-5, Hike-in, Permit required, 12 person max, Stock allowed, Reservations accepted, Elev: 7960ft/2426m, Tel: 307-344-2160. GPS: 44.157355, -110.335911

230 • B1 | Yellowstone NP - Fox Creek (6M7)

Dispersed sites, Tents only: $3, Hike-in, Permit required, 12 person max, Reservations accepted, Elev: 8231ft/2509m, Tel: 307-344-2160. GPS: 44.134679, -110.297373

231 • B1 | Yellowstone NP - Mariposa Lake (6M3)

Dispersed sites, Tents only: $3, Hike-in, Permit required, 8 person max, Reservations accepted, Elev: 8998ft/2743m, Tel: 307-344-2160. GPS: 44.153255, -110.237079

232 • B1 | Yellowstone NP - Snake River (8C1)

Dispersed sites, Tents only: $3, Hike-in, Permit required, 8 person max, Reservations accepted, Elev: 6959ft/2121m, Tel: 307-344-2160. GPS: 44.168662, -110.586759

233 • B1 | Yellowstone NP - Snake River (8C2)

Dispersed sites, Tents only: $3-5, Hike-in, Permit required, 12 person max, Stock allowed, Reservations accepted, Elev: 7065ft/2153m, Tel: 307-344-2160. GPS: 44.146653, -110.525839

234 • B1 | Yellowstone NP - Snake River (8C4)

Dispersed sites, Tents only: $3-5, Hike-in, Permit required, 12 person max, Stock allowed, Reservations accepted, Elev: 7194ft/2193m, Tel: 307-344-2160. GPS: 44.170296, -110.488169

235 • B1 | Yellowstone NP - Snake River Ford (8C6)

Dispersed sites, Tents only: $3, Hike-in, Permit required, 8 person max, Reservations accepted, Elev: 6982ft/2128m, Tel: 307-344-2160. GPS: 44.175108, -110.568964

236 • B1 | Yellowstone NP - Snake River Stock (8C7)

Dispersed sites, Tents only: $5, Hike-in, Permit required, 12 person max, Reservations accepted, Elev: 6969ft/2124m, Tel: 307-344-2160. GPS: 44.168886, -110.579651

237 • B1 | Yellowstone NP - Two Ocean Trail Jct (6M4)

Dispersed sites, Tents only: $3-5, Hike-in, Permit required, 12 person max, Stock allowed after 7/20, Reservations accepted, Elev: 8589ft/2618m, Tel: 307-344-2160. GPS: 44.152071, -110.260971

238 • B2 | Yellowstone NP - Cliff Creek (6Y5)

Dispersed sites, Tents only: $3, Hike-in, Permit required, 20 person max, Reservations accepted, Elev: 7873ft/2400m, Tel: 307-344-2160. GPS: 44.169087, -110.101112

239 • B2 | Yellowstone NP - East Confluence (6Y4)

Dispersed sites, Tents only: $3-5, Hike-in, Permit required, 20 person max, Stock allowed, Reservations accepted, Elev: 7839ft/2389m, Tel: 307-344-2160. GPS: 44.160168, -110.118915

240 • B2 | Yellowstone NP - North Thorofare (6T2)

Dispersed sites, Tents only: $3, Hike-in, Permit required, 20 person max, Reservations accepted, Elev: 7869ft/2398m, Tel: 307-344-2160. GPS: 44.142124, -110.104246

241 • B2 | Yellowstone NP - South Thorofare (6T1)

Dispersed sites, Tents only: $3-5, Hike-in, Permit required, 20 person max, Stock allowed, Reservations accepted, Elev: 7871ft/2399m, Tel: 307-344-2160. GPS: 44.139958, -110.103902

242 • B2 | Yellowstone NP - South Yellowstone River (6Y2)

Dispersed sites, Tents only: $3, Hike-in, Permit required, 12 person max, Reservations accepted, Elev: 7839ft/2389m, Tel: 307-344-2160. GPS: 44.144031, -110.126212

243 • B2 | Yellowstone NP - Three Mile Bend (6Y6)

Dispersed sites, Tents only: $3-5, Hike-in, Permit required, 20 person max, Stock allowed, Reservations accepted, Elev: 7835ft/2388m, Tel: 307-344-2160. GPS: 44.186203, -110.109989

www.ingramcontent.com/pod-product-compliance
Lightning Source LLC
Chambersburg PA
CBHW081230090426
42738CB00016B/3249